DUNS SCOTUS LIBRARY
LOURDES COLLEGE
SYLVANIA, OHIO
WITHDRAWN

D0142720

K96

# STATISTICAL ANALYSIS FOR THE SOCIAL SCIENCES

# STATISTICAL ANALYSIS FOR THE SOCIAL SCIENCES

### Norman R. Kurtz
*Brandeis University*

**Allyn and Bacon**
*Boston • London • Toronto • Sydney • Tokyo • Singapore*

**Series Editor:** *Sarah L. Kelbaugh*
**Editor-in-Chief, Social Sciences:** *Karen Hanson*
**Editorial Assistant:** *Jennifer Muroff*
**Marketing Manager:** *Brooke Stoner*
**Editorial–Production Administrator:** *Donna Simons*
**Editorial–Production Service:** *Shepherd, Inc.*
**Composition and Prepress Buyer:** *Linda Cox*
**Manufacturing Buyer:** *Megan Cochran*
**Cover Administrator:** *Jenny Hart*
**Electronic Composition:** *Shepherd, Inc.*

Copyright © 1999 by Allyn & Bacon
A Viacom Company
160 Gould Street
Needham Heights, MA 02494

Internet: www.abacon.com

All rights reserved. No part of the material protected by this copyright notice may be reproduced or utilized in any form or by any means, electronic or mechanical, including photo-
copying, recording, or by any information storage and retrieval system, without written
permission from the copyright owner.

**Library of Congress Cataloging-in-Publication Data**
Kurtz, Norman R.
  Statistical analysis for the social sciences  /  Norman R. Kurtz.
     p.    cm.
  Includes bibliographical references and index.
  ISBN 0-205-28972-X
  1. Social sciences—Statistical methods.   I. Title.
HA29. K937   1998
519.5—dc21                                               98-23707
                                                              CIP

Printed in the United States of America
10   9   8   7   6   5   4   3   2   1      03   02   01   00   99   98

*For Loretta*

# CONTENTS

# PREFACE

Statistics is not the kind of subject matter that readily attracts us, and statistics courses are not likely to compete for most-sought-after classroom experiences. In part this is due to an undeserved reputation for being a difficult mathematics course. Although statistics can be mathematical, most introductory books in social statistics are not difficult because of their mathematical expectations. Some skill in addition, subtraction, multiplication, and division is usually sufficient. The subject also might be less than enthusiastically received and sought out because there is some mystery about what it is good for and what advantage is to be gained by mastering it. Statistics might be seen as a realm of study reserved for a small minority given to unusual pursuits. However, being able to use and understand statistical material is an essential part of everyday life. It is important simply in order to be an intelligent and critical consumer of daily newspapers, popular magazines, daily polls, and numerical descriptions on television. It also enables us to deal more wisely with such crucial choices as health care programs, investments, political choices, and reports on our social and physical surroundings. A basic understanding of the wide array of numerical descriptions that appear before us is important not only to avoid being misled and to be able to recognize misinformation but also—and even more important—to understand what is happening in the world around us.

The purpose of this book is to provide you with the capacity to be a critical consumer of statistical information. It will give you a solid grounding in the skills of statistical descriptions and build a foundation from which you can move on to more advanced statistical courses. These goals are achieved in two ways. First, the book is written in a clear and simple style. Every effort has been made to exclude extraneous material that may be of interest to experts in the subject matter but is not essential to understanding the basic ideas that drive statistical descriptions. In addition, much attention is paid to vocabulary and the definition of terms, on the assumption that if the meaning of key terms is unclear, you will get lost in the professional lingo of statistics. Second, the content is organized in a way that makes clear the logic underlying each procedure and shows how one idea is linked to the next. The presentation shows that statistical models are organized around a general conceptual model that is disarmingly simple and also clarifies the meaning of statistical conclusions. Effort has also been made to use mathematical notations that minimize unnecessary confusion and maximize the capacity to cover material without turning you off with unimportant details.

Each procedure is illustrated with an example that makes plain the logic and meaning of the results. Care has been taken to prevent the content of examples from interfering with understanding the statistical procedures.

Much effort has been placed on making the book readable so that you will stick with it through the end, yet care has been taken to avoid shortchanging you on conceptual content. A simplified introduction to statistics would be of little value if it left you poorly informed about the underlying conceptual content that makes the conclusions of statistical analyses legitimate and trustworthy. Much of the difficulty in mastering statistical methods rests on the *somewhat different way of thinking about things* represented by statistical approaches. Thus, it is essential, at the introductory level, to get a good grasp on the underlying concepts that justify statistical approaches and conclusions. This book will not leave you short in that regard. You will gain a thorough understanding of how numerical results are arrived at and what they mean, and you will understand the logic that justifies the role of statistics in the research process.

This book consists of 12 chapters. The first three focus on methods for preparing and presenting statistical descriptions. Chapters 4, 5, and 6 present the logic that makes it possible to describe larger populations based on smaller samples representing them. Chapter 7 illustrates the logic and process for testing hypotheses, and Chapters 8 and 9 apply hypothesis testing to comparisons based on two samples. Chapter 10 describes analysis of variance techniques that make it possible to evaluate more than two samples. Chapter 11 presents regression and correlation and shows the conceptual link to the material on analysis of variance presented in Chapter 10. Chapter 12 reviews selected statistical techniques for evaluating the strength of the association between discrete measures.

Each chapter ends with a glossary of key terms, reviews of symbols and formulas, and exercises. While computers have dramatically altered statistical analysis at every level, learning the subject matter may be substantially enhanced with problem sets that illustrate how problems are solved and decisions are made and that show the rationale behind the techniques. The exercises at the end of each chapter are intended to support such learning. In addition, each chapter suggests computer assignments for your software that further enhance the learning process.

## ACKNOWLEDGMENTS

I appreciate the efforts of all of the editorial staff of Allyn and Bacon, especially the consistent support and counsel of Sarah Kelbaugh, Series Editor, the efforts of Jennifer Muroff, Editorial Assistant, and the recognition by Karen Hanson, Editor-in-Chief, Social Sciences, of the potential of the book. My special thanks to Kennie Harris, project editor, and the staff at Shepherd, Inc., who patiently assisted and guided me through the production process.

I am indebted to the many students who have inspired my teaching and insisted on clear exposition of statistical content. I am also thankful for the support of Nicole, Brian, and Laura, who never let me down. My very special thanks to Loretta whose patience in reading, commenting on, and proofing the text seemed unending. It would not have happened without her.

I am also grateful to the following reviewers for their insightful comments throughout the book's development: Diane Louise Balduzy, Massachusetts College of Liberal Arts; Ruth Dunkle, University of Michigan; Robin Franck, Southwestern University; Rebecca F. Guy, University of Memphis; and Jon Lorence, University of Houston.

# 1

# SOCIAL STATISTICS AND MEASUREMENT
## *The Purpose of Social Statistics*

The purpose of this book is to help you understand and use numbers to describe social phenomena. The body of methods used for such numerical descriptions is known as *statistics*. The first section of this chapter provides a basic overview of statistics and the role that statistical procedures play in social research. The second section discusses measurement. To understand social statistics, you need to know how measurement is defined and applied in social research.

## WHAT IS STATISTICS?

People have always been driven to describe the world in which they live and the experiences that are important in their lives. Early records of such descriptions consist of paintings in caves and carvings in wood and stone, and through time an unbelievable variety of descriptive techniques has evolved. Today we take for granted the many available ways to describe what we see and experience. Prose is used by many to describe sensory and emotional experiences from many perspectives. Others use poetry to create moving rhythmic descriptions that embody a great capacity for emotional engagement with nature and human experience. Some use oils or drawings, concentrating on stimulating the human capacity to experience the world through visual descriptions. Yet others use music, sculpture, and countless other media to share the world of their experience.

Each approach, whatever its method, enriches the ability to better understand and apprehend the world. To the extent that we are knowledgeable about the different media, our intellectual and emotional capacities to appreciate, respect, understand, and better use the world around us are enhanced.

Statistics is simply another method of describing the world, though it is unique because it describes the world with numbers. Statistics counts; measures sizes, quantities, and densities; and looks at associations between two or more numerical descriptions. As a consequence, statistics can provide unique insights about the world around us.

As with all descriptive media, to appreciate and benefit from numerical descriptions you must understand the rules and logic around which such descriptions are organized. As is true of any descriptive medium, statistical descriptions can be done well or poorly, and in some cases it takes special training to know the difference between the two. If you are going to analyze something with numbers, you need to do it correctly, and this book will help you do that. It will provide you with a basic introduction to numerical techniques that statisticians use to describe the world. You will become a critical user of such numerical descriptions and will be able to create your own. Some descriptions are relatively simple and can be comprehended easily, whereas others are organized around more sophisticated logic, requiring commitment and hard work to understand. This book makes a special effort to explain the logic and methods of statistical descriptions.

## *The Problem in Doing It with Numbers*

It is no secret that many people feel less comfortable with numbers than they do with words. This is understandable because words are the everyday medium of social exchange, and most people feel fairly comfortable using words to express their concerns and messages. People also routinely use numbers in verbal exchanges, but usually numbers are not the primary medium of communication. Many people feel less comfortable being confronted with tables of numbers, equations, or other complex numerical presentations.

Moreover, we have been exposed to some strong negative messages regarding numbers, especially statistics, so we approach them with a sense of uncertainty and distrust. For example, many of us have heard the phrase "There are liars, damn liars, and statisticians," implying that statisticians have a propensity to be dishonest and, when using numbers, are likely to tell lies. No studies exist to substantiate that statisticians are generally more dishonest than the public at large, nor is it plausible that this is so. In addition, most of us likely have been lied to far more often with words than with numbers. The distrust of numbers that is associated with statistics might reflect the frustration people feel when confronted with numerical descriptions that are hard to understand. It is also true that some people use numerical descriptions without understanding their limitations or original intent or even misuse them to achieve some purpose unfairly. This book will help you understand statistical descriptions, be sophisticated enough to distinguish more accurate from less accurate numerical representations, and recognize when others are misusing numbers or going beyond their original intent.

Some might feel that using numbers to describe people and their activities is dehumanizing. Thus, we hear that no one wants to be "just a number." And, although numbers might be used by people who are driven by poor motivations or are pursuing inappropriate goals to dehumanize others, the likelihood is greater that words are used to do the same. When you consider the everyday use of clinical, psychological, sociological, political, religious, and other words by the general public to sort, categorize, and dismiss others around them, the risk represented by numbers must be far less. Most of us likely have been called bad names far more often than bad numbers, and we are more likely offended by adjectives that others apply to us than numbers. Thus, it seems that the use of numbers should be no more problematic than the use of words. In either case, it is important to understand what numbers mean and how to use them properly and for the right purposes.

Another issue in learning to understand and use statistics is that the subject matter of statistics is based on mathematics, and many people feel that they do not have a natural bent for numbers or sufficient mathematical background to understand the material. Even those who feel comfortable with arithmetic might approach a statistics course with some apprehension. Given this uncertainty, some may conclude that it is best to stay away from the subject matter altogether. It is true that statistical methods are based on sophisticated mathematical principles and logic, but the good news is that you do not have to be a mathematical whiz to understand and use statistical methods. Most introductory texts for social statistics (such as this one) can be mastered by anyone who is able to add, subtract, multiply, and divide.

Contrary to what many people think, the difficulty in learning introductory statistics is not a function of the mathematics involved but is due to several other issues. First, statistical methods are organized around *formulas* made up of abstract symbols. Such symbols are convenient shorthand notations to seasoned users, but they can appear meaningless and confusing to those not experienced in their use. Special effort is made throughout this book to explain the meaning and function of each formula to avoid any guesswork about what is going on. Second, students who enroll in social statistics courses frequently have had less positive experiences in mathematics courses and have every right to be apprehensive about managing the content of a statistics text. Rest assured that every effort is made here to present all mathematical procedures at a level that meets the needs of even the most timid user. Also, the mathematics involved is far simpler than it might seem at first glance. Third, and perhaps the real barrier for newcomers to statistics, is that often it is difficult to understand "what is going on" or "what the purpose or point is" in the presentation of statistical procedures. This problem arises because statistical methods are organized around logic that is not immediately obvious. However, once you understand the logic around which statistical procedures are organized and what the procedures are "driving at," the subject matter can be mastered without much difficulty. This book makes special effort to explain and lay out the logic and purpose of the methods that are presented to help you understand exactly what each statistical method is attempting to achieve. You will be able to draw your own conclusions about the usefulness of their numerical descriptions.

## A Framework for Statistical Work

Statisticians describe the world with numbers by counting, ranking, and measuring quantities, sizes, opinions, feelings, and other dimensions. For example, statisticians might *count* the number of individuals belonging to different religious organizations, evaluate how individuals *rank* the performance of the city mayor on a scale of 1 to 5, or calculate the *amount* of disposable income that is available to a family. In more complex descriptions, they examine the association between two or more measures.

The materials that statisticians work with are called **variables.** A variable is any entity that can take on more than one value. Thus, gender is a variable with the values male or female. Age is a variable that can take on values ranging from the first day of life to more than 100 years. Some variables, such as gender, take on only two values, whereas others, such as age, can be represented by a large number of different values.

Although variables are the basic working material of statistics, the focus is on the values that a variable takes over a *sample* (or group) of observations (or cases). The different values that a variable has for a sample of observations is referred to as the **distribution** of the variable. Usually, statisticians do not want to describe only one case; rather, they focus on a large number of cases and on how the different values of a variable are distributed across the individuals in their sample.

Assume, for example, that your home community has a population of 5,000 people. The community can be described in terms of gender, that is, the percentage of males and females residing there. If 55% of 5,000 people are females and 45% are males, that is the distribution of the gender variable in the community. Further, the community can be described in terms of age. A list of the ages of the 5,000 inhabitants is the distribution of the age variable in the community. Note that each variable that is used to describe the community—whether it be gender, age, income, religious preference, level of education, and so on—has a specific distribution. Also, the distribution of any variable in the community might differ from that of another community.

You will soon feel comfortable with the terms *variable* and *distribution of a variable* because they will be used throughout this book. Variables and their distributions are the materials around which the work of statistics is organized.

Usually, statisticians collect information on variables from **samples.** Samples are small groups selected to represent larger populations. A statistician studying your community of 5,000 people very likely would use only a small sample of the 5,000 because it is too expensive and time consuming to talk to all 5,000 people. Moreover, as you will learn as you study this book, you need not include all 5,000 because precise information about the community can be obtained from a small sample of the 5,000 if the sample is properly selected and studied. Studying small samples of large populations not only is more efficient but also can reduce the amount of human error associated with compiling information on large numbers of individuals. In studying the community of 5,000, it might be necessary to use a sample of only 200 or fewer individuals to get an accurate description of the whole community. The size of the sample required is a function of the diversity of the population. The greater the diversity, the larger the sample needed to ensure that all the different elements in the population are represented.

Let's define more precisely the terms *sample* and *population*. A **population** is the entire set of entities on which you are focused. If you are interested in studying all the students at your college or university, the total number of students is your population. If you are studying all college students in the state, the number of all such students in the state is your population. Researchers define the boundaries of populations according to the subject matter of their research.

A *sample* is a subset of a population. When researchers use the word sample, they mean a *representative sample,* which is a subset of a population that is selected to represent all the elements of a population. Whenever the word sample is used here, the reference is to a representative sample.

Numbers are used to describe both populations and samples. However, numbers that describe characteristics of population members are referred to as **parameters,** and numbers that describe samples are referred to as **statistics.** Sample statistics can also be thought of as estimates of the population parameters they represent.

## Descriptive Statistics and Inferential Statistics

Statistical methods can be divided into *descriptive* and *inferential* techniques. **Descriptive statistics** consist of exactly what the name implies: They are methods for organizing numerical descriptions of social phenomena. Generally, statistical descriptions consist of different ways of organizing and presenting the distribution of values for a variable. **Inferential statistics** consist of methods for using sample statistics to draw inferences about population parameters. Most research is based on inferential statistics because it is too difficult, too expensive, and unnecessary to study entire populations. This book introduces you to the logic and methods that make statistical inference possible.

## The Role of Statistics in Social Research

The general purpose of statistics is to describe things with numbers, but statistical methods play an important part in the broader activity of social research. The following example shows how statistics fits into the research process. This example is a simplification of how things really work, but it will give you a good idea of the importance of statistical descriptions in social research.

A theoretical proposition suggests that physical propinquity (closeness) increases the likelihood of social interaction between members of groups that historically have avoided interaction. The authors of the study were concerned about whether increased contact between blacks and whites, due to a decline in segregation and especially residential segregation, has led to an increase in friendships between the two racial groups.[1]

---

[1] This proposition is paraphrased from a study reported by Lee Sigelman, Timothy Bledsoe, Susan Welch, and Michael W. Combs, "Making Contact? Black–White Social Interaction in an Urban Setting," *American Journal of Sociology* 101:1306–32. (Copyright 1996 The University of Chicago Press.) The discussion following here draws on material from the article but considerably simplifies the study.

**Theory** is an important component of social research. It represents how the researcher thinks about the subject being researched. In general, a theory is the researcher's notion about how things work. One issue that concerned the authors of "Making Contact? Black–White Social Interaction in an Urban Setting" was whether increased physical and social closeness influenced the likelihood of interracial friendships. It seems reasonable that greater propinquity increases the opportunity for social contact, which should undermine negative stereotypes and open the door for interracial friendships.

Although the proposition that propinquity increases the likelihood of interracial friendships may be useful on a theoretical level, it is too abstract for purposes of research. Research is organized around things that can be measured, ranked, or counted. This means that the proposition about group membership and aspirations must be reduced to elements that can be measured. The authors did this by **operationalizing** the primary concepts of the theory. Operationalizing a concept consists of specifying the means for observing the intent or content of the concept. Propinquity was operationalized using several measures (independent variables, discussed shortly), including the percentage of black residents in the neighborhood; whether one works in the city or in the suburbs; whether one attends church; early life neighborhood composition; and early life school composition. Friendship was operationalized in a scale consisting of a number of questions regarding interracial friendships. For our purposes assume that the variable of friendship could take one of two values: either you do or you do not have a close interracial friendship.

Once researchers operationalize their variables, they develop **hypotheses.** These are statements specifying the relationship between two or more variables. They are important working tools for researchers because they are statements that can be tested with data based on observations. As you will see, much statistical work is organized around testing hypotheses. A potential hypothesis for our example is the following: *There is no relationship between the percentage of black residents in the neighborhood and the likelihood of their forming close interracial friendships.* The hypothesis can be tested by examining the differences in the percentage of black residents in the neighborhood and the presence of friendships between blacks and whites.

The example serves to illustrate the different roles that variables can play in the research process. **Independent variables,** also referred to as *predictors,* are presumed to bring about or be associated with changes in a **dependent variable.** Dependent variables, also referred to as *outcomes,* are those influenced by independent variables. In our example, some of the independent variables are the percentage of black residents in the neighborhood, whether one works in the city or in the suburbs, and so on. The dependent variable is close interracial friendships. By nature, variables are not independent or dependent; rather, the role they play depends on the theoretical model that the researcher develops. Thus, in one case friendship might serve as an independent variable to predict one outcome and in another case, such as the example here, friendship is the dependent variable, or the outcome predicted by the independent variables.

Once the theory is in place and the variables specified, instruments for collecting the data must be developed. Data can be collected a variety of ways, including interviews, mailed questionnaires, and observations. An important part of data collection is specifying the *population of reference*. The researcher must determine the boundaries of the population to which the research findings apply. Whatever the population of reference, a sampling strategy must be organized to represent the population. If the reference is to the entire population of the United States, a complex sampling procedure would be necessary to ensure representation. If the reference is to a small community, sampling would be less complex, but the study results would be more limited because they would apply only to that community. The authors of our study used a large midwestern urban area to test their hypotheses. Their interest in blacks and whites in both urban and suburban settings required a sampling strategy for representing such areas. They developed data collection instruments, selected a sample from the population of reference, and collected the data.

As you might suspect, the results of their study were not simple and straightforward. They found "that interracial friendship is much more predictable for whites than for blacks."[2] For whites, living in an interracial neighborhood, attending school with blacks, and being middle-aged all predicted such friendships, whereas for blacks the only predictor was having attended school with whites. In general, propinquity did foster interracial friendships.[3]

**Statistical methods** are crucial at this point in the research process. These methods provide the basis for deciding whether the observed differences in the measures of propinquity and the presence of interracial friendships are significant. A *significant difference* is one in which the values of an independent variable make a real difference in those of the dependent variable. The example serves to illustrate the role that statistics plays in research.

Figure 1.1 shows the ideal steps in the research process. Much of researchers' effort is devoted to developing conceptual schemes that provide a framework for generating propositions about the relationships between the concepts of their theories. In turn, these propositions lay the groundwork for defining variables and developing testable hypotheses. A population of reference must be defined and a sampling strategy developed to represent the population relevant to the theoretical interests. Data collection instruments must be created to gather the information from sample members to test the hypotheses. Only after collecting the data and then preparing it for analysis are researchers ready to apply formal statistical methods to organize and analyze those data.

Figure 1.1 makes it obvious that statistics plays only a small role in the overall research process. That role might seem minor, but it is crucial because it provides the basis for deciding whether a hypothesis should be accepted or rejected

---

[2] Ibid., p. 1324.

[3] Ibid. The study contains much more substance, and the results are more complex. A reading of the article would enhance the appreciation of how research works.

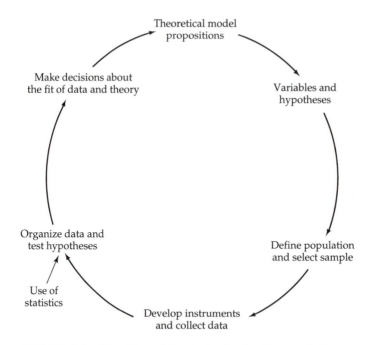

Theoretical model
propositions

Make decisions about
the fit of data and theory

Variables and
hypotheses

Organize data and
test hypotheses

Define population
and select sample

Use of
statistics

Develop instruments
and collect data

**FIGURE 1.1    The Use of Statistics in the Research Process**

and determines whether the proposition suggested by the original theory is cred-
ible. Thus, the role of statistics is often essential in determining the future direction of theoretical speculations in scientific work.

Generally, social data are collected through the use of questionnaires, interviews, or other formats for recording observational data. Let's return to our example of describing the community of 5,000 people. Suppose that you select a sample of 250 people and ask them questions related to social characteristics,
including their gender, age, and family income. You develop a code sheet to assign
numbers to the responses for each variable on which data are collected.

To analyze the data with a computer, you need to transfer the data to a format that is compatible with the software you will use for the analysis. Such formats generally consist of a spreadsheet in which the rows represent the respondents, or cases, and the columns represent the variables, as shown in Table 1.1.
The rows of the spreadsheet contain the cases, which are numbered sequentially
from 1 down the left-hand column. The variables begin in column 2 with age,
gender, education, and so on. The spreadsheet in Table 1.1 shows that case 1 is 29
years old, is a male (0 = male, 1 = female), has 12 years of formal education, and
so on. Note that the values of the variables are represented with numbers. Each
number represents a response. Age is recorded using a number corresponding to
years. Gender is represented by 0s and 1s, where 0 = male and 1 = female.

TABLE 1.1    **Spreadsheet Format**

| Case | Age | Gender | Education | Religious Preference | Marital Status | Political Preference | Residence |
|------|-----|--------|-----------|----------------------|----------------|----------------------|-----------|
| 1 | 29 | 0 | 12 | 2 | 2 | 2 | 1 |
| 2 | 23 | 1 | 14 | 4 | 1 | 4 | 1 |
| 3 | 37 | 1 | 16 | 3 | 2 | 1 | 1 |
| 4 | 46 | 0 | 10 | 5 | 4 | 2 | 2 |
| 5 | 34 | 1 | 14 | 1 | 1 | 3 | 5 |

Marital status is represented by assigning a number to being single, married, formerly married, and so on.[4] The computer then counts the number of 1s, 2s, and 3s and reports the number of cases with that value. As a general rule, data entered on spreadsheets are represented by numbers and are referred to as *numerics.* Variables represented with letters are referred to as *alphas.* Although the computer is most adept at dealing with numeric data, alpha representations are sometimes desirable for purposes of display. Thus, you could use M = male and F = female. The computer, using the data entered in the spreadsheet, can produce basic descriptive numerical summaries of data, graphs, charts, and other complex statistical evaluations.

## *Summary*

The purpose of this section was to provide an introduction to the subject matter of statistics. Statistics is defined as a body of methods for providing numerical descriptions. This book is concerned primarily with descriptive statistics and inferential statistics. The former consists of basic methods for displaying numerical descriptions, the latter of methods that make it possible to describe large populations on the basis of inferences from small samples.

The role and importance of statistics in the total research process was illustrated with an example. Given all the other tasks that are involved in doing research, the role of statistics might seem relatively minor, but it is crucial because often statistical results represent key evidence in determining whether the propositions and theories that drive a research endeavor are worthy of further support. The following section introduces the concept of measurement and defines how it is used in social research.

---

[4]You can assign any numbers you want to variable values, but each response to a question must have a unique number.

## MEASUREMENT

### *The Concept of Measurement*

Measurement is the backbone of all scientific endeavor. Advances in scientific knowledge depend on the capacity of scientists to develop more precise measurements of the subject under investigation. **Measurement** has been defined as "the assignment of numerals to aspects of objects or events according to rule."[5] According to this definition, measurement is any consistent set of rules for assigning numbers to phenomena. Given that statistics is concerned with describing things with *numbers,* the business of how numbers are assigned deserves some attention.

Numerical measuring devices such as clocks, rulers, speedometers, thermometers, and others are used by everyone without giving much thought to how these tools were created. Everyday measuring devices provide numerical descriptions that have immediate relevance, providing a sense of time, length, speed, temperature, and so on. Although we might not often think about the rules that were used to create these measures, each measure is organized around a very specific set of conditions.

### *Four Criteria for Measuring Devices*

In doing research and scientific work, it is important to know what the rules and conditions are for assigning numbers to objects or events. Prior to examining the general types of measurements used in social science, it is worthwhile to examine the four conditions that any measuring device must meet to be useful. A device must have (1) *reliability* and (2) *validity* and (3) be *exhaustive* and (4) be *mutually exclusive.*

#### *Reliability*

A scale is **reliable** if, when used to repeat a measurement of the same object under the same conditions, it produces the same results. For example, you step on a bathroom scale, and it registers your weight. Then you step off the scale and back on it, and it registers the same weight. This measurement is reliable. It has *reproduced* the same value under the same conditions. This condition is also known as the *criterion of reproducibility.*

Whereas most people give little thought to the reliability of the different measuring devices they use, in any scientific discipline reliability always is of great concern. Although some standard measures, such as weight and height, are easy to reproduce, others—those that interest social scientists the most—might not be. Social scientists measure, for example, social class, social achievement, satisfaction with social services, and participation in deviant behavior, all of which are both important and difficult to measure. For example, we all have a commonsense

[5] S. Smith Stevens, "Measurement," in Garry M. Maranell, ed., *Scaling: A Sourcebook for Behavioral Scientists* (Chicago: Aldine, 1974), pp. 27–28. The discussion that follows is based in part on the material presented by Stevens, in Maranell, pp. 22–41.

notion of what social class is and might use the term in everyday discourse, but it is another matter to devise a measurement scheme that is reliable for assigning people to a set of social classes. Not only is there disagreement on the criteria that should be used, but developing operational indices that satisfy commonsense notions of what social class really consists of is difficult. And whatever criteria are used, how individuals are assigned to social class categories should not be a function of who is using the tool or the conditions under which it is applied. The criterion of reliability requires that a measuring device be such that the same people are assigned to the same social class regardless of who uses the instrument and the setting in which it is applied.

Social science relies heavily on measurements that are based on responses that people give to questionnaires. Here reliability is a matter of whether a respondent is likely to give the same answer to a question if the process is repeated. It may be that answers are influenced by the time of the day that the data were collected, events that transpired just before the questionnaire was completed, who was present when the questions were answered, or even the setting in which the information was collected. For example, adolescents might answer differently to questions on their drinking behavior if the survey is conducted in their homes or in their classroom at school.

To deal with these problems, social scientists go to great effort to standardize their instruments, including examining at length the problems of reliability they might encounter. Although a detailed discussion of these issues is beyond the scope of this book, remember that a good measuring device is reliable only if it produces the same results under the same conditions.

## *Validity*

Whereas reliability deals with reproducibility, **validity** refers to whether a measuring device measures what it was intended to measure. For example, we expect a thermometer to provide information on temperature; if it does that, it is a valid measure. If an outdoor thermometer reads 82° F, we prepare for a balmy, comfortable day. If the same thermometer registers 30° F, we prepare for a cooler day by wearing a jacket. On the basis of utility, a thermometer provides valid information on temperature, and we are in position to respond appropriately.

Measuring devices are valid for specific purposes. Although a thermometer provides information on the temperature of a room, it provides no information on the social comfort level of a room. Other factors can make a room seem more or less comfortable, such as a strange odor, inadequate lighting, or the presence of certain people.

Going beyond the intent of measuring devices is problematic with respect to some social data. Thus, although it is assumed sometimes that intelligence tests reflect native intellectual capacity, these measures are confounded by such things as social experience, family income, and so on. Social class assignments might be assumed to reflect how people see themselves when, more likely, they are statements of how researchers see people.

In addition, a measuring device can be reliable but not valid. A bathroom scale might consistently over- or under-report weight, which would make it reliable but provide an invalid measure of actual weight.

As with reliability, issues of validity are always of concern in scientific endeavors. Although agreement might exist on what to measure, devising the instruments to capture the subject of interest might not be so easy. For example, we might all understand what is meant by *social aspirations* but have a very difficult time finding a tool that embodies what we think we mean by that term. Moreover, given that data for social research are collected through questionnaires or interviews, validity is a function of whether those who answer the questions respond to the real intent of the question. For example, if you are interested in measuring drinking behavior, the resulting measures are valid only to the extent that the questions result in accurate information on that behavior. The accuracy of responses is a function of the questions asked, how the respondent feels about the questions, the situation in which the questions are presented, and how the respondent thinks the information they give will be used.

Validity in social science measurements is a function of at least several factors, including skill in constructing questions that will produce the information intended, the sensitivity and personal nature of the information sought, the difficulty that respondents have producing the information, and the accuracy of their memory. Moreover, some are more reluctant to share their thoughts or to discuss their personal behavior with outsiders, creating variation in responses. Furthermore, some information is difficult for people to remember, resulting in inaccurate responses due simply to faulty recollection. Also, the subjects that social scientists address frequently involve personal or private aspects of life. The difficulty of obtaining accurate measures of, for example, sexual activity or illegal behavior is apparent, but assessing more mundane aspects, such as political and religious beliefs, life satisfaction, academic potential, or suitability for employment are difficult as well.

Developing accurate tools for measurement is not trivial, as it remains the basis on which all scientific investigation rests. Advances in the ability to better understand human behavior will depend on increasing the capacity to measure more precisely.

### Exhaustive

A good measuring device must meet the condition of exhausting the possibilities of what it is intended to measure. All the elements that are the target of a measuring device must be represented by some value on a scale. If a measuring device cannot assign values to these elements, it is not very useful. For example, if you want to measure political party preference, all the target population's party choices must be represented on the scale. Suppose that you developed a scale consisting of Democrats, Republicans, and Independents but some of the population were Socialists. This scale would not be **exhaustive.**

Many social measures include the category "other." This category lumps together individuals whose preferences represent a very small percentage of the respondents. However, even when it represents only a small percentage, this category fails to provide information about their preferences. As the percentage of "other" respondents increases, the scale becomes less informative.

### Mutually Exclusive
**Mutually exclusive** means that each observation fits one and only one of the scale categories. If a scale were developed to measure ethnicity and some of the respondents fit into more than one of the scale's categories because of ethnic roots, the scale would not meet the criterion of being mutually exclusive. To address this problem, you would need to add additional scale categories that reflected the wider range of ethnic heritages. Scales are structurally adequate if they are such that *all the members of the sample* fit one (exhaustive) and *only one* scale category (mutually exclusive).

## Types of Scales

Three types of measurement scales are used in social research: nominal, ordinal, and interval. (Another type of measurement discussed here is the ratio scale, which is a special type of interval scale. But beyond defining it, the scale will receive no further attention in this book.) Special attention is given to a unique nominal scale—the dichotomous scale—because its properties are somewhat different from those of other nominal scales in that it is similar to an interval scale when treated mathematically. Moreover, statistical methods have been developed to evaluate dichotomous measures. Each scale type conforms to the definition of measurement in that they embody predetermined rules for assigning numbers.

### Nominal Scales
Also referred to as *qualitative* (or *categorical*) scales, **nominal scales** consist of categories for sorting or classifying objects or events on the basis of some quality or attribute. Examples of such scales are political and religious preferences, ethnic heritage, native language, and marital status.

Suppose that you develop a scale for classifying the members of your statistics class in terms of their major fields of study. Your scale might consist of the categories shown in Table 1.2. If the scale includes all the majors represented in the class (exhaustive) and if everyone fit into one and only one of the categories (mutually exclusive), the scale would be adequate. It is possible that some of your classmates are pursuing double majors, such as sociology and economics. If so, the scale would need to be modified to include categories for double majors. The scale must also be reliable to obtain consistent responses on majors, and it must be valid in that the majors must be among those offered at the school.

Our definition of measurement includes the phrase "assigning numbers according to rule," implying that the categories of nominal scales be labeled with numbers. Typically, this is not done when reporting nominal scales because the numerals assigned to the scale categories serve only as *labels* and cannot be interpreted or manipulated mathematically. For example, if you assigned numbers to

**TABLE 1.2    Major Field of Study**

Sociology
Psychology
Social Work
Anthropology
Economics

the scale categories in Table 1.2 so that sociology = 1, psychology = 2, social work = 3, anthropology = 4, and economics = 5, it would not mean that psychology, with its label 2, has twice the value of sociology (1), nor could you add a psychology major (2) to a social worker (3) and end up with an economist (5). Thus, numbers assigned to nominal scale categories serve only as distinguishing labels and do not represent a numerical value for the categories. Usually, nominal data being prepared for computer analysis are assigned numbers because software programs are more adept at dealing with numbers than with names; again, however, numbers serve only as identifiers or labels.

### Ordinal Scales

**Ordinal scales** consist of categories that rank observations from least to most or from most to least. Examples include the position of individuals finishing a race (first, second, and third) or in a social class (upper, middle, and lower); scales that organize entities or events in terms of categories such as very favorable, favorable, neutral, unfavorable, and very unfavorable; and any scheme for logically organizing observations in an ascending or a descending order.

In contrast to numerals used in nominal scales, numerals used in ordinal scales are more than labels in that they reflect a lower or a higher position on the scale. For example, the social aspirations of a sample of 75 individuals in Table 1.3 shows how such a scale can be displayed. Those with the lowest aspirations have been assigned a 1 and those with the highest a 5. The numbers have meaning in that those assigned 5 have higher aspirations than those assigned 4, those assigned 4 have higher aspirations than those assigned 3, and so on. This means that if $4 > 3$ and $5 > 4$, then $5 > 3$.

Numbers assigned this way do not provide information on the size of the difference between the scale categories. From Table 1.3 you know that those assigned 4 have higher aspirations than those assigned 2, but you do not know exactly how much higher. It would be inappropriate to conclude that 4 indicates twice as much social aspiration as 2 or that those assigned 1 have only half of the aspirations of those assigned 2. We know only that 4 is higher than 2 but not how much higher.

Thus, the numerals on ordinal scales serve only as *ranks for ordering observations from least to most in terms of the characteristic measured* and fail to indicate the precise amount of the characteristic that is present.

**TABLE 1.3    Social Aspirations (n = 75)**

| Social Aspirations | | | | | |
|---|---|---|---|---|---|
| 1<br>Very Low | 2<br>Low | 3<br>Moderate | 4<br>High | 5<br>Very High | Total |
| 5 | 10 | 25 | 20 | 15 | 75 |

### Interval Scales

**Interval scales** have all the properties of nominal and ordinal scales, but not only do they consist of mutually exclusive categories and order objects from least to most, they specify the exact amount of the measured characteristic that is present. Examples of interval scales include a ruler, a weight scale, age, number of years of formal education, hourly wage, and so on. The intervals of all these scales are of equal size. That is, the distance between 1 and 2 inches on a ruler is precisely the same as that between 2 and 3 inches or 7 and 8 inches. Because all intervals are of equal size, they can be divided into increasingly smaller equal units, allowing for even more precision. Thus, an inch can be divided into halves, quarters, eighths, sixteenths, thirty-seconds, and so on. Theoretically, the categories of interval scales are infinitely divisible into smaller equal parts, allowing for increasing precision.

The property of *infinite divisibility* means that interval scales have an infinite continuum of points or numerical values. Thus, such scales are referred to as *continuous measures*, whereas nominal and ordinal scales, consisting of *discrete* categories, are referred to as *discrete measures*. Continuous scales provide exact measures of the *amount* of a characteristic present, whereas discrete scales consist of counts of the number of observations appearing in a *finite* set of categories.

Inasmuch as interval scales measure exact quantities, the numerical values of the scales can be treated mathematically. For example, someone who is 20 years old is twice as old as someone who is 10 and only half as old as someone who is 40. Mathematical procedures can be applied to the numerals of interval scales, which are then subject to sophisticated analyses.

### Ratio Scales

The **ratio scale** is a special form of interval scale. It differs in that it has a true *zero point*, that is, a point at which the measured characteristic is known to be absent. Although the commonly used Fahrenheit thermometer has a zero on its scale, it is not a true zero point in that zero is not intended to represent the absence of heat. A Kelvin thermometer, however, has a true zero point at which, theoretically, heat is absent. The advantage of using a ratio scale is that it identifies the point of origin of a measured characteristic.

Many measures used in social research meet the requirements of a ratio scale. For example, some people have zero income, and some adults have zero years of formal education. Of course, this does not mean that people live without resources or that those with no formal education have experienced no learning. While ratio scales represent an important refinement in interval scale measurement, for most statistical procedures they are treated as interval measures. Thus, ratio scales are not identified separately but are included in the more general category of *interval scales* and *continuous measures*.

### Dichotomous Scales

**Dichotomous scales** are nominal scales that consist of only two categories but have unique properties that set them apart from the more general class of nominal measures. Examples of dichotomous scales are measures of gender (male and female), yes-no and true-false questions, or any other measure that consists of only two categories. Dichotomous measures are unique in that numbers assigned to them can be manipulated mathematically. Suppose that you have a dichotomous measure of gender so that males = 0 and females = 1. If you have a sample of 10 people, of which 2 are males and 8 are females, you can add their scale values—$0 + 0 + 1 + 1 + 1 + 1 + 1 + 1 + 1 + 1 = 8$—and divide the sum by the sample size (10), so that $8/10 = .80$. The value .80 has meaning in that the proportion of females is .80. With the scale values of 0 and 1, this result can be achieved only when you have the ratio of 2 males to 8 females. This is a clear and unambiguous description of the characteristic of gender for the sample. For many purposes, the numerical values assigned to dichotomous scales can be treated as though they were interval scale values, and for this reason they are treated as a special case. In addition, many statistical procedures have been developed to deal with dichotomous data, indicating that such measures deserve special attention.

### Summary of Measurement

Measurement is the basis for all systematic inquiry because it provides tools for recording differences between things in the worlds of observation and behavior. At the most elementary level, measurement scales are simply devices for sorting things with common characteristics. In scientific undertakings, measurement is the most basic and important part of any investigation. The tools used for measurement must meet four criteria: (1) They must be *reliable* so that, when used to measure the same unit under the same conditions, they produce the same results; (2) they must be *valid* by actually measuring what they intend to measure; (3) the categories of a scale must be *exhaustive* so as to include all members with the measured characteristic; and (4) they must be *mutually exclusive* so that each measured element fits only one scale category or value.

Five types of scales have been discussed. *Nominal* scales categorize observations in terms of qualities or attributes. *Ordinal* scales go one step beyond and provide ordered categories that rank observations from least to most in terms of some characteristic. Both nominal and ordinal scales are made up of discrete categories. *Interval* and *ratio* scales are more complex, consisting of intervals of equal size that make it possible to precisely determine the amount of a characteristic present in each observation. *Dichotomous* scales are unique nominal scales in that, numerically, they can be treated like interval measures.

## A STRATEGY FOR LEARNING

Acquiring any new body of information requires a strategy. Throughout the book, emphasis is placed on knowledge that is essential for mastering the methods of statistics. Tips and hints on the logic that ties the techniques of statistics into a systematic body of methods are also given. An important part of learning any discipline is mastering its vocabulary by incorporating it into your speech and writing. This means making a conscious effort not only to learn and remember new terms as they appear, but also to use those terms when discussing the subject matter. As an aid, a summary of key terms is provided at the end of each chapter. It is also important to remember primary symbols that are part of the language of statistics, so a summary of the symbols introduced in each chapter is provided. In addition, the formulas introduced in each chapter are summarized as a quick reference at the end. While some of the more basic formulas that appear frequently may stick in your memory, it is not important to try to memorize formulas.

Each chapter concludes with a problem set. It is appropriate, given the ready availability of computers, to ask why you should bother to calculate solutions by hand. Can't the computer do it all and do it better? First, doing problems by hand is the easiest way to really learn and understand what statistics is about. If you don't understand how the basic models for statistical analysis work, you are not likely to understand the method except in the most superficial way. Understanding that comes through calculation is particularly important if you plan to go into advanced statistics courses. While advanced statistical models rely more than ever on computers, understanding the models, their limitations, and the meanings of their results depends heavily on knowing how basic statistical calculations work.

Second, it is important to do hand calculations because a great many occasions call for statistical calculations of data that are not available on a computer or that, if available, can be calculated by hand in far less time than it would take to organize the effort electronically. Many of you will take jobs whose responsibilities include working with numbers and data from various sources. Many everyday data sets are not computerized, so the capacity to quickly calculate summary descriptive and inferential statistics is a real advantage.

The role of the computer is equally important. The number of introductory statistics courses without a computer component is dwindling rapidly. As part of learning basic statistics, this book assumes you will complete exercises on the computer. Likely, you will be expected to learn to use a statistical software package with a computerized database. Each chapter in this book will suggest potential computer exercises that you can apply to your database. For example, as part of Chapter 1, you may want to become familiar with the contents of the database used for your course. It is important to recognize the key variables in the database, and given the discussion of measurement, to be able to identify the type of scale represented by each variable in your data set. You may also want to review the variables, selecting a variable that may serve as an important dependent measure and then identifying several independent measures that might influence the value of the dependent measure. Of course, the primary goal is to become familiar with the specific software used in the course and the general character of the database.

## CHAPTER SUMMARY

This chapter's purpose was to introduce the subject of statistics and provide a sense of what to expect in this book. Statistics is a body of methods for describing the world with numbers. The two primary methods discussed here are descriptive and inferential statistics. Whereas the former includes methods for displaying numerical descriptions, the latter makes it possible to describe large populations on the basis of inferences from small samples.

The role of statistics in research was illustrated with an example. Given all that is involved in doing research, the role of statistics seems relatively minor, but it is crucial because often statistical results contain the key evidence for determining whether the theoretical propositions are worthy of further support.

The second topic of this chapter was measurement, which provides the tools for recording differences and assigning numbers to the world of observation and behavior. The minimum criteria for any measuring device include having reliability and validity and being exhaustive and mutually exclusive. Five types of scales are discussed: nominal, dichotomous, ordinal, interval, and ratio. Dichotomous scales are considered separately from other nominal scales because, for many numerical purposes, they can be treated like interval measures. In dealing with numerical descriptions, you always need to be aware of the type of scale you are using. Special statistical techniques exist for analyzing data produced by each scale type. In later chapters you will find that the type of scale used to derive data restricts the type of statistical analysis that can be conducted. The next chapter discusses methods used to organize and display data that result from the use of various measures.

An important part of learning any new discipline is mastering its vocabulary. Therefore, you must concentrate on learning and remembering new terms as they appear in each chapter. As an aid, a summary of key terms, symbols, and formulas is given at the end of each chapter to provide a review of the chapter's contents.

## KEY TERMS

**dependent variable**   A variable whose values are affected by an independent variable; also referred to as a *criterion* or an *outcome*.

**descriptive statistics**   Statistical methods used to present the character and distribution of some measured phenomenon.

**dichotomous scale**   A nominal scale consisting of only two categories.

**distribution**   The different values that a variable has for a sample of observations.

**exhaustive**   The capacity of a scale to include values for all the elements represented by a measure.

**hypothesis**   A statement specifying the relationship between two or more variables.

**independent variable**   A variable that affects or predicts a dependent variable; also referred to as a *predictor*.

**inferential statistics**   Statistical methods used to draw inferences about population characteristics on the basis of observations of a sample.

**interval scale**   A continuous scale in which the exact distance between the points on the scale is known; this provides a measure of the quantity (or amount) of the property that the measured object possesses.

**measurement**   The assignment of numbers to aspects of objects or events according to rule.

**mutually exclusive**   The capacity of a scale for classifying objects into one and only one scale category.

**nominal scale**   A scale for classifying objects or events according to some quality or attribute.

**operationalize**   Specifying the procedures that must be undertaken to measure what is intended by a variable.

**ordinal scale**   A scale that ranks (orders) objects from least to most or most to least without establishing the exact distances between the ranks.

**parameter**   Any number describing a population.

**population**   The entire set of entities of concern.

**ratio scale**   An interval scale with a true zero point.

**reliability**   The capacity of a scale to provide reliable results such that repeated measures of the same object under the same conditions give the same results.

**sample**   A representative subset of a population.

**statistic**   Any number describing a sample.

**statistical methods**   The body of methods used to develop numerical descriptions.

**theory**   An explanation of how things work.

**validity**   The capacity of a scale to measure what it is intended to measure.

**variable**   An entity that can take on more than one value.

## EXERCISES

1. Select a research article from a professional journal such as the *American Journal of Sociology,* the *American Sociological Review,* or some other research journal in the social sciences or human services. Answer the following questions:

   a. What is the primary theoretical proposition addressed in the article?
   b. Describe how the dependent variable(s) is operationalized.
   c. Describe how the primary independent variables are operationalized.
   d. What conclusions are drawn at the end of the article?

2. The following variables are frequently encountered in social research. Identify the level of measurement usually associated with each:

   Age
   Gender
   Ethnic origin
   Marital status
   Religious preference
   Years of formal education completed
   Occupation
   Income
   Number of siblings
   Birth order of siblings
   Political preference

3. Give two examples illustrating the character of a reliable scale.

4. Give two examples illustrating the character of a valid scale.

5. Give an example illustrating a scale that is reliable but not valid.

6. What is the difference between the scale properties of mutually exclusive and exhaustive?

7. What is the difference between a nominal and an ordinal scale?

8. What is the difference between an ordinal scale and an interval scale?

9. What is the difference between a discrete measure and a continuous measure?

10. What is unique about a dichotomous scale?

11. What is measurement?

# 2

# DISPLAYING DATA

The purpose of this chapter is to present methods and techniques for describing numbers assigned to a sample of observations with respect to some measurement. Measurement is concerned with assigning numbers to observations. Given that social research is usually based on relatively large numbers of observations, presentations must be done with care so the import of the numerical description is accurate and clear to users. We will examine the concept of a frequency distribution, methods for creating relative frequency displays, and the use of tables and graphs for data display. While research is generally based on samples, the techniques described here are used whether the data is based on observations of a sample or an entire population.

Although the following content is not difficult to understand, be sure to become familiar with the new terms. Much of the difficulty in following any new subject matter is due to new and strange vocabulary, and this is also true in statistics. A commitment to mastering these terms will help you understand the rest of the text more easily.

## FREQUENCIES AND FREQUENCY DISTRIBUTIONS

A **frequency** is the number of observations with a common property. If you select a sample of 115 voters and 45 of them are Democrats, the frequency of Democrats is 45. A **frequency distribution** shows all the frequencies of an interrelated set of observations. The frequency distribution of the sample of 115 voters is shown in Table 2.1. The *variable* is political party affiliation, the measurement is a *nominal scale*, and the scale consists of three categories: Democrats, Republicans, and Independents. The symbol *f* designates the frequencies of the scale categories, and *n* represents the total number of observations. Note that the sum of the frequencies must equal *n*.

The distribution of outcomes for ordinal scales, which also consist of limited categories, can be presented similarly. Suppose that you measured, using a five-point ordinal scale, the extent to which students were satisfied with the pace of a

**TABLE 2.1  Political Party Affiliations**

| | |
|---|---|
| ($n = 115$) | |
| **Party** | $f$ |
| Democrat | 45 |
| Republican | 45 |
| Independent | 25 |
| Total | 115 |

course they are enrolled in. The results are shown in Table 2.2. Whereas most of the students, 36, were either very satisfied or satisfied, as many as 14 were dissatisfied or very dissatisfied.

In the case of interval data, the number of scale categories potentially can be very large because interval scales, by definition, consist of a continuous set of scale values and each observation can have a unique value. Consequently, presenting distributions of interval measures requires more extensive consideration.

For example, the distribution of values resulting from a measurement might consist of a simple listing of the individual score for each sample member. The listing may be presented as a **disordered array** or an **ordered array.** A disordered array is a random listing of sample values presented in the order in which the data were collected. An ordered array lists the observations in order from the lowest to the highest or the highest to the lowest value.

Presenting the entire **array** of observed values has the advantage of displaying the specific value of each observation or member of the sample, as shown in Table 2.3. The table presents an ordered array of the body weights of a sample of 77 individuals. The advantage of presenting the entire array is that all the data on that measurement are available to the audience. The disadvantage is that the large number of observations and the resulting large amount of data become overwhelming, making it difficult to assess their importance. Given that the purpose of numerical presentations is to help you better understand what is being reported, the confusion created by too much data is counterproductive and should be avoided.

A glance at the array in Table 2.3 will show values from 102 to as high as 198; beyond that, however, all the detail of the numbers makes it difficult to say much about the sample of body weights. Arrays can be simplified by recasting them into

**TABLE 2.2  Level of Satisfaction with Pace of Course**

| Very Satisfied | Satisfied | So-So | Dissatisfied | Very Dissatisfied | Total |
|---|---|---|---|---|---|
| ($n = 60$) | | | | | |
| 24 | 12 | 10 | 6 | 8 | 60 |

**TABLE 2.3   Ordered Array of Body Weights**

$(n = 77)$

| | | | | | | |
|---|---|---|---|---|---|---|
| 102 | 130 | 143 | 152 | 156 | 164 | 174 |
| 108 | 132 | 143 | 152 | 157 | 165 | 177 |
| 110 | 133 | 143 | 153 | 158 | 166 | 178 |
| 111 | 133 | 146 | 154 | 158 | 166 | 179 |
| 114 | 134 | 147 | 154 | 160 | 168 | 183 |
| 117 | 136 | 147 | 155 | 161 | 168 | 185 |
| 119 | 137 | 147 | 155 | 161 | 169 | 185 |
| 121 | 139 | 149 | 155 | 161 | 169 | 188 |
| 122 | 141 | 150 | 156 | 162 | 171 | 191 |
| 123 | 141 | 150 | 156 | 163 | 173 | 196 |
| 128 | 142 | 151 | 156 | 163 | 174 | 198 |

**grouped frequency distributions,** which consist of *class intervals*, each of which represents a limited range of the original values.

For example, the array of body weights in Table 2.3 can be recast into 10-pound intervals, as shown in Table 2.4. The use of class intervals results in a display that is immediately more informative than the original one. The right-hand column headed by the symbol *f* contains the number of individuals in each weight category. For example, 18 persons weighed somewhere between 150 and 159 pounds, whereas 15 weighed between 160 and 169 pounds.

**TABLE 2.4   Grouped Frequency Distribution for Body Weights**

$(n = 77)$

| Class Limits | *f* |
|---|---|
| 190–199 | 3 |
| 180–189 | 4 |
| 170–179 | 7 |
| 160–169 | 15 |
| 150–159 | 18 |
| 140–149 | 11 |
| 130–139 | 8 |
| 120–129 | 4 |
| 110–119 | 5 |
| 100–109 | 2 |
| Total | 77 |

TABLE 2.5  Stated Class Limits and Exact Class
Limits for Body Weights

(*n* = 77)

| Stated Class Limits | Exact Class Limits | f |
|---|---|---|
| 190–199 | 189.5–199.5 | 3 |
| 180–189 | 179.5–189.5 | 4 |
| 170–179 | 169.5–179.5 | 7 |
| 160–169 | 159.5–169.5 | 15 |
| 150–159 | 149.5–159.5 | 18 |
| 140–149 | 139.5–149.5 | 11 |
| 130–139 | 129.5–139.5 | 8 |
| 120–129 | 119.5–129.5 | 4 |
| 110–119 | 109.5–119.5 | 5 |
| 100–109 | 99.5–109.5 | 2 |
| | Total | 77 |

There is a trade-off in converting an ordered array to a grouped frequency distribution. An ordered array displays the value of each of the 77 body weights. The grouped frequency distribution presents body weights only in terms of 10-pound intervals, and although it displays the number of individuals in each weight interval, it does not provide information on individual weights. However, the grouped frequency display is more informative in providing a sense of how weights are distributed in the sample. Some of the detail provided by the array is sacrificed for a gain in information on the distribution of body weights. The example shows that in presentations, especially to audiences not sophisticated in the use of numerical descriptions, grouped frequency distributions might be more informative than the entire array.

Two requirements must be met in constructing grouped frequency distributions. First, the class intervals must be of equal size; otherwise, the presentation might be misinterpreted. In the example of body weights, each class interval consists of an exact range of 10 pounds. It would be confusing and misleading if some of the intervals were 5 pounds, some 10, and yet others 15 in that readers might overlook the differences in interval widths.

Second, the *exact* limits of the intervals must be established so that each observation fits into one and only one interval. Table 2.5 shows both the *stated class limits* and exact class limits for the example of body weights. Stated limits are rounded off to avoid presenting an unnecessary, visually distracting amount of digits. Numerical data should always be presented in a way that reduces the potential for confusion and misunderstanding, and stated limits serve that purpose. However, for results to be accurate, mathematical calculations must be based on the exact limits of the intervals. Therefore, it must be clear whether an observation of 109.5 pounds should be placed in interval 100–109 or interval 110–119.

   Rules for exact class limits resolve ambiguity for cases at the margins of the intervals. The rule adopted for our example follows. An observation of 109.5 is rounded up to 110 and is in the interval 110–119; an observation of 109.4 is rounded down to 109 and is in the interval 100–109. Given the rule, the exact class limits for Table 2.5 become 99.5–109.5, 109.5–119.5, and so on. The proper interpretation of the exact class limits, looking at the first interval, is that interval 100–109 includes *all values equal to or greater than 99.5 and less than 109.5*. Thus, a value of 99.5 is in the interval, but one of 109.5 is in the next interval, 110–119. Interval 2 includes all values equal to or greater than 109.5 and less than 119.5 and so on. The rule provides for mutually exclusive categories.

   After the array of values is grouped into intervals, information on the exact value of any one observation within the interval is forfeited. Table 2.5 shows that 15 individuals weigh from 159.5 to 169.5, but the exact weight of any one individual in the interval is unknown. The best estimate for any one weight is the midpoint of the interval. Using the midpoint to estimate the weight of individuals in an interval is based on the *principle of least error*. The midpoint on the long term will result in less error than any other point within the interval. For example, using the midpoint to represent a 10-point interval with boundaries of 159.5 and 169.5 would never result in an error greater than 5 points, which would occur only if the real value were located at either end of the interval. If the lower limit of 159.5 were used instead of the midpoint, and the actual value were 169.3, it would be off by almost 10 points, an error considerably greater than 5 points.

   The exact midpoint (mpt) for any interval can be calculated using the following formula:

$$\mathrm{mpt} = l_i + \frac{w_i}{2} \tag{2.1}$$

where     $l_i =$ the exact lower limit of an interval

   $w_i =$ the width of the interval

Applied to interval 159.5–169.5, Formula 2.1 shows the midpoint to be

$$\mathrm{mpt}(159.5\text{–}169.5) = 159.5 + \frac{10}{2}$$

$$= 159.5 + 5$$

$$= 164.5$$

   On the basis of the principle of least error, the best estimate for the weight of any individual in interval 159.5–169.5 is 164.5. After the midpoint for one interval has been calculated, the midpoints of the remaining intervals are obvious. Thus, the interval below the one we calculated would be 154.5, and the one above would be 174.5.

   The width of the intervals is important to consider when constructing grouped frequency distributions. If the intervals are too wide, much of the information contained in the original data might be lost. If the intervals are too narrow, too many intervals will result, and the original goal of simplifying the array of individual scores might not be met. In our example of weights, if the intervals were 20 pounds wide, much information on the distribution of individual weights would be lost. If the intervals were only 2 pounds, little would be gained in terms of simplifying the original array. The choice of interval widths should focus on providing the audience with the most informative and least confusing display of data.

A rule of thumb states that data arrays be recast into no fewer than 10 and no more than 20 intervals. In our example, the weights ranged from 99.5 to 199.5 for a range of 100 pounds, and we used 10 intervals in grouping the data. If the weight range had been from 49.5 to 249.5 pounds with 200 or more individuals, 15- or even 20-pound intervals might have provided a more informative display.

## RELATIVE FREQUENCIES

Often it is more convincing to display frequency distributions relative to some standard. Relative frequency displays provide such a medium. Three commonly used relative frequencies are *ratios*, *proportions*, and *percentages*. Each reports frequencies of observations relative to some base or standard.

### Ratios

The most general relative frequency is the common **ratio.** A ratio is simply *one number divided by another.* For example, the ratio of the number of sociology majors to psychology majors is

$$\frac{\text{Sociologists}}{\text{Psychologists}}$$

If you have 60 students and 40 are sociologists and 20 are psychologists, the ratio of sociologists to psychologists is $40/20 = 2.00$, which means that there are two sociology majors for every psychology major. Rather than present the ratio of sociologists to psychologists, you could calculate the ratio of psychologists to sociologists, or $20/40 = .5$, indicating that there are .5 psychologists for every sociologist. Although the information is the same, the two presentations feel somewhat different. It might be easier to comprehend the ratio of 2 sociologists for every psychologist rather than .5 psychologists for every sociologist. The general formula for a ratio is

$$\text{Ratio} = \frac{f_1}{f_2} \tag{2.2}$$

where     $f_1$ = the frequency of the first value

$f_2$ = the frequency of the second value

Ratios are very useful in that they allow comparisons of very different measures. For example, you can calculate the ratio of students to teachers, tuition dollars to classroom hours, dollars to staff, clients to clinic hours, automobiles to households, or whatever your interests might be. Quite literally, they can be used to compare apples and oranges. You can calculate ratios for all levels of measurement, whether interval, ordinal, nominal, or dichotomous. This is true because ratios are based on the number of observations with a common value. They are powerful descriptive tools because they are easily understood and frequently serve the interest at hand. The ease by which ratios can be calculated should not lead to underestimating their power and utility. As you progress through this text, you will also find that *much of statistical analysis is organized around ratios,* so we will return to the idea of the ratio frequently.

## *Proportions*

A **proportion** is a special ratio by which a subset of frequencies in a distribution is divided by the total number of frequencies. Simply stated, a proportion is a *ratio of a part to the whole:*

$$\text{Proportion} = \frac{\text{Part}}{\text{Whole}}$$

In contrast, the more general ratio discussed previously can be thought of as a *part divided by a part:*

$$\text{Ratio} = \frac{\text{Part}}{\text{Part}}$$

For a frequency distribution, a proportion can be expressed as

$$\text{Proportion} = \frac{f_i}{n} \tag{2.3}$$

where    $f_i$ = the frequency of a subset of a distribution

$n$ = the total number of members in the distribution

The proportion of sociologists relative to 60 sociology and psychology majors would be

$$\frac{\text{Sociologists}}{\text{Sociologists} + \text{Psychologists}}$$

and applying Formula 2.3 to the sample of 40 sociologists and 20 psychologists, we find that

$$\frac{40}{40 + 20} = .67$$

The proportion of sociologists out of the group of 60 sociology and psychology majors is .67. Further, the proportion of psychologists is

$$\frac{20}{20 + 40} = .33$$

Note that the sum of the two proportions, .67 + .33, is 1.00. It is always true that the sum of the proportions of the frequencies of a distribution must total 1.00. By calculating the proportions, we know that the number of sociologists relative to the total number is .67 and that the number of psychologists relative to the total number is .33.

Another way to think about proportions is that changing the original observations to proportions is a **linear transformation** of the frequency distribution. In our example, the original distribution of sociologists and psychologists was transformed from a scale of values that was 40 + 20 = 60 to one that was .67 + .33 = 1.00. The transformation is useful because it is easier to understand, especially when large numbers of observations are involved. Moreover, the transformation enables us to convert quite different measures to a standard distribution of values that extends from .00 to 1.00. The proportion of sociologists to psychologists, females to males, or particular religious preference to all religious preferences has immediate intuitive meaning and is readily understood by a variety of audiences. In addition, distributions based on different sample sizes can be compared by transforming them to proportions. Further examples of using proportions are provided later in this chapter.

## Percentages

A **percentage** is a proportion multiplied by 100:

$$\text{Percentage} = \frac{f_i}{n} \times 100 \tag{2.4}$$

The percentage of sociologists in the group of 60 majors is

$$\frac{40}{60} \times 100 = 66.7\%$$

whereas the percentage of psychologists is

$$\frac{20}{60} \times 100 = 33.3\%$$

The sum of the percentages of all the frequencies of a distribution always equals 100. Thus, the sum of the percentages of sociologists and psychologists is 66.7 + 33.3 = 100. Converting the frequencies of a distribution to percentages represents another linear transformation in which the original frequencies are converted to a new number scale extending from 0.00 to 100. Using percentages, we have transformed the original frequency distribution of 40 + 20 = 60 to 66.7 + 33.3 = 100. The advantages to using percentages are the same as those to using proportions, and their use is so common in everyday affairs that they are generally understood and appreciated by everyone.

The percentages in the example above are rounded to one decimal point. As a general rule, reported percentages should be rounded to one decimal beyond what is important for understanding the original measure. Thus, the original concern with sociology and psychology majors was in terms of whole individuals, so the reported percentage is rounded to one decimal beyond the whole individual. It provides sufficient precision to understand the original concern.

As is true with ratios and proportions, percentages can be applied to all levels of measurement, including interval, ordinal, nominal, and dichotomous scales, because they are based on the number of observations related to the categories of some measurement device. Proportions and percentages also may be cumulated to display the number of observations above or below any point in a distribution. However, such accumulations are appropriate only for interval and ordinal measurements. Recall that the categories of nominal scales have no fixed order, so it does not matter whether Republicans precede Democrats, or vice versa, on a scale of political party preference. Therefore, it does not make sense to think in terms of observations above or below the categories of a nominal scale.

Cumulating observations *down* a scale indicates the relative number of observations above a point, whereas cumulating them *up* indicates the relative number below a point on the scale. Table 2.6 shows the scores of 115 individuals on an examination. This cumulative frequency distribution shows each exam score as well as proportions and percentages. For purposes of illustration, the proportions are cumulated down the frequencies, and the percentages are cumulated up the frequencies.

The cumulative proportion, CP, from the highest to the lowest score, shows that .06 scored 100, .14 scored 99 or higher, .24 scored 98 or higher, and so on. By subtraction, we also know that $1.00 - .24 = .76$; this proportion scored less than 98.

**TABLE 2.6   Frequencies, Proportions, and Percentages of Examination Results**

| | | | ($n = 115$) | | |
|---|---|---|---|---|---|
| **Exam Score** | $f$ | **P** | **CP** | **%** | **C%** |
| 100 | 7 | .06 | .06 | 6.0 | 100.0 |
| 99 | 9 | .08 | .14 | 8.0 | 94.0 |
| 98 | 12 | .10 | .24 | 10.0 | 86.0 |
| 97 | 15 | .13 | .37 | 13.0 | 76.0 |
| 96 | 18 | .16 | .53 | 16.0 | 63.0 |
| 95 | 17 | .15 | .68 | 15.0 | 47.0 |
| 94 | 12 | .10 | .78 | 10.0 | 32.0 |
| 93 | 10 | .09 | .87 | 9.0 | 22.0 |
| 92 | 6 | .05 | .92 | 5.0 | 13.0 |
| 91 | 3 | .03 | .95 | 3.0 | 8.0 |
| 90 | 6 | .05 | 1.00 | 5.0 | 5.0 |
| Totals | 115 | 1.00 | | 100.0 | |

Note: $f$ = frequency, P = proportion, CP = cumulated proportion, % = percentage, and C% = cumulated percentage.

Continuing with Table 2.6, note that the sum of the proportions column, P, equals 1.00 and that the cumulated proportions, CP, equal 1.00. Thus, the original distribution of frequencies, $f$, that included 115 observations was transformed to a new distribution with values ranging from .00 to 1.00.

Also in Table 2.6, the cumulated percentages, C%, were cumulated from the highest to the lowest score, showing that 5.0% scored 90, 8.0% scored 91 or lower, 13.0% scored 92 or lower, and so on. If you subtract 13.0% from 100, you find that 87.0% scored higher than 92.

In presenting proportions and percentages, you must be careful when working with small numbers of observations. As $n$ declines below 100, proportion and percentage values can change dramatically with the relocation of a few cases. Reporting the results of small samples only in terms of proportions and percentages may be misleading. For example, Table 2.7 reports the racial characteristics for two groups of 12 observations each. If only the proportions and percentages were reported, it would appear that group 1 had a much larger number of Other (.583) than group 2 (.500) and significantly fewer Black (.167 to .250). However, the difference in real numbers consists of one less Black and one more Other in group 1. Therefore, when few observations are involved, the shift of even one case can result in a substantial difference in proportions and percentages and perhaps in misinterpretation. As a rule of thumb, proportions and percentages should not be reported for less than 50 observations, and the actual numbers on which they are based should also be reported.

Proportions and percentages are useful and informative for presenting numerical descriptions. They consist of linear transformations that convert frequencies into standard form. Proportions transform the frequencies of a distribution regardless of the number of original observations to a relative scale of .00 to 1.00, whereas percentages transform them to a relative scale of .00 to 100.00. The transformations are useful because they are widely understood, easily interpreted, and allow comparisons of groups with different numbers of observations. Table 2.8 presents data on the examination scores of two classes. Determining whether the performances of the two classes are similar from the original frequency distributions is difficult. Table 2.9 displays the two frequency distributions with the

**TABLE 2.7   Frequencies, Proportions, and Percentages of Racial Composition of Two Groups**

| Race | Group 1 | | | | Group 2 | | |
|------|---|------|------|---|---|------|------|
| | $f$ | P | % | | $f$ | P | % |
| Black | 2 | .167 | 16.7 | | 3 | .250 | 25.0 |
| White | 3 | .250 | 25.0 | | 3 | .250 | 25.0 |
| Other | 7 | .583 | 58.3 | | 6 | .500 | 50.0 |
| Total | 12 | 1.000 | 100.0 | | 12 | 1.000 | 100.0 |

**TABLE 2.8** **Frequencies of Examination Scores for Two Classes**

| | Frequencies | |
|---|---|---|
| Score | Class A | Class B |
| 100 | 10 | 47 |
| 95 | 20 | 94 |
| 90 | 30 | 141 |
| 85 | 30 | 141 |
| 80 | 20 | 94 |
| 75 | 10 | 47 |
| Totals | 120 | 564 |

proportions and percentages. It is immediately clear that the distributions in the two classes are the same. Transforming the original frequency distributions to proportions or percentages shows that there was no difference in the performances of class A and class B.

## Summary

Relative frequencies are useful numerical descriptions because they present frequencies relative to some standard. Ratios compare the relationship of one frequency to another on the same or different measure. Proportions and percentages transform a distribution of values to a common standard, allowing for easy interpretation and comparisons of frequencies within and between groups. Another way to present samples of observations is by using tables, discussed next.

**TABLE 2.9** **Frequencies, Proportions, and Percentages for Examination Scores for Two Classes**

| | Class A | | | Class B | | |
|---|---|---|---|---|---|---|
| Exam Scores | $f$ | P | % | $f$ | P | % |
| 100 | 10 | .083 | 8.3 | 47 | .083 | 8.3 |
| 95 | 20 | .167 | 16.7 | 94 | .167 | 16.7 |
| 90 | 30 | .250 | 25.0 | 141 | .250 | 25.0 |
| 85 | 30 | .250 | 25.0 | 141 | .250 | 25.0 |
| 80 | 20 | .167 | 16.7 | 94 | .167 | 16.7 |
| 75 | 10 | .083 | 8.3 | 47 | .083 | 8.3 |
| Totals | 120 | 1.000 | 100.0 | 564 | 1.000 | 100.0 |

Note: $f$ = frequency, P = proportion, and % = percentage.

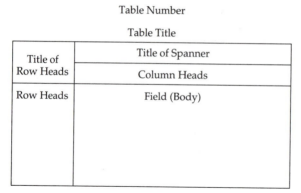

**FIGURE 2.1   Typical Table Components**

## USING TABLES FOR DISPLAY

Numerical descriptions are not always easy to understand, so presentations must be structured to be user friendly. A convenient way to make such descriptions comprehensible is with tables. Some basic rules and conventions need to be followed when constructing and using statistical tables. Figure 2.1 describes a table's major components. If there is more than one table in a document, they are numbered sequentially. If the report consists of several chapters, tables can be referenced with two numbers, such as 1.1, 1.2, and 2.1, where the first number identifies the chapter and the second is the number of the table in the chapter.

Tables should always have a *title* that clearly informs readers of the contents of the table. A title should be brief and should indicate the variables described in the table. Table 2.10 is titled "Political Party Preferences," informing the reader that it provides information on the political party preferences of a sample of individuals. Statistical tables also need to inform readers of the number of observations that are included in the table. This information may appear in the table title or in the table itself.

The top of the column in the left-hand side of the table, referred to as the **row head,** informs readers of the contents of the rows of the table. The titles of the rows appear below the row head and contain the names or values of the rows of the table. Thus, the row head in Table 2.10 contains the name "Political Party Preference," and the names of party preferences, Democrat, Republican, and Independent, are the row titles.

The **spanner** informs the reader of the content of the table's columns, and the **column heads** present the names of the values of the variable in the spanner. Table 2.10 presents only one variable, which appears in the row head, so the spanner contains only the frequency of the variable of political party preference. The **field** or *body* of the table contains the data of interest. In our example, it shows the number of individuals preferring each political party.

**TABLE 2.10   Political Party Preferences**

**(n = 254)**

| Preference | f |
|---|---|
| Democrat | 112 |
| Republican | 116 |
| Independent | 26 |
| Total | 254 |

Whereas tables that report on one variable are known as **univariate displays,** those reporting on two variables are called **bivariate displays.** In bivariate displays, one variable appears in the rows and the other in the columns. Bivariate displays are also referred to as **contingency tables** in that they show the contingency, or relationship, between two variables. If the presentation involves an independent and a dependent variable, usually the dependent variable appears in the rows and the independent variable in the columns. However, some place the independent variable in the rows. Usually if percentages are included, they are calculated in the direction of the independent variable, which is also known as the control variable.

Table 2.11 displays the contingency between religious affiliation and political party preference. The body of the table shows the political party preferences of a sample of 469 individuals indicating their affiliation as Catholic, Protestant, Jewish, or Other. Religious affiliation is assumed to be the independent variable, whereas political party affiliation, seen as a function of religion, is treated as the dependent variable. The row totals show the number of individuals preferring each of three political parties, whereas the column totals indicate the number of individuals affiliated with each of four religious groups. Each cell of the table

**TABLE 2.11   Political Party Preference and Religious Affiliation**

**(n = 469)**

| Political Party Preference | Religious Affiliation | | | | Row Totals |
|---|---|---|---|---|---|
| | Catholic | Protestant | Jewish | Other | |
| Democrat | 94 (58.4) | 47 (30.0) | 43 (48.3) | 26 (41.9) | 210 (44.8) |
| Republican | 49 (30.4) | 93 (59.2) | 21 (23.6) | 31 (50.0) | 194 (41.4) |
| Independent | 18 (11.2) | 17 (10.8) | 25 (28.1) | 5 (8.1) | 65 (13.8) |
| Column totals | 161 (34.3) | 157 (33.5) | 89 (19.0) | 62 (13.2) | 469 (100.0) |

shows the contingency between a religious affiliation and a political party preference. The table shows both the frequency and the percentage for each cell.

Conventionally, the percentages are calculated for the independent variable (the columns) to reflect the percentage of a political party preference associated with each religious group. If you add the column percentages for each religious group, they will total 100. Thus, in the column for Catholics, the percentages are $58.4 + 30.4 + 11.2 = 100.0$.

The percentages could be calculated for the rows, which might be of interest, but if both the column and the row percentages are presented, the table might appear numerically busy and be confusing to readers. As a general rule, the busier a table is with numerical detail, the more likely it will be avoided or ignored. The trade-off is to present as much numerical description as you need to get your message across while avoiding excessive detail that will discourage readers from studying the description.

Note that the table presents the percentages for both the row and the column totals, also referred to as the *marginal* totals. These show how the sample of 469 individuals is distributed across the categories of political party preference and religious affiliation. From the marginal totals, we know that 44.8% are Democrat, 41.4% are Republican, and 13.8% are Independent. We also know that 34.3% are Catholic, 33.5% are Protestant, 19% are Jewish, and 13.2% are Other.

Some presentations involve more than one independent variable. Those with two independent variables are referred to as **multivariate displays.** In such displays, the independent variables are usually displayed in the columns and the dependent variable in the rows. Figure 2.2 is a display illustrating religious affiliation, social class position, and political party preference. The addition of social class produces three subcategories for religious affiliation, including upper, middle, and lower social class. The display offers more information but is more visually complex. Although such displays can be important and be of help in some cases, making them too complex defeats the original purpose: providing a clear description of the data.

| Political Preference | Catholic | | | Protestant | | | Jewish | | | Other | | | Total |
|---|---|---|---|---|---|---|---|---|---|---|---|---|---|
| | U | M | L | U | M | L | U | M | L | U | M | L | |
| Democrat | | | | | | | | | | | | | |
| Republican | | | | | | | | | | | | | |
| Independent | | | | | | | | | | | | | |
| Total | | | | | | | | | | | | | |

U = upper, M = middle, and L = lower class.

**FIGURE 2.2   Religious Affiliation, Social Class, and Political Party Preference**

# USING GRAPHIC DISPLAYS

An important tool for displaying numerical data is the use of graphs. The following section reviews some basic graphic methods. We will consider a frequency histogram, frequency polygons, bar charts, and pie charts. Before looking at the different graphic displays, let's review the Cartesian coordinate system, which serves as the basis of many graphs.

## *The Cartesian Coordinate System*

The **Cartesian coordinate system** is composed of two number scales placed **orthogonally** (at right angles) to each other, as shown in Figure 2.3. The point at which the two lines intersect, 0, is called the *point of origin.* On the **horizontal axis** (x), values to the right of the point of origin are positive and values to the left of the point of origin negative. On the **vertical axis** (y), values above the point of origin are positive and values below the point of origin negative. The horizontal axis is also called the **abscissa** and the vertical axis the **ordinate.**

If the coordinate system is presenting the distribution of one variable, the values of the variable are presented on the x-axis and the frequencies on the y-axis. If the coordinates are presenting the relationship between two variables, the independent variable is presented on the x-axis and the dependent variable on the y-axis.

Figure 2.3 shows that the upper right-hand quadrant of the coordinate system, quadrant I, displays those cases in which both x and y values are positive. Quadrant II contains the outcomes where x is negative and y positive, quadrant III

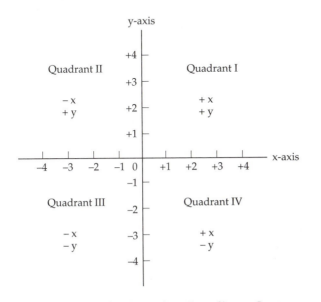

**FIGURE 2.3    The Cartesian Coordinate System**

where both x and y are negative, and quadrant IV where x is positive and y negative. In graphic presentations, only the quadrants involving actual cases are displayed. Most scales used in social research assume positive values, so quadrant I is used the most.

## Frequency Histograms

A **frequency histogram** is a graph that shows the frequency distribution of an interval variable. It portrays the frequency or number of observations for the intervals of the scale. The bars correspond to the interval widths. Figure 2.4 shows a histogram of the data on body weights presented in Table 2.4 (see also Table 2.12). The 10-pound intervals for the weights appear on the x-axis and the frequency of each weight interval on the y-axis. The bars of the histogram are created by drawing vertical lines from the exact lower and upper limits of each interval for weight up to the frequencies on the y-axis that correspond with the interval. Whereas the exact limits of the intervals are used to construct the histogram, the visual display often presents only the stated limits, as shown in Figure 2.4.

Each bar represents an area that is proportional to the frequency of cases in the interval. Thus, the bar for interval 100–109, with two cases, contains 2/77, or .03, of the total area of the bars; interval 110–119, with five cases, contains 5/77, or .07, of the area; and the sum of the areas of all the bars equals 1.00. Thus, the size of each bar is an accurate reflection of the proportion of cases represented by each interval.

A **relative frequency histogram** is one in which the frequencies on the y-axis are converted to proportions or percentages, as shown in Figure 2.5. Both types of histogram result in identical graphs, but the relative frequency histogram shows the proportion or percentage of observations located in each interval.

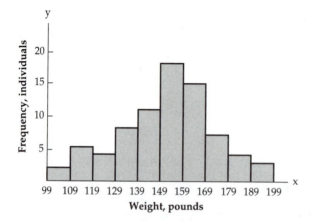

**FIGURE 2.4   Histogram of Body Weights ($n = 77$)**

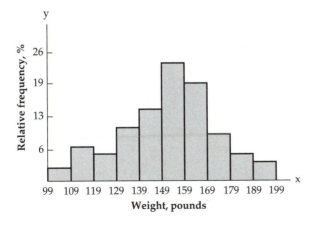

**FIGURE 2.5   Histogram of the Relative Frequency Distribution of Body Weights ($n = 77$)**

## Frequency Polygons

A **frequency polygon** is similar to a histogram. However, rather than using bars to represent the number of observations in each interval, a frequency polygon uses a line to connect the *midpoints* of the intervals and their frequencies. The midpoints represent the intervals on the basis of the principle of least error (discussed earlier). Whereas the exact limits of the intervals can be used to determine the midpoints, the stated limits can be used to present the frequency polygon, as shown in Figure 2.6.

The visual image produced by a frequency polygon is quite different from that of a histogram even though the data are the same. Although no rules govern which graph is more appropriate in any given case, the frequency histogram and

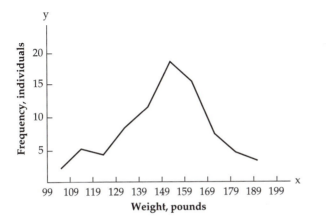

**FIGURE 2.6   Frequency Polygon of Body Weights ($n = 77$)**

the frequency polygon are alternatives for displaying the same data. Caution must be used when interpreting the points on a frequency polygon's line. The only points on the line that can be associated with specific values in the original measure are those at the midpoints of the intervals. This is true because the exact locations of the observations within each interval are unknown and because estimates of points at the upper or lower end of the intervals would risk greater error than the midpoints.

## Cumulative Frequency Polygons

Cumulated frequencies (discussed earlier) can also be displayed using a **cumulative frequency polygon.** Table 2.12 presents the data on the body weights of 77 individuals. The columns of the table show the frequency for each weight class, the cumulated frequency (CF), and the cumulated proportion (CP). The frequencies are cumulated from the lower to the upper limit of the weight categories (they could have been cumulated from the upper to the lower limit as well).

Figure 2.7 displays the cumulated data. When connecting the points of each interval, you must base the cumulative line on the points at the exact upper limits of the interval. The upper limits of the interval are used because the line is intended to reflect the cumulation of all values from the exact lower limit to the exact upper limit of each interval. In Figure 2.7, the line begins at the exact upper limit of 109.5 because it represents the cumulation of all values greater than 99.5 but less than 109.5. The second point is at the exact upper limit of 119.5 and so on.

The ordinate in Figure 2.7 presents not only the frequencies but also a scale reflecting the relative frequencies in terms of percentages. If the actual frequencies

**TABLE 2.12    Stated Class Limits and Exact Class Limits for Body Weights**

| Exact Class Limits | $f$ | CF | CP |
|:---:|:---:|:---:|:---:|
| $(n = 77)$ | | | |
| 189.5–199.5 | 3 | 77 | 1.00 |
| 179.5–189.5 | 4 | 74 | .96 |
| 169.5–179.5 | 7 | 70 | .91 |
| 159.5–169.5 | 15 | 63 | .82 |
| 149.5–159.5 | 18 | 48 | .62 |
| 139.5–149.5 | 11 | 30 | .39 |
| 129.5–139.5 | 8 | 19 | .25 |
| 119.5–129.5 | 4 | 11 | .14 |
| 109.5–119.5 | 5 | 7 | .09 |
| 99.5–109.5 | 2 | 2 | .02 |
| Total | 77 | | |

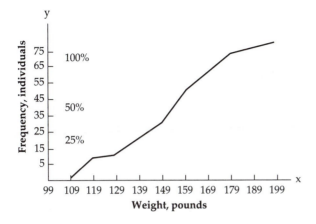

**FIGURE 2.7　Cumulative Frequency Distribution of Body Weights, Lowest to Highest ($n = 77$)**

on the ordinate are transformed to percentages or proportions, the figure is referred to as a **relative cumulative frequency polygon.**

Figure 2.7 cumulates the observations from the lower to the upper limit of the scale, but they could have been cumulated from the upper to the lower limit as well. The cumulative line would be based on the exact lower limits of the interval, beginning with interval 189.5. The visual impact of the two cumulative frequency polygons is quite different, as can be seen by comparing Figure 2.7 with Figure 2.8. Whether you cumulate the values of a distribution up or down depends on whether you want to present the distribution in terms of values above or below a given point on the line.

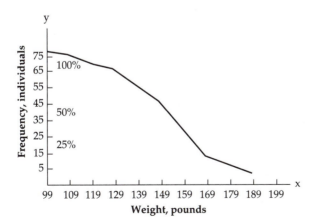

**FIGURE 2.8　Cumulative Frequency Distribution of Body Weights, Highest to Lowest ($n = 77$)**

Cumulative frequency polygons are also known as **ogives,** an architectural term used to describe the interior of a vaulted arch. The shapes of curves resulting from cumulated frequencies have the characteristic appearance of an ogive, as can be seen in Figures 2.7 and 2.8.

Frequency histograms, frequency polygons, and cumulative frequency polygons are basic graphic models for describing the frequency distributions of interval measures. The graphs are based on the Cartesian coordinate system, and each provides a somewhat different perspective of the data. More complex graphic displays can be constructed. For example, the distributions of two samples can be superimposed in graphic displays and so on. Computer software programs for statistical analysis provide a large number of graphic options that are effective in communicating the message of numerical descriptions.

Graphs also are useful for presenting ordinal and nominal data. The following three models—bar charts, sliding bar charts, and pie charts—are some of the types of graphs used for presenting discrete data.

## Bar Charts

Graphic displays of ordinal and nominal data are more limited because the distances between the points of such scales are unknown. Thus, ordinal scales rank observations from most to least but do not provide information on the distance between the ranks. Nominal scales categorize data only in terms of qualitative differences; the order of the scale categories is arbitrary. As a consequence, graphs of discrete data are limited to representations of the proportion of cases in the ranks or nominal categories of such scales.

Figure 2.9 presents a **bar chart** of educational attainment by gender and race. Race is categorized as White and Black, and gender is shown with different shadings in the bars, the lightest shade being both genders, the medium shade male, and the darkest shade female. The length of the bars represents the percentage of individuals in each group attaining a high school degree and a bachelors degree or more in 1992. Virtually no gender differences exist for either blacks or whites in high school graduation, but whites of either gender are somewhat more likely to complete high school than blacks. College graduation is equally likely for black males and females, but only about half as many blacks complete college as whites. There is also some gender variation among whites, with white males somewhat more likely to complete college than white females. The bar chart presents the distribution of three dichotomous nominal measures, including race, gender, and educational attainment, on the vertical axis. The horizontal length of the bars shows the proportion related to each nominal category. This type of display is known as a **horizontal bar chart.** The chart can be inverted so that the nominal categories are on the horizontal axis and the frequencies on the vertical axis. This is referred to as a **vertical bar chart.**

The bars represent segments that are proportional to the number of cases in each category. Whereas the length of the bar reflects the exact proportion of cases

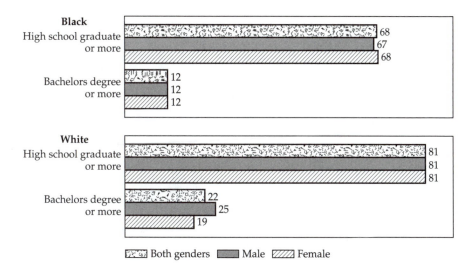

**FIGURE 2.9   Percentage of Persons Age 25 and Older by Educational Attainment, Gender, and Race**

Source: Claudette Bennett, *Current Population Reports, Population Characteristics, The Black Population in the United States, March 1992,* U.S. Department of Commerce, Economics and Statistics Administration, Bureau of the Census, p. 8.

in each category, the width of the bars and the distance between the bars are arbitrary because the precise difference between the discrete categories of nominal and ordinal scales is not established by such measures.

## Sliding Bar Charts

The frequencies of two discrete variables, one of which is a dichotomy, can be displayed using a **sliding bar chart.** In such a graph, the vertical axis is located near the center of the chart, and the area on either side of the axis represents the two categories or values of the dichotomous measure. Horizontal bars representing the categories of the second variable intersect the vertical axis, so that the lengths of the bars on either side of the axis represent the proportion of cases falling in one or the other categories of the dichotomy. Figure 2.10 shows a sliding bar chart organized around the dichotomy of race, categorized as Black and White. The vertical axis is intersected by occupational categories. The chart illustrates the difference in blacks and whites across these occupational categories. Thus, 14.1% of black males are in managerial or professional specialties, whereas 26.8% of white males are in such occupations.

Perhaps the most popular use of the sliding bar chart is to describe the age and gender profile of a population. The resulting graphs are referred to as **population pyramids** because their shape approximates the figure of a pyramid. Figure 2.11 shows the age and gender profile of the population of the United States. The

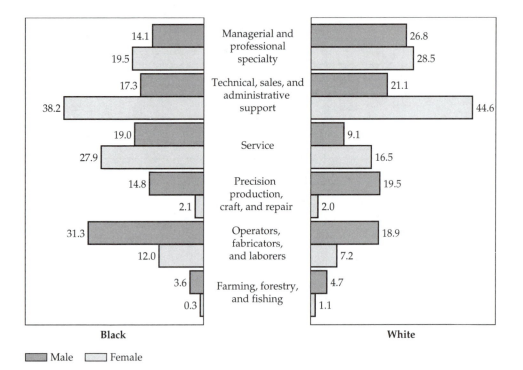

**FIGURE 2.10   Occupational Distribution of the Employed Civilian Labor Force by Gender and Race (Annual Averages)**
Source: Claudette Bennett, *Current Population Reports, Population Characteristics, The Black Population in the United States, March 1992,* U.S. Department of Commerce, Economics and Statistics Administration, Bureau of the Census, p. 8.

x-axis shows the number of people in millions, and the horizontal bars show age in terms of 5-year intervals. The vertical axis bisects the horizontal bars, with females on the right and males on the left. The graph provides a rather clear image of the gender and age profile of the U.S. population in 1990.

## Pie Charts

**Pie charts** provide another way to describe data. Such charts consist of a circle that is divided proportional to the number of cases in each category of a discrete scale. It is constructed by dividing the degrees of a circle into the proportions or percentages represented by the scale categories. A circle contains 360 degrees (written as 360°), and because percentages are based on parts per 100, the percentages contained in the scale categories are multiplied by 360. Thus, a scale category equal to 1% is represented by 3.6°, 10% by 36°, and so on.

Figure 2.12 presents the sources of revenue for public institutions of higher education. Tuition pays the greatest share, 40.4%, and so the proportion of the circle representing tuition is 360° × .404 = 145.4°.

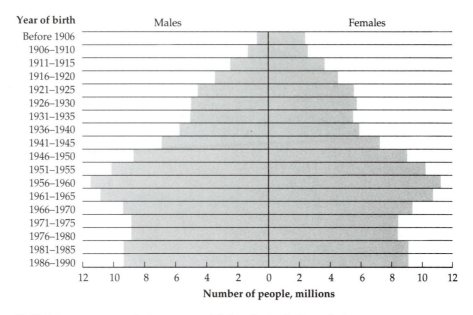

FIGURE 2.11   Population Pyramid for the U.S. Population
The population pyramid for the United States in 1990 shows the impact of low birth rates during the Depression (births in 1931–35), the higher birth rate of the Baby Boom generation (births in 1946–60), the decline in fertility in the 1960s and 70s, and the slight resurgence in fertility in the 1980s. Source: U.S. Bureau of the Census, 1990 Census of Population and Housing.

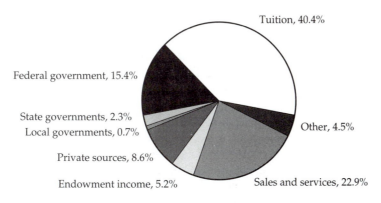

Total revenues = $54.9 billion

FIGURE 2.12   Sources of Current–Fund Revenue for Public Institutions of Higher Education
Source: U.S. Department of Education, National Center for Education Statistics, Integrated Postsecondary Education Data System (IPEDS), "Finance, FY91" survey.

## COMPUTER EXERCISES: SOME SUGGESTIONS

The material in this chapter has great potential for computer exercises. Applying your software to the material can help you both learn to use the computer for developing basic data displays and understand the content of the chapter. The first exercise could consist of using the computer to organize a basic data set. Initially, you may want to review the list of variables you will be working with, become familiar with the variable values, and if not completed for the data set, assign value labels to the variables. You can create frequency tables, including grouped frequencies, and produce proportions and percentages for frequency distributions. You can cumulate frequencies or percentages. As part of these exercises, become familiar with the procedures for labeling tables, producing percentages for either rows or columns or both. You will find that the less content placed in a table, the more visually appealing it is and the easier it is to understand. You may also want to create tables using percentages for very small samples to see the distortion that occurs when frequencies for table cells are limited.

Your statistical software package likely contains options for creating various types of charts. You can create charts appropriate for interval, ordinal, and nominal data. You may also want to experiment with more complicated charts in which you superimpose one frequency display upon another. The software packages available make it relatively easy to produce many different types of tabular displays just by learning a few basic commands. Learning to use a statistical software package is an important part of preparing yourself for the future.

## CHAPTER SUMMARY

The skill with which data are displayed determines whether research findings will be communicated and understood. It is especially important to invest time in developing clear presentations, especially when intended for audiences not trained in statistical methods. Remember that the purpose of numerical descriptions is to provide more insight and a better understanding of complex phenomena. That purpose can be attained only by presentations that are readily understood and appreciated by potential users.

Frequency distributions and grouped frequency distributions are means for simplifying large numbers of observations and lengthy data arrays. Relative measures, such as simple ratios, proportions, and percentages, make comparing data sets easier because they transform large numbers of observations to simplified standard scales.

Tables can also be used to provide a more immediate visual display of data. Graphic displays represent further visual aids in data presentation. Frequency histograms, polygons, and cumulative polygons are common ways to present interval data. Bar charts, sliding bar charts, and pie charts can be used to represent ordinal and nominal measures. Computer software provides a wide range of possibilities for describing all levels of measurement. Such displays offer powerful tools for data presentation and are important vehicles for presenting complicated data sets to interested users and audiences.

The next chapter introduces additional ways to summarize data, including measures of central tendency (averages) and measures of variation (differences). The descriptions they provide focus on summary numerical values that describe entire distributions of observations. These numerical summaries are the workhorses of statistics in that they are the values around which most statistical models are organized.

## KEY TERMS

**abscissa**   The x- (horizontal) axis in the Cartesian coordinate system.

**array**   A data display in which every observation is presented.

**bar chart**   A graph for displaying ordinal or nominal data in which the length of the bars is proportional to the percentage of cases in the scale categories.

**bivariate display**   A chart showing the frequencies of two variables. If one variable is treated as independent, it usually appears in the columns and the dependent variable in the rows.

**Cartesian coordinate system**   Two numbered lines placed at right angles to each other. The point of intersection of the two is equal to zero; positive values are to the right and above the intersect and negative values to the left and below the intersect.

**column head**   The title of the columns designating the contents of the columns of the table.

**contingency table**   A display showing the joint distribution (contingency) between two variables.

**cumulative frequency distribution**   A display of a frequency distribution in which observations are cumulated up or down the categories of the scale.

**cumulative frequency polygon**   A graphic display of an interval variable in which the scale values are shown on the x-axis and frequencies on the y-axis; the graph shows the cumulation of the frequencies from either the lowest to the highest or the highest to the lowest score.

**disordered array**   A display of observations that are not ordered from the lowest to the highest or highest to the lowest value.

**field**   The body of a table in which data are presented.

**frequency**   Outcomes or observations that have a common property.

**frequency distribution**   A display of the frequencies of values across all the categories of a scale.

**frequency histogram**   A chart displaying the frequencies of an interval measure with bars that are proportional in size to the number of observations in a category.

**frequency polygon**   A graph in which the frequencies of scale categories are displayed by a line joining the midpoints of the categories in reference to their frequency.

**grouped frequency distribution**   A distribution in which observations are grouped into intervals and the number or frequency of observations in each interval is shown.

**horizontal axis**   The x-axis, or horizontal line, of a graph based on the Cartesian coordinate system.

**horizontal bar chart**   A chart with horizontal bars displaying the proportion of cases in discrete categories.

**linear transformation**   Changing a scale of frequencies to another scale, usually a standard scale that allows the comparison of different measures.

**multivariate display**   A data display in which the values for more than two variables are presented.

**ogive**   A term describing the interior of a vaulted arch, which is also the characteristic shape of a cumulative frequency polygon.

**ordered array**   A display of observations that are ordered least to most.

**ordinate**   The y- (vertical) axis in the Cartesian coordinate system.

**orthogonal**   In reference to lines, it means that they are at right angles to each other.

**percentage**   The ratio of a subset of scores to the total number of scores in a distribution multiplied by 100.

**pie chart**   A circle graph in which categories are represented by "pie slices" proportional to the percentage of scores in the categories.

**population pyramid**   A sliding bar chart displaying the age of the population across gender.

**proportion**   The ratio of a subset of scores to the total number of scores.

**ratio**   One number divided by another. The ratio $f_1$ to $f_2$ is $f_1 : f_2$ or $f_1/f_2$.

**relative cumulative frequency polygon**   A frequency polygon based on the cumulated values of a distribution that have been transformed to proportions or percentages.

**relative frequency histogram**   A histogram displaying proportions or percentages of cases in the categories of an interval scale.

**row head**   The title of the rows designating the contents of the rows of a table.

**sliding bar chart**   A graph for displaying the joint distribution of a dichotomous scale and any other type of measure.

**spanner**   The headings for columns in a table.

**univariate display**   The display of the distribution of one variable.

**vertical axis**   The y-axis, or upright line, of a graph based on the Cartesian coordinate system.

**vertical bar chart**   A chart with vertical bars displaying the proportion of cases in a discrete category.

## SYMBOLS

| | |
|---|---|
| $f$ | The symbol for the frequency of observations in a scale category |
| mdt | The midpoint of the exact limits of a grouped frequency distribution |
| P | Proportion |
| % | Percentage |
| x | The horizontal axis of the Cartesian coordinate system. It is also called the abscissa and is treated as the independent variable. |
| y | The ordinate (vertical) axis of the Cartesian coordinate system; can be treated as a dependent variable |
| X | The symbol for a value or score in a distribution. |

## FORMULAS

$$mdt = l_i + \frac{w_i}{2}$$

Formula for locating the midpoint of the category of a grouped frequency distribution.

$$Ratio = \frac{f_1}{f_2}$$

Formula showing that a ratio is one number divided by another.

$$Proportion = \frac{f_i}{n}$$

Formula showing that a proportion equals some part of a distribution divided by the whole distribution.

$$Percentage = \frac{f_i}{n} \times 100$$

Formula showing that a percentage equals some part of a distribution divided by the whole and multiplied by 100.

## EXERCISES

**1.** The following array of ages resulted from a survey of 90 individuals. Create an ordered array of the data.

| | | | | | | | | |
|---|---|---|---|---|---|---|---|---|
| 60 | 38 | 43 | 43 | 70 | 28 | 64 | 40 | 38 |
| 41 | 25 | 39 | 69 | 37 | 41 | 57 | 20 | 75 |
| 46 | 65 | 81 | 46 | 52 | 23 | 59 | 46 | 29 |
| 11 | 36 | 57 | 14 | 13 | 41 | 81 | 15 | 34 |
| 52 | 50 | 27 | 56 | 53 | 63 | 73 | 66 | 45 |
| 57 | 04 | 40 | 39 | 29 | 32 | 33 | 38 | 59 |
| 20 | 83 | 34 | 70 | 36 | 25 | 38 | 40 | 33 |
| 15 | 14 | 63 | 38 | 52 | 12 | 44 | 79 | 58 |
| 92 | 51 | 67 | 88 | 24 | 47 | 91 | 24 | 20 |
| 77 | 48 | 42 | 45 | 30 | 34 | 57 | 41 | 41 |

**2.** In the array above, what is the ratio of persons 65 years and older to those younger than 65?

**3.** What is the ratio of persons younger than 20 years to those 50 and older?

**4.** What proportion of the group is older than 50 years?

**5.** What proportion of the group is older than 30 years?

6. What proportion is either 20 to 30 or 50 to 60 years old?

7. What percentage of the group is exactly 60 years old?

8. What percentage of the group is 40 to 60 years old?

9. Cumulate the proportions for the ordered array from the youngest to the oldest.

10. Cumulate the percentages for the ordered array from the oldest to the youngest.

11. What proportion of the individuals is younger than 25 years?

12. What proportion of the individuals is younger than 70 years?

13. What percentage of the group is older than 50?

14. What percentage of the group is older than 14?

15. Recast the array of ages into a grouped frequency distribution of 10-year intervals.

16. What are the exact limits of the interval for those in their 50s?

17. What is the midpoint of the interval for those in their 60s?

18. What would be the exact limits of the interval for 11-year-olds if you used 7-year intervals?

19. What would be the midpoint of the interval for 11-year-olds if you used 7-year intervals?

20. Draw a histogram of data on age using 10-year intervals.

21. Draw a frequency polygon using 10-year intervals.

22. Draw a cumulative frequency polygon cumulating the 10-year interval data beginning with the youngest age category.

23. Draw a bar chart describing the data on drug use presented below. The bars should be proportional to the percentage of users in each drug category.

**Drug Use Type, Age 12 and Older: 1996 (percentage who have ever used drugs)**

| Drug | Percentage |
| --- | --- |
| Marijuana | 32.0 |
| Inhalants | 5.6 |
| Hallucinogens | 9.7 |
| Cocaine | 10.3 |
| Heroin | 1.1 |
| Stimulants | 4.7 |
| Sedatives | 2.3 |
| Tranquilizers | 3.6 |
| Alcohol | 82.6 |
| Cigarettes | 71.6 |

Source: Adapted from data presented in *Preliminary Results from the 1996 National Household Survey on Drug Abuse,* Substance Abuse and Mental Health Administration, U.S. Department of Health and Human Services, Washington, D.C., July 1997, p. 57.

24. The data in the following table indicate the gender distribution of employees in various health occupations. Draw a sliding bar chart that indicates the relationship between gender and health occupation. (The axis of the chart is gender, and the bars represent the proportions of females and males in each category.)

### Health Occupation and Gender, 1995

| | Gender | | |
|---|---|---|---|
| Occupation | Male | Female | Total |
| Dentist | 134,230 | 20,770 | 155,000 |
| Pharmacist | 108,460 | 61,540 | 170,000 |
| Physician | 523,908 | 169,092 | 693,000 |
| Physicians' assistants | 25,740 | 29,260 | 55,000 |
| Registered nurses | 136,413 | 1,840,587 | 1,977,000 |
| Dieticians | 6,392 | 87,608 | 94,000 |
| Inhalation therapists | 37,506 | 56,494 | 94,000 |
| Physical therapists | 38,740 | 91,260 | 130,000 |
| Speech therapists | 7,189 | 83,811 | 91,000 |

Source: Adapted from data reported in the U.S. Department of Commerce, Bureau of the Census, *Statistical Abstract of the United States: 1996,* 116th ed., Washington, D.C., p. 405.

25. The following data on health care expenditures were reported for 1994. Draw a pie chart that shows the percentage of expenditures for the various categories in which funds were spent.

### Health Care Expenditure by Object, 1994

| Type of Expenditure | Percentage |
|---|---|
| Hospital care | 40.7 |
| Physician services | 22.8 |
| Dentist services | 5.1 |
| Other professional services | 6.0 |
| Home health care services | 3.1 |
| Drugs and drug sundries | 9.4 |
| Eyeglasses and appliances | 1.6 |
| Nursing home care | 8.7 |
| Other health services | 2.6 |

Source: Adapted from data presented in the U.S. Bureau of the Census, *Statistical Abstract of the United States: 1978,* 116th ed., Washington, D.C., 1996, p. 112.

# 3

# NUMERICAL SUMMARIES OF DATA

Distributions of variables are the basic materials of social research. Because social research usually involves large numbers of observations, a variety of methods have been developed for organizing data into displays that are informative and meaningful. Chapter 2 reviewed some of the techniques for data display, including frequency distributions, relative frequency distributions, and tabular and graphic displays. Each method provides a unique description and perspective of the distribution of a variable.

This chapter continues the discussion of techniques for numerical descriptions of distributions. However, instead of simply reorganizing distributions and their frequencies for presentation, we will look at techniques for deriving single numerical values that describe an entire distribution of observations. The numerical descriptions reviewed here include measures of central tendency and measures of variation. These techniques provide simple, easy-to-understand descriptions of distributions, and two in particular, the mean and the variance, turn out to be the workhorses of statistical models. They are workhorses in that the mathematical models central to statistical analysis are organized around means and variances or other descriptors that serve as their surrogates.

Recall from Chapter 1 that samples are ordinarily used by researchers to learn about populations. Entire populations are too large, unwieldy, or expensive to study in detail, so it is assumed that if a sample represents the population, the sample characteristics should provide a good estimate or be quite similar to those of the population. The terms *estimate* and *similar* are important because, although a properly selected sample should provide a good representation of the population, the fact that it is only a subset of the whole means that it is not an *exact* replica of the population. For this reason, sample characteristics are referred to as *estimates* of population characteristics. As we will see later, the logic and methods of statistical inference make it possible to determine how good an estimate of a population a sample is. The numerical descriptors of the mean and the variance play a key role in those determinations.

# MEASURES OF CENTRAL TENDENCY

The **measures of central tendency** discussed here include the mode, the median, and the mean.[1] Each measure provides unique information about a distribution. The use of the techniques is restricted by the type of scale used for measurement. For example, modes can be used for nominal, ordinal, or interval measures; medians can be calculated for ordinal and interval data; and means can be used only with interval data and, with some caution, can be applied to ordinal measures.

## The Mode

The **mode** is defined as the most frequent value in a distribution and can be thought of as the most popular outcome for a variable. The mode for the data in Table 3.1 is sociology because it was chosen as a major by more undergraduate social science majors than any other major. Sociology majors represent a total of 149 of the 641 majors. The next most popular majors are political science and social psychology. Note that reporting the mode provides information only on the most frequent or popular outcome.

The mode for *grouped frequency distributions* is the midpoint of the interval that has the greatest number of observations. In Table 3.2, the mode for group 1 is 144.5 because it is the midpoint of the interval that has the greatest number of observations: 23 out of 80 cases.

A distribution can have more than one mode, as shown by group 2 in Table 3.2. Interval 170–179 has the most observations, 21, but an almost equal number, 20, appears in interval 120–129. Although the former interval has one more case than the latter, the difference is only one case, and the distribution would properly be described as having two modes, or as **bimodal,** with modes of 124.5 and 174.5.

**TABLE 3.1   Undergraduate Majors**

| Major | f |
| --- | --- |
| Anthropology | 97 |
| Economics | 104 |
| Political Science | 110 |
| Psychology | 72 |
| Social Psychology | 109 |
| Sociology | 149 |
| Total | 641 |

[1]Other measures of central tendency include the geometric and harmonic means, but they are not used frequently in social research and go beyond the purpose of this text.

**TABLE 3.2    Body Weights for Two Groups**

| Weights | Group 1 $(f_1)$ | Group 2 $(f_2)$ |
|---|---|---|
| 190–199 | 3 | 3 |
| 180–189 | 2 | 8 |
| 170–179 | 4 | 21 |
| 160–169 | 10 | 7 |
| 150–159 | 13 | 9 |
| 140–149 | 23 | 6 |
| 130–139 | 12 | 7 |
| 120–129 | 7 | 20 |
| 110–119 | 3 | 3 |
| 100–109 | 3 | 2 |
| Total | 80 | 86 |

The two categories are almost equally popular. A distribution can have more than two modes, but if it has more than three modes, describing the distribution in terms of a most popular outcome loses its meaning.

The mode is a useful but somewhat limited measure of central tendency. It is useful because it is the only measure of central tendency that can be used to describe the distribution of nominal as well as ordinal and interval variables. Further, if the most frequent or popular outcome is of interest, the mode provides that information. However, it is limited because it considers only one feature of a distribution: the location of the greatest number of observations. Other important differences, such as the number of observations above and below the mode or the distance between the modal value and other values, are not taken into consideration.

## The Median

The **median** is defined as the point in a distribution above and below which exactly half the observations lie. The median is the exact midpoint in the distribution. Symbolized by md, the median is determined differently for an array with an odd number of observations than it is for one with an even number. The formulas are as follows:

$$\text{Odd number} = \frac{n+1}{2} \tag{3.1}$$

$$\text{Even number} = \frac{n}{2} \text{ and } \frac{n+2}{2} \tag{3.2}$$

In the case of an odd number of observations, the median is simply the middle observation; an equal number of observations fall above and below it. In Table 3.3,

| TABLE 3.3 | Distribution of Odd and Even Size |
| --- | --- |

| Distribution 1<br>($n = 5$) | Distribution 2<br>($n = 6$) |
| --- | --- |
| 198 | 197 |
| 179 | 193 |
| 172 | 189 |
| 167 | 187 |
| 154 | 183 |
|  | 179 |

distribution 1 contains 5 cases. Using Formula 3.1, we see that the median is $(5 + 1)/2 = 3$, or the third value counting up from the bottom score or down from the top score. The median value for distribution 1 is identified as 172.

Distribution 2 contains an even number of observations, 6, so the median is $6/2 = 3$ and $(6 + 2)/2 = 4$, or the third and fourth scores in the distribution. Counting from the top or the bottom, the third and fourth scores are 187 and 189. Thus, we use the *two middle* scores of the distribution to represent the median. Both can be reported as the location of the median; alternatively, the average of the two values, $(187 + 189)/2 = 188$, can be reported. In the case of both the odd and the even distributions, the median identifies the middle case of the distribution.

Formula 3.3 is used to determine the midpoint for a grouped frequency:

$$md = l_i + i \left( \frac{\frac{n}{2} - f_m}{f_i} \right) \tag{3.3}$$

where  $n$ = the total number of observations

$\frac{n}{2}$ = $n$ divided by 2 (identifies the interval in which the median is located, which is interval $i$)

$l_i$ = the exact lower limit of interval $i$

$i$ = the width of interval $i$

$f_m$ = the number of observations in the intervals below interval $i$

$f_i$ = the number of observations in interval $i$

Table 3.4 shows the grouped frequency distribution of the weekly earnings of 70 individuals. The goal in determining the median is to locate the observation at the exact midpoint of the distribution. Recall that in a grouped frequency distribution the exact value of observations within the intervals is unknown but that, according to the principle of least error, the value at the midpoint of the interval is the estimate of least error for any individual observation. You begin by

**TABLE 3.4    Weekly Earnings**

**(n = 70)**

| Earnings | f | CF |
|---|---|---|
| 390–399 | 3 | 70 |
| 380–389 | 4 | 67 |
| 370–379 | 6 | 63 |
| 360–369 | 8 | 57 |
| 350–359 | 19 | 49 |
| 340–349 | 10 | 30 |
| 330–339 | 9 | 20 |
| 320–329 | 6 | 11 |
| 310–319 | 3 | 5 |
| 300–309 | 2 | 2 |
| Total | 70 | |

identifying the interval in which the middle observation is located. To do this, divide the total number of observations by 2, or $70/2 = 35$.

The value 35 informs us that the median is located at some point in the interval containing the thirty-fifth observation. Counting frequencies from the bottom of the distribution, we find that $2 + 3 + 6 + 9 + 10 = 30 + 19 = 49$. The thirty-fifth observation is located among the 19 cases in the interval 350–359. Remember that the exact limits of intervals are always used in calculations; in our example, they are 349.5–359.5. Using Formula 3.3, we can find the median:

$$\text{md} = l_i + i \left( \frac{\frac{n}{2} - f_m}{f_i} \right)$$

$$= 349.5 + 10 \left( \frac{\frac{70}{2} - 30}{19} \right)$$

$$= 349.5 + 10 \left( \frac{5}{19} \right)$$

$$= 349.5 + 2.63$$

$$= 352.13$$

The median of the distribution is 352.13, or exactly half the weekly earnings of the 70 individuals are greater than \$352.13 and exactly half are less. Insofar as the median is the midpoint of a distribution, it also represents the fiftieth percentile; that is, 50% of the cases are above the median and 50% are below.

TABLE 3.5    Weekly Earnings

| | ($n = 70$) | |
| --- | --- | --- |
| Earnings | *f* | CF |
| 390–399 | 21 | 70 |
| 380–389 | 0 | 49 |
| 370–379 | 0 | 49 |
| 360–369 | 0 | 49 |
| 350–359 | 19 | 49 |
| 340–349 | 0 | 30 |
| 330–339 | 9 | 30 |
| 320–329 | 6 | 21 |
| 310–319 | 3 | 15 |
| 300–309 | 12 | 12 |
| Total | 70 | |

The median, while identifying the point above and below which half the observations lie, is insensitive to differences between observations located above and below the median, as shown in Table 3.5. Here, the weekly earnings from Table 3.4 have been relocated so that the 10 observations in interval 340–349 are in interval 300–309 and all the earnings above interval 350–359 are in interval 390–399. The median would remain unchanged because half the earnings would still be above and below $352.13. However, the relocation of these cases would dramatically change the distribution of weekly earnings, so the information provided by the median about the total distribution is limited. Still, if you want to know where the middle case is located, only the median provides that information, and in many cases that is exactly what you need to know.

The examples here used interval scale measures. You can also find the midpoint for ordinal distributions. In ordinal scales, the median locates the *rank* above and below which half the observations lie. This information might be helpful, but when you interpret the value, you must remember that the median value identifies only the midpoint of the ranked scores.

The third measure of central tendency, the **mean,** is unique because it takes into account the value of each observation. Whereas the mode locates the position of the most popular value and the median the value at the middle of the distribution, the mean is based on the exact value of each observation.

## *The Arithmetic Mean*

Generally, when we think of the average for a distribution of scores, it is the arithmetic mean that we have in mind. The **arithmetic mean,** symbolized by $\overline{X}$, is the sum of all the values in a distribution divided by the total number of observations:

$$\overline{X} = \frac{\Sigma X_i}{n} \qquad (3.4)$$

where      $\Sigma X_i$ = the sum of the individual values beginning with the first through the last score

$n$ = the total number of scores

Suppose you completed five exams in a course and received the following grades: 98, 93, 87, 84, and 76. Using Formula 3.4, you would find the arithmetic mean as follows:

$$\overline{X} = \frac{98 + 93 + 87 + 84 + 76}{5}$$

$$= \frac{438}{5}$$

$$= 87.6$$

Note that each observation contributes its proportional share to the final outcome. Whereas in calculating the median, only the number of observations above and below the midpoint are taken into account, the mean uses the *actual numerical value* of each observation. In addition, if any one of these values changes, the mean is altered. This was not the case with the median, as can be seen by comparing Tables 3.4 and 3.5.

The mean can be thought of as the *point of balance* in a distribution in that the sum of the distances of the observations below the mean is equal to the sum of the distances of the observations above the mean. Assume that you have a distribution of seven values: 1, 1, 3, 3, 6, 7, and 7. The mean of the distribution is

$$\frac{1 + 1 + 3 + 3 + 6 + 7 + 7}{7} = \frac{28}{7} = 4$$

Figure 3.1 illustrates that 4 is the point of balance. If you compare the sums of the distances of the scores below the mean to those above the mean, you will find that they are equal. The three scores below the mean include two 3s that are 1 unit below and two 1s that are 3 units removed from the mean, for a total distance from the mean of $1 + 1 + 3 + 3 = 8$ units. The three scores above the mean include one 6 that is 2 units and two 7s that are 3 units removed, for a total distance of $2 + 3 + 3 = 8$ units, which equals the distance of the scores below the mean. As a point of balance, the mean is sensitive to the relocation of any observation in the distribution. If one of the four values in our example were changed (e.g., if a 1 became a 0), the mean would change as well:

$$\frac{0 + 1 + 3 + 3 + 6 + 7 + 7}{7} = \frac{27}{7} = 3.86$$

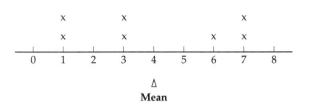

**FIGURE 3.1 The Mean as a Point of Balance**

As the point of balance in a distribution, the mean provides a unique description of the distribution. For this reason the mean is very useful in higher-order statistical models and calculations.

Computation of the mean for grouped data must assume that the actual values of the individual observations within each interval are unknown. Table 3.6 shows a distribution of weekly earnings. The distribution shows the number of individuals, *f*, in each income category, but the exact earnings of any one individual is unknown. Using the principle of least error, we find that the best estimate for the earnings of any individual in the categories of the distribution is the midpoint of the category. For example, the best guess of the income for any of the nine individuals in the category $359.5–$369.5 is the midpoint of the interval: $364.5.

Based on the midpoint, Formula 3.5 provides an accurate estimate of the mean for the grouped frequency distribution.

$$\overline{X} = \frac{\Sigma f_i m_i}{n} \tag{3.5}$$

where     $f_i$ = the number of cases in an interval

$m_i$ = the midpoint of an interval

$\Sigma f_i m_i$ = the sum of the products of the frequency and midpoint of each interval, $f_i m_i$

$n$ = the total number of observations

The formula instructs you to multiply the frequency (number of observations) of each interval by the midpoint, sum the products, and then divide the sum by the total number of observations. Table 3.6 shows the weekly incomes of 80 individuals as well as the midpoints of the intervals and the product, *fm*. On the basis of that information, the mean income of the sample of 80 individuals is calculated to be

$$\overline{X} = \frac{27,730.0}{80}$$

$$= 346.63$$

**TABLE 3.6    Weekly Earnings**

| Earning Interval | f | m | fm |
|---|---|---|---|
| 389.5–399.5 | 2 | 394.5 | 789.0 |
| 379.5–389.5 | 1 | 384.5 | 384.5 |
| 369.5–379.5 | 3 | 374.5 | 1,123.5 |
| 359.5–369.5 | 9 | 364.5 | 3,280.5 |
| 349.5–359.5 | 17 | 354.5 | 6,026.5 |
| 339.5–349.5 | 23 | 344.5 | 7,923.5 |
| 329.5–339.5 | 15 | 334.5 | 5,017.5 |
| 319.5–329.5 | 6 | 324.5 | 1,947.0 |
| 309.5–319.5 | 2 | 314.5 | 629.0 |
| 299.5–309.5 | 2 | 304.5 | 609.0 |
| Totals | 80 | | 27,730.0 |

Another method for calculating the mean for grouped data is given in Formula 3.6. Although the formula gives the same answer as Formula 3.5, it incorporates some basic ideas that are conceptually interesting:

$$\overline{X} = \overline{X}' + \frac{\Sigma f_i x_i}{n}(i) \qquad (3.6)$$

where    $\overline{X}'$ = the midpoint of the interval for the guessed mean. With $\overline{X}'$, you can select the midpoint of any interval, and you will get the correct answer, but if you select the interval containing the midpoint of the distribution, the computations will be easier.

$f_i$ = the frequencies of each interval

$x_i$ = the "computation variable" (a new scale of values that is multiplied by the interval frequencies rather than the midpoint). The computation variable, $x_i$, begins with 0 at the interval of the guessed mean; intervals above are assigned values +1, +2, +3, and so on in ascending order and those below −1, −2, −3, and so on in descending order.

$n$ = the number of observations

$i$ = the width of the intervals

Table 3.7 presents the data on weekly income. The formula indicates that you first select the midpoint of the interval in which you guess the mean will be located. You need not be concerned about guessing the correct interval because any interval you select will result in the correct answer. However, the closer your guess is to the interval in which the mean actually is located, the easier the calculations will be to make. The best guess can be arrived at by dividing the number

**TABLE 3.7   Weekly Earnings**

| Earning Interval | $f$ | $x$ | $fx$ |
|---|---|---|---|
| 389.5–399.5 | 2 | +5 | +10 |
| 379.5–389.5 | 1 | +4 | +4 |
| 369.5–379.5 | 3 | +3 | +9 |
| 359.5–369.5 | 9 | +2 | +18 |
| 349.5–359.5 | 17 | +1 | +17 |
| 339.5–349.5 | 23 | 0 | 0 |
| 329.5–339.5 | 15 | −1 | −15 |
| 319.5–329.5 | 6 | −2 | −12 |
| 309.5–319.5 | 2 | −3 | −6 |
| 299.5–309.5 | 2 | −4 | −8 |
| Totals | 80 | | 17 |

of cases by 2, $80/2 = 40$, and then counting the frequencies from the bottom of the distribution until the interval containing the fortieth case is located. In our example, it would be $2 + 2 + 6 + 15 = 25$, and the next interval, 339.5–349.5, contains 23 cases, so the fortieth case is in that interval.

Second, you assign the computation variable, beginning with 0, to the interval in which you guess the mean to lie, and then assign ascending positive values to the intervals above and descending negative values to the intervals below, as shown in Table 3.7. The computation variable is a linear transformation of the values for the midpoint of each interval, simplifying the calculations that were done using Formula 3.5. Third, you multiply the frequency of each interval by the value of its computation variable, $fx$. Fourth, you sum the products and divide the sum by $n$. The result of the division is multiplied by the width of the interval, $i$, and the product is added to the guessed mean.

The computation is shown using the data in Table 3.7. The table contains the frequencies, $f$, the computation variable, $x$, and the product, $fx$. The mean was guessed to lie in interval 339.5–349.5, so $\overline{X}' = 344.5$. Applying Formula 3.6, we see that

$$\overline{X} = \overline{X}' + \frac{\Sigma f_i x_i}{n}(i)$$

$$\overline{X} = 344.5 + \frac{17}{80}(10)$$

$$= 344.5 + (.213)(10)$$

$$= 344.5 + 2.13$$

$$= 346.63$$

which is the same as the answer derived using Formula 3.5. The computations using Formula 3.6 with the computation variable are somewhat easier than using the midpoints of the intervals, as shown in Formula 3.5.

While computers can quickly give results for the calculations shown for grouped data, frequently data are not computerized. Yet, it may be important to report the medians or means. The calculations, as shown here, are readily accomplished.

## Group Means

Frequently, you will encounter data that report the means for several groups, so that you must calculate the mean for the combined groups. The mean of a group of means is sometimes referred to as the **grand mean.** If all the groups are the same size, the procedure is straightforward. You simply sum the means of the groups and divide the sum by the number of groups. However, if the groups are of unequal size, the computation must ensure that each group's contribution to the grand mean is weighted in proportion to its size. Formula 3.7 accounts for differences in group size:

$$G\overline{X} = \frac{\Sigma n_i \overline{X}_i}{N} \tag{3.7}$$

where     $n_i \overline{X}_i =$ the size of the group multiplied by its mean

$N =$ the number of all the group members

For example, in Table 3.8, class A with 65 members should make a smaller contribution to the grand mean than class B with 110 members. Using Formula 3.7, you find that the grand mean for the example is

$$G\overline{X} = \frac{65(87)+110(92)+85(89)+200(96)+60(84)}{65+110+85+200+60}$$

$$= \frac{5,655+10,120+7,565+19,200+5,040}{520}$$

$$= \frac{47,580}{520}$$

$$= 91.50$$

**TABLE 3.8   Means of Groups**

| Groups | $\overline{X}$ | $n$ |
|--------|----------------|-----|
| A      | 87             | 65  |
| B      | 92             | 110 |
| C      | 89             | 85  |
| D      | 96             | 200 |
| E      | 84             | 60  |
| Total  |                | 520 |

The grand mean is also referred to as a **weighted mean** because the contribution of each score is weighted by the number of members in the group.

## Two Properties of the Mean

The arithmetic mean provides a unique description of a distribution and as such is a workhorse of statistics. Two properties make it unique. The **first property of the mean** is that the sum of the differences between the individual scores and the mean equals zero. That might be obvious, given that the mean has already been described as the point of balance in a distribution where the distances of the scores above the mean equal those of the scores below the mean. The mean is the only value for which the property is true, making it a unique descriptor. The property is expressed as

$$\Sigma(X - \overline{X}) = 0 \tag{3.8}$$

This assertion can be tested with the example in Table 3.9. Column A shows a distribution of five scores ranging from 198 to 153 and the sums and means of those scores. Column B shows the difference between the mean of 175 and the original scores; the sum of those differences equals zero. Column D shows the difference between a value smaller than the real mean (174) and scores in the distribution; the sum of those differences is equal to +5, which is greater than zero. Column F shows the difference between a score larger than the mean (176); the sum of those differences is equal to –5, which is less than zero. Thus, only the sum of the differences around the mean will always equal zero. The differences around any other value will always result in a sum other than zero.

The **second property of the mean** is that the squared differences between the individual scores and the mean equals a minimum value. No other value will result in a smaller sum of squared differences. The property is expressed as

$$\Sigma(X - \overline{X})^2 = \text{the minimum value} \tag{3.9}$$

**TABLE 3.9   Differences and Squared Differences between Scores and the Mean**

| A | B | C | D | E | F | G |
|---|---|---|---|---|---|---|
| | **Mean Value** | | **Value Less Than Mean** | | **Value Greater Than Mean** | |
| **Score** | $X - 175$ | $(X - 175)^2$ | $X - 174$ | $(X - 174)^2$ | $X - 176$ | $(X - 176)^2$ |
| 198 | +23 | 529 | +24 | 576 | +22 | 484 |
| 185 | +10 | 100 | +11 | 121 | +9 | 81 |
| 172 | –3 | 9 | –2 | 4 | –4 | 16 |
| 167 | –8 | 64 | –7 | 49 | –9 | 81 |
| 153 | –22 | 484 | –21 | 441 | –23 | 529 |
| $\Sigma = 875$ | 0 | 1,186 | +5 | 1,191 | –5 | 1,191 |
| $\overline{X} = 175$ | | | | | | |

Referring to Table 3.9, we see that this formula illustrates the property of the minimum value by showing that the sum of the squared differences around the true mean is the smallest value. Column C shows that the sum of the squared differences around the mean is 1,186. Column E shows that the sum of the squared differences for 174 is larger (1,191), and column G shows that 176 is also larger and equal to 1,191.

The importance of the two properties of the mean is that the mean and sum of the squared differences around the mean provide unique descriptions of distributions; thus, these two values can be used to represent distributions in higher-order calculations.

## *Summary of Measures of Central Tendency*

Each of the measures of central tendency provides a different description of a distribution. The mode identifies the value that appears most often in a distribution and can be used to describe nominal, ordinal, and interval measures. The weakness of the mode is that it ignores all other information about values in a distribution except the most frequent one. However, if you want to know which score or value appears most often in a distribution, the mode is exactly what you need.

The median identifies the point above and below which half the cases are located. It is the middle value of a distribution. Its weakness is that it ignores the location of scores above or below the midpoint. For example, all the scores above the median could be equal to the value directly above the median, whereas those below could equal the most extreme value below, and the median would not be affected. Thus, the location of cases at the extremes of the distribution is ignored. In some cases, this is desirable because of the need to minimize the effect of extreme scores. For example, if you have a group of five individuals with incomes of $21,000, $22,000, $23,000, $24,000, and $150,000, the arithmetic mean of the group would be $48,000, a value nowhere near any of the five incomes because of the influence of the highest income. The median of $23,000 is more informative about the income of the five individuals because you know that half had more and half had less than that income. The median can be used to describe distributions resulting from ordinal and interval measures.

The mean identifies the point of balance in a distribution because it takes into account the actual values of observations or their distances from the mean. It assumes that the data are a continuous measure and so is best suited for interval data. However, means are frequently computed for ordinal data and can be interpreted in terms of the positions they represent on the ordinal scale.

The two properties of the mean make it a unique descriptor of a distribution, and as such it plays an important role in higher-order statistical calculations and models. As you advance through this text, you will find virtually every chapter dealing with some application of the arithmetic mean.

Although measures of central tendency are useful for nominal, ordinal, and interval measures, they do not provide useful descriptions of dichotomous distri-

| Measures of Central Tendency | Levels of Measurement | | |
|---|---|---|---|
| | Nominal | Ordinal | Interval |
| Mode | x | x | x |
| Median | | x | x |
| Mean | | | x |

**FIGURE 3.2  Measures of Central Tendency and Measurement**

butions. The mode identifies only which of the two categories has the most members; the median or midpoint is not meaningful for only two categories; and the mean is always $n/2$, or half the number of observations. Figure 3.2 shows the relationship of the measures of central tendency to the three types of measurements.

In some distributions, one measure of central tendency might be at the same location in a distribution as another. In only one case are the mean, median, and mode in the same location (they coincide)—namely, when a continuous distribution of values is unimodal and symmetrical. In this case, the distribution of values above the mean is a mirror image of that below the mean.

Table 3.10 presents the distribution of weight for three groups. Frequency polygons of the distributions are shown in Figure 3.3 with the locations of the three measures of central tendency.

**TABLE 3.10  Body Weights for Three Groups**

| Body Weights | Group A | Group B | Group C |
|---|---|---|---|
| 190–199 | 1 | 1 | 2 |
| 180–189 | 2 | 2 | 3 |
| 170–179 | 4 | 4 | 15 |
| 160–169 | 7 | 7 | 5 |
| 150–159 | 14 | 14 | 6 |
| 140–149 | 24 | 24 | 3 |
| 130–139 | 14 | 1 | 2 |
| 120–129 | 7 | 1 | 5 |
| 110–119 | 4 | 2 | 10 |
| 100–109 | 2 | 6 | 16 |
| 90–99 | 1 | 18 | 13 |
| Totals | 80 | 80 | 80 |
| Mode | 144.5 | 144.5 | 104.5/174.5 |
| Median | 144.5 | 144.5 | 121.5 |
| Mean | 144.5 | 135.7 | 133.5 |

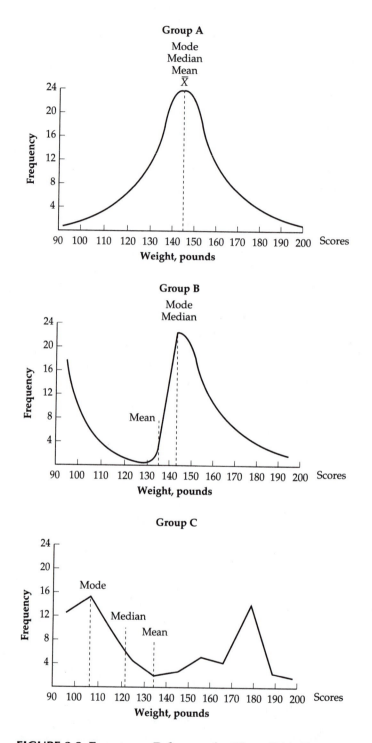

**FIGURE 3.3  Frequency Polygons for Three Distributions of Body Weights**

In group A, the mode, median, and mean are identical. Figure 3.3 indicates that group A, with the same mean, median, and mode, is a symmetrical distribution. The line of the curve to the right of the mean, median, and mode is a mirror image of that to the left. In later chapters you will see that this particular distribution serves as an important theoretical model in statistics.

Group B has a mode and median that are the same, 144.5, but the mean is lower, 135.7. The shape of the frequency polygon in Figure 3.3 shows that the mean is pulled down in the distribution by the large number of scores, 18, in the lowest weight category, 90–99. However, the median, 144.5, is unaffected by the low scores because the number of scores above and below the median did not change. Similarly, the mode remained at 144.5 because that interval continued to have the greatest number of observations, 24.

All three measures of central tendency differ in group C. The distribution is bimodal, with peaks at both 104.5 and 174.5. The median is 121.5 and the mean 133.5. The effect of the differences in the measures of central tendency on the shape of the distribution for group C is shown in Figure 3.3.

The three measures of central tendency are most frequently used to describe samples. However, remember that most research is based on samples, so the measures of central tendency are used as *estimates* of the populations represented by the samples. The mean is the measure of central tendency that plays the most important role in higher-order statistical calculations as an estimator of population characteristics.

The symbol for the population mean is the Greek letter "mu" ($\mu$). An important part of statistical analysis is determining whether the sample mean, $\overline{X}$, is a good estimate of the population parameter, $\mu$.

## MEASURES OF VARIATION

Measures of central tendency provide a single value that describes an entire distribution of scores. Although the mean, median, and mode give slightly different perspectives of a distribution, all emphasize the similarities of the observations. It is equally important to know about the differences, or *variation*, within a distribution. Two methods for estimating variation include measures for interval scale data and, for discrete measures, the index of qualitative variation.

The importance of **measures of variation** (also referred to as *measures of dispersion*) can be illustrated with an example. The distribution of poverty was evaluated for the two communities of Urbanville and Central City. Poverty was evaluated by comparing the number of poor households per 100 on the basis of an analysis of a sample of 10 census tracts in each community.[2] Both communities had a sum of 217 poor households over the 10 tracts, resulting in an average of 21.7 poor households per community, as shown in Table 3.11. If only the

---

[2] Densely populated areas in the United States are divided into census tracts, which are small geographic areas defined by the National Bureau of the Census for population counts.

TABLE 3.11    Poverty Households per 100
in Two Communities

| Urbanville | Central City |
|------------|--------------|
| 24.5 | 27.4 |
| 23.8 | 24.6 |
| 23.1 | 23.0 |
| 22.4 | 22.5 |
| 21.7 | 21.8 |
| 21.0 | 21.6 |
| 21.0 | 20.9 |
| 20.3 | 19.7 |
| 19.6 | 18.1 |
| 19.6 | 17.4 |
| 217.00 | 217.00 |
| $\overline{X} = 21.7$ | $\overline{X} = 21.7$ |

mean were available to describe the distribution of poverty for the two communities, the conclusion would be that they are identical. Both have an average of 21.7 poor households per 100. However, a brief glance at the two distributions indicates that they are so different that using only the mean of 21.7 to describe them would be misleading. The number of poor households in Urbanville does not deviate much from the mean of 21.7; the highest number of poverty households is 24.5 and the lowest 19.6. Given that the sample is a good representation of all the census tracts in Urbanville, we can safely assume that other census tracts in the community would have poverty rates somewhere near 21.7.

Central City presents a quite different picture. Some census tracts have substantially more poor households than others, from a high of 27.4 to a low of 17.4 per 100. Assuming that the 10 census tracts are a good representation of Central City, the results suggest that other census tracts in the community are likely to exhibit substantial scatter around the mean of 21.7. This indicates that, in the case of Central City, the mean is not as good a representation of poverty as it is for Urbanville. The census tracts in Urbanville are more homogeneous in terms of the number of poor households and in Central City more heterogeneous.

What we need is a summary number, one that is similar to the mean and that informs us about the *variation*, **dispersion,** or **scatter** of poverty in the census tracts of the two communities. Combined with the mean, such a number would provide a more complete description. Methods for these numerical descriptions of variation are discussed in the remainder of this chapter.

## Variation of Continuous Distributions

Measures of variation for continuous distributions considered here are the range, the semi-interquartile range, the variance, and the standard deviation.

### Range

The **range** of a distribution is the highest value in the distribution minus the lowest value. From Table 3.11, the ranges for the distributions of poverty in the two communities are 24.5 − 19.6 = 4.9 for Urbanville and 27.4 − 17.4 = 10 for Central City. As you might expect, the range for Urbanville, 4.9, is smaller than that for Central City, 10. The difference in the two ranges underscores the fact that census tracts in Urbanville are much more homogeneous with respect to poverty than they are for Central City.

The range provides useful information about a distribution by describing the distance between the lowest and the highest scores. It is especially helpful to review the range of variables before analyzing a data set to get a sense of variables that have high rather than low variation. The range is also helpful in identifying distributions with unexpected extreme scores, referred to as **outliers.** Outliers are scores that are much larger or smaller than the expected outcomes and can be indicative of measurement or other types of error that require special attention.

Although the range is useful for defining the extremes of the distribution, it is limited because it accounts for only the highest and the lowest scores and ignores all the other values between the extremes. For example, if Central City had 27.7 poor families per 100 in the first nine census tracts and 17.4 in the tenth, the range would remain the same, 27.4 − 17.4 = 10. If that were the only information available about poverty in Central City, it would be quite misleading, suggesting much variation when in fact all but one of the census tracts would have 27.4 poor families per 100.

The size of the range is also a function of the number of observations (sample size). Theoretically, and in the case of many empirical phenomena, the more cases available or the larger the sample size, the greater the likelihood of including extreme values. Usually, extreme values are rare and thus are more likely to be included with large samples than with small ones. Including more extreme values in larger samples results in a larger range.

### Semi-Interquartile Range

The problem of using only the two extreme scores of a distribution can be offset by using the **semi-interquartile range,** which is a measure of variation based on the **quartiles** of a distribution. Quartiles divide distributions into four equal parts. The semi-interquartile range is defined as the average of the difference between the third and the first quartile:

$$\text{Semi-interquartile range} = \frac{Q_3 - Q_1}{2} \qquad (3.10)$$

where $Q_1$ = the first quartile = $(n + 1)/4$

$Q_3$ = the third quartile = $3(n + 1)/4$

The semi-interquartile range for the 10 census tracts of Urbanville and Central City in Table 3.11 is determined by the following:

$Q_1 = (n + 1)/4 = (10 + 1)/4 = 2.75$ units above the lowest score, which is the position of the value at the first quartile (twenty-fifth percentile) of the distribution

$Q_3 = 3(n + 1)/4 = 3(10 + 1)/4 = 8.25$ units above the lowest score, which is the position of the value at the third quartile (seventy-fifth percentile) of the distribution

The value of the score at the first quartile for Urbanville is between the second and the third scores of the distribution. The above calculations for $Q_1$ show that it is exactly 2.75 scores from the bottom, or .75 of the distance between the scores of 19.6 and 20.3, which is 20.3 − 19.6 = .70 units × .75 = .53, and .53 + 19.6 = 20.13. The third quartile is 8.25 scores from the bottom, or .25 of the distance between 23.1 and 23.8, which is .70 units × .25 = .17, and .17 + 23.1 = 23.27. Applying Formula 3.10, we find that the semi-interquartile range for Urbanville is

$$\frac{Q_3 - Q_1}{2} = \frac{23.27 - 20.13}{2} = \frac{3.14}{2} = 1.57$$

The same procedures are used to derive the values for Central City; $Q_1$ is exactly 2.75 scores from the bottom, or .75 of the distance between the scores of 20.9 and 19.7, which is 20.9 − 19.7 = 1.20 units × .75 = .90, and 19.6 + .90 = 20.50. The third quartile is 8.25 scores from the bottom, or .25 of the distance between 24.6 and 23.0, which is 1.60 units × .25 = .40, and 23.0 + .40 = 23.40. Using Formula 3.10, we find that the semi-interquartile range for Central City is

$$\frac{Q_3 - Q_1}{2} = \frac{23.40 - 20.50}{2} = \frac{2.90}{2} = 1.45$$

The results show that using the interquartile range considerably diminishes the variation for both communities. Removing the extreme 25% of the census tracts from the bottom and top of the distribution results in a lower interquartile range for Central City than Urbanville. Using the interquartile range eliminates the effect of the extreme scores by excluding them. The measure is useful when extreme scores are a problem but is limited in that it can mask real differences in a distribution. Its real shortcoming is that it fails to consider the value of each observation in the distribution.

The next two measures considered here, variance and standard deviation, are based on the value of each score in a distribution and are the primary methods used to assess the variation of continuous variables. Like the mean, they are work-horses in statistical estimates and models, and as we will see, most statistical models are organized around the mean and variance (or standard deviation) or measures that serve as their surrogates.

### Variance

We examined two properties in the discussion of the mean. Recall that the second property was that the sum of the squared differences between individual observations and the mean equals a minimum value, $\Sigma(X - \overline{X})^2$ = minimum. **Variance,** symbolized by $s^2$, is based on this unique minimum value; it equals the average of the squared differences around the mean, as shown in the following formula:

$$s^2 = \frac{\Sigma\left(X - \overline{X}\right)^2}{n-1} \qquad \textbf{(3.11a)}$$

This formula instructs you to subtract the mean from each score in the distribution, square each difference, sum the squared differences, and divide the sum by the number of scores less 1. Because the calculation is based on the squared differences, the results are never negative. The formula provides an estimate of the variance for the population from a sample.[3] However, using a sample to estimate variance for a population is likely to result in an underestimate of the population variance. This is because samples, and especially small samples, are less likely to include extreme scores in the population. Extreme values are fewer in the population and thus less likely to be included in the sample, leading to an underestimate. The denominator $n - 1$ rather than $n$, the actual sample size, is used to compensate for this underestimate. Reducing the denominator by 1 slightly increases the estimate. The effect of $n - 1$ is greatest when the sample size is small and the risk of underestimating the real variance in the population is greatest. As sample size increases, the effect of reducing the denominator by 1 diminishes, and even with samples as small as 30 the effect is negligible. We will return to the subject of estimation in Chapter 6, which discusses the logic of statistical inference.

Frequently, $\Sigma(X - \overline{X})^2$ is symbolized in abbreviated form as $\Sigma x^2$. Formula 3.11a then becomes

$$s^2 = \frac{\Sigma x^2}{n-1} \qquad \textbf{(3.11b)}$$

Table 3.12 shows the distributions of scores for Urbanville and Central City and the differences of the means and the sums of the squared differences. Applying Formula 3.11a, we find that the variances for the two distributions are as follows:

$$s^2 = \frac{\Sigma\left(X - \overline{X}\right)^2}{n-1}$$

Urbanville $\qquad s^2 = \dfrac{26.46}{10-1} = 2.94$

Central City $\qquad s^2 = \dfrac{79.34}{10-1} = 8.82$

---

[3] The equation for the population variance is $\sigma = \dfrac{\Sigma\left(X - \mu\right)^2}{N}$; however, most research is based on sample estimates because population values such as $\mu$ are not available.

**TABLE 3.12    Variance for Poverty in Urbanville and Central City**

| Urbanville ($n = 10$) | | | Central City ($n = 10$) | | |
|---|---|---|---|---|---|
| $X$ | $X - \bar{X}$ | $(X - \bar{X})^2$ | $X$ | $X - \bar{X}$ | $(X - \bar{X})^2$ |
| 24.5 | 2.8 | 7.84 | 27.4 | 5.7 | 32.49 |
| 23.8 | 2.1 | 4.41 | 24.6 | 2.9 | 8.41 |
| 23.1 | 1.4 | 1.96 | 23.0 | 1.3 | 1.69 |
| 22.4 | .7 | .49 | 22.5 | .8 | .64 |
| 21.7 | 0 | 0 | 21.8 | .1 | .01 |
| 21.0 | −.7 | .49 | 21.6 | −.1 | .01 |
| 21.0 | −.7 | .49 | 20.9 | −.8 | .64 |
| 20.3 | −1.4 | 1.96 | 19.7 | −2.0 | 4.00 |
| 19.6 | −2.1 | 4.41 | 18.1 | −3.6 | 12.96 |
| 19.6 | −2.1 | 4.41 | 17.4 | −4.3 | 18.49 |
| 217.0 | | 26.46 | 217.0 | | 79.34 |
| $\bar{X} = 21.7$ | | | $\bar{X} = 21.7$ | | |

Variance takes into account the value of each observation. The results confirm our intuitive sense that the variance in poverty in the census tracts of Central City is much larger than in Urbanville.

The values resulting from calculating variance are a function of the original measurement scale used to generate the data. In the case of Urbanville and Central City, we know only that 8.82 is larger than 2.94. However, the standard deviation provides a method for transforming observed variances to a standard form that is more easily understood and compared.

### Standard Deviation

A frequently used measure of variation is the **standard deviation.** Symbolized by $s$, for a sample value, the standard deviation is defined as the square root of variance, as shown in the following formulas:

$$s = \sqrt{\frac{\Sigma\left(X - \bar{X}\right)^2}{n - 1}} \qquad (3.12a)$$

$$s = \sqrt{\frac{\Sigma x^2}{n - 1}} \qquad (3.12b)$$

Applied to the distributions of the two communities, the standard deviation for Urbanville is

$$s = \sqrt{2.94} = 1.71$$

and that for Central City

$$s = \sqrt{8.82} = 2.97$$

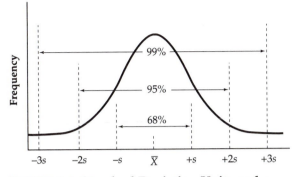

**FIGURE 3.4 Standard Deviation Units and a Bell-Shaped Curve**

Again, the results confirm our intuitive sense about the difference in poverty between Urbanville and Central City. The standard deviation, *s*, is a useful numerical descriptor because it can be interpreted in terms of *standard deviation units* for any continuous distribution. Taking the square root of the variance represents a linear transformation for any continuous measure in which $1s = 1$ standard deviation unit, $2s = 2$ standard deviation units, and $3s = 3$ standard deviation units. The standard deviation units can be the basis for powerful statements about a distribution.

For Urbanville, $1s = 1.71$, $2s = 2(1.71) = 3.42$, and $3s = 3(1.71) = 5.13$. For Central City, $1s = 2.97$, $2s = 2(2.97) = 5.94$, and $3s = 3(2.97) = 8.91$. Further, if the distribution of the variable in the population is bell shaped in form, such that the mode, median, and mean are equal, the frequency polygon appears as shown in Figure 3.4. The theoretical model of the bell-shaped curve is useful because it is known that about 68% of all observations are within 1 standard deviation unit below and 1 standard deviation unit above the mean, 95% are between 2 standard deviation units above and below the mean, and 99% are between 3 standard deviation units above and below the mean, as shown in Figure 3.4. The areas associated with the standard deviation units may be represented as follows:

$-1.00$ to $+1.00$ $s = 68\%$ of the area of the curve

$-2.00$ to $+2.00$ $s = 95\%$ of the area of the curve

$-3.00$ to $+3.00$ $s = 99\%$ of the area of the curve

What does this mean in terms of the poverty rates of the two communities? If we assume that the distributions of poor households in census tracts for the populations of the two communities are bell shaped, we can use the model and standard deviations to estimate their poverty rates.

In Urbanville, with $s = 1.71$, it is estimated that 68% of all census tracts will have a poverty rate between ±1.71 units below and above the mean (21.7), 95% of the tracts will have a poverty rate between ±2(1.71) units below and above the mean, and 99% of the tracts will have a poverty rate between ±3(1.71) units below and above the mean. Thus, for Urbanville

±1s = 1(1.71) ± 21.7 = 19.99–23.41 poor households in 68% of its census tracts

±2s = 2(1.71) ± 21.7 = 18.28–25.12 poor households in 95% of its census tracts

±3s = 3(1.71) ± 21.7 = 16.57–26.83 poor households in 99% of its census tracts

Thus, it is estimated that 68% of all the census tracts in Urbanville will have between 19.99 and 23.41 poor households, 95% will have between 18.28 and 25.12, and 99% will have between 16.57 and 26.83. Notice that the higher the percentage of census tracts included, the wider the estimated boundaries of poverty. Earlier, in discussing variance, we saw that larger samples are more likely to include extreme scores. Similar logic underlies what happens when your estimates go from 68% to 99% of the census tracts.

The larger standard deviation of Central City results in wider boundaries. The following shows what would be expected in Central City:

1s = 2.97 ± 21.7 = 18.73–24.67 poor households in 68% of its census tracts

2s = 2(2.97) ± 21.7 = 15.76–27.64 poor households in 95% of its census tracts

3s = 3(2.97) ± 21.7 = 12.79–30.61 poor households in 99% of its census tracts

This example illustrates the effect of low as opposed to high standard deviations. The rate of poverty in Urbanville is predictable within fairly narrow boundaries, whereas the prediction for Central City involves larger boundaries. A lower standard deviation allows for greater precision. As we will see in the next chapter, the numerical descriptions provided by the standard deviation and standard deviation units are powerful tools for data analysis.

### Chebyshev's Theorem

According to Figure 3.4, the areas related to standard deviation units are defined when the distribution of the variable represents a bell-shaped curve; that is, the standard deviation is relatively small, and most of the scores are grouped around the mean, declining symmetrically away from the mean. However, some distributions have large standard deviations, indicating that most of the scores are not grouped near the mean and the underlying population of scores may not be **symmetrical** and bell shaped in that the distribution may be skewed either to the left or to the right of the mean. Under these conditions, use of the bell-shaped model might be questionable.

However, **Chebyshev's theorem** states that even when distributions have large standard deviations and are skewed rather than bell shaped, the values of a distribution will be within boundaries that are a close approximation of the bell-shaped distribution. Formula 3.13 describes the boundaries according to Chebyshev's theorem:

$$1-\left(\frac{1}{k^2}\right) \tag{3.13}$$

where $k$ is any standard deviation value greater than 1.

The theorem states that for any distribution, regardless of shape, the proportion of observations within 2 standard deviation units is $1 - \left(\frac{1}{2^2}\right) = .75$ and within 3 standard deviation units is $1 - \left(\frac{1}{3^2}\right) = .89$. Thus, even with a highly skewed distribution, 75% of the observations will be within 2 standard deviations of the mean, and 89% will be within 3 standard deviations of the mean. The theorem indicates that using the bell-shaped distribution to interpret standard deviation units is useful, even with distributions that are not bell shaped.

### Alternatives for Calculating s² and s

Formulas 3.11a and 3.12a are based on squared differences around the mean. An alternative method does not require the calculation of the mean but is based on the **sums of the squares** of the original scores in a distribution. The formulas related to this alternative are used in more advanced statistical calculations, and it is helpful to become familiar with the method. The following formula shows the procedure:

$$s^2 = \frac{\sum X_i^2 - \frac{\left(\sum X_i\right)^2}{n}}{n-1} \tag{3.14}$$

where    $\sum X_i^2$ = the sum of the squared observed values

$\left(\sum X_i\right)^2$ = the sum of the observed values squared

The standard deviation is given in the following formula:

$$s = \sqrt{\frac{\sum X_i^2 - \frac{\left(\sum X_i\right)^2}{n}}{n-1}} \tag{3.15}$$

An application of the formulas is shown with the data in Table 3.13. The sums-of-squares equation provides results identical to those found using the squared differences around the mean.

For Urbanville, the variance and standard deviation are as follows:

$$s^2 = \frac{4735.36 - \frac{\left(217\right)^2}{10}}{10-1}$$

$$= \frac{4735.36 - 4708.90}{9}$$

$$= 2.94$$

**TABLE 3.13   Variance for Poverty in Urbanville and Central City**

| | Urbanville (n = 10) | | Central City (n = 10) | |
|---|---|---|---|---|
| | $X$ | $X^2$ | $X$ | $X^2$ |
| | 24.5 | 600.25 | 27.4 | 750.76 |
| | 23.8 | 566.44 | 24.6 | 605.16 |
| | 23.1 | 533.61 | 23.0 | 529.00 |
| | 22.4 | 501.76 | 22.5 | 506.25 |
| | 21.7 | 470.89 | 21.8 | 475.24 |
| | 21.0 | 441.00 | 21.6 | 466.56 |
| | 21.0 | 441.00 | 20.9 | 436.81 |
| | 20.3 | 412.09 | 19.7 | 388.09 |
| | 19.6 | 384.16 | 18.1 | 327.61 |
| | 19.6 | 384.16 | 17.4 | 302.76 |
| Totals | 217.0 | 4,735.36 | | 4,788.24 |

and

$$s = \sqrt{2.94} = 1.71$$

For Central City, the variance and standard deviation are as follows:

$$s^2 = \frac{4788.24 - \dfrac{(217)^2}{10}}{10 - 1}$$

$$= \frac{4788.24 - 4708.90}{9}$$

$$= 8.82$$

and

$$s = \sqrt{8.82}$$

$$= 2.97$$

The answers are identical to those when we used the squared differences around the means approach.

### $s^2$ and s for Grouped Data

Another formula must be used to compute the variance and standard deviation for grouped frequency distributions. The following formula is based on the midpoints of the intervals and is similar in structure to the sums-of-squares approach used in Formula 3.14:

$$s^2 = \frac{\Sigma f_i m_i^2 - \frac{\left(\Sigma f_i m_i\right)^2}{n}}{n-1} \qquad (3.16)$$

where          $\Sigma f_i m_i^2$   means to square the midpoint of each category, multiply the squared value by its frequency, and sum the products

$\dfrac{\left(\Sigma f_i m_i\right)^2}{n}$   means to multiply the frequency of each category by its midpoint, sum the products, square the sum of the products, and divide by $n$

The standard deviation for grouped data can be calculated by taking the square root of the variance, as shown in the following formula:

$$s^2 = \sqrt{\frac{\Sigma f_i m_i^2 - \frac{\left(\Sigma f_i m_i\right)^2}{n}}{n-1}} \qquad (3.17)$$

Table 3.14 presents test score data for a sample of 62 individuals. The values ranged from 50 to 99 (recall that the exact limits of the intervals are 49.5 to 99.5). The variance for the grouped frequency distribution is determined using Formula 3.16.

$$s^2 = \frac{381,308 - \frac{4,814^2}{62}}{62-1}$$

$$= \frac{381,308 - 373,783.81}{61}$$

$$= \frac{7524.19}{61}$$

$$= 123.35$$

and

$$s = \sqrt{123.35}$$

$$= 11.11$$

The results show that the variance for the distribution is 123.35 with a standard deviation of 11.11. Given that the mean for the distribution is 77.65, we can expect the following:

$1s = 11.11 \pm 77.65 = 68\%$ of the test scores for the population will be between 66.54 and 88.76 points

$2s = 2(11.11) \pm 77.65 = 95\%$ of the test scores for the population will be between 55.43 and 99.87

$3s = 3(11.11) \pm 77.65 = 99\%$ of the test scores for the population will be between 44.32 and 110.98

**TABLE 3.14   Test Scores: A Grouped Frequency Distribution**

**(*n* = 62)**

| Interval | *f* | *m* | *fm* | *m²* | *fm²* |
|---|---|---|---|---|---|
| 95–99 | 5 | 97 | 485 | 9,409 | 47,045 |
| 90–94 | 7 | 92 | 644 | 8,464 | 59,248 |
| 85–89 | 4 | 87 | 348 | 7,569 | 30,276 |
| 80–84 | 8 | 82 | 656 | 6,724 | 53,792 |
| 75–79 | 14 | 77 | 1,078 | 5,929 | 83,006 |
| 70–74 | 12 | 72 | 864 | 5,184 | 62,208 |
| 65–69 | 3 | 67 | 201 | 4,489 | 13,467 |
| 60–64 | 6 | 62 | 372 | 3,844 | 23,064 |
| 55–59 | 2 | 57 | 114 | 3,249 | 6,498 |
| 50–54 | 1 | 52 | 52 | 2,704 | 2,704 |
| Totals | 62 | | 4,814 | | 381,308 |
| | $\overline{X} = 77.65$ | | | | |

## Coefficient of Variation

Means, variances, and standard deviations for any distribution are a function of the numerics of the original scale used to collect the data. Thus, the means and variances for Urbanville and Central City are a function of the number of poor households per 100 in census tracts. If you calculated the means and variances for a distribution of hourly incomes, the results would be based on hourly incomes. Consequently, it is difficult to get a sense for how the variance of one variable compares to that of another. We all know the adage that you can't compare apples and oranges, but in many cases that is precisely what is of interest. Moreover, anyone can compare apples with apples. It is a real gain to be able to compare things that are ordinarily difficult to compare. The **coefficient of variation** provides a basis for comparing the variances of distributions using different measures. This coefficient, symbolized by *V*, is equal to the ratio of the variance to the mean:

$$V = \frac{s}{\overline{X}} \tag{3.18}$$

Suppose that you are interested in the relative variation of entrance exam scores for a class of premed students and a class of social science students. The premed exam had a maximum score of 500 and the social science exam 300. The mean exam score for premed students was 390 with a standard deviation of 21, whereas the mean exam score for social science majors was 225 with a standard deviation of 24. The results would be

$$\text{Premed} = \frac{21}{390} = .054 \qquad \text{Social science} = \frac{24}{225} = .107$$

indicating a greater relative variation among social science students than among premed students.

## Variation of Discrete Distributions

Estimates for variance and standard deviation that have been discussed relate to distributions based on interval or continuous measures. Those methods cannot be used for distributions of discrete measures, that is, for nominal and ordinal scales. The **index of qualitative variation (IQV)** provides a measure for assessing the variation of discrete distributions.

The IQV is a procedure that compares the *observed* variation of a distribution to its maximum variation. The estimate is based on the ratio of observed differences to the maximum *expected* differences that could occur given the measurement, as shown in the following formula:

$$IQV = \frac{\text{Observed variation}}{\text{Maximum expected variation}} \times 100 \qquad (3.19)$$

The ratio of observed variation to maximum expected variation deserves special attention because it is basic to statistical thinking. In Formula 3.19, the **maximum expected variation** literally is the maximum difference that could occur given the measurement that was used, whereas **observed variation** is the amount of that maximum that was observed in the sample. Suppose that you have a sample of 49 majors in seven academic fields. Table 3.15 contrasts the minimum and maximum variation that could occur with the sample. Minimum variation occurs if all 49 sample members choose the same academic major, such as economics, as shown in Table 3.15. The variation in the distribution is zero because all the individuals have the same major. Maximum variation occurs when sample members are equally distributed across scale categories. In our example, the 49 sample members are equally divided across the seven majors, representing the maximum possible variation.

**TABLE 3.15   Minimum and Maximum Distributions across Seven Majors**

| Major Field | Minimum Variation | Maximum Variation |
|---|---|---|
| Anthropology | 0 | 7 |
| Economics | 49 | 7 |
| History | 0 | 7 |
| Political Science | 0 | 7 |
| Psychology | 0 | 7 |
| Social Psychology | 0 | 7 |
| Sociology | 0 | 7 |
| Totals | 49 | 49 |

TABLE 3.16    Graduate Majors and Two Seminars

| Major | Seminar 1 | | Seminar 2 | |
|---|---|---|---|---|
| | Observed | Maximum | Observed | Maximum |
| Anthropology | 2 | 5 | 8 | 7 |
| Political Science | 17 | 5 | 6 | 7 |
| Psychology | 1 | 5 | 9 | 7 |
| Sociology | 0 | 5 | 5 | 7 |
| Total | 20 | | 28 | |

The observed and maximum expected variations are equal to the sum of the products of all possible pairs of frequencies in the scale categories. Table 3.16 shows the majors of graduate students enrolled in two seminars. The majors include anthropology, political science, psychology, and sociology. Seminar 1 had a total of 20 students, and seminar 2 had 28.

Beginning with seminar 1, the observed variation, OV, is the sum of the products of all possible pairs of frequencies observed across the majors. Identifying all possible pairs can be accomplished by beginning with the frequency of the top category and pairing it with each frequency below, then selecting the second frequency from the top and pairing it with those below, and so on. The procedure can be illustrated using the category labels of majors:

[(anthropologists × political scientists) + (anthropologists × psychologists) + (anthropologists × sociologists)] + [(political scientists × psychologists) + (political scientists × sociologists)] + [psychologists × sociologists]

The series exhausts all possible pairs of categories. The frequencies for each category are used in performing the calculations. The observed variation for seminar 1 is

$$OV = [(2 \times 17) + (2 \times 1) + (2 \times 0)] + [(17 \times 1) + (17 \times 0)] + [1 \times 0]$$

$$= [34 + 2 + 0] + [17 + 0] + [0]$$

$$= 53$$

Similarly, the maximum variation for seminar 1 is

$$MV = [(5 \times 5) + (5 \times 5) + (5 \times 5)] + [(5 \times 5) + (5 \times 5)] + [5 \times 5]$$

$$= [25 + 25 + 25] + [25 + 25] + [25]$$

$$= 150$$

The ratio of the observed to the maximum variation for seminar 1 is

$$IQV = \frac{53}{150} \times 100$$

$$= .35\,(100)$$

$$= 35\%$$

The solution indicates that the observed distribution of majors in seminar 1 represents 35% of the maximum possible variation that 20 students could have over four categories of majors. Similarly, the IQV for seminar 2 is

$$OV = [(8 \times 6) + (8 \times 9) + (8 \times 5)] + [(6 \times 9) + (6 \times 5)] + [9 \times 5]$$

$$= [48 + 72 + 40] + [54 + 30] + [45]$$

$$= 289$$

$$MV = [(7 \times 7) + (7 \times 7) + (7 \times 7)] + [(7 \times 7) + (7 \times 7)] + [7 \times 7]$$

$$= [49 + 49 + 49] + [49 + 49] + [49]$$

$$= 294$$

$$IQV = \frac{289}{294} \times 100$$

$$= .98(100)$$

$$= 98\%$$

The observed variation in seminar 2 represents 98% of the maximum variation, indicating that the 28 students came close to exhibiting the maximum variation possible across four categories of majors. The results for the two seminars are intuitively satisfying because seminar 1, with most students majoring in political science (17 out of 20), displayed a much lower percentage of the maximum potential variation (35%) than seminar 2, with a fairly equal number of majors in each category, which had 98%.

The IQV is useful for evaluating the variation of discrete measures. It compares the observed scatter in a distribution against the maximum scatter that could have occurred. The ratio of observed to maximum expected variation is conceptually interesting because, as we will find, many statistical models are organized around similar ratios.

## Summary of Variation

Measures of variation inform us about the extent of the scatter in the observations of a distribution. Several measures for interval data were discussed. The range describes the total extent of scatter in a distribution by subtracting the lowest observed value from the highest. This description is useful, especially for initial reviews of distributions of variables, because it provides a sense of how wide the sample observations are dispersed. It is limited because it is based only on the lowest and highest scores and ignores all other observations.

The semi-interquartile range removes the influence of the extreme values by focusing on the average of the differences between the first and third quartiles. Again, it is limited because it fails to account for the value of each observation.

Variance and standard deviation provide the most useful estimates because the value of each score contributes to the final result. Calculations of both are based on the property of the mean: $\Sigma(X - \overline{X})^2$ = a minimum value that represents a unique description of the distribution. The standard deviation is especially useful because it can be interpreted using a bell-shaped curve and standard deviation units. The use of the bell-shaped curve is considered in greater detail in the next chapter.

## COMPUTER EXERCISES: SOME SUGGESTIONS

The numerical summaries of central tendency and variation are central to statistical models. Learning to produce and interpret these values using your computer software is important. You may begin by identifying several frequency distributions of interval measures from your data set. You may want to have two or more ungrouped frequency distributions as well as a grouped frequency distribution. Have the computer provide you with the modes, medians, and means of the distributions. You may also want to produce frequency histograms of the distributions and examine differences in the shapes of the histograms and the relationship of the differences to the measures of central tendency. You can also produce the range, variance, and standard deviation for the distributions that you have selected. Compare the values for the different distributions, and review their influences on the frequency histograms.

## CHAPTER SUMMARY

Measures of central tendency and variation provide numerical descriptions of the distributions of variables. Measures of central tendency focus on the similarity of the observations, whereas measures of variation focus on the differences.

The mean and standard deviation (or variance) are workhorses for statistical models. They are the numerical descriptors around which most statistical models are organized. The process of statistical inference, that is, generalizing findings from samples to the populations they represent, depends especially on the mean and variance. The symbols representing these measures, for both samples and populations, are important, and you should become familiar with them. They include:

| | | | |
|---|---|---|---|
| Sample mean | $\overline{X}$ | Population mean | $\mu$ |
| Sample variance | $s^2$ | Population variance | $\sigma^2$ |
| Sample standard deviation | $s$ | Population standard deviation | $\sigma$ |

## KEY TERMS

**arithmetic mean**    Another term for the mean or the point of balance in a distribution.

**bimodal distribution**    A distribution with two modal or popular outcomes.

**Chebyshev's theorem**    Distributions with large standard deviations that are skewed still approximate a normal distribution.

**coefficient of variation**    Ratio of the variance to the mean, which provides an indication of relative variation.

**dispersion**    A term describing the variation or scatter of the scores in a distribution.

**first property of the mean**    The sum of the differences between the mean and the individual scores of a distribution is equal to zero.

**grand mean**    The mean of the means of two or more distributions.

**group means**    The average of two or more group means.

**index of qualitative variation (IQV)**    A measure of the ratio of the observed variation to the maximum variation across the categories of nominal or ordinal distributions.

**maximum expected variation**    The maximum variation that could occur in a distribution.

**mean**    The point of balance in the distribution of an interval variable. Each value in the distribution contributes its proportional share to the value of the mean.

**measures of central tendency**    A generic term applied to measures of the mode, median, and mean.

**measures of variation**    A generic term applied to methods for determining the scatter or dispersion of scores in a distribution.

**median**    The midpoint in a distribution of interval or ordinal measures. It is the point above and below which exactly half the observations are located.

**mode**    The most frequently appearing score for interval, ordinal, or nominal measures. It is the most popular score in a distribution.

**observed variation**    The variation observed in a distribution.

**outliers**    Unexpectedly extreme scores.

**quartiles**    The units that result from dividing a distribution into four equal parts.

**range**    A measure of variation showing the difference between the highest and the lowest scores in the distribution of an interval measure.

**scatter**    A term referring to the variation or dispersion of scores in a distribution.

**second property of the mean**    The sum of the squared differences between the mean and the scores of a distribution is equal to a minimum value.

**semi-interquartile range**    The difference between the first and third quartiles of an interval distribution.

**standard deviation**   The square root of variance. It describes the scatter in a distribution.

**sums of the squares**   An alternative method for computing variance on the basis of the sums of scores and sums of squared scores.

**symmetrical**   Applied to a distribution, it obtains when the distribution of values on the left of the mean mirrors those on the right.

**variance**   The average of the sums-of-squares differences around the mean. Variance describes the scatter of the observations for interval measures.

**weighted mean**   A grand mean of means in which the contributions are weighted by the number of members in each group.

## SYMBOLS

| | |
|---|---|
| md | Median |
| $\overline{X}$ | Sample mean |
| $\mu$ | Population mean |
| $G\overline{X}$ | Group mean |
| IQV | Index of qualitative variation |
| $s^2$ | Sample variance |
| $\sigma^2$ | Population variance |
| $s$ | Sample standard deviation |
| $\sigma$ | Population standard deviation |
| $Q$ | Semi-interquartile range |
| $V$ | Coefficient of variation |

## FORMULAS

$$md = \frac{n+1}{2}$$

The median for an array with an odd number of observations

$$md = \frac{n}{2} \text{ and } \frac{n+2}{2}$$

The two formulas used to determine the mean for arrays with an even number of observations

$$md = l_i + i\left(\frac{\frac{n}{2} - f_m}{f_i}\right)$$

The median for a grouped frequency distribution

$$\overline{X} = \frac{\Sigma X_i}{n}$$

The mean for an array of interval scores

$$\overline{X} = \frac{\Sigma f_i m_i}{n}$$

The mean for a grouped frequency distribution

$$G\overline{X} = \frac{\Sigma n_i \overline{X}_i}{N}$$

The mean of two or more means

$$IQV = \frac{\text{Observed variation}}{\text{Maximum variation}} \times 100$$

Index of qualitative variation

$$Q = \frac{Q_3 - Q_1}{2}$$

Semi-interquartile range

$$s^2 = \frac{\Sigma (X - \overline{X})^2}{n-1}$$

Variance based on squared differences around the mean.

$$s^2 = \frac{\Sigma x^2}{n-1}$$

Variance, where $\dfrac{\Sigma x^2}{n-1} = \dfrac{\Sigma (X - \overline{X})^2}{n-1}$

$$s^2 = \frac{\Sigma X^2 - \dfrac{(\Sigma X)^2}{n}}{n-1}$$

Variance based on sums of the squares

$$s = \sqrt{\frac{\Sigma (X - \overline{X})^2}{n-1}} = \sqrt{\frac{\Sigma x^2}{n-1}}$$

Standard deviation based on squared differences around the mean

$$s = \sqrt{\frac{\Sigma X^2 - \dfrac{(\Sigma X)^2}{n}}{n-1}}$$

Standard deviation based on the sums of the squares

$$s^2 = \frac{\Sigma f_i m_i^2 - \dfrac{(\Sigma f_i m_i)^2}{n}}{n-1}$$

Variance for grouped frequency distributions

$$s^2 = \sqrt{\frac{\Sigma f_i m_i^2 - \dfrac{(\Sigma f_i m_i)^2}{n}}{n-1}}$$

Standard deviation for grouped frequency distributions

$$1 - \left(\frac{1}{k^2}\right)$$

Chebyshev's theorem

$$V = \frac{s}{\overline{X}}$$

Coefficient of variation

## EXERCISES

1. John received the following scores on a series of exams: 85, 74, 90, 78, and 74. What are the mode, median, and mean for his exams?

2. Mary received scores of 86, 38, 90, 81, and 90 on the same series of exams. What are the mode, median, and mean for her exams?

3. Which measure of central tendency gives the best impression of John's performance? Which gives the best impression of Mary's performance? Explain your choice for each.

4. Which measure of central tendency gives the worst impression of John's performance? Which gives the worst impression of Mary's performance? Explain your choice for each.

5. If the instructor were to agree that John and Mary could drop the exam with the lowest score, what would their means be?

6. The following distributions represent the performance of two classes on an exam.

| Class 1 | Class 2 |
|---------|---------|
| 98 | 98 |
| 97 | 91 |
| 94 | 89 |
| 93 | 83 |
| 90 | 83 |
| 90 | 83 |
| 90 | 79 |
| 88 | 78 |
| 87 | 76 |
| 85 | 74 |
| 82 | 72 |
| 81 | 71 |
| 80 | 69 |
| 77 | 68 |
| 73 | 67 |

   a. What is the mode for each class?
   b. What is the median for each class?
   c. What is the mean for each class?
   d. What is the range for each class?
   e. What is the semi-interquartile range for each class? Which class is affected most by using the semi-interquartile range rather than the range?
   f. What is the variance and standard deviation for class 1?
   g. What is the variance and standard deviation for class 2?
   h. Explain why the variances differ for the two classes.
   i. Draw frequency polygons for the distributions of the two classes using an unbroken line for class 1 and a broken line for class 2.
   j. What are the values for 1, 2, and 3 standard deviation units for the two classes?
   k. Use the sums of the squares solution to calculate the variance and standard deviation for the two classes.

**7.** The following grouped frequency distribution of age was noted:

| Age Interval | f |
|---|---|
| 90–99 | 8 |
| 80–89 | 12 |
| 70–79 | 14 |
| 60–69 | 22 |
| 50–59 | 31 |
| 40–49 | 20 |
| 30–39 | 18 |
| 20–29 | 13 |
| 10–19 | 10 |
| 0–9 | 7 |
| Total | 155 |

**a.** What is the mode for the distribution?
**b.** What is the median for the distribution?
**c.** What is the mean for the distribution?
**d.** What is the range for the distribution?
**e.** What are the variance and standard deviation for the distribution?

**8.** Polyglot was a community of approximately equal numbers of citizens representing six ethnic groups. The membership of two popular social clubs in the town was reviewed in terms of ethnic representation. The following data resulted:

| Ethnic Group | Club 1 | Club 2 |
|---|---|---|
| African | 3 | 8 |
| Italian | 8 | 10 |
| French | 12 | 11 |
| German | 6 | 9 |
| Greek | 28 | 7 |
| Spanish | 33 | 9 |
| Totals | 90 | 54 |

**a.** What is the IQV for club 1?
**b.** What is the IQV for club 2?
**c.** Which club was most representative of the six ethnic groups?

**9.** The mean IQ scores for five senior high school classes were $n_1 = 117$, $\overline{X}_1 = 109$; $n_2 = 321$, $\overline{X}_2 = 103$; $n_3 = 412$, $\overline{X}_3 = 114$; $n_4 = 119$, $\overline{X}_4 = 121$; and $n_5 = 297$, $\overline{X}_5 = 116$. What is the grand mean for the five classes?

# 4

# A CONTINUOUS PROBABILITY DISTRIBUTION

## The Normal Distribution

To this point, we have examined some basic concepts and methods for describing the distribution of a variable. Chapter 1 provided a perspective of the role that statistics plays in social research. The importance of measurement and the various types of scales used in social science were also discussed. Chapter 2 reviewed a variety of techniques for organizing and displaying data, including arrays, frequency distributions, grouped frequency distributions, tables, charts, and graphs. Each method of presentation is an important tool for developing numerical descriptions of the distributions of variables. Chapter 3 introduced two primary numerical summaries of distributions including measures of central tendency and variance.

This chapter considers the role of **probability** in statistical descriptions. Probability theory is a complex subject that represents a major field of study on its own. Our concern with probability is limited to the role that it plays in statistical work. The focus here is on understanding how probability models are used to make decisions about numerical descriptions.

Recall that variables are observable entities that can take on two or more values. They are the raw materials that researchers work with to describe the activities and characteristics of populations. However, researchers seldom can afford to study entire populations. Rather, they select relatively small samples that represent the populations they are interested in and then generalize their findings from the samples to the populations.

Generalizing from sample findings to populations is based on *statistical inference,* which is the process of inferring population characteristics from sample observations. More specifically, statistical inference makes it possible to *estimate,* or infer, a population parameter from a sample statistic. The process of using sample findings to estimate population parameters is based on probability. Simply stated, probability is used to assess the likelihood that an observed sample statistic represents a population parameter. The purpose of this chapter is to describe how probability is used in statistical inference. More specifically, the model of probability considered here is the *normal probability distribution*, which relates to continuous or interval measures.

# THE ROLE OF PROBABILITY

## An Overview

The role of **probability** in statistical inference can be illustrated with an example involving coin tosses. A single toss of a coin has two possible outcomes: a head or a tail. If the toss is fair, the most likely outcome for a series of tosses is expected to be about half heads and half tails. This **theoretical expectation** is based on the assumption that if heads and tails are equally likely on a single toss, in the long run the most likely outcome on a series of tosses should consist of about half heads and half tails. The long-run expectation is based on what is expected if a coin is tossed an infinite number of times. The outcome of an infinite number of tosses may be thought of as the *real distribution*, or the population, of coin tosses.

The long-run expectation for the outcomes of a coin toss is the theoretical distribution of outcomes; it is not empirical—that is, it is not something we can see. The distributions of variables in populations are equivalent to the theoretical distribution of an infinite number of coin tosses because normally they are not available. In real life, researchers do not deal with an infinite number of outcomes, and social researchers do not analyze distributions of variables for entire populations. Rather, they work with small samples that represent subsets of populations. However, samples are important because the distribution of variables in samples provides the basis for estimating real and unknown population values.

However, a sample provides *only* an estimate. In fact, if repeated samples are drawn from the same population, the outcomes will vary somewhat from sample to sample. They will vary because, in the process of randomly drawing sample members, chance differences in who is selected will result in variations in sample outcomes. The fluctuation in sample results is referred to as *random variation.* Although random variation in sample results reminds us that samples do not perfectly represent populations, in the long run the sample outcomes should be close enough to the real population values to provide reliable estimates.

The logic of random variation in sampling outcomes can be illustrated by returning to our example of coin tosses. Suppose that you take a small sample of coin tosses (say 20) and you end up with an outcome of 9 heads and 11 tails. Remember, the theoretical expectation is half heads and half tails, so the expectation is that we should get about 10 heads and 10 tails. Although the outcome of 9 heads and 11 tails does not meet our expectation, you would hardly be surprised at that outcome, nor would you cry foul and insist that the tosses were unfair. Rather, you would likely accept the outcome of 9 heads and 11 tails as reasonable variation from what was expected. Intuitively, you know that the difference between your ideal expectation and what actually happens is due to chance variation in outcomes. We can accept some variation from ideal expectations, especially when using a small sample.

You also recognize that if you engage in repeated experiments of 20 tosses, you will end up with some variation in outcomes, such as 9 heads and 11 tails, 12 heads and 8 tails, 11 heads and 9 tails, 7 heads and 13 tails, and so on. This is called *random variation* from ideal expectations, and it is expected, even when everything is done to ensure that the coin is tossed fairly.

However, if the difference between what you expect and what you observe becomes more extreme, such as 2 heads and 18 tails or 1 head and 19 tails, you might begin to question the fairness of the tosses. It is one thing to have outcomes vary somewhat from your ideal expectations but quite another to have extreme variations. Put another way, outcomes that are close to our expectations are likely to be seen as caused by chance or the luck of the draw, whereas outcomes that are far removed from our expectations suggest that something other than chance is at work. This is true even though we are aware that there is some chance that extreme outcomes, or long shots, can happen.

The whole business of expected and unexpected outcomes and the luck of the draw is somewhat more manageable if you assign probabilities to outcomes. Probabilities provide a more precise definition of the point between what is seen as a chance difference and what is too extreme to be due to chance. Methods for calculating probabilities make it possible to assess the likelihood of outcomes. In the context of social research, probability methods make it possible to assess the likelihood of observing a sample value given a population expectation. Calculating the probabilities of events can be complicated, as it requires the use of sophisticated mathematics. However, most researchers do not calculate probabilities directly for sample observations; if it were necessary for researchers to do so, it is likely that far less research based on probabilities would be done.

Fortunately, it is not necessary to calculate probabilities from scratch because models have been developed that make it possible to determine the probabilities of outcomes with relative ease. If you take the time to learn how to use the models, you can determine the probabilities of outcomes without resorting to a lot of mathematics. The general character of such probability models can be illustrated with a relative frequency distribution such as was discussed in Chapter 2.

## Probability and Relative Frequencies

The probability of a particular outcome for a variable may be defined as the ratio of successful outcomes to the total number of outcomes as shown in the following formula:

$$p = \frac{r}{n} \tag{4.1}$$

where      $p$ = the probability

$r$ = the subset of outcomes of concern

$n$ = the total number of outcomes

The expression is similar to that used for a proportion, $\dfrac{f}{n}$ (see Formula 2.3 in Chapter 2), except that Formula 4.1 uses the symbol $r$ rather than $f$ in the numerator. Recall that the symbol $f$ represents the frequencies of a particular variable value. The symbol $r$ has a more general reference to some subset of outcomes of the total sample. The frequency distribution of the weights of 77 individuals, shown in Table 4.1, can be used to illustrate the application of Formula 4.1. If the frequency for each weight category is seen as a subset of the total sample of body weights, then $\dfrac{r}{n}$ provides the relative frequency for each weight interval. The results are shown in Figure 4.1. For purposes of illustration, the relative frequency for each interval appears above the bar in the chart. Thus, the proportion of individuals weighing between 100 and 109 pounds is 2/77 = .026, those between 110 and 119 pounds is 5/77 = .065, and so on. If you add up all relative frequencies, the sum equals 1.00.

The relative frequency for each weight interval also represents the probability of observing someone in that weight category. If our sample represents a larger population, we can infer that the probability of seeing individuals in the population weighing between 100 and 109 pounds is .026, or about 2.6% of the time we would expect to encounter someone in that weight category in the population. Similarly, the probability of someone weighing between 150 and 159 pounds is .233, or 23.3%, and so on. The probabilities simply represent the proportion of individuals in each category.

**TABLE 4.1   Body Weights: Grouped Frequency Distribution**

| Body Weights | $f$ | $r/n$ |
|:---:|:---:|:---:|
| 190–199 | 3 | .039 |
| 180–189 | 4 | .052 |
| 170–179 | 7 | .091 |
| 160–169 | 15 | .195 |
| 150–159 | 18 | .233 |
| 140–149 | 11 | .143 |
| 130–139 | 8 | .104 |
| 120–129 | 4 | .052 |
| 110–119 | 5 | .065 |
| 100–109 | 2 | .026 |
| Total | 77 | 1.000 |

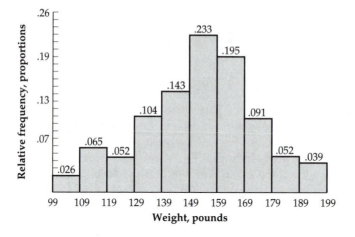

**FIGURE 4.1   Relative Frequency Histogram of
Body Weights**

A small sample of observations, such as the 77 weights, is useful for illustrating the concept of probability, but in practice such distributions usually are not composed. Remember, although researchers work with samples, their real concern is estimating population values represented by the samples. It follows that the **probability distribution** of concern to the researcher is that of the *variable in the population.* However, we know that populations usually are not available to researchers, so it is not practical to construct probability distributions for variables in populations. This also suggests that determining probabilities for underlying population distributions is much more complicated than the simple proportions describing our sample of body weights. Fortunately, it is not necessary to calculate directly the probabilities of events in populations. *Theoretical probability distributions* have been constructed that make it possible to determine the probabilities of the outcomes of most variables.

The frequency histogram of body weights described in Figure 4.1 consists of a small and finite set of observations. Frequency histograms of the distributions of variables in populations differ in two important ways. First, because populations are very large, histograms describing them consist of a great number of observations (Figure 4.2). In other words, they involve many frequencies. Second, if the variable is a continuous scale of interval measures, the number of potential values that the variable can take on is also very large. As shown in Figure 4.2, the large number of frequencies results in a histogram of bars with many different heights, and the large number of values on the x-axis means the widths of the bars become very narrow. Figure 4.2 illustrates the change in the appearance of a histogram with as few as 24 interval categories. Increases that approach an infinitely large number of observations will result in so many bars that the chart will appear as a smooth curve rather than bars, as shown in Figure 4.3.

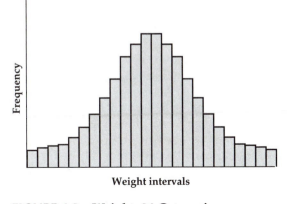

**Weight intervals**

**FIGURE 4.2    Weight: 24 Categories**

Third, many *continuous* variables assume the form of a **bell-shaped distribution,** such as the one in Figure 4.3. Given that distributions of many variables have a similar form, the bell-shaped curve can be used as a model to determine the probabilities of outcomes for a large number of measures. The model identifies areas associated with particular values of a variable. Once the area in which an observation occurs is established, the probability of the observation also can be determined by identifying the proportion of the area above and below the location of the observation. The model that makes this possible is referred to as the **normal probability distribution,** or the *normal curve.* The normal probability distribution has a number of characteristics that make it especially useful as a model for researchers.

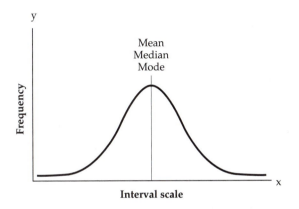

**FIGURE 4.3    The Bell-Shaped Distribution**

# THE NORMAL PROBABILITY DISTRIBUTION

## Characteristics of the Normal Distribution

The normal distribution has several unique characteristics that you should be familiar with (Figure 4.3 provides a visual illustration of these characteristics):

1. The normal distribution is *bell shaped,* with the most frequent observations at the midpoint. As you move to the left and right of the center of the distribution, the frequencies diminish in number. Because the observations at the midpoint are the most frequent ones, they also are the most probable occurrences. Similarly, as you move away from the midpoint, the observations become less frequent and the probability of their occurrence declines as well (see Figure 4.3).
2. The normal distribution is a **symmetrical distribution,** so that the left half of the curve is a mirror image of the right half.
3. The mean, median, and mode *coincide;* thus, the point of balance (mean), the midpoint (median), and the most frequent occurrence (mode) of the distribution are all located at the same point on the curve.
4. The normal distribution is a **continuous probability distribution,** so that, theoretically, the number of values the variable can assume on the x-axis is infinite because the units of the scale on the x-axis can be divided into infinitely smaller equal parts. Thus, the model can be used for very precise measures.
5. The normal distribution is an *asymptotic* distribution, so that, although the line of the curve descends as you move away from the center of the distribution, it never actually joins the line of the x-axis (**asymptosis**). This means that as you move away from the center or mean of the distribution, the probability of observations becomes less likely; that is, the frequencies decline and approach zero. But zero is never achieved because, at least theoretically, there is always some probability, however remote, that a more extreme observation than the last most extreme one could be observed. Thus, the distribution allows for even the most extreme outcomes.
6. The *total area* under the curve is equal to 1, and any value on the x-axis bisects the curve into two parts: the portion of the curve above the value and the portion below the value. The portion above the curve can be thought of as the probability of values equal to or larger than an observed value, whereas the portion below is the probability of the values equal to or smaller than an observed value. The two portions are proportions of 1.00, and the sum of the two portions always equals 1.00.

Given that the proportions of the curve above and below an observation can be established, probability statements about any observation on the x-axis can be made. For example, if an observation bisects the curve so that .95 of the area lies below it and .05 above, it can be said that 95% of the observations are expected to be less and 5% are expected to be greater than the observation. It can also be said that the probability of seeing a value less than the observation is .95 and the probability of seeing a value greater than the observation is .05. The potential of the normal probability model for identifying the location of observations on the curve and making probability statements about the area above and below them makes the model most useful to researchers.

## Empirical Normal Probability Distributions

The normal probability distribution is a theoretical model that has been derived mathematically. It is useful because many variables encountered in the empirical world have frequency distributions that are similar in form to the theoretical model. Although **empirical normal distributions** have a form similar to the theoretical model, each empirical distribution has its own mean and standard deviation in keeping with the type of measuring device used. Thus, body weights have a specific range of values and are located on the segment of the number line relevant to body weight values. The segment of numbers for body weights differs from that used by a Fahrenheit thermometer, achievement scores on an IQ test, or the annual earnings of members of a community.

Thus, all empirical measures are located on some segment of the number line that potentially extends from an infinite negative value to an infinite positive value. The position of a particular measure on the number scale is a function of the empirical values it spans. The location of means is also a function of the empirical values, as shown in Figure 4.4.

Differences in standard deviations of empirical distributions influence the peakedness (referred to as **kurtosis**) of their curves. A small standard deviation suggests that observations are clustered near the mean, resulting in a more peaked distribution. Such peaked distributions are referred to as **leptokurtic,** as shown in Figure 4.5. A large standard deviation occurs when observations are scattered farther from the mean and toward the tails of the distribution, producing a flatter curve. Flat distributions are referred to as **platykurtic.** Distributions that have

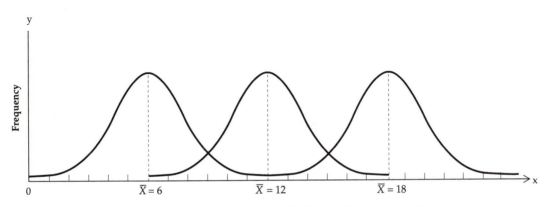

**FIGURE 4.4   Empirical Normal Distributions: Different Means and Equal Standard Deviations**

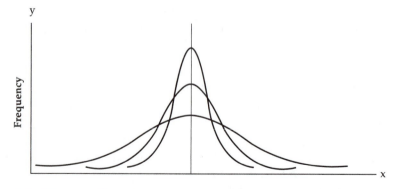

**FIGURE 4.5    Three Empirical Normal Distributions: Unequal Standard Deviations and Equal Means**

moderate peakedness are similar to the theoretical normal curve and are known as **mesokurtic.** Despite the differences in the means and standard deviations of various measurements, all empirical normal curves are similar in that they approximate the form or shape of the theoretical normal probability model.

Although empirical normal distributions approximate the theoretical normal model, the location of their means and the value of their standard deviations vary, so the area associated with observations fluctuates from one variable to the next. This means that the area above and below empirical observations is not fixed and would need to be recalculated for each observation to determine probabilities. Fortunately, such onerous calculations can be avoided by transforming empirical measures to the values of the fixed standard scale used by the theoretical normal probability model.

## The Standard Normal Probability Distribution

The theoretical model differs from empirical distributions because it is based on a fixed **standard normal probability distribution,** known as the **Z-score** scale. The value at the midpoint of the scale is 0; values to the right are +1, +2, +3, and higher; and values to the left are −1, −2, −3, and lower. The mean of the distribution is always 0 because that is the point of balance in the distribution and the standard deviation is always 1. Given that the values on the x-axis are fixed, an observation with a particular value is always at the same location; and, because the area of the curve above and below any observation on the x-axis can be determined, the probability of any observation can be known as well.

Even more important, any interval measure can be transformed to the Z-score scale. Figure 4.6 shows the character of the scale on the x-axis. Although means and standard deviations vary for different empirical measures, the Z-score scale always has a mean of 0 and a standard deviation of 1. Therefore, 1 standard deviation unit above *and* below the mean always equals ±1.00, 2 standard deviation units equal ±2.00, and 3 standard deviation units equals ±3.00.

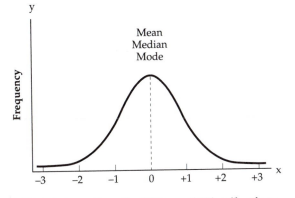

**FIGURE 4.6 Standard Normal Distribution:
The Z-Score Scale**

The values of empirical distributions are transformed to Z-scale values using Formula 4.2. The formula converts the values of the original measures to the values of the Z-score scale by subtracting the mean of the empirical distribution from each observed value and dividing the result by the standard deviation of the empirical distribution:

$$Z = \frac{X - \overline{X}}{s} \tag{4.2}$$

Given that the mean and standard deviation can be easily calculated for interval scale data, the Z-score transformation has wide applicability. You need only assume that the distribution in the population approximates that of a bell-shaped curve.

Assume that the underlying distributions of poverty across the census tracts of Urbanville and Central City (see Table 4.2) are normal in form. The transformed values would thus be calculated using Formula 4.2. The Z score for Urbanville's first score is

$$Z = \frac{X - \overline{X}}{s} = \frac{24.5 - 21.7}{1.71} = \frac{2.80}{1.71} = 1.64$$

and the Z value for Central City's first score is

$$Z = \frac{27.4 - 21.7}{2.97} = \frac{5.70}{2.97} = 1.92$$

The transformation of the original empirical values to Z values is linear; changing the values of the original measure to Z values does not alter the relative position of the scores to each other.

Earlier it was stated that distributions transformed to the Z scale always have means equal to 0 and standard deviations equal to 1. You can check this assertion by computing the mean and standard deviation for the Z-score distributions of poverty for Urbanville and Central City, and given rounding errors, it will demonstrate the assertion.

**TABLE 4.2   Z-Score Transformation for Poverty in Urbanville and Central City**

| Urbanville | | Central City | |
|---|---|---|---|
| X | $Z = X - \bar{X}/s$ | X | $Z = X - \bar{X}/s$ |
| 24.5 | +1.64 | 27.4 | +1.92 |
| 23.8 | +1.23 | 24.6 | +.98 |
| 23.1 | +.82 | 23.0 | +.44 |
| 22.4 | +.41 | 22.5 | +.27 |
| 21.7 | .00 | 21.8 | +.03 |
| 21.0 | −.41 | 21.6 | −.03 |
| 21.0 | −.41 | 20.9 | −.27 |
| 20.3 | −.82 | 19.7 | −.67 |
| 19.6 | −1.23 | 18.1 | −1.21 |
| 19.6 | −1.23 | 17.4 | −1.45 |
| 217.0 | | 217.0 | |
| $\bar{X} = 21.7$ | | $\bar{X} = 21.7$ | |
| $s_1 = 1.71$ | | $s_2 = 2.97$ | |

## Areas under the Standard Normal Curve

The area of the curve associated with each Z score is fixed. Once the values of a measure are transformed to the Z scale, the area associated with each Z score is defined, and the probability of its occurrence can be determined. Table B.1 (see Appendix B) shows the proportion of the area of the curve above and below Z values. Column A contains the Z values from .00 to 4.00. Column B shows the area either to the left of a minus Z score or the right of a plus Z score. Column C shows the area both to the left of a minus Z score and to the right of a plus Z score. The areas in columns B and C are located on the tails of the distribution.

Column D shows the area between the $\bar{X}$ and the Z for either a minus or plus Z score, and column E shows the area between the $\bar{X}$ and the Z values for minus and plus scores. The areas in columns D and E are located between the Z value and $\bar{X}$.

For example, column B shows the area beyond Z = 1.50 (which can be either +1.50 or −1.50) as .0668. Column C shows the area beyond both +1.50 and −1.50 as .1336, which is the sum of the areas for +1.50 = .0668 and −1.59 = .0668. Column D shows the area between the $\bar{X}$ and Z for 1.50 = .4332, and column E shows the area between the $\bar{X}$ and +1.50 and −1.50 as .8664, which is the sum of +1.50 = .4332 and −1.50 = .4332. If you add columns C and E, you find .1336 + .8664 = 1.0000.

Also, if you add the area in columns B and D, .0668 + .4332 = .5000, or exactly half the area of the curve. The same results will obtain for any Z score. The areas for Z = +1.50 are shown in Figure 4.7.

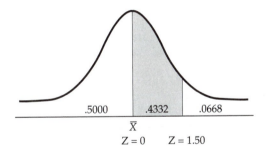

**FIGURE 4.7   Areas under the Curve for Z = + 1.50**

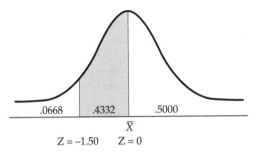

**FIGURE 4.8   Areas under the Curve for Z = –1.50**

Figure 4.8 shows the area for Z = –1.50, and (as you might expect), given that the normal curve is symmetrical, the areas for Z = –1.50 are identical to those for Z = +1.50. Thus, the areas shown in the columns of Table B.1 can be used for assessing both negative and positive Z scores.

Given that we can identify the area related to Z scores, we can make probability statements about a value converted to a Z score. In our example of Z = 1.50, we can say that any value equal to or more extreme than +1.50 will occur only .0668, or 6.68%, of the time (see column B in Table B.1). Given that the total area of the curve is equal to 1.00, you also know that the probability of a Z score equal to or less than +1.50 is 1.0000 – .0668 = .9332. Given the symmetry of the curve, the same is true for Z = –1.50 as for Z = +1.50.

You also can identify the area of a ± value. For example, the area beyond both +1.50 and –1.50 equals .1336 (see column C in Table B.1). The unshaded portion of the curve in Figure 4.9 identifies the area for ±1.50. It shows that .0668 of the area is on the left tail of the curve and .0668 is on the right, for a total area of .1336 (see column C in Table B.1). You could say that the probability of seeing scores more extreme than either +1.50 or –1.50 is .1336, or you would expect such scores to occur about 13.36% of the time.

The area between ±1.50 (see column E in Table B.1) equals .8664. The shaded area of Figure 4.9 shows that the area between –1.50 and the mean is .4332; the area between +1.50 and the mean is also .4332, for a total of .8664. The probability of

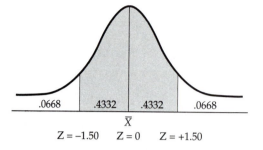

**FIGURE 4.9    Areas under the Curve for
Z = ±1.50**

seeing scores between +1.50 and –1.50 is .8664, or you would expect such scores to occur about 86.64% of the time.

The real value of Table B.1 and the areas related to Z scores is that you can transform any set of values regardless of their original metrics to Z scores. Once they are transformed to Z scores, Table B.1 shows the probabilities associated with any Z value.

Note that the shaded areas in Figures 4.7 and 4.8 relate to only one side of the normal curve; that is, they relate to only one tail of the distribution (the area shown in column B of Table B.1). Column B is titled "one-tailed," meaning that the values in the column are the probabilities of Z scores on either the right or the left tail of the curve. Similarly, column D in Table B.1 shows the **one-tailed probabilities** for the area between the $\overline{X}$ and Z scores.

The unshaded area in Figure 4.9 encompasses both sides of the curve, and in reference to Table B.1, column C presents the probabilities associated with both tails of the distribution, which are referred to as **two-tailed probabilities.** They are used to assess the probability of the occurrence of both plus and minus Z values. We return to the idea of one- and two-tailed probabilities in Chapter 7, which discusses hypothesis testing.

Table B.1 in the appendix is useful not only for determining the probabilities of Z scores representing observed events, but you can also determine the Z score associated with a particular probability. Suppose that you want to know the Z score associated with a one-tailed probability of .05. You move down column B until you locate the closest value to .05, which is .0495, and the Z value associated with it in column A is 1.65. For a two-tailed probability of .05, go to column C until you locate the value of .05, and the associated Z score in column A is 1.96.

The standard normal probability distribution and the Z-score transformation provide a simple model for assessing the probabilities associated with observed values. However, the use of the model is based on the assumption that the **underlying distribution** of the variable in the population approximates that of the normal curve. If the underlying distribution is not normal, conclusions about the area associated with a particular score might be in error. However, recall that Chebyshev's theorem (discussed in Chapter 3) indicates that even when distributions diverge from the ideal normal form, the area associated with particular Z values is not distorted dramatically.

Two other characteristics of distributions, skewness and kurtosis, provide information on whether a distribution is normal in form. Combined with the mean and variance, they represent the four descriptors of any distribution.

## SKEWNESS AND KURTOSIS

Every distribution of scores can be described in terms of four characteristics referred to as the *moments* of a distribution. The four moments are represented symbolically as follows:[1]

$$\text{Mean} = m_1 = \frac{\Sigma\left(X - \overline{X}\right)}{n} = \overline{X}$$

$$\text{Variance} = m_2 = \frac{\Sigma\left(X - \overline{X}\right)^2}{n} = s^2$$

$$\text{Skewness} = m_3 = \frac{\Sigma\left(X - \overline{X}\right)^3}{n} = s^3$$

$$\text{Kurtosis} = m_4 = \frac{\Sigma\left(X - \overline{X}\right)^4}{n} = s^4$$

The first moment, the *mean*, represents the point of balance in a distribution, and from Chapter 3 we know that the differences around the mean equal zero. Thus, the **first moment of a distribution,** the *mean*, is equal to zero. The **second moment of a distribution,** *variance*, describes the extent to which the observations in a distribution are scattered around the mean or the point of balance. It is equal to the average of the squared differences around the mean and symbolized by $s^2$. Given that the values are the sums of squares, variances always have a positive sign. **Skewness,** the **third moment of a distribution,** provides an estimate of the symmetry of the distribution and conceptually is the average of the cubed differences around the mean. It can have both negative and positive values. *Kurtosis*, the **fourth moment of a distribution,** is the average of the fourth power around the mean and has only positive values. It indicates whether the scores are clustered relatively close to the mean or farther away.

Recall that a symmetrical distribution is such that observations to the right of the mean are a mirror image of those to the left. The normal curve, a bell-shaped distribution, is symmetrical, but not all symmetrical distributions are bell shaped (normal). Any distribution with identical left and right sides to the mean

---

[1] The actual formulas for calculating skewness and kurtosis go beyond the purposes of this presentation, but it is important to be familiar with the concepts and the descriptions they provide of a distribution.

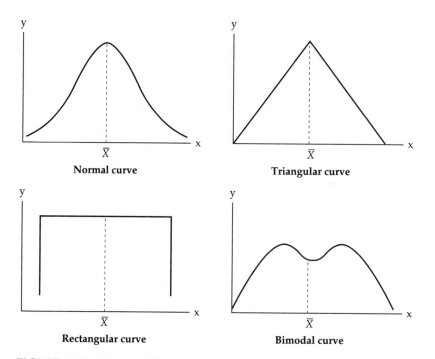

FIGURE 4.10    Types of Symmetrical Distributions

is symmetrical. Figure 4.10 presents four examples of symmetrical distributions, and only one of them, the upper left, is normal.

A distribution can be skewed either to the left, a **negative skew,** or to the right, a **positive skew.** In a negatively skewed distribution, a larger number of the observations to the left of the mean extend farther toward the tail of the distribution than do those to the right (see Figure 4.11). If the skew is positive, more observations extend farther toward the right tail of the curve. When a distribution is skewed to either the left or the right, the mean, median, and mode no longer coincide. The mean, on the x-axis, shifts to accommodate the more numerous observations toward the tail and maintain the point of balance. The mode remains at the peak (the point at which most of the observations occur), and the median or midpoint, like the mean, is pulled toward the side of the skew to account for additional scores toward the tail of the distribution.

Skewness affects the proportion of the area above and below the mean so that the distribution no longer conforms to the areas associated with standard deviation units and the Z scores of the standard normal distribution. For example, the area for 1 standard deviation unit above the mean in a positively skewed distribution is greater than the area below the mean. The inverse is true for a negatively skewed distribution, as can be seen in Figure 4.11.

Although the extent of the skewness of a distribution is evaluated mathematically, its effect can be illustrated. We know that about 95% of the area of the stan-

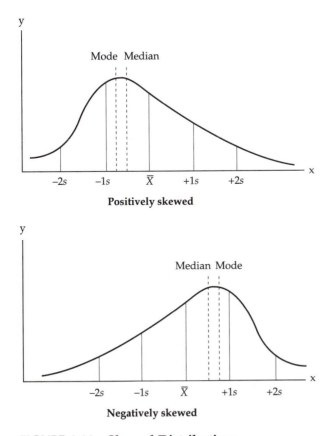

**FIGURE 4.11  Skewed Distributions**

dard normal distribution lies between –2 and +2 standard deviation units (check this by looking up the area associated with $Z = 2.00$ in Table B.1). Extreme skews may reduce the area from 95% to about 75%. However, the effect of slightly skewed distributions is negligible. More advanced statistics texts discuss procedures for evaluating skewness.

Kurtosis relates to the peakedness of a curve. If a relatively large proportion of observations are close to the mean, the distribution becomes peaked and is described as leptokurtic, as shown in Figure 4.12. If the observations are relatively far from the mean, the distribution becomes flatter and is referred to as platykurtic. A mesokurtic distribution is one that has a bell shape, characteristic of the standard normal distribution. Figure 4.12 shows the three types. The problem encountered in using the normal curve model to interpret the areas associated with leptokurtic distributions is that more observations are located in the first standard deviation unit and fewer in the second and third than the standard model anticipates. In the case of platykurtic distributions, fewer cases than expected are in the first standard deviation unit and more are in the second and third than is appropriate for interpreting areas using the standard normal model.

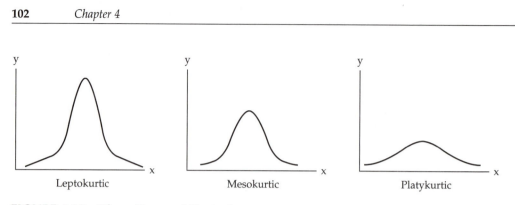

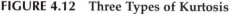

**FIGURE 4.12   Three Types of Kurtosis**

## COMPUTER EXERCISES: SOME SUGGESTIONS

This chapter introduced a model for making probability statements about observations. There are no direct computer exercises that relate to the content of this chapter. However, when we consider statistical testing in later chapters, you will find that the computer will automatically provide the probability of your results. You might consider a few procedures by returning to the frequency distributions you created for the previous chapter. There it was suggested that you examine the measures of central tendency and variation for your distributions. You now know about two additional descriptors of a distribution to the mean and variance, skewness and kurtosis. You can produce those values and become familiar with the criteria used by the software for these measures to assess whether your distributions meet the expectations for the normal distribution.

## CHAPTER SUMMARY

The purpose of this chapter was to introduce you to the concept of a continuous probability distribution and how it is used by social researchers. The standard normal distribution represents an especially useful model because any continuous measure can be transformed to the Z scale, on which the normal distribution is based. Once measures are transformed to the Z scale, the normal probability distribution can be used to determine the probabilities associated with any Z value. Moreover, the probabilities are easy to determine using Table B.1, which shows the proportion (and probabilities) associated with any Z score. The Z-score table provides ready information on the probabilities of observed outcomes.

The standard normal curve model is based on the assumption that the underlying distribution of the variable approximates the shape or form of the normal distribution. The underlying distribution of a variable refers to the distribution of the variable in the population. Two measures are helpful in determining whether a variable's distribution fits the normal curve: skewness and kurtosis. A distribution with little skew and mesokurtic peakedness suggests the approximation of a normal distribution.

Not all variables are continuous, so because the standard normal distribution is intended for continuous measures, another model must be used for discrete data such as ordinal and nominal measures. The next chapter introduces a **discrete probability distribution:** the binomial distribution.

## KEY TERMS

**asymptosis**   A characteristic of the normal curve such that the line of the curve never touches or coincides with the x-axis; this means that the distribution represented by the curve is always open to more extreme scores than the last, most extreme score observed.

**bell-shaped distribution**   A distribution in which most scores are clustered around the mean, declining in frequency symmetrically to the left and right as you move away from the mean.

**continuous probability distribution**   A probability distribution based on a scale of continuous interval measures.

**discrete probability distribution**   A probability distribution based on discrete measures such as ordinal and nominal scales.

**empirical normal distribution**   A bell-shaped distribution characterizing an observed distribution of scores based on values of the real number line.

**first moment of a distribution**   The mean or point of balance in a distribution.

**fourth moment of a distribution**   The peakedness or kurtosis of a distribution.

**kurtosis**   The peakedness of a distribution.

**leptokurtic**   A relatively peaked distribution indicating an unusual proportion of scores near the mean.

**mesokurtic**   A moderately peaked distribution shaped like the normal distribution.

**negative skew**   An asymmetrical distribution with a larger proportion of scores away from the mean on the left side of the curve.

**normal probability distribution**   A probability distribution of continuous values that has a bell-shaped, symmetrical form.

**one-tailed probability**   Probabilities associated with negative or positive Z scores. The probability is equal to the proportion of the area below a negative or above a positive Z score.

**platykurtic**   A relatively flat distribution indicating an unusual proportion of the scores located away from the mean toward the two tails of the distribution.

**positive skew**   An asymmetrical distribution with a larger proportion of the scores away from the mean to the right side of the curve.

**probability**   The proportion of a subset of outcomes to the total number of outcomes.

**probability distribution**   The distribution of all possible outcomes for a variable showing the probability associated with each outcome.

**second moment of a distribution**   The variance of a distribution; it describes the extent to which scores are scattered around the mean.

**skewness**   The departure of a distribution from symmetry.

**standard normal probability distribution**   A normal probability distribution based on Z scores that always have a mean equal to 0 and a standard deviation equal to 1.

**symmetrical distribution**   A distribution that has a form such that the right half is a mirror image of the left half.

**theoretical expectation**   In probability it refers to the distribution of outcomes expected in the long run.

**third moment of a distribution**   Skewness, which is the departure of a distribution from symmetry.

**two-tailed probability**   The probability associated with Z scores below and above the mean. The probability is equal to the proportion of the area below a negative Z score plus the area above a positive Z score.

**underlying distribution**   The distribution of a variable in the population.

**Z score**   Scores of a standardized scale where the mean always equals 0 and the standard deviation always equals 1.

## SYMBOLS

| | |
|---|---|
| $m_1$ | First moment of a distribution |
| $m_2$ | Second moment of a distribution |
| $m_3$ | Third moment of a distribution |
| $m_4$ | Fourth moment of a distribution |
| Z | Z score |

## FORMULAS

$$m_1 = \frac{\Sigma(X - \overline{X})}{n}$$

$$m_2 = \frac{\Sigma(X - \overline{X})^2}{n}$$

$$m_3 = \frac{\Sigma(X - \overline{X})^3}{n}$$

$$m_4 = \frac{\Sigma\left(X - \overline{X}\right)^4}{n}$$

$$Z = \frac{X - \overline{X}}{s}$$

## EXERCISES

1. Describe six characteristics of the normal probability distribution.

2. What is the difference between an empirical normal distribution and a standard normal distribution?

3. What effect does a change in the mean have on the form of an empirical normal distribution?

4. What effect does a change in the standard deviation have on the form of an empirical normal distribution?

5. What does a relatively small standard deviation do to the shape of an empirical normal distribution?

6. What does a relatively large standard deviation do to the shape of an empirical normal distribution?

7. The following weights were recorded for a group of 10 people: 180, 179, 177, 169, 165, 164, 160, 158, 154, and 142.
   a. What are the mean and standard deviation of the distribution?
   b. Transform the original distribution of body weights to standardized (Z) scores.
   c. Use the model of the standard normal distribution and identify the area below and above each of the standardized scores.

8. Jennifer scored 17 for the Bush Team, which had a mean score of 14.5 with a standard deviation of 1.2. Beth scored 30 for the Downtown Team, which had a mean of 28 with a standard deviation of 2. Which player had the better score with respect to the team she represented?

9. What is the probability for a Z score equal to or more extreme than +1.96?

10. What is the probability for a Z score equal to or more extreme than −1.96?

11. What is the probability for a Z score equal to or more extreme than ±1.96?

12. What proportion of the curve lies above a Z score of +2.58?

13. What proportion of the curve lies below a Z score of +2.58?

14. What proportion of the curve lies above a Z score of −2.58?

15. What proportion of the curve lies below a Z score of −2.58?

16. What proportion of the curve lies in the smaller portions of a Z score of ±2.56?

17. What proportion of the curve lies in the larger portions of a Z score of $\pm 2.56$?

18. What is the Z score associated with a one-tailed probability of .02?

19. What is the Z score associated with a two-tailed probability of .02?

20. What is the Z score associated with a two-tailed probability of .015?

21. What is the Z score associated with a one-tailed probability of .25?

22. The sample of individuals from community A were tested for social sensitivity, where a high score represents greater sensitivity.

| Score | f |
|-------|---|
| 90–99 | 5 |
| 80–89 | 9 |
| 70–79 | 12 |
| 60–69 | 16 |
| 50–59 | 25 |
| 40–49 | 17 |
| 30–39 | 14 |
| 20–29 | 8 |
| 10–19 | 4 |
| 00–09 | 3 |

   a. What is the mean for the distribution?
   b. What is the standard deviation for the distribution?
   c. Draw a frequency polygon of the distribution. Does it appear symmetrical?
   d. On the basis of your graph, how would you describe its kurtosis?
   e. Assuming that the underlying distribution is normal, what is the likelihood of seeing a score as great as 85 in community A?
   f. What is the probability of seeing a score of 70?
   g. What is the probability of seeing a score of 22?
   h. Would a score of 19 or 79 be more likely?

23. The following distribution of social sensitivity scores was observed for community B.

| Score | f |
|-------|---|
| 90–99 | 3 |
| 80–89 | 4 |
| 70–79 | 6 |
| 60–69 | 7 |
| 50–59 | 8 |
| 40–49 | 9 |
| 30–39 | 12 |
| 20–29 | 18 |
| 10–19 | 21 |
| 00–09 | 25 |

   a. What is the mean for the distribution?
   b. What is the standard deviation for the distribution?
   c. Draw a frequency polygon of the distribution. Is it symmetrical?
   d. On the basis of your graph, how would you describe its kurtosis?

**24.** The following distribution of social sensitivity scores was observed for community C.

| Score | f |
|-------|-----|
| 90–99 | 11 |
| 80–89 | 10 |
| 70–79 | 13 |
| 60–69 | 11 |
| 50–59 | 12 |
| 40–49 | 10 |
| 30–39 | 12 |
| 20–29 | 11 |
| 10–19 | 10 |
| 00–09 | 13 |

**a.** What is the mean of the distribution?
**b.** What is the standard deviation of the distribution?
**c.** Draw a frequency polygon of the distribution. Does it appear to be symmetrical?
**d.** On the basis of your graph, how would you describe its kurtosis?

**25.** Describe the differences among the three distributions of sensitivity scores in terms of variance, skewness, and kurtosis.

# 5

# A DISCRETE PROBABILITY DISTRIBUTION
## *The Binomial Distribution*

The previous chapter discussed the characteristics of a continuous probability distribution, the normal distribution. The model of the standard normal distribution is important because it enables us to assign probabilities to the outcomes of continuous variables. On a more practical level, it means that you can determine the probability of any value in a distribution if it represents a normal distribution. All you need to do is calculate the mean and the standard deviation, and then you can determine the Z score and use Table B.1 in Appendix B to assess the probability of any observation.

Recall that continuous variables consist of measurements with an infinite number of equidistant points on a number scale. Discrete variables differ because they consist of measures that include a relatively small number of discrete scale categories. For example, the discrete variable of gender consists of only two outcomes: male and female. In using this measure, we simply count the number of individuals who are male and female. Discrete measures provide information on the number of observations that fall in the categories of nominal and ordinal scales. Recall from Chapter 2 that these scales are more limited in terms of mathematical manipulations. However, it is still important to determine the probability of observations in **discrete probability distributions.** This chapter discusses a model that forms the basis for determining such probabilities: the binomial probability distribution.

## *CHARACTERISTICS OF THE BINOMIAL PROBABILITY DISTRIBUTION*

The **binomial probability distribution** describes the probabilities associated with discrete random variables. The distribution of the variable must satisfy certain conditions for the model to be applicable. Before looking at the conditions, let's review the language used to describe binomial models. In the binomial model, the outcome for any sample observation is usually referred to as a **trial,** whereas a series of trials is referred to as an **experiment.** For example, in a repeated drawing of samples of 30 members from a population of males and females, the outcome on each draw of 30 members is a trial and the total number of draws of 30 the experiment. The conditions that must be met for the binomial model include the following:

1. The variable must be dichotomous; that is, it can have only two possible outcomes, such as male or female, users or nonusers of a service, liberals and conservatives, and so on. The two outcomes are labeled $p$ and $q$, where $p$ equals one of the dichotomous outcomes and $q$ the other. In trials such as a coin toss, $p$ = heads is one outcome and $q$ = tails is the other.
2. The probabilities associated with the two outcomes must remain the same for each trial in the experiment. If the probability of drawing a male is .50 on the first trial (or draw), it must be .50 on all remaining trials in that experiment. Moreover, the sum of the probabilities for $p$ and $q$ must always equal 1.00. Thus, if $p$ = .50, then $q$ = .50, and their sum is 1.00. If $p$ = .35, then $q$ = .65, and their sum is 1.00.
3. Each trial in an experiment must be an **independent event,** which means that what occurs on the first trial does not influence the outcome on the second. Thus, drawing a male on the first trial cannot influence or change the probability of drawing a male on the second trial. A coin coming up heads on the first toss is presumed to have no effect on the likelihood of heads on the second toss.
4. The trials in an experiment must be identical or meet the same conditions. Simply stated, you cannot change the rules in the middle of an experiment.

Given these four conditions, the binomial model is appropriate for determining the probability associated with the various outcomes of an experiment. For example, if you design an experiment such that you draw 10 individuals from a population that has an equal number of males and females (i.e., $p$ = $q$ = .50) and the outcome is 7 males and 3 females, the binomial model shows the probability of the outcome.

## THE BINOMIAL MODEL AND ITS APPLICATION

The calculation of binomial probabilities is based on the work of Jacob Bernoulli, who lived in the last half of the seventeenth century. The procedure, referred to as the **Bernoulli frequency function,** is based on the factorial and is given by

$$P(r) = (_nC_r)\, p^r q^{n-r} \tag{5.1}$$

where

$$(_nC_r) = \frac{n!}{r!(n-r)!}$$

and

$n$ = the number of trials in the experiment

$r$ = the number of the $p$ outcomes in the experiment

$p$ = the proportion of times $p$ is expected to occur in any one trial

$q$ = the proportion of times $q$ is expected to occur in any one trial

$p^r$ = the number of times $p$ occurs in a specific trial

$q^{n-r}$ = the number of times $q$ occurs in a specific trial

The expanded form of Formula 5.1 is

$$P(r) = \frac{n!}{r!(n-r)!} p^r q^{n-r} \qquad (5.2)$$

Suppose that you were to draw a sample of 8 individuals from a population consisting of equal numbers of males and females and your sample contained 6 males and 2 females. If the population were made up of an equal number of males and females, you would expect your sample to contain about equal numbers of males and females. However, in our example we ended up with 6 males and 2 females. What is the probability of that happening when both appear in equal numbers in the population? First, you must know what the probability is of drawing a male from the population on any single draw. Our population contains an equal number of males and females, the probability of drawing a male on any single draw equals .50, and the same is true for a female.

Second, to use the binomial model, you must assume that the probability of selecting a male or female remains unchanged for each of the 8 draws. This means that you must return each draw to the population prior to the next draw so the number in the population remains the same for each draw. Failing to return each draw would change the probability on successive draws. Returning each draw also assures independence because the outcome on one draw does not influence that of others. By Formula 5.2,[1] the probability of 6 males in 8 draws, symbolized by $P(6)$, from a population of equal numbers of males and females is .1094, or 11%:

$$P(6) = \frac{8!}{6!(8-6)!} \left(\frac{1}{2}\right)^6 \left(\frac{1}{2}\right)^2$$

$$= \frac{8 \times 7 \times 6 \times 5 \times 4 \times 3 \times 2 \times 1}{6 \times 5 \times 4 \times 3 \times 2 \times 1 \times (2 \times 1)} \left(\frac{1}{2}\right)^6 \left(\frac{1}{2}\right)^2$$

[1] Instead of using the fraction ½ to represent $p$ and $q$, you could use the proportion .50 and get the same results.

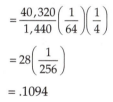

$$= \frac{40{,}320}{1{,}440}\left(\frac{1}{64}\right)\left(\frac{1}{4}\right)$$

$$= 28\left(\frac{1}{256}\right)$$

$$= .1094$$

The Bernoulli frequency function can be used to determine the probability of any outcome, as in our example.

All possible outcomes in an experiment can be displayed using the **binomial expansion** $(p + q)^n$. The expanded expression of $(p + q)^n$ is shown in Formula 5.3, which is its algebraic description. If you find the algebra too challenging, the term can be assessed by following the computational instructions on the basis of simple arithmetic (see the following numbered list):

$$\left(p+q\right)^{n} = p^{n} + np^{n-1}q + \frac{n(n-1)}{2!}p^{n-2}q^{2} \tag{5.3}$$

$$+\frac{n(n-1)(n-2)}{3!}p^{n-3}q^{3}\ldots$$

$$+\frac{n(n-1)(n-2)\ldots(n-k)}{k!}pq^{n-k}+q^{n}$$

Formula 5.3 describes all possible outcomes for $p$ and $q$ for a given number of trials. The meaning of the terms of the binomial can be described more clearly by reference to our example of 8 draws in repeated trials where males ($p$) equal females ($q$). The expanded term for $n = 8$ and $p = q = \frac{1}{2}$ is

$$(p + q)^8 = p^8 + 8(p^7q) + 28\ (p^6q^2) + 56(p^5q^3)$$

$$+ 70(p^4q^4) + 56(p^3q^5) + 28(p^2q^6) + 8(pq^7) + q^8$$

The expression $(p + q)^8$ may be read as (males + females)$^8$, which is the number of trials or the sample size. The individual terms for the binomial expansion can be determined quite simply using the following steps:

1. The first term is always $p^n$. In our example, where $n = 8$, the *exponent* of $p$ is 8 and the term is $p^8$. The term has a *coefficient* of 1, so it is really $1(p^8)$; however, the coefficient of 1 is not written but understood. The term indicates that an outcome of all males in a trial of 8 draws can occur in only one way; that is, a male must be drawn on each of the 8 trials.
2. The second term is $8(p^7q)$. The *exponent* of $p$ is always one less than the first term. In our example, the exponent in the first term was 8, so for the second term it is $8 - 1 = 7$. The outcome $q$ appears in the second term with no exponent, indicating that the second term represents an outcome of 7 males and 1 female. (Note that the sum of the exponents of $p$ and $q$ must always equal the number of trials, or $n$; in our example it is 8.) The coefficient in the second

term always equals *n*. In our example, *n* = 8, which informs us that the outcome of 7 males and 1 female can occur eight different ways. The female outcome can occur on the last draw (MMMMMMMF), on the second-to-last draw (MMMMMMFM), and so on to the first draw (FMMMMMMM).

3. The third term is 28($p^6q^2$). Looking at the second and third terms, we see that the exponent of *p* in each successive term is reduced by 1 and that of *q* increased by 1. In our example, the second term, $p^7q$, becomes $p^6q^2$ in the third term, $p^5q^3$ in the fourth term, and so on. The coefficient for the third term is based on calculations related to the previous or second term. Multiply the coefficient in the second term, which is 8, by the exponent for *p*, which is 7, and 8 × 7 = 56; then divide the product by the exponent of *q* plus 1. The exponent of *q* in the second term is 1, and adding 1, the sum is 2. Dividing 56 by 2 gives 28, which is the coefficient of the third term.

4. The fourth and all successive terms are derived in the same way as the third term. Thus, the exponents of *p* and *q* in the fourth term are $p^5q^3$. The coefficient is the product of the coefficient and the exponent of the preceding or third term, which is 28 × 6 = 168 divided by the exponent of *q* plus 1, 2 + 1, which is 168/3 = 56. The steps are repeated to the final term, $q^8$. Table 5.1 shows that the outcomes are symmetrical—i.e., the bottom half of the distribution is a mirror image of the top half. This is only true when *p* = *q*.

The expansion $(p + q)^n$ reveals all possible outcomes for a binomial experiment. Table 5.1 illustrates the expanded term for eight trials in greater detail. The first column shows the terms of the expansion. Columns 2 and 3 show the steps for calculating the probability for each term, and column 4 shows the probabilities.

The coefficients of the terms in column 1 indicate the number of ways in which the outcome for each term can occur; the exponents of *p* and *q* define the outcome. In the first term, $p^8$, the coefficient is 1, indicating that all males can be drawn in only one way, that is, if a male is selected on each of the eight draws. The coefficient of the second term, 8($p^7q$), indicates that 7 males and 1 female can be drawn in eight ways; the third term, 28($p^6q^2$), indicates that 6 males and 2 females can be drawn in 28 ways; and so on. Notice that the larger the coefficient, the greater the probability of the outcome. Thus, 70($p^4q^4$), where males equal females, can occur in 70 ways and has a probability of .2734, whereas that of $p^8$, with a coefficient of 1, can occur in only one way and has a probability of .0039.

Column 2 shows the expression in column 1 with the values of *p* and *q*, where each occurs ½ of the time. Column 3 shows the outcome displaying the product of *p* and *q* for each outcome. Because *p* = *q* in our example, the denominator is the same for each outcome. Notice also that the denominator is the sum of the coefficients in column 2, which becomes the numerator in column 3: 1 + 8 + 28 + 56 + 70 + 56 + 28 + 8 + 1 = 256. The total number of events that can occur in an experiment with 8 draws is 256, and the probability of any specific outcome is the ratio of the number of ways in which the outcome can occur to the total number of out-

**TABLE 5.1**  **Population Where Number of Males Equals Females: Possible Outcomes of Eight Draws**

| 1 | 2 | 3 | 4 |
|---|---|---|---|
| $p^8$ | $= (\frac{1}{2})^8$ | $= 1/256$ | $= .0039$ |
| $8(p^7q)$ | $= 8[(\frac{1}{2})^7(\frac{1}{2})]$ | $= 8/256$ | $= .0313$ |
| $28(p^6q^2)$ | $= 28[(\frac{1}{2})^6(\frac{1}{2})^2]$ | $= 28/256$ | $= .1094$ |
| $56(p^5q^3)$ | $= 56[(\frac{1}{2})^5(\frac{1}{2})^3]$ | $= 56/256$ | $= .2188$ |
| $70(p^4q^4)$ | $= 70[(\frac{1}{2})^4(\frac{1}{2})^4]$ | $= 70/256$ | $= .2734$ |
| $56(p^3q^5)$ | $= 56[(\frac{1}{2})^3(\frac{1}{2})^5]$ | $= 56/256$ | $= .2188$ |
| $28(p^2q^6)$ | $= 28[(\frac{1}{2})^2(\frac{1}{2})^6]$ | $= 28/256$ | $= .1094$ |
| $8(pq^7)$ | $= 8[(\frac{1}{2})(\frac{1}{2})^7]$ | $= 8/256$ | $= .0313$ |
| $q^8$ | $= (\frac{1}{2})^8$ | $= 1/256$ | $= .0039$ |

Note: The probability could have been derived using proportions for $p$ and $q$ rather than fractions. Thus, rather than $p = \frac{1}{2}$ and $q = \frac{1}{2}$, we could have used $p = .50$ and $q = .50$. The final probabilities, of course, would be the same. Fractions are used here because they more clearly show that the probability of the outcomes is their ratio to the total number of outcomes, as shown in column 3.

comes. This is in keeping with our original definition of probability in Chapter 4, where it was stated that the probability of an event is the proportion of outcomes it represents of the total number of outcomes. Thus, the probability of $p^8$ is 1/256 because $p^8$ can occur in only 1 out of the 256 possible outcomes, $8(p^7q) = 8/256$ because it represents 8 of the 256 outcomes, and so on.

Further, if you add the probabilities in column 4, you will find that the sum is equal to 1.00. (The sum may deviate slightly from 1 because of rounding.) This conforms with the requirement that the sum of the individual probabilities of the events in an experiment must always equal 1.00.

If you examine the structure of the outcomes in Table 5.1, you will also notice that the binomial probability distribution is symmetrical. Figure 5.1 presents a relative frequency histogram and polygon of the distribution and shows that the form is very similar to that of the normal curve for continuous distributions. In fact, if the number of draws were increased from 8 to 100, the curve would approximate a smooth line, and its shape would be almost indistinguishable from the bell shape of the normal curve. The close similarity is most apparent when $p = q = 1/2$, and this has important implications for dealing with distributions of discrete variables. However, before continuing, let's discuss the form of the curve when $p \neq q$.

The more unequal $p$ and $q$, the more the form of the distribution will deviate from the bell-shaped (normal) curve. Suppose that you drew a sample of 5 individuals ($n = 5$) from a population in which 60% (.60) were employed and

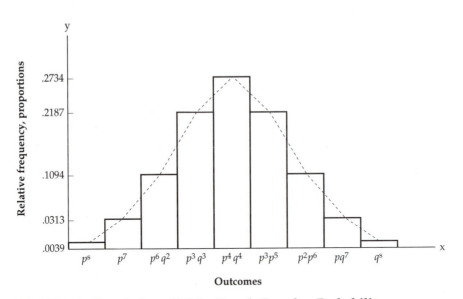

**FIGURE 5.1    Population of Males Equals Females: Probability Distribution for $n = 8$**

40% (.40) unemployed. The probability distribution, using the binomial expansion, would be

$$(p + q)^5 = p^5 + 5(p^4q) + 10(p^3q^2) + 10(p^2q^3) + 5(pq^4) + q^5$$

$$(.60 + .40)^5 = (.60)^5 + 5[(.60)^4(.40)] + 10[(.60)^3(.40)^2]$$
$$+ 10[(.60)^2(.40)^3] + 5[(.60)(.40)^4] + (.40)^5$$

$$= .0778 + .2592 + .3456 + .2304 + .0768 + .0102$$

The distribution of the probabilities is not symmetrical, as the probability of drawing 5 employed persons is .0778 and drawing 5 unemployed only .0102. This is because the proportion of employed persons in the population, .60, is greater than the unemployed, .40. A graph of the outcomes, shown in Figure 5.2, confirms the lack of symmetry for the distribution.

The degree of symmetry is a direct function of the discrepancy between $p$ and $q$. For example, if 4 out of 5 persons were employed in the population, the probability distribution for a sample of 5 draws ($n = 5$, $p = .80$, $q = .20$) would be:

$$(p + q)^5 = p^5 + 5(p^4q) + 10(p^3q^2) + 10(p^2q^3) + 5(pq^4) + q^5$$

$$(.80 + .20)^5 = .3277 + 5[(.4096)(.20)] + 10[(.5120)(.04)]$$
$$+ 10[(.64)(.008)] + 5[(.80)(.0016)] + .003$$

$$= .3277 + .4096 + .2048 + .0512 + .0064 + .0003$$

The probability of drawing a sample of 5 employed persons is high, .3277, and that of drawing 5 unemployed persons very low, .0003, because most of the

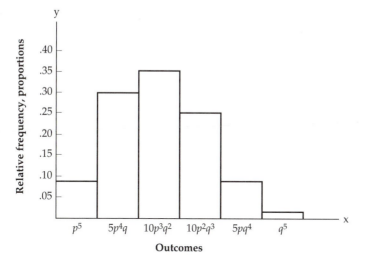

**FIGURE 5.2   Population of Employed (.60) and Unemployed (.40): Probability Distribution for** $n = 5$

population, .80, is employed. The asymmetry of the distribution is shown in Figure 5.3. The most likely events are clustered to the left of the distribution, representing the high proportion of employed persons.

Using the binomial expansion or Bernoulli's frequency function to determine probabilities associated with observations for everyday research would be difficult for large samples. As sample size increases, so does the difficulty of the computations. The term $(p + q)^8$ is relatively simple to expand, but if the number increases as little as $(p + q)^{15}$, the computational effort increases markedly; social research is not often based on samples as small as 15. Fortunately, tables have been constructed to list the probabilities associated with various sample sizes and $p$ and $q$ values. Table B.2 in Appendix B provides the probabilities for selected outcomes of $p$ and $q$ for samples up to 15. Other references are available that list probabilities for 100 or more observations. In Table B.2, the number of trials, $n$, is presented in the extreme left column. The next column, $r$, is the number of occurrences for $p$, and the probability for $p$ on any one trial is presented across the top of the table. Thus, if $n = 8$ and $r = 4$ (four $p$ outcomes, or $p^4q^4$) and the probability on any draw is $p = .50$, the probability of $p^4q^4$ is .273. That is, drawing four $p$s in eight draws will occur 27.30% of the time.

Another alternative available for determining probabilities for binomial outcomes with large samples is a Z-score transformation. Here, the probabilities of outcomes can be determined using the standard normal curve model and Table B.1 in Appendix B.

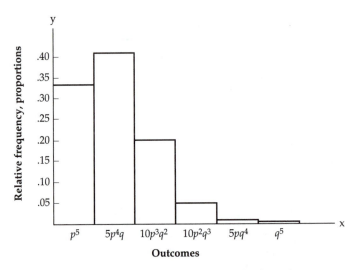

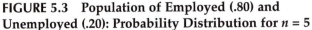

**FIGURE 5.3    Population of Employed (.80) and Unemployed (.20): Probability Distribution for $n = 5$**

## TRANSFORMING BINOMIAL DATA TO CONTINUOUS FORM WITH Z SCORES

Earlier it was stated that as sample size increases, when $p = q$, the distribution of binomial outcomes increasingly resembles that of the normal distribution. As we will see, however, if $n$ is large enough, the normal distribution will be approximated even when $p$ and $q$ are not exactly equal. More important, discrete binomial data can be evaluated using the model of the continuous probability distribution of the standard normal curve. The procedure consists of estimating the population mean, $\mu$, and standard deviation, $\sigma$, for the binomial distribution and using these estimates to approximate Z scores for binomial outcomes. Note that the estimates are for the population values, $\mu$ and $\sigma$, rather than for the sample values, $\overline{X}$ and $s$. To use the approximation, however, $nP$ and $nQ$ must be greater than or equal to 10.[2]

The mean is estimated as follows:

$$\mu = nP \tag{5.4}$$

[2] Preferences vary for the criterion. Quinn McNemar, *Psychological Statistics* (New York: John Wiley and Sons, 1969), p. 45ff, suggests that $nP \geq 5$ and $nQ \geq 5$ may be used. Robert Parsons, *Statistical Analysis: A Decision-Making Approach* (New York: Harper and Row, 1974), p. 284, suggests that $nP \geq 5$ or $nQ \geq 5$ and $n > 30$ is appropriate. The alternative suggested here is somewhat conservative and requires a somewhat larger sample, but it is assumed that when $n$ is small, the binomial or table values will provide the information with little effort.

where    $n$ = the sample size or number of observations

$P$ = the probability of $p$ on a single trial in the population

And the standard deviation is estimated by

$$\sigma = \sqrt{nPQ} \tag{5.5}$$

where    $n$ = the sample size or number of observations

$P$ = the probability of $p$ on a single trial in the population

$Q$ = the probability of $q$ on a single trial in the population

Suppose we select a sample of 25 members from a population where the number of males equals females. The population mean and standard deviation for the distribution would be

$$\mu = nP = 25(.50)$$

$$= 12.5$$

$$\sigma = \sqrt{nPQ} = \sqrt{25(.50)(.50)}$$

$$= \sqrt{6.25}$$

$$= 2.5$$

Once the mean and standard deviation are known, the Z score for any specific binomial outcome can be determined using the following approximation:

$$Z = \frac{|r - nP| - .5}{\sqrt{nPQ}} \text{ to } \frac{|r - nP| + .5}{\sqrt{nPQ}} \tag{5.6}$$

where    $r$ = the binomial outcome of concern

$n$ = the sample size or number of observations

$P$ = the probability of $p$ for any single trial in the population

$Q$ = the probability of $q$ for any single trial in the population

$\pm.5$ = Yates correction for continuity

Recall that the Z-score model is based on the assumption that the measure is continuous or interval, but binomial measures are discrete and lack the characteristic of a continuous distribution of values. A correction must be made for violating the assumption of continuity, and the **Yates correction** can do this. The Yates correction, $\pm.5$, treats $r$, the outcome, as though it were at the midpoint of an interval, with the upper and lower limits of the interval defined by $|r - nP| - .5$ and $|r - nP| + .5$. While the correction for continuity does not change the discrete distribution to a continuous form, it accounts for the discrete measure by making the boundaries in which the Z score is located somewhat wider to correct for treating a discrete measure as though it were continuous.

Suppose you draw a sample of 25 individuals from a population where males $= p = .50$ and females $= q = .50$ and the outcome is 9 males ($r = 9$) and 16 females. Applying Formula 5.6, we find the Z score for $r = 9$ as follows:

$$Z = \frac{|r - nP| - .5}{\sqrt{nPQ}} \text{ to } \frac{|r - nP| + .5}{\sqrt{nPQ}}$$

$$= \frac{|9 - (25)(.50)| - .5}{\sqrt{25(.50)(.50)}} \text{ to } \frac{|9 - (25)(.50)| + .05}{\sqrt{25(.50)(.50)}}$$

$$= \frac{|-3.5| - .5}{\sqrt{6.25}} \text{ to } \frac{|-3.5| + .5}{\sqrt{6.25}}$$

$$= \frac{-3}{2.5} \text{ to } \frac{-4}{2.5}$$

$$Z = \qquad -1.2 \text{ to } -1.6$$

The solution tells us that the discrete outcome of 9 males in a sample of 25 lies somewhere between the Z values of –1.2 and –1.6. The values are negative because the outcome of 9 males is below the midpoint: 12.5 of the 25 trials. The probabilities associated with the Z scores, according to Column B in Table B.1 (Appendix B), are .1151 and .0548. Given $p = q$, the outcome of 9 males is somewhere near the midpoint of the two values, which is .0831. If you had used the Bernoulli frequency function to find the answer, you would have found it to be .0812, which is very close to the midpoint between the two values found here.

The width of the intervals of the Z scores is a function of the size of the sample. The larger $n$, the narrower the interval and the closer the approximation to the normal curve. Suppose that our sample consisted of 100 members and the proportion of males in the population remained at .50. The proportion of 9 males out of our original sample of 25 = .36. If we drew the same proportion, .36 out of a sample of 100, the results would be 36 males and 64 females. The probability would be as follows:

$$Z = \frac{|36 - (100)(.50)| - .5}{\sqrt{100(.50)(.50)}} \text{ to } \frac{|36 - (100)(.50)| + .5}{\sqrt{100(.50)(.50)}}$$

$$= \frac{|-14| - .5}{\sqrt{25}} \text{ to } \frac{|-14| + .5}{\sqrt{25}}$$

$$= \frac{-13.5}{5} \text{ to } \frac{-14.5}{5}$$

$$Z = \qquad -2.7 \text{ to } -2.9$$

The Z values of –2.7 and –2.9 are a much narrower interval than was the case when $n = 25$, and the probabilities of .0035 and .0019 provide a more precise estimate of the probability of drawing 36 males in a sample of 100. While $P = Q = .50$ in the foregoing examples, if the criteria $nP \geq 10$ and $nQ \geq 10$ are met, the approximation can be used even when $p \neq q$. Table B.2 in Appendix B provides probabilities for $P \neq Q$.

## COMPUTER EXERCISES: SOME SUGGESTIONS

Discrete probability distributions play an important role in statistical analysis. Computer exercises that focus on dichotomous distributions will be helpful. You can go to your data file and identify a group of dichotomous measures. You can also use this method to develop more skills in recoding variables. Thus, your data set is likely to contain a number of nominal measures consisting of three or four categories with frequencies that do not satisfy the categories. In routine data analysis, such measures are recoded and collapsed to dichotomies. The computer also provides an opportunity to develop more skills in creating and interpreting two-by-two contingency tables with various presentations of row and column percentages. In addition, your software will contain procedures for determining the probabilities associated with binomial outcomes, which can be used to parallel the material covered in this chapter.

## CHAPTER SUMMARY

The binomial distribution is a model that allows you to determine the probabilities for dichotomous outcomes. When the number of observations is small (10 or less), the Bernoulli frequency function provides the exact probabilities of binomial outcomes. If you are interested in all the probabilities associated with a binomial experiment, the binomial expansion provides a display of those outcomes. As $n$ becomes large, however, the calculations necessary for the Bernoulli and binomial expansion become cumbersome, and the approximation to the continuous distribution and the Z scale provides a convenient alternative. On an applied level this means that you can determine the probability for any dichotomous event that meets the assumptions of the binomial model, and as we will see in the following chapter, probability plays a key role in statistical inference.

## KEY TERMS

**Bernoulli frequency function**   An expression describing the probability of any single event in a distribution of binomial outcomes.

**binomial expansion**   An expression describing the probabilities for all outcomes in a binomial experiment given by $(p + q)^n$.

**binomial probability distribution**   A distribution describing the probabilities of discrete events for a dichotomous set of independent outcomes.

> **discrete probability distribution**   A distribution based on discrete measures, such as ordinal and nominal scales.
>
> **experiment**   A series of interrelated trials.
>
> **independent event**   An experiment in which the outcome for any one trial has no influence on the outcomes of other trials.
>
> **trial**   One event in an experiment consisting of a series of events.
>
> **Yates correction**   A correction in the formula estimating Z scores for binomial outcomes given that discrete measures are evaluated using a model for continuous measures.

## SYMBOLS

$P(r)$        The probability ($P$) of a defined outcome ($r$)

$(p + q)^n$     The binomial term

## FORMULAS

$\mu = np$ 

Mean for binomial data

$\sigma = \sqrt{npq}$

Standard deviation for binomial data

$({}_nC_r)p^r q^{n-r}$

Equals $\dfrac{n!}{r!(n-r)!}p^r q^{n-r}$

$(p + q)^n$

Equals $p^n + np^{n-1}q + \dfrac{n(n-1)}{2!}p^{n-1}q^2$

$+ \dfrac{n(n-1)(n-2)}{3!}p^{n-2}q^3 + \ldots +$

$+ \dfrac{n(n-1)(n-2)\ldots(n-k)}{k!}pq^{n-k} + q^n$

$Z = \dfrac{|r - nP| - .5}{\sqrt{nPQ}}$ to $\dfrac{|r - nP| + .5}{\sqrt{nPQ}}$

Z-score transformation for binomial data

## EXERCISES

1. Describe the conditions under which continuous and discrete probability distributions are useful.

2. Give an example describing a discrete event.

3. Expand the term $(p + q)^{10}$.

4. A researcher drew a random sample of 10 individuals. The sample contained 7 males and 3 females. What is the probability of the outcome if $p$ = males = .50 in the population?

5. The researcher drew a second random sample of 10 individuals. The sample contained 1 male and 9 females. What is the probability of this event if males = $p$ = .50 in the population?

6. The researcher drew another random sample of 10 individuals, this time for a population where males = $p$ = .60. The sample contained 7 males and 3 females. What is the probability of the occurrence?

7. The researcher drew one more random sample of 10 individuals where males = $p$ = .60. The sample contained 2 males and 8 females. What is the probability of the outcome?

8. Use the Bernoulli frequency function to determine the probability of drawing 5 losing numbers in 9 draws if the probability of a losing number = $p$ = .30.

9. Use the Bernoulli frequency function to determine the probability of drawing 4 losing numbers in 5 draws if the probability of a losing number = $p$ = .70.

10. Use the Bernoulli frequency function to calculate the probability of having 6 rainy days out of 12 if the probability of a rainy day = $p$ = .23.

11. Use Table B.2 in Appendix B to evaluate the probability of a sample with 12 males in a sample of 14 when males = $p$ = .50.

12. Use Table B.2 in Appendix B to evaluate the probability of a sample with 10 females and 4 males when males = $p$ = .50.

13. Use Table B.2 in Appendix B to evaluate the probability of winning 3 games out of 11 when winning = $p$ = .60.

14. Use Table B.2 in Appendix B to evaluate the probability of 6 heads out of 9 tosses when heads = $p$ = .50.

15. A sample of 30 students was interviewed from a population in which half the students were liberal and half conservative.
    a. Estimate the mean for the distribution in the population.
    b. Estimate the standard deviation for the distribution in the population.
    c. What are the Z scores for having 19 liberals in the sample when liberals = $p$ = .50?
    d. What are the probabilities of the Z scores?
    e. What are the Z scores for having 9 conservatives in the sample when liberal = $p$ = .50?
    f. What are the probabilities of the Z scores in question e?

16. A sample of 60 individuals was drawn from a population in which .70 were blue-collar workers and the remainder white-collar workers. The sample, however, contained 30 blue-collar workers.
    a. Estimate the mean for the distribution in the population.
    b. Estimate the standard deviation for the distribution in the population.
    c. What are the Z scores for the outcome of the 30 blue-collar workers?
    d. What are the probabilities of the Z scores?
    e. What are the Z scores for observing 40 blue-collar workers?
    f. What are the probabilities associated with question e?

# 6

# THE BASIS OF STATISTICAL INFERENCE

Whereas inference refers to the general process of drawing conclusions from evidence, **statistical inference** relates to conclusions based on statistical evidence. Statistical evidence usually consists of numerical information derived from a sample to draw inferences about the characteristics of a population. The purpose of this chapter is to present the chain of reasoning that makes statistical inference possible. First, we consider some basic ideas about sampling and then examine the logic around which statistical inference is organized. Finally, we discuss some methods for estimating, or inferring, unknown population parameters.

## *RANDOM SAMPLING*

A population is the entire set of entities of interest. The boundaries of a population are a matter of definition, depending on the goals and resources of the researcher. For example, if the purpose is to find out the drinking patterns of a particular community, the members of that community are the population of reference. If the goal is to evaluate the drinking patterns of a state, all the individuals in the state make up the population of reference. The larger the population, the more complex its composition, and the broader the goals of the research, the more difficult it is to represent the population adequately.

When researchers use the term *sample,* they usually mean a **representative sample,** assuming that it represents a population. Whether a sample is representative of a population is a function of how the sample is selected. The best method for selecting a representative sample is by random selection procedures. Such procedures are the most likely ones to avoid the introduction of bias in the selection process. Samples selected using random selection methods are known as *random samples.*

A random sample is one in which all members of the population have an *equal and independent* chance of being selected for the sample. If a population consists of 1,000 members and each has 1/1000 chance of being included in the sample, they have an equal chance. *Independence* means that each member's chance of being included in the sample is independent of the chance of the selection of some other population members. Random samples are also referred to as **probability samples** because all members of the population have some probability of being included in the sample.

Populations of interest to researchers are often made up of complex subgroups that require special expertise in designing sampling procedures to ensure that the criteria of equal and independent opportunity are met. However complex, the basis for selection is **simple random sampling.**[1] Simple random sampling consists of procedures whereby sample members are selected through some random process. A random process most of us are familiar with is the lottery. In one form of the lottery, the names of all the members of the population are written on slips of paper, placed in a drum, and thoroughly mixed. Then slips are drawn at random from the drum. However, the use of the lottery would be somewhat awkward for most research purposes, and more efficient methods have been devised.

One frequently used method for selecting a random sample is the *random numbers table*. These are exactly what the name implies: lists of randomly generated numbers. Table B.10 in Appendix B displays random numbers. Suppose that you have a population of 40 members and want to draw a random sample of 10 members. You begin by numbering the members of the population from 1 through 40 in any order. Then you turn to a random numbers table (Table B.10) and select a starting point anywhere in the table.

Suppose that you begin with the block of numbers shown in Table 6.1 (also located on the second page of Table B.10). The selected blocks begin in the second column of blocks from the left of the page and in the fifth row from the top of the table. If the population of concern consists of fewer than 100 members (our example consists of 40), you use pairs of numbers and begin selection by moving either across the rows of the blocks or down the columns. When you encounter a number in the blocks from 1 through 40, the person with that number in your population is selected to be a sample member. You continue the process until you select the required number of sample members. In our example, we want to select 10 members. Begin by moving across the rows of the blocks in Table 6.1. The first number encountered between 1 and 40 is 01, and the second is 27; then 02, 21 (02 is encountered again and skipped because we have already chosen 02), (27 is encountered again and is skipped because it already has been chosen). Continuing, we encounter 17, 05, 31, 10, 36, and 04. Thus, the members of the sample are those individuals in the population who previously were assigned the numbers 01, 27, 02, 21, 17, 05, 31, 10, 36, and 04. The selected numbers have been underlined in Table 6.1.

---

[1] The discussion of sampling is limited to what is necessary to understand the logic of statistical inference. For further detail, you should consult specialized texts on sampling.

**TABLE 6.1    Random Numbers Table Segment**

| 86 | 83 | 42 | 99 | <u>01</u> | 68 | 41 | 48 | <u>27</u> | 74 |
|----|----|----|----|----|----|----|----|----|----|
| 69 | 97 | 92 | <u>02</u> | 88 | 55 | <u>21</u> | <u>02</u> | 97 | 73 |
| 93 | <u>27</u> | 88 | <u>17</u> | 57 | <u>05</u> | 68 | 67 | <u>31</u> | 56 |
| 68 | <u>10</u> | 72 | <u>36</u> | <u>21</u> | 94 | <u>04</u> | 99 | 13 | 45 |
| 62 | 53 | 52 | 41 | 70 | 69 | 77 | 71 | 28 | 30 |

You could have selected the sample by moving down the columns of numbers rather than the rows, and the sample members would have included 27, 10, 02, 17, 36, 01, 21, 05, 04, and 31.

If the population consists of 100 to 999 members, selections are made using sets of three numbers rather than pairs; and if the population is from 1,000 to 9,999, sets of four numbers are used. The importance of using a random numbers table is that it removes personal bias from the selection process, and the two criteria, that all members of the population have an equal and independent chance of being selected, are satisfied by the procedure.

## ACCURACY AND ERROR IN SAMPLING

A sample represents a population accurately **(accuracy)** if the **sample statistic** is equal to the population parameter. For example, if the mean weight of a population is 142 pounds and a sample is drawn that has a mean weight of 142, the sample is accurate in that it gives the correct information about the population weight. **Error** exists when the sample statistic and the population parameter differ. Error in sampling can be grouped into two classes: **systematic error** and **random error.** Systematic error, also referred to as **bias,** occurs when there is a flaw in the sampling procedure such that not all elements in the population have an equal and independent chance of being included in the sample. Systematic error is the result of a flawed sampling strategy. The only means for correcting systematic error is to revise the sampling procedures so that they are appropriate for selecting a representative sample.

However, even when proper random sampling procedures are used and everything is done right, some difference between the sample statistic and the real population parameter is likely to exist. Such error, random error, or sampling variability, results because of chance factors that influence the outcomes of random selection procedures. The character of **chance variation** can be illustrated using an example of drawing members from a population with equal numbers of males and females. Even if everything is done correctly, a range of outcomes is possible, as shown in Table 6.2. Each of the outcomes has some chance of occurring.

Common sense leads us to believe that usually we can expect about half males and half females if they are equal in number in the population, and Table 6.2 shows that this result has the highest probability of occurrence: .2734. However, the distribution of outcomes in Table 6.2 indicates that considerable variation can

**TABLE 6.2    Potential Outcomes ($n = 8$):**
**Males = $p = .50$; Females = $q = .50$**

| | |
|---|---|
| $p^8$ | .0039 |
| $8p^7q$ | .0313 |
| $28p^6q^2$ | .1094 |
| $56p^5q^3$ | .2188 |
| $70p^4q^4$ | .2734 |
| $56p^3q^5$ | .2188 |
| $28p^2q^6$ | .1094 |
| $8pq^7$ | .0313 |
| $q^8$ | .0039 |

exist in sampling results. Any of the displayed outcomes can occur, even when proper random sampling procedures are followed. In fact, equal numbers of males and females are expected only 27.34% of the time, whereas variations as great as 7 males and 1 female have a 3.13% chance of occurring. Even results of all males or all females can be expected 0.39% of the time. And remember, the variation shown in Table 6.2 will occur when the number of males and females is equal in the population and when the procedures for drawing the sample are truly random. This suggests that variability is not a trivial issue, and it will occupy much of our attention in the following discussion.

The example can be used to illustrate another point. Research is based on measures of variables describing characteristics of **sample members.** The variables are referred to as **random variables** because the sample selection procedures result in random variation in the variable values. The presence of random variation means that, if repeated samples are drawn from the same population, the estimates provided by the samples will not be the same. Rather, they will exhibit the kind of variation shown in Table 6.2. Thus, most of the sample estimates will be around $p^5q^3$, $p^4q^4$, and $p^3q^5$, but occasionally, because of random variation, more extreme values such as $p^6q^2$, $p^2q^6$, $p^7q$, $pq^7$, and even $p^8$ or $q^8$ can occur.

In the everyday world of research, it is not possible to draw repeated samples and review their distributions. Researchers usually can afford to select only one sample, and population estimates must be based on information from that sample. Given the one sample, the researcher must decide whether the sample estimates of the population parameters are satisfactory. The logic of statistical inference provides the rationale for making such judgments.

## THE LOGIC OF STATISTICAL INFERENCE

The logic of statistical inference is organized around three distributions: the **distribution of the population,** the **distribution of the sample means,** and the **distribution of the sample.** The role of each distribution is central to the process of inference. Theoretically, statistical inference can be organized around any numerical index that describes the distribution of a variable, such as the mean, the median, or the standard deviation. However, the index most commonly used is the mean, and the discussion on inference that follows focuses on this measure.

## The Distribution of the Population

A variable is distributed in a specific form in a given **population.** For example, the distribution of age in any population has a specific form. This simply means that if the age of every member of the population were known and the ages displayed in terms of a frequency polygon, the resulting graph would show the form, or shape, of that distribution. The distribution of variables in some populations may be bell shaped, skewed to the right or the left, bimodal, rectangular, and so on. Whatever form they take, it is the real distribution for that variable in the population. Also, every variable in the population has a mean and a standard deviation (represented by the symbols $\mu$ and $\sigma$, respectively).

The problem is that entire populations can seldom be studied, nor can the value of every population member be known for the variables involved in a research endeavor. Consequently, the real shapes of the distributions of variables in populations are unknown. The only information available to the researcher about population parameters is the estimates provided by samples. If samples were always accurate representations of populations, there would be no problem; however, regardless of the care taken, sampling error due to random variation is always present. The extent of the size of the sampling error then becomes the issue. The second distribution, the distribution of the sample means, provides the basis for estimating the amount of error of a sample estimate.

## The Distribution of the Sample Means

The distribution of the sample means is exactly what the name implies: a distribution of sample means. The distribution is the result of drawing a large number of samples of a particular size from the same population, calculating the mean for each sample, and then creating a distribution from the means of the samples. The distribution of the sample means has three important characteristics that lie at the heart of statistical inference:

1. The distribution of means will approximate the form of a normal distribution regardless of the original distribution of the variable in the population if the size of each of the samples is equal to or greater than 30.
2. The mean of the distribution of means, symbolized by $\mu_{\bar{X}}$, always will equal the real population mean, $\mu$.
3. The standard deviation (referred to as the standard error) of the sampling distribution of the means, $\sigma_{\bar{X}}$, has a fixed relationship to the standard deviation of the population, $\sigma$, which plays a crucial role in determining the amount of error due to sampling variability.

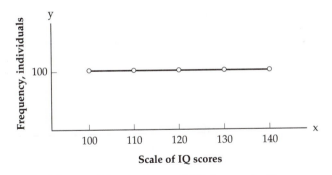

**FIGURE 6.1   Distribution of IQ Scores in the Population (*N* = 500)**

These three characteristics are derived from an important theorem, known as the **central limit theorem,** and deserve close attention because they make it possible to estimate sampling error or determine how good a sample estimate of the population is without knowing the real population value.

*The first characteristic* is that the distribution of the sample means will approximate the form of a normal distribution regardless of the original distribution of the variable in the population. For this to be true, the size of each sample in the distribution of sample means must be equal to or greater than 30. Suppose that you have a population of 500 members, all of whom have one of five IQ scores, including 100, 110, 120, 130, and 140. Assume further that the variable of IQ is distributed in the population so that each of the five IQ scores is held by 100 members. The form of the distribution of IQ scores in the population is shown in Figure 6.1.

The distribution of IQ scores in the population does not begin to approximate a normal distribution. Rather, because each of the five IQ scores has a frequency of 100, the distribution is a straight line. However, according to the central limit theorem, if repeated samples, each containing 30 or more members, are drawn from the population and the mean IQ is calculated for each sample, the distribution of the sample means will be normal in form. Although we have already stated that this characteristic holds true only when sample sizes are equal to or larger than 30, even with samples of as few as 2 members, the distribution begins to approximate that of a normal curve.

Suppose that 25 samples of only 2 members each are drawn from the population of 500. The expected sample results are shown in Table 6.3.[2] The table displays the IQs of the two members in each sample and their mean. Thus, in the first sample, the first member had an IQ of 100, as did the second. The mean of the two

[2] In a real experiment, the sample results would not appear as orderly as shown. The outcomes would be randomly distributed and vary somewhat from those in the table. The table outcomes are ideal, but in a real experiment, variations from what is shown would be modest, and the general conclusions the same.

**TABLE 6.3    Sampling Distribution of the Means: 25 Samples of 2 Members Each from a Population of Five IQs**

| First Member | Second Member | $\overline{X}$ | First Member | Second Member | $\overline{X}$ | First Member | Second Member | $\overline{X}$ |
|---|---|---|---|---|---|---|---|---|
| 100 | 100 | 100 | 110 | 130 | 120 | 130 | 110 | 120 |
| 100 | 110 | 105 | 110 | 140 | 125 | 130 | 120 | 125 |
| 100 | 120 | 110 | 120 | 100 | 110 | 130 | 130 | 130 |
| 100 | 130 | 115 | 120 | 110 | 115 | 130 | 140 | 135 |
| 100 | 140 | 120 | 120 | 120 | 120 | 140 | 100 | 120 |
| 110 | 100 | 105 | 120 | 130 | 125 | 140 | 110 | 125 |
| 110 | 110 | 110 | 120 | 140 | 130 | 140 | 120 | 130 |
| 110 | 120 | 115 | 130 | 100 | 115 | 140 | 130 | 135 |
|  |  |  |  |  |  | 140 | 140 | 140 |

sample members is $(100 + 100)/2 = 100$. The second sample consists of IQs of 100 and 110, for a mean of $(100 + 110)/2 =105$ and so on.

A frequency distribution of the outcomes of means can be created, as shown in Table 6.4. The most frequent outcome is the mean of 120, which occurs five times. The least frequent outcomes are the means of 100 and 140, each of which occurs only once. The distribution is symmetrical around the mean of 120.

If the frequency distribution of sample means in Table 6.4 is plotted, according to the central limit theorem their distribution should be more similar to the normal curve than the straight line of the original distribution of the population. Figure 6.2 shows this to be true. The distribution of the 25 sample means resembles a pyramid, and although it does not have a smooth bell shape, it is a much closer approximation to the normal curve than the original straight line of the population, and this approximation occurred

**TABLE 6.4    Outcomes of Means**

| $\overline{X}$ Outcomes | $f$ |
|---|---|
| 100 | 1 |
| 105 | 2 |
| 110 | 3 |
| 115 | 4 |
| 120 | 5 |
| 125 | 4 |
| 130 | 3 |
| 135 | 2 |
| 140 | 1 |

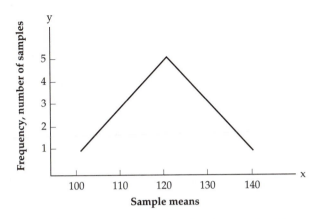

**FIGURE 6.2    Sampling Distribution of the Means: 25 Samples of 2 Members Each from a Population of Five IQs**

using samples with only 2 members. If the sample size were increased, the approximation would improve, and once its size was 30 or greater, the shape of the distribution of the sample means would be indistinguishable from that of the normal curve.

The importance of this characteristic is that the shape of the distribution of the sample means is that of a normal distribution. This signifies that any sample mean comes from a distribution of means that is normal in form regardless of the distribution of the variable in the population. Moreover, because the shape of the distribution of means is normal, the location of any observed sample mean can be determined by using the standard normal probability distribution. To understand the importance of this, we need to consider the second characteristic of the distribution of the means.

*The second characteristic* is that the mean of the sampling distribution of the means, symbolized by $\mu_{\bar{x}}$, will equal the population mean, $\mu$. This assertion can be tested with our example of the population of 500 IQ scores. The real mean of the population of the IQ scores is

$$100(100) + 110(100) + 120(100) + 130(100) + 140(100)/500 = 60{,}000/500 = 120 = \mu$$

If you calculate the mean of the sample means in Table 6.3, you will find it to be $100 + 105 + 110 + \ldots + 130 + 135 + 140 = 3{,}000/25 = 120 = \mu_{\bar{x}}$, which is identical to $\mu$, the original population mean. Thus, regardless of the distribution of the variable in the population, not only does the distribution of the sample means approximate the normal distribution but the mean of the distribution, $\mu_{\bar{x}}$, equals the true population mean, $\mu$.

In reference to the first characteristic, every sample mean comes not only from a normal distribution of means but also from a distribution with a mean that equals the true (but unknown) population mean, $\mu_{\bar{x}} = \mu$. Thus, we know that 68% of all sample means are likely to be ± 1 standard deviation, 95% will be

± 2 standard deviations, and 99% will be ± 3 standard deviations above or below the real population mean. The practical significance of these two characteristics is dramatic. Any sample mean that you encounter, regardless of which original measure or distribution produced the mean, comes from a normal distribution, and there is a 68% chance that it is only ± 1 standard deviation away from the real and unknown population mean.

*The third characteristic* is that the standard deviation of the distribution of the sampling means, called the **standard error of the mean** and symbolized by $\sigma_{\bar{X}}$, has a fixed relationship to the standard deviation of the population. The standard error of the mean is equal to the population standard deviation, $\sigma$, divided by the square root of the sample size:

$$\sigma_{\bar{X}} = \frac{\sigma}{\sqrt{n}} \tag{6.1}$$

Formula 6.1 shows that the standard error of the distribution of sample means, $\sigma_{\bar{X}}$, varies directly with $\sigma$. As $\sigma$ increases, $\sigma_{\bar{X}}$ increases, and as $\sigma$ decreases, $\sigma_{\bar{X}}$ decreases. Thus, the standard error is a function of $\sigma$, which is the amount of variation that the variable has in the population. If a variable in the population has a lot of variability, the standard error will be large; if it has little variability, it will be small. This is an important point to understand because the size of the standard error indicates the level of difficulty in getting a good estimate of a population characteristic using a sample. A large standard error indicates that using the sample, $\bar{X}$, to estimate the population, $\mu$, is subject to more error than a small standard error, which makes sense intuitively. Suppose that you have a group of 500 individuals who are between 25 and 35 years old and another group of 500 who are between 1 and 100 years old. Clearly, it is easier to get a sample with a mean close to that of the population with ages 25 to 35 than the population with ages from 1 to 100. In the former case, you could use a fairly small sample and get a good estimate because there is so little scatter (variation) in the ages of the population. In the latter, you would have to use a much larger sample to get as good an estimate.

Table 6.5 illustrates what happens to the standard error, $\sigma_{\bar{X}}$, for different values of $\sigma$ when the sample size remains the same. When $\sigma = 3$, the standard error of the mean is only 1.5, but when $\sigma = 5$, it is 2.5. Again, the relationship is important because the size of $\sigma$ affects our ability to estimate the population mean using a sample mean. Variables with a lot of natural variation in the population are more difficult to estimate with samples than are variables with less variation.

Formula 6.1 also shows that the size of $\sigma_{\bar{X}}$ can be influenced by the sample size in that $\sigma_{\bar{X}}$ varies inversely with the sample size. If you hold $\sigma$ constant and increase the size of the sample, $\sigma_{\bar{X}}$ decreases; if you decrease the sample size, $\sigma_{\bar{X}}$ increases. Table 6.6 shows the effect of changes in $n$ when $\sigma = 3$. When $n = 4$, the value of $\sigma_{\bar{X}} = 1.5$, but if $n$ is increased to 9, $\sigma_{\bar{X}} = 1.0$. This illustrates that if a variable has a lot of variation in the population, you can improve your estimate by using a larger sample. Again, this seems correct intuitively. If you use a large sample, you are more likely to include a broad range of the population values, resulting in a sample mean that provides a better estimate of the real population value;

**TABLE 6.5   The Effect of $\sigma$ on $\sigma_{\bar{x}}$**

| $\sigma = 3, n = 4$ | $\sigma = 5, n = 4$ |
|---|---|
| $\sigma_{\bar{x}} = \dfrac{3}{\sqrt{4}}$ | $\sigma_{\bar{x}} = \dfrac{5}{\sqrt{4}}$ |
| $= \dfrac{3}{2}$ | $= \dfrac{5}{2}$ |
| $= 1.5$ | $= 2.5$ |

and, if you select a sample so large that it includes the entire population, there will be no error in your estimate whatsoever. The important point is that sample size makes a difference in estimating population parameters. A larger sample will result in a smaller standard error, $\sigma_{\bar{x}}$, than will a small sample. However, as we will see later, there are diminishing returns on increases in sample size.

## The Distribution of the Sample

Although you must know about the role of the distribution of the population and the distribution of the sample means, in everyday research the *only* distribution the researcher deals with directly is that of the **sample.** Usually, the distribution of the population is inaccessible, and such parameters as $\mu$ and $\sigma$ are unknown. In fact, the reason for using a sample is to get an estimate of the population values. Also, usually it is not possible to select repeated samples to generate the distribution of the sample means and calculate $\mu_{\bar{x}}$ or $\sigma_{\bar{x}}$.

Instead, the researcher has one sample available and must make an estimate of the population parameters on the basis of information from the sample. From the preceding discussion we know that judging how precise the estimate is of the sample mean, $\bar{X}$, requires that we know the value of the standard error, $\sigma_{\bar{x}}$. However, according to Formula 6.1, the estimate of $\sigma_{\bar{x}}$ is based on $\sigma$, the standard deviation of the population, which is unknown. Fortunately, William S. Gosset, while studying variations in brewing materials for the Guiness Brewery in Dublin, Ireland, found that a good estimate of $\sigma_{\bar{x}}$ could be made using the

**TABLE 6.6   The Effect of $n$ on $\sigma_{\bar{x}}$**

| $\sigma = 3, n = 4$ | $\sigma = 3, n = 9$ |
|---|---|
| $\sigma_{\bar{x}} = \dfrac{3}{\sqrt{4}}$ | $\sigma_{\bar{x}} = \dfrac{3}{\sqrt{9}}$ |
| $= \dfrac{3}{2}$ | $= \dfrac{3}{3}$ |
| $= 1.5$ | $= 1$ |

standard deviation of the sample, *s*, rather than σ, if you use *n* – 1 in the denominator rather than *n*. Because of restrictions on publishing imposed by his employer, he published his findings under the name Student, and the resulting statistic became known as Student's *t*. Formula 6.2 indicates Gosset's contribution to the standard error:

$$\sigma_{\bar{X}} = \frac{s}{\sqrt{n-1}}$$ (6.2)

This formula differs in two respects from Formula 6.1. First, the formula uses the sample standard deviation, *s*, in the numerator rather than the population standard deviation, σ. This is important because, whereas σ is rarely available, *s* can be calculated readily for any sample.

Second, $\sqrt{n}$ is replaced in the denominator by $\sqrt{n-1}$. Reducing the denominator by 1 makes it possible to estimate $\sigma_{\bar{X}}$ using *s* rather than σ. The rationale is as follows: In drawing a sample, especially if the sample is small, values that lie farther from the mean and are fewest in the population tend to be underrepresented in the sample. This underrepresentation of extreme values means that the sample standard deviation, *s*, will be somewhat smaller than the real population value, σ. Given that *s* is likely to be smaller than σ in the numerator, an underestimate of $\sigma_{\bar{X}}$ may result.

However, the potential for an underestimate due to *s* can be compensated for by reducing the denominator; thus $\sqrt{n-1}$ is used rather than $\sqrt{n}$. Gosset demonstrated that $\frac{s}{\sqrt{n-1}}$ provides an unbiased estimate of $\sigma_{\bar{X}}$. The effect of reducing *n* by 1 is greatest when the sample size is small. As *n* becomes large, subtracting 1 has a diminishing effect. This makes sense because large samples are more likely to include extreme values in the population and less likely to underestimate $\sigma_{\bar{X}}$ than small samples. The good news is that the only information you need to estimate $\sigma_{\bar{X}}$ are the sample values *n* and *s*.

## Summary of the Logic of Statistical Inference

The logic of statistical inference establishes the foundation for inferring population characteristics from sample observations. The logic is organized around three distributions. The distribution of the variable in the population is what researchers want to know. However, information on entire populations usually is not available because it is too difficult and costly to acquire. Thus, population values are estimated by using samples.

The distribution of the sample means, like the distribution of the population, usually is not available, but knowledge about the character of the distribution is what makes statistical inference possible. First, the distribution of the sample means is always normal in form, so any sample mean is part of a normal distribution of means. Second, the standard error of the mean, $\sigma_{\bar{X}}$, represents the variation a variable has in the population. And, given $\sigma_{\bar{X}}$, we can determine the accuracy of a sample estimate. Fortunately, $\sigma_{\bar{X}}$ is easy to estimate.

**TABLE 6.7**   **Symbols for the Mean and Standard Deviation for the Three Distributions of Statistical Inference**

| Distribution | Mean | Standard Deviation |
|---|---|---|
| Distribution of the population | $\mu$ | $\sigma$ |
| Distribution of the sample means | $\mu_{\bar{X}}$ | $\sigma_{\bar{X}}$ |
| Distribution of the sample | $\bar{X}$ | $s$ |

You need to know only the sample size, $n$, and its standard deviation, $s$, both of which are readily available.

The distribution of the variable in the sample usually is all the researcher has. Using $n$ and $s$ from the sample, $\sigma_{\bar{X}}$ can be calculated, informing us of the amount of variation our measure has in the population. Knowing this, we can assess how good an estimate our sample mean is of the population mean. The remainder of this chapter reviews how the standard error of the mean is used to make population estimates. Table 6.7 summarizes the symbols used to describe the three distributions. Familiarize yourself with these symbols because they will be used throughout the discussion that follows. Two applications used frequently are point estimates and interval estimates.

## POINT ESTIMATES FOR POPULATION MEANS

Any sample statistic is a **point estimate** of a population represented by a sample. Thus, means, medians, and standard deviations are examples of point estimates. Because of its descriptive properties and utility in higher-order calculations, the mean is most frequently used as a point estimate of $\mu$. An estimate can be very precise or can be subject to considerable error. Precision is a function of how close the sample mean, $\bar{X}$, is to the real population mean, $\mu$. The **error of an estimate** is equal to the absolute difference between the sample mean and the population mean, or $|\bar{X} - \mu|$. Of course, the problem is that no information usually exists about $\mu$, so the error cannot be determined simply by subtracting $\mu$ from $\bar{X}$.

However, we can use our knowledge of the distribution of the sample means to assess how likely it is that the point estimate is a good fit to the population value. We know that the distribution of the sample means is a normal distribution when $n \geq 30$, so any sample mean comes from a normal distribution. We also know that the distribution of sample means has a mean, $\mu_{\bar{X}}$, and a standard error, $\sigma_{\bar{X}}$. Figure 6.3 illustrates the theoretical normal distribution. Any observed sample mean is located somewhere in the distribution. Using the model of the standard normal distribution, we can determine how good an estimate a sample mean provides of an unknown population mean. The goodness of the estimate is a function of the standard error, $\sigma_{\bar{X}}$. When $\sigma_{\bar{X}}$ is large, the estimate provided by the $\bar{X}$ of $\mu$ is less precise than when it is small.

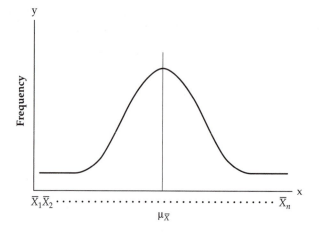

**FIGURE 6.3   Theoretical Distribution of the Sample Means**

The use of point estimates can be illustrated using the samples from the two communities and poverty. When the example was introduced in Chapter 3, it consisted of small samples of 10 census tracts. The properties of the distribution of the sample means require sample sizes of at least 30. Assume that both our samples are increased to 37 and that their means and standard deviations remain unchanged, as shown in Table 6.8.

Both communities have an average of 21.7 poor households per census tract, but Urbanville has little variation, $s = 1.71$, whereas Central City has greater variation, $s = 2.97$. Although the sample $\overline{X}$ and $s$ are available for both communities, we have no information on their population values. The concern is whether the means of 21.7, based on the sample of 37 census tracts, provide a good estimate of their population parameters.

Using Formula 6.2, we can calculate the standard errors for the two communities, as shown in Table 6.9. The standard errors indicate how much variation poverty has in the total population of census tracts in the two communities. The standard errors can be interpreted using the areas of the standard normal distribution. For Urbanville, 68% of all sample means would include the real population mean within $\pm 1$ $\sigma_{\overline{x}}$ units, or .285 points above and below the mean, and for Central City it would be $\pm.495$ points. By extension, 95% of all sample means would include the real population mean for Urbanville and be within 2 standard deviation units, or $\pm 2(.285) =$

**TABLE 6.8   Means and Standard Deviations**

| Urbanville | Central City |
|:---:|:---:|
| $n = 37$ | $n = 37$ |
| $\overline{X} = 21.7$ | $\overline{X} = 21.7$ |
| $s = 1.71$ | $s = 2.97$ |

**TABLE 6.9    Standard Error Terms for Urbanville and Central City**

| Urbanville | Central City |
|---|---|
| $\sigma_{\bar{X}} = \dfrac{s}{\sqrt{n-1}}$ | $\sigma_{\bar{X}} = \dfrac{s}{\sqrt{n-1}}$ |
| $= \dfrac{1.71}{\sqrt{37-1}}$ | $= \dfrac{2.97}{\sqrt{37-1}}$ |
| $= .285$ | $= .495$ |

±.570, and 99% would be within ±3(.285) = ±.855 points. For Central City, the 95% limits would be ±2(.495) = ±.990 points, and at 99% they would be ±3(.495) = ±1.485.

The difference in the standard errors indicates that a sample mean from Urbanville is more likely to provide a good point estimate of the real population mean than one from Central City. The example shows that the larger the sample standard deviation, $s$, and subsequently $\sigma_{\bar{X}}$, the less precise the point estimate the $\bar{X}$ is of $\mu$. The standard error provides information helpful in deciding how precise a sample estimate might be of a population parameter.

## CONFIDENCE INTERVALS AND POPULATION MEANS

A primary application of the standard error is in developing *confidence interval estimates*. Confidence intervals use the same information as point estimates but differ in that they include a specified probability that the lower and upper limits of the interval will include the real population mean. As in point estimates, the sample mean plays a key role because the lower and upper values of the interval are anchored below and above the mean. The width of the intervals is a function of the probability, or confidence, that the interval will contain the true population value, $\mu$. Such interval estimates are commonly referred to as **confidence limits.**

Confidence limits for the mean, symbolized by CL, are determined by

$$\text{CL} = \bar{X} - Z\sigma_{\bar{X}} \text{ to } \bar{X} + Z\sigma_{\bar{X}} \qquad (6.3)$$

The formula shows that the width of the interval around the mean is a function of the Z value and the standard error of the mean, $\sigma_{\bar{X}}$. The $\sigma_{\bar{X}}$ takes into account the amount of variation that the variable has in the population. If $\sigma_{\bar{X}}$ is small, the confidence limits will be narrower and more precise. If $\sigma_{\bar{X}}$ is large, the confidence interval will be wider and less precise.

The Z value in the formula represents the level of probability (confidence) that the interval will contain the real population mean. The more confident you want to be that the limits include $\mu$, the larger the Z value and the wider the confidence limits. Thus, if you want to be 95% confident, the Z value corresponding to 95% of the area of the normal curve is used, which is ±1.96. If you want 99%

**TABLE 6.10    95% and 99% Confidence Limits for Urbanville
Mean = 21.7; Standard Error = .285**

---

**95% Limits; Z = 1.96**

---

$CL_{.95}$ = 21.7 – 1.96(.285) to 21.7 + 1.96(.285)

21.7 – .559 to 21.7 + .559

21.141 to 22.259

---

**99% Limits; Z = 2.58**

---

$CL_{.99}$ = 21.7 – 2.58(.285) to 21.7 + 2.58(.285)

21.7 – .735 to 21.7 + .735

20.965 to 22.435

---

confidence, the corresponding Z value is ±2.58. Column E in Table B.1 (Appendix B) identifies the area between the ±Z value and the mean.[3]

There is an inverse relationship between the level of confidence and the precision, or width, of a confidence interval. The greater the confidence, the wider the limits and the less the precision. Suppose that you were to use confidence limits to guess the mean age of students enrolled in an undergraduate statistics course. If you use very wide limits, such as 10 to 65 years, you will have great confidence that the intervals include everyone in the class but very little precision. To report that the ages of class members range somewhere between 10 and 65 is to say very little. The intervals are so wide that they fail to provide precise information about the age of the group. If you use narrow limits, such as 18 to 22 years, you will have much more precision but might lose confidence that the limits actually include enough of the class members to contain the real mean of the group. The wide limits give you confidence but lack precision. The narrow limits give you precision but reduce your confidence. The example illustrates the choices that researchers must make in choosing the width of confidence limits. Generally, 95% and 99% confidence limits are used, but the width of the limits should be a function of how much precision is required given the purpose at hand.

Table 6.10 shows the confidence limits for both the 95% and the 99% level for poverty in Urbanville. The small standard error of .285 (see Table 6.9) has 95% limits that extend only from 21.141 to 22.259, and even at the 99% level the limits are quite precise: 20.965 to 22.435.

Central City's confidence limits, shown in Table 6.11, fail to approach the precision of Urbanville's because of the larger standard error. At the 95% level, the limits are 20.730 to 22.670, and at the 99% level they increase to 20.423 to 22.977.

---

[3] The Z score associated with a level of confidence (e.g., 95%) can be determined from column E in Table B.1 (Appendix B). Column E shows the area between the Z score and the mean both below and above the mean. Confidence limits always refer to values below and above the mean, which can be located in column E, and its corresponding Z score. The Z score associated with the 95% confidence value is 1.96, and for the 99% level it is 2.58.

**TABLE 6.11    95% and 99% Confidence Limits for Central City
Mean = 21.7; Standard Error = .495**

| 95% Limits; Z = 1.96 |
| :---: |
| $CL_{.95}$ = 21.7 − 1.96(.495) to 21.7 + 1.96(.495) |
| 21.7 − .970 to 21.7 + .970 |
| 20.730 to 22.670 |

| 99% Limits; Z = 2.58 |
| :---: |
| $CL_{.99}$ = 21.7 − 2.58(.495) to 21.7 + 2.58(.495) |
| 21.7 − 1.277 to 21.7 + 1.277 |
| 20.423 to 22.977 |

The limits are less precise for Central City than Urbanville. Note that for both communities, as the confidence level increased from 95% to 99%, the limits became wider and less precise. The trade-off between confidence and precision is clear.

What is the utility of the information we obtain from the confidence limits? We are trying to determine whether our sample mean is a good estimate of the real population mean. Whereas the real population mean is a fixed value, sample means fluctuate from one sample to another because of random variation in sample selection. Confidence limits establish the boundaries within which the real population mean *might* be located given our sample estimates. Given our sample mean and standard error for Urbanville, we can conclude that 95% of the time the confidence interval of 21.141 to 22.259 will include the true population mean. Conversely, 5% of the time the confidence limits will not include the population mean; that is, it could be below or above the limits of 21.141 and 22.259. You can increase the confidence of including Urbanville's real population mean by using 99% limits, but you lose precision because the width of the intervals increases to 20.965 to 22.435.

The important information provided by the confidence limits is that Urbanville's sample mean of 21.7 is likely a good estimate of the real mean of its total population of census tracts. The low standard error for Urbanville results in relatively precise intervals at the 95% level of confidence, and even the 99% level results in narrow and precise limits.

Central City, with a larger standard error, has wider confidence limits and thus less precision. At the 95% level, the confidence limits extend from 20.730 to 22.670, compared to Urbanville's limits of 21.141 to 22.259. At the 99% level, the confidence limits for Central City increase to 20.423 to 22.977. The real population mean for the census tracts of Central City is likely to differ more from its sample mean of 21.7 than is true for Urbanville.

Note that Central City's intervals provide the same confidence as do Urbanville's but are less precise. Also, the difference in precision is a function of the difference in their standard errors. Central City has a larger standard error, indicating that poverty in the population varies more across its census tracts than is true for Urbanville. The conclusion is that small standard errors allow for more precise estimates of population parameters than do large standard errors.

The real purpose of confidence limits is to get an estimate of the location of the real population mean. We know from the logic of statistical inference and, more specifically, from the characteristics of the distribution of the sample means that every sample mean comes from a distribution of means that is normal in form. We also know that the distribution of the means is such that $\mu_{\bar{X}} = \mu$, and the standard error, $\sigma_{\bar{X}}$, informs us about the amount of variation that a variable has in the population. Although $\mu$ is unknown, we can use $\sigma_{\bar{X}}$ and $\bar{X}$ to construct confidence limits that provide an estimate of the boundaries within which the unknown $\mu$ is likely to be located.

If you were to draw repeated random samples of 30 or more members from the total population of census tracts for either community, you would find that the means and standard errors of the samples would vary somewhat. Some would be greater than our values, and some would be less. If you were to compute confidence limits around each of the sample means, you also would find that the confidence limits would vary somewhat with each sample. However, most of the limits would overlap and include the unknown population mean. As a matter of fact, at the 95% level, 95 out of 100 samples would produce confidence limits that include $\mu$, and at the 99% level 99 out of 100 would do so.

Figure 6.4 shows the distribution of 20 random samples and their confidence limits around an unknown $\mu$. The horizontal lines represent the 95% confidence

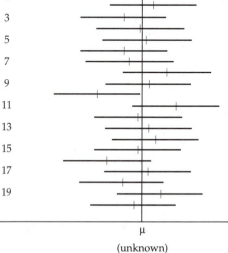

**FIGURE 6.4   Twenty Samples and Their Confidence Limits**

level for each of the 20 samples. Figure 6.4 shows that for all the 20 sample outcomes except one, sample 10, the intervals around the sample means include the true population mean. In the real world of research, only one sample is drawn, but the confidence limits around that sample mean are likely to include the population mean.

Confidence limits indicate the precision of a sample estimate. Narrow (precise) confidence limits, such as those of Urbanville, give confidence that the sample mean of 21.7 is very close to its real population mean. The wider limits of Central City indicate that the sample estimate of 21.7 is subject to more error. The larger standard error suggests that a larger sample is needed to get as reliable an estimate for Central City as for Urbanville. The exercises at the end of this chapter will give you an opportunity to construct confidence limits for other distributions and to see the influence of various standard error terms.

## CONFIDENCE LIMITS AND SAMPLE SIZE

What do researchers do when faced with large standard errors and imprecise estimates, such as those for Central City? If you have advance information that a particular measurement has a lot of variation, you can improve the quality of the sample estimate by drawing a larger sample. Recall from the discussion of Formula 6.2 that the size of the standard error is a function not only of the size of the standard deviation but also of sample size. If the standard deviation does not change and sample size is increased, the standard error becomes smaller. Also, recall the logic that, given a random selection procedure, a large sample is more likely to provide a precise estimate of a population than a small sample. Carrying the logic to an extreme, if the sample becomes so large that it encompasses the entire population, there will be no error whatsoever in the estimate.

Table 6.12 shows the effect of larger sample sizes on the standard error of Central City. Assume that for every sample the standard deviation remains the same; that is, $s = 2.97$.[4] A sample of 37 has a standard error of .495, but when $n$ is increased to 100, $\sigma_{\bar{x}}$ is reduced to .299, and at 400 it becomes .149. The effect of sample size on the width of the confidence limits is also shown in Table 6.12. Increases in sample size reduce the width of the intervals, resulting in a more precise estimate.

However, increases in sample size reach a point of diminishing returns, depending on the amount of variation that a measurement or variable has in the population. As a general rule, to reduce the standard error by half, the sample size must be quadrupled. Table 6.13 illustrates the effect of increases in sample size from $n = 37$ to $n = 1,000$ for Urbanville and Central City. In the case of Urbanville, increasing the sample to 100 reduces the width of the interval to the point where it provides very precise information on the location of $\mu$. However, because of the

---

[4] In fact, the standard deviations would vary somewhat from sample to sample, but the differences would not be great, and for purposes of illustration we will assume that they remain the same.

**TABLE 6.12**   **Effect of Sample Size on the Standard Error for Central City**

| $n = 37$ | $n = 100$ | $n = 400$ |
|---|---|---|
| $\sigma_{\overline{X}} = \dfrac{2.97}{\sqrt{37-1}}$ | $\sigma_{\overline{X}} = \dfrac{2.97}{\sqrt{100-1}}$ | $\sigma_{\overline{X}} = \dfrac{2.97}{\sqrt{400-1}}$ |
| $= \dfrac{2.97}{6}$ | $= \dfrac{2.97}{9.95}$ | $= \dfrac{2.97}{19.97}$ |
| $= .495$ | $= .299$ | $= .149$ |

**95% Confidence Limits for Central City for Three Sample Sizes**

$n = 37, \sigma_{\overline{X}} = .495, \overline{X} = 21.7, Z = 1.96$

$CL_{.95} = 21.7 - 1.96(.495)$ to $21.7 + 1.96(.495)$

20.730 to 22.670

$n = 100, \sigma_{\overline{X}} = .299, \overline{X} = 21.7, Z = 1.96$

$CL_{.95} = 21.7 - 1.96(.299)$ to $21.7 + 1.96(.299)$

21.114 to 22.286

$n = 400, \sigma_{\overline{X}} = .149, \overline{X} = 21.7, Z = 1.96$

$CL_{.95} = 21.7 - 1.96(.149)$ to $21.7 + 1.96(.149)$

21.408 to 21.992

**TABLE 6.13**   **The Effect of Increases in Sample Size for Urbanville and Central City**

| $n$ | $\sigma_{\overline{X}}$ | $CL_{.95}$ | Interval Width |
|---|---|---|---|
| | | Urbanville: $s = 1.71$ | |
| 37 | .285 | 21.141 to 22.259 | 1.118 |
| 100 | .172 | 21.363 to 22.037 | .674 |
| 200 | .121 | 21.463 to 21.937 | .474 |
| 400 | .086 | 21.531 to 21.869 | .338 |
| 700 | .065 | 21.573 to 21.827 | .254 |
| 1,000 | .054 | 21.594 to 21.806 | .212 |
| | | Central City: $s = 2.97$ | |
| 37 | .495 | 20.730 to 22.670 | 1.940 |
| 100 | .299 | 21.114 to 22.286 | 1.172 |
| 200 | .210 | 21.288 to 22.112 | .824 |
| 400 | .149 | 21.408 to 21.992 | .584 |
| 700 | .112 | 21.481 to 21.919 | .438 |
| 1,000 | .094 | 21.516 to 21.884 | .368 |

larger standard error for Central City, a sample of more than 200 is required to attain the precision of Urbanville with a sample of 100. Notice also that the gain in precision for Central City with samples larger than 400 diminishes. Increasing sample size in Central City from 400 to 1,000 results in narrowing the confidence limits by only .216 points (.584 − .368 = .216). Given the additional cost and effort of using a sample of 1,000 as opposed to 400 and the small additional gain in precision, such an increase in sample size would be difficult to justify.

A question frequently asked in social research is, How large should a sample be? The answer is partly a function of information on the size of the standard error, $\sigma_{\bar{x}}$. To derive a precise estimate of $\mu$ when $\sigma$ is large, we must increase the size of the sample. If you have information on the standard error of the population, the sample size required to achieve a particular confidence limit can be calculated using

$$n = \left( \frac{\sigma Z}{i} \right)^2 \tag{6.4}$$

where $i$ = the width of the interval.

Suppose you know that a variable has standard deviation, $\sigma$, in the population of 9.28 and you want 95% confidence limits that are no wider than ±1.5 points. The sample size necessary to achieve this can be determined by

$$n = \left( \frac{(9.28)(1.96)}{1.5} \right)^2$$

$$= (12.13)^2$$

$$n = 147$$

The results show that you would need a sample of about 147 members to have a standard error that would produce 95% confidence limits that are 1.5 points below and above the mean.

## CONFIDENCE LIMITS AND PROPORTIONS

The discussion of estimation and confidence limits dealt exclusively with procedures for continuous measurements, but confidence limits can be created for discrete data as well. Recall from Chapter 5 that the mean and standard deviation can be calculated for dichotomous data if $np \geq 10$ and if $nq \geq 10$. Further, if $n \geq 30$, it is possible to determine the **standard error of the sample proportion, $\sigma_p$,** which is comparable to the standard error of the mean. The $\sigma_p$ is calculated using the following formula:

$$\sigma_p = \frac{\sqrt{npq}}{n} \tag{6.5}$$

Suppose that a random sample of 50 individuals is drawn from a community and it is found that .40 favored a civic project, whereas .60 opposed it. The data meet the criteria for establishing confidence limits because $n \geq 30$, $np = 50(.40) = 20 \geq 10$, and $nq = 50(.60) = 30 \geq 10$. The standard error of the sample proportion, according to Formula 6.5, is

$$\sigma_p = \frac{\sqrt{50(.40)(.60)}}{50} = \frac{3.46}{50} = .069$$

Once $\sigma_p$ is known, the confidence limits are determined by

$$\text{CL} = p - Z\sigma_p \text{ to } p + Z\sigma_p \qquad (6.6)$$

The 95% confidence limits for our example are

$$\text{CL}_{95} = .40 - 1.96(.069) \text{ to } .40 + 1.96(.069)$$

$$= .265 \text{ to } .535$$

The results indicate that the limits of .265 and .535 will contain the real population proportion, $P$, 95% of the time. As in the case of the mean, confidence limits are a function of the size of the standard error, the sample size, and the degree of confidence desired. A larger sample would have produced a smaller standard error, resulting in narrower confidence limits. Narrow limits provide more precise information on the location of the population proportion than do wide limits.

## COMPUTER EXERCISES: SOME SUGGESTIONS

Understanding statistical inference is essential to learning statistical analysis. The topic also lends itself to interesting computer exercises that will illustrate some of the major issues of sampling. Your software will have procedures for selecting random samples from your data set. Select three or four independent samples of the same size from your total cases. Then select several interval variables and compare the basic statistics of the samples. Differences between the means, variances, and standard deviations will clearly illustrate the concept of sampling variation.

Also, select several independent samples each of different sizes, so you have three or four small, three or four medium, and three or four large samples. Then select several interval variables and compare the basic statistics. First compare the statistics within the groups of small, medium, and large samples. This should illustrate that small sample means will differ more than large sample means. Because of sampling variation, this may not occur for everyone selecting the samples, but over all the class selections, that will be the case. The variances and standard deviations can also be compared, and the overall results should show that small samples tend to underestimate variance. After completing the within-group statistics, compare the basic statistics across the samples of different sizes. Also compare the sample results to the statistics for the entire data set. You will find that large samples give better estimates of the total population than smaller samples.

You can also produce confidence limits around the means of the various samples that are selected. The difference in the confidence limits should show that large samples provide greater precision than small ones, but that the gains from medium to large samples are less than those from small to medium samples. You can also select several dichotomous measures and use various samples to develop confidence limits around proportions. Computer exercises should be particularly helpful in reinforcing the conceptual content of this chapter.

## CHAPTER SUMMARY

Data for social research are generally derived from samples with the intent of inferring the sample findings to the population. Given that random sampling procedures are used, the logic of statistical inference provides a clear rationale for estimating an unknown population, $\mu$, from an observed sample, $\overline{X}$. Given that the distribution of the sample means is always a normal distribution, we know that any sample mean comes from a normal distribution. Thus, we can use the model of the standard normal distribution to assess how precise an estimate the sample, $\overline{X}$, is of the population, $\mu$. The information can be used to create interval estimates regarding the location of the unknown population mean. Interval estimates, more commonly referred to as confidence limits, make it possible to assess how much confidence can be placed in the $\overline{X}$ as an estimator of $\mu$.

The capacity to evaluate how precise an estimate is provided by a sample observation of the population is the foundation on which inferential research rests. In addition, other methods are available to test directly the goodness of fit between sample statistics and known or expected population parameters. These methods are organized around hypothesis testing and are considered in the next chapter.

## KEY TERMS

**accuracy**   An accurate sample exists when the sample statistic is approximately equal to the population parameter.

**bias**   In sampling, error that results from a flaw in the sampling design such that some elements of the population are systematically omitted or overrepresented in the sample.

**central limit theorem**   A theorem that provides the basis for statistical inference around logic associated with the distribution of the population, the distribution of the sample means, and the distribution of the sample.

**chance variation**   Variation in sample outcomes that is due to random processes.

**confidence limits**   The lower and upper limits of an interval likely to contain the true population mean.

**distribution of the population**   The real distribution of a variable in the population.

**distribution of the sample**   Distribution of the variable in the sample; the data that researchers usually work with.

**distribution of the sample means**   The distribution of the means of a series of samples drawn from a population.

**error**   Exists when a sample statistic differs too much from a population parameter.

**error of an estimate**   The absolute difference between a sample estimate and the real population parameter.

**point estimate**   A statistic such as the mean, median, or standard deviation, which provides an estimate of that value for the population.

**population**   The entire set of entities of interest.

**probability sample**   A sample obtained in such a manner that each object in the population has an equal and independent chance of being selected.

**random error**   Error resulting from variation due to random or chance factors.

**random variables**   Variables describing sample characteristics; referred to as random variables because they are subject to random variation due to variability in drawing sample members.

**representative sample**   A sample that represents the population in terms of the interests at hand.

**sample**   A subset of a population, usually presumed to be representative of the population.

**sample member**   The individual unit of a sample.

**sample statistic**   A number describing a characteristic of a sample. In inference, the sample statistic used most often is the mean.

**simple random sampling**   Sample selection procedures using a random process, such as a random numbers table.

**standard error of the mean**   The standard deviation of the distribution of sample means.

**standard error of the sample proportion**   The standard deviation of the distribution of a sample proportion.

**statistical inference**   The process of estimating unknown population parameters using information derived from sample statistics.

**systematic error**   Error in sampling due to a flaw in the sampling design that systematically distorts the capacity of the sample to represent the population.

## SYMBOLS

| | |
|---|---|
| $\mu$ | Population mean |
| $\sigma$ | Standard deviation of the population |
| $\mu_{\bar{x}}$ | Mean of the distribution of sample means |
| $\sigma_{\bar{x}}$ | Standard error of the mean |
| $\overline{X}$ | Sample mean |
| $s$ | Standard deviation of the distribution of the sample |
| $\sigma_p$ | Standard error of a sample proportion |
| $\mu_p$ | Mean of a population proportion |
| CL | Confidence limits |

## FORMULAS

$$\sigma_{\bar{x}} = \frac{\sigma}{\sqrt{n}}$$    Standard error of the mean

$$\sigma_{\bar{x}} = \frac{s}{\sqrt{n-1}}$$    Student's estimate of the standard error

$$CL = \overline{X} - Z\sigma_{\bar{x}} \text{ to } \overline{X} + Z\sigma_{\bar{x}}$$    Confidence limits for the mean

$$n = \left(\frac{\sigma Z}{i}\right)^2$$    Estimate for sample size

$$\sigma_p = \frac{\sqrt{npq}}{n}$$    Standard error of proportions

$$CL = p - Z\sigma_p \text{ to } p + Z\sigma_p$$    Confidence limits for a proportion

## EXERCISES

1. A population of 600 members was identified and numbered from 000 to 599. Use a random numbers table to select a sample of 50 members. List the numbers of those selected.

2. In exercise 1, what is the probability of any one member being selected when you use the random numbers table?

3. Name and describe the role of each of the three distributions involved in the logic of statistical inference.

4. Plot a graph of the distribution of the population of the six outcomes for the toss of a die. Note that the graph should be such that the frequencies appear on the ordinate and the outcomes of the tosses on the abscissa.

5. Plot the distribution of the sample means for tosses of two dice using a frequency polygon. The sequence of outcomes is demonstrated below. What can you say about the distribution of outcomes?

| Die 1 | Die 2 | Mean | Die 1 | Die 2 | Mean |
|-------|-------|------|-------|-------|------|
| 1 | 1 | 1 | . | . | . |
| 1 | 2 | 1.5 | . | . | . |
| 1 | 3 | 2 | . | . | . |
| 1 | 4 | 2.5 | . | . | . |
| 1 | 5 | 3 | 6 | 1 | 3.5 |
| 1 | 6 | 3.5 | 6 | 2 | 4 |
| 2 | 1 | 1.5 | 6 | 3 | 4.5 |
| . | . | . | 6 | 4 | 5 |
| . | . | . | 6 | 5 | 5.5 |
| . | . | . | 6 | 6 | 6 |

6. Explain the relationship between changing values of $n$ and $\sigma$ and the resulting $\sigma_{\bar{x}}$.

7. What is the basis for the argument that $\dfrac{s}{\sqrt{n-1}} = \dfrac{\sigma}{\sqrt{n}}$?

8. A researcher had a sample of 40 members, and the standard deviation of the population was 5. What is the standard error of the mean?

9. What would happen to the standard error of the mean if the researcher's sample size were increased to 100?

10. Two students had the following scores on weekly exams:

| Student 1 | | Student 2 | |
|-----------|-----|-----------|-----|
| 89 | 85 | 100 | 84 |
| 88 | 84 | 98 | 82 |
| 87 | 84 | 96 | 80 |
| 87 | 83 | 94 | 78 |
| 87 | 83 | 92 | 76 |
| 86 | 83 | 90 | 74 |
| 86 | 82 | 88 | 72 |
| 85 | 81 | 86 | 70 |

a. What is the mean for each student?
b. What is the standard deviation for each student?
c. What is the standard error of the mean for each student?
d. Establish confidence limits for the two students at the 95% level. Explain the difference between the results.

    **e.** Establish confidence limits for the two students at the 99% level. Explain the difference between the results.

    **f.** Why do wider limits increase confidence that the population parameter is included in the limits, but narrower limits are preferable?

**11.** A sample of 40 workers were polled on their opinions about job security. It was found that .45 felt positive about the matter, whereas .55 felt negative.

    **a.** What is the standard error of proportions for the outcome?

    **b.** What would the confidence limits be at the 95% level?

    **c.** What would the confidence limits be at the 99% level?

# 7

# TESTING HYPOTHESES

## *One-Sample Tests*

Chapter 6 examined the logic of statistical inference which shows that you can estimate an unknown population parameter with a sample statistic. The role of estimating population parameters is crucial because usually only sample statistics are available. Point estimates are single-sample values that provide an estimate of a particular population parameter, such as the mean. Interval estimates or confidence limits establish a range of values within which an unknown population parameter is likely to be located.

In this chapter the discussion of statistical inference is continued, but the focus will be on *hypotheses.* Hypothesis testing is the basis for decision making in statistical analysis. We review the basics of hypothesis testing and how it is used to compare a statistical value from a sample to some known or expected population parameter. Generally, the procedure is one in which a hypothesis about a population parameter is proposed and then a sample statistic is used to test the hypothesis. If the sample statistic is in agreement with the population expectation, the hypothesis is supported, but if it differs, the hypothesis is rejected.

## WHAT IS A HYPOTHESIS?

The common definition of a **hypothesis** is that it is an assertion that is subject to verification or proof. In statistical decision making, the assertion made by a hypothesis is tested with information from a sample. In reference to statistical inference, a more precise definition of a hypothesis is that it is a statement about a population parameter that is verified with a sample statistic. Remember that hypotheses are always statements about the population, and verification is based on information from a sample.

It would seem that testing a hypothesis is a straightforward procedure in which the data necessary to test the hypothesis are marshaled, and then, given the evidence, the hypothesis is either accepted as true or rejected as false. However, for valid philosophical and logical reasons, the process is somewhat more complicated. Decisions about hypotheses are based on the *criterion of falsifiability*, which is the notion that although it is possible to determine whether a hypothesis is false, it is much more difficult, if not impossible, to prove that a hypothesis is true. If the evidence from a sample is contrary to the hypothesis, the hypothesis cannot be true and thereby is proven false. However, if the evidence agrees with the hypothesis, it does not prove the hypothesis true. It means only that, given the evidence available from the sample under consideration, the hypothesis is *not proven false*. If additional samples and evidence are collected, the hypothesis might be proven false, so it would be inappropriate to conclude that it is true.

For example, you might hypothesize that all swans are white, and from a large number of observations you may see only white swans. The criterion of falsifiability indicates that it would be inappropriate to conclude that you have proven true the hypothesis that all swans are white. There may be swans that you have not seen that are not white. However, you can prove the hypothesis false. If you encounter a swan that is not white, your hypothesis is falsified and you have established the fact that all swans are not white. Of course, the more evidence supporting a hypothesis, the more tenable it becomes and the less likely that it is false.[1]

The concept of falsifiability influences the way in which **statistical hypotheses** are structured and tested. Researchers work with two general kinds of hypotheses: the **null hypothesis,** $H_0$, which asserts that a population parameter does not differ from some value, and the **directional hypothesis,** $H_1$, which states that the value of the population parameter is either greater or less than that proposed by $H_0$. The remainder of this chapter illustrates hypothesis testing.

## HYPOTHESIS TESTING: THE STANDARD-ERROR-OF-THE-MEAN TEST

The role and application of hypotheses will be illustrated with examples for one-sample tests. Generally, one-sample tests evaluate an expected or known population parameter using a sample statistic. The statistical tests considered here include the **standard-error-of-the-mean test, Student's *t* test,** the **standard-error-of-proportions test,** and the **chi-square test.**

---

[1] For a detailed discussion of falsifiability and hypothesis testing, see Karl R. Popper, *The Logic of Discovery* (New York: Harper Torch Books, 1968).

## *Example 7.1*

Assume that a population has a mean age of 66.9 and a standard deviation of 5.9. A representative sample of 75 individuals is selected from the population, the mean age of which is 68.3 years. In summary, the data are

Expected mean age of the population = $\mu$ = 66.9

Standard deviation of the population = $\sigma$ = 5.9

Sample mean age                                     = $\overline{X}$ = 68.3

The concern is whether the sample mean of 68.3 supports the belief that the age of the population is 66.9. Obviously, 68.3 does not equal 66.9, but the difference could be due to random variation in sample outcomes. The purpose of testing the difference is to determine whether the difference is too large to be due to random variation. The following hypotheses could be tested:

$H_0$: $\mu$ = 66.9      The population mean does not differ from 66.9.
$H_1$: $\mu$ > 66.9      The population mean is greater than 66.9.

The null hypothesis states that the mean age of the population is equal to the expected value of 66.9. Note that the symbol $\mu$ is used because hypotheses are always statements about population parameters. The symbolic statement, $H_0$: $\mu$ = 66.9, is read "the population mean does not differ from 66.9." The null hypothesis is referred to as a *no-difference statement* because it posits that no difference exists between the age of the population and 66.9; that is, it is neither less than nor greater than 66.9. Given that the null hypothesis is a neither-less-nor-greater-than statement, it is also referred to as nondirectional.[2] It does not posit a difference in either direction; that is, that the population is younger or older than 66.9.

The research hypothesis, based on the information provided by the sample, states that the population mean is either less or greater than some value, depending on whether the sample value (statistic) is less or greater than the hypothesized population parameter. As with the null hypothesis, the research hypothesis is always a statement about the population parameter. In our example it states that the population mean is greater than 66.9 because our sample value, 68.3, is greater.

The research hypothesis is also referred to as a directional hypothesis because it states the direction of the difference. In our example, the potential directional hypotheses are

$H_1$: $\mu$ < 66.9
$H_2$: $\mu$ > 66.9

Given that our sample, $\overline{X}$ = 68.3, is greater than the hypothesized value of 66.9, the appropriate directional hypothesis is $H_1$: $\mu$ > 66.9, which states that the mean age

---

[2] Some texts present $\mu \neq$ 66.9 as an alternative hypothesis to $H_0$. If $H_0$ is shown false, then the alternative, that $\mu$ differs from 66.9, can be concluded. Given that the alternative provides no new information beyond the inverse of $H_0$: $\mu$ = 66.9, it is not treated separately here.

of the population is greater than 66.9. Thus, the direction of the research hypothesis, whether it is < or >, is determined by whether the sample results are expected either to be less than or to exceed the population parameter.

The decision to reject a hypothesis is based on a *test statistic,* which is numerical information provided by the sample. Thus, the hypothesis $H_0$: $\mu$ = 66.9 is an assertion about a population parameter that is tested with a statistic derived from a sample. The numerical result of the sample is referred to as the *test statistic.* If the sample findings disagree with the hypothesis, it is rejected; if they agree, it is not rejected. According to the **criterion of falsifiability,** if the existing evidence does not support the null hypothesis, it is proven false. If it supports the null hypothesis, it does not prove that it is true, only that it is not false.

The research hypothesis is a more specific statement that posits the direction of the difference. In our example, $H_1$ is that the population mean is greater than 66.9. If we find that the sample evidence supports $H_1$, then we conclude that the population mean is greater than 66.9.

How do you know whether you should use the null or a research hypothesis? The decision is up to the researcher, but it is a decision that should be made at the outset of the research, not after the evidence is in. The decision should be based on what is reasonable, given existing knowledge, and what the researcher expects, given the theoretical model driving the research. If the existing evidence is unclear and the direction of the difference cannot be specified given theoretical expectations, the null hypothesis is appropriate. If prior knowledge suggests a direction of difference and it is in agreement with theoretical expectations, a directional hypothesis is the choice. Stating and choosing hypotheses after the data are analyzed is generally considered inappropriate because then the hypotheses did not come about as the result of theoretical speculation, and it may be unethical and subject to bias to state them after the fact.

For the purposes of this text, and for understanding the basics of hypothesis testing with various statistical models, the examples that follow will test both the null and, when appropriate, a directional hypothesis. However, you should understand that when you conduct research, decisions about hypotheses are determined by the issues at hand.

## *Level of Significance*

An important question in testing hypotheses is, How much difference must there be between what is *expected for the population* and what is *observed in the sample* to reject $H_0$ or accept $H_1$? The answer to this question is a function of the **level of significance,** which is the point at which the difference between what is observed and what is expected is too great to be due to chance or random variation.

Assume that you draw a random sample of 30 members from a population presumed to contain half males and half females. Given the distribution of males and females in the population, you expect about an even number of males and females in the sample. However, you would not be surprised if the sample contained 16 males and 14 females or 13 males and 17 females. You would assume that such small sampling variations from the population expectation are due to chance differences in sampling outcomes. However, if the results were 2 males and 28 females, you might feel less comfortable in assuming that the difference in what is expected for the population and observed in the sample is due to chance. If you are satisfied that appropriate sampling procedures were used, you might begin to wonder whether the population expectation is correct. You might conclude that the difference is too great to be due to random variation in sampling outcomes and decide that the population contains fewer males than females.

There is a risk in arriving at this conclusion. A difference, even as great as 2 males and 28 females, may be due to chance. Recall from the discussion of discrete probabilities in Chapter 5 that extreme outcomes, such as 2 males and 28 females, can occur even if they are equal in number in the population. This outcome, if males do equal females, has a very small probability of occurrence, so small that you may feel safe in concluding that the sample results are not due to chance; rather, they are evidence that fewer males than females exist in the population.

As the difference increases between what is expected for the population and what is observed in the sample, the likelihood that the difference is due to chance declines. The level of significance is based on that logic and consists of establishing a level or specific point at which the differences are considered too great to be due to chance.

The level of significance for testing a hypothesis is established by the researcher and consists of setting a point beyond which the sample differs too much from what is expected, given random variation in sample outcomes. The decision recognizes that sampling outcomes will vary somewhat from expectations. A line is drawn between what is considered a small difference and a large difference, that is, between a difference due to chance and one so great that it may not be a chance event, and this indicates a real difference from what was expected.

Small differences from what is expected are those with a high probability of occurrence; that is, they are likely to be observed frequently. Large differences are those with a low probability of occurrence and not likely to be observed. The level of significance then is a *level of probability*. As shown in Figure 7.1, the level of significance divides outcomes into those that are probable and likely due to random variation and those that are improbable and not likely but that represent real differences from what is expected. Improbable outcomes are referred to as *significant* because they differ substantially from what was expected for the population.

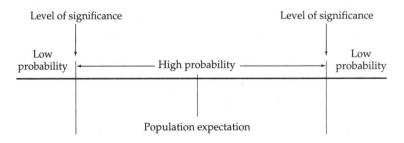

**FIGURE 7.1    Level of Significance: High and Low Probabilities**

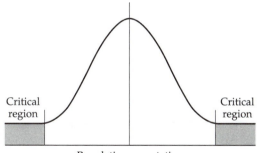

Population expectation

**FIGURE 7.2    The Critical Region for Rejecting the Null Hypothesis**

Deciding whether a sample observation and population expectation differ is based on the probability of the occurrence of the difference. In Chapters 4 and 5 we discussed probability distributions for evaluating outcomes for both continuous and discrete measures. If the assumptions of the theoretical distributions are met, models such as the standard normal distribution and the binomial distribution can be used to determine the probability of sample outcomes.

Figure 7.2 illustrates the level of significance applied to the normal distribution. The midpoint of the distribution represents the population expectation. The vertical lines at the tails of the distribution represent the level of significance, or that point beyond which outcomes are considered too far removed from the mean to be due to chance. The shaded area at either end of the distribution is known as the **critical region.** It is critical because a sample result falling in that area is considered significantly different from what was expected for the population. Note that the critical region is both above and below the mean or the population expectation because sample results may be either less than or greater than the population expectation.

The critical region is also referred to as the **region of rejection** for the null hypothesis because outcomes in the region call for the rejection of $H_0$. In our example, the expectation is that the mean age of the population is 66.9; thus, our null hypothesis is $H_0$: $\mu = 66.9$. If the sample outcome differs too much from the expected population mean, that is, if the probability of the sample outcome falls in the critical region, then $H_0$ will be rejected.

Whereas the critical region is the region of rejection for the null hypothesis, it is the **region of acceptance** for the directional hypothesis. If the outcome is such that it falls in the critical region above the mean, $H_1$: $\mu >$ is accepted; if it falls in the critical region below the mean, $H_1$: $\mu <$ is accepted.

## *Stating the Hypothesis: Example 7.1*

Suppose that we decide to test $H_0$: $\mu = 66.9$ by setting the level of significance at $\alpha = .05$. By establishing the level of significance at .05, we decide that $H_0$ will be

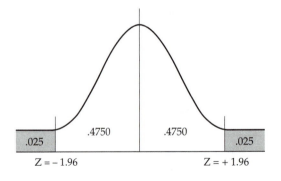

.4750    .4750

.025    .025

Z = − 1.96    Z = + 1.96

**FIGURE 7.3    The Critical Region for the Null Hypothesis: α = .05**

rejected if the sample $\overline{X}$ differs so much from μ = 66.9 that its probability is .05 or less. In other words, $H_0$ will be rejected only if the sample result is so far removed from 66.9 that it occurs only 5 or less out of 100 times.

Figure 7.3 shows the critical region for the .05 level of significance. The area of .05 is equally divided between the two tails of the distribution so that each tail contains .025 of the area of the curve. The reason for dividing .05 equally between the two tails is that $H_0$ is nondirectional. It is proven false if the sample results are either so much less than 66.9 that they occur only .025 or less of the time or so much greater than 66.9 that they occur only .025 or less of the time. Note also that at the .05 level of significance 95% of the area is between the critical regions on the two tails. This means that 95% of the sample results are values that are between the two critical regions on the tails and thus will support $H_0$: μ = 66.9. Because $H_0$ is tested using both the left and the right tails of the curve, it is referred to as a **two-tailed test.** Note also that the .05 two-tailed probability corresponds with a Z score of ±1.96 (see Column C in Table B.1 in Appendix B). This means that any $Z \geq 1.96$ has a two-tailed probability of .05 or beyond.

In our example the expected age for the population was 66.9, but our sample of 75 members had a mean age of 68.3. Given the standard deviation of age in the population, 5.9, is the difference between what we expect and what we observe too great to be due to chance at α = .05? The standard-error-of-the-mean test is used to calculate the probability of the difference and is given by Formula 7.1.

## *Application of the Standard-Error-of-the-Mean Test*

### *Description*

Formula 7.1 shows that the Z score is based on a ratio of the difference between the observed mean age and the expected mean age *to* the variation of age in the population. The size of the Z score is based on whether the difference between what was observed, $\overline{X}$, and what was expected, μ, is large relative to the variation of the measure, $\sigma_{\bar{X}}$. Recall that the standard error of the mean, $\sigma_{\bar{X}}$, is an estimate of how much variability a measure has in the population, as shown in the expansion of Formula 7.1:

$$Z = \frac{\bar{X} - \mu}{\sigma_{\bar{X}}} = \frac{\dfrac{\bar{X} - \mu}{\sigma}}{\sqrt{n}} \qquad (7.1)$$

where          $\bar{X}$ = the observed sample mean

$\mu$ = the hypothesized or expected population mean

$\dfrac{\sigma}{\sqrt{n}}$ = the standard error of the mean, $\sigma_{\bar{X}}$

The test statistic resulting from the formula is a Z score that is used to evaluate the probability of the difference between the observed and the expected values.

Special attention should be given to the conceptual ratio represented by Formula 7.1 because it serves as a general conceptual model for all statistical tests. Statistical tests are organized around ratios of the difference between some observed and expected value *to* the variation of the measure in the population:

$$\frac{\text{Observed sample mean} - \text{Expected population mean}}{\text{Variation in the population}}$$

Ratios resulting in relatively small values suggest that differences are a function simply of the random variation of the measure, whereas relatively large values are seen as differences that go beyond what is anticipated given random variation of the measurement in the population. Although formulas for statistical significance become more complex than Formula 7.1, they are based on the same general ratio. According to Formula 7.1, the test statistic is

$$Z = \frac{68.3 - 66.9}{5.9/\sqrt{75}}$$

$$= \frac{68.3 - 66.9}{5.9/8.66}$$

$$= \frac{1.4}{.68}$$

$$= 2.06$$

The significance of the test statistic, $Z = 2.06$ for the null hypothesis, $H_0 = 66.9$, is determined using the normal probability distribution in Table B.1 in Appendix B. Column C for two-tailed tests in the table shows that $Z = 2.06$ has a two-tailed probability of .0384, which is beyond .05 and falls in the region of rejection for the null hypothesis. Thus, we can reject $H_0$ and accept $H_1$. The conclusion is that given the evidence from the sample, $\bar{X} = 68.3$, the expectation for the population, $\mu = 66.9$, might be inappropriate. The population may be somewhat older than the expected 66.9.

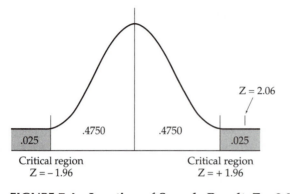

**FIGURE 7.4   Location of Sample Result: Z = 2.06**

Figure 7.4 illustrates the decision. Given that $H_0$ is nondirectional, the critical region for $\alpha = .05$ includes both tails of the distribution with half the area, .025, on the left and half, .025, on the right. Our test statistic of Z = 2.06 is on the right tail of the distribution and, given the two-tailed test, column C in Table B.1 shows it has a probability of .0197, which clearly is in the region of rejection of .025.

From another perspective, the critical region consists of .025 + .025 = .05, which means that 5% of all sample outcomes will result in rejecting $H_0$. Our sample statistic was one that occurred less than 5% of the time. The area between the critical regions, .4750 + .4750 = .9500, shows that 95% of all sample outcomes lead to the acceptance of $H_0$, but that was not true for our sample outcome.

We can also determine the specific probability associated with Z = ±2.06. The two-tailed probability is given in column C of Table B.1 and is .0394, which indicates that a score as extreme or more extreme than Z = ±2.06 will occur only about 3.94% of the time.

The significance of the research hypothesis, $H_1 > 66.9$, is tested using column B of Table B.1 of the normal probability distribution. If we test the one-tailed hypothesis at the .05 level, the Z score associated with the nearest value, .0495 in column B, is 1.65. Our Z = 2.06 is more extreme than 1.65. Column B shows the one-tailed probability of 2.06 to be .0197, which clearly is in the critical region on the right tail of the normal distribution. Note also that the one-tailed probability for 2.06 in column B, .0197, is exactly half a two-tailed probability, .0394, shown in column C. This is always the case because directional probabilities deal with only one tail of the distribution, whereas null (nondirectional) hypotheses deal with both tails. Figure 7.5 illustrates the **one-tailed test**. If $H_1$ is tested at .05, Z = 2.06 with a probability of .0197 is well within the region of acceptance. Again, the exact level of probability for Z = 2.06 is known from column B of the Z-score table. It is .0197, which indicates that a one-tailed difference as extreme or more extreme than Z = 2.06 will occur only 1.97% of the time. We can conclude that the mean age of the population not only differs from 66.9 but also is likely to be higher than 66.9.

The example illustrates statistical decision making for a sample value *greater* than the population expectation. In other situations, of course, the sample result is

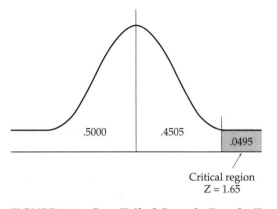

FIGURE 7.5   One-Tailed Sample Result: Z = 2.06

*less* than expected for the population (the Z score has a negative rather than a positive value). In such cases, the observed value is on the left side of the distribution. Figure 7.6 shows the critical regions for directional hypotheses for α = .01. Whether the test statistic is a negative or positive value, if the sample result is greater than the Z score associated with .01, which is 2.33, $H_0$ is rejected and $H_1$ accepted.

Researchers are free to select whatever levels of significance are appropriate to their task, but the level of significance should be selected prior to calculating the test statistic. The assumption is that the level of significance is a function of the theoretical issues at stake and the amount of error appropriate for rejecting $H_0$ and accepting $H_1$. Given that computer software packages for statistical analysis automatically produce the specific probabilities associated with test statistics, they are readily available to researchers. As a result, the focus often is on the actual probability level of the statistic. Although this might be justifiable where the differences are small from a preestablished level of significance, decisions should not be made after the fact.

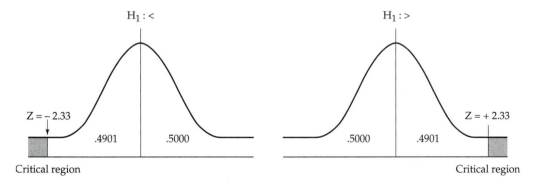

FIGURE 7.6   Critical Regions for One-Tailed Test When α = .01

**TABLE 7.1    Levels of Significance and Their Z Scores**

| α | One-Tailed Hypothesis | Two-Tailed Hypothesis |
|---|---|---|
| .05 | 1.65 | 1.96 |
| .01 | 2.33 | 2.58 |

Statistically significant results indicate only that, given some level of significance, they are not due to chance or to random variation associated with sample outcomes. Statistical significance should not be confused with substantive significance, that is, whether the result is important. Whether something is substantively significant is a function of its importance in the context of some meaningful set of relationships.

The most frequently used levels of significance in social research are .01 and .05. Although nothing is sacred about these levels, they are convenient, and it is helpful to remember the Z scores associated with them, shown in Table 7.1. Given that the probabilities of Z scores associated with one- and two-tailed hypotheses for .01 and .05 levels of significance are easy to remember, an alternative method for making decisions about hypotheses can be used. For example, any two-tailed hypothesis can be rejected at the .05 level if you have a $Z \geq \pm 1.96$. In our example, on finding $Z = 2.06$, given that it is greater than 1.96, $H_0$ can be rejected because we know that a value of 2.06 will be farther out on the tail of the curve than 1.96. Similarly, $H_0$ can be rejected at the .01 level for any Z value equal to or greater than $\pm 2.58$. For a one-tailed test, any value equal to or greater than $\pm 1.65$ allows for acceptance at .05, and a Z score equal to or greater than $\pm 2.33$ is required to accept a one-tailed hypothesis at the .01 level.

Conceptually, the test statistic resulting from the standard-error-of-the-mean test indicates that the ratio of the difference between the observed sample mean and the expected population mean *to* the standard error (the variation of the measure in the population) is too great to be due to chance.

The use of one- and two-tailed hypotheses may seem confusing at first, but in practice they are readily distinguished. Hypotheses containing an = sign are nondirectional and require two-tailed tests. Those using < or > signs are directional and use one-tailed tests.

## Summary

The standard-error-of-the-mean test is used to assess the difference between an observed sample mean and an expected or known population mean. The test can be used only when the population parameter, μ, and σ are known. The test statistic used to estimate the difference between $\overline{X}$ and μ is a Z score that can be interpreted using the normal probability distribution. However, to ensure that the assumptions of the central limit theorem apply, the sample must be $\geq 30$. The following is a summary of the requirements that must be met to use the standard-error-of-the-mean test:

1. The variable must consist of an interval measure, $n \geq 30$.
2. The population value $\sigma$ must be known.
3. The distribution of the variable in the population must be normal in form.

## THE RISK OF ERROR

In our example, we rejected $H_0$: $\mu = 66.9$ because our sample of 75 members had a mean age of 68.3, which was greater than expected given the variation of age in the population. We concluded that the difference between our sample observation and the population expectation was too great to be due to chance. In fact, if the population mean actually were 66.9, the two-tailed probability of a sample mean as extreme or more extreme than 68.3 is less than .0394. We decided that if the result had a probability less than .05, $H_0$ would be rejected. However, our decision to reject $H_0$ could be wrong. In fact, every time you make a decision regarding $H_0$ at a chosen level of probability, you run the risk of making an error.

Two types of error can occur. The first occurs whenever $H_0$ is rejected; it is known as the risk of a **Type I error** and consists of rejecting $H_0$ as false when it is true. It also consists of deciding that the difference between what is observed and what is expected is too great to be due to chance when the difference is in fact due to chance. Type I errors are also referred to as **alpha errors** and are symbolized by $\alpha$.

The second type of error occurs whenever $H_0$ is accepted; it is known as a **Type II error** and consists of accepting $H_0$, when it is false. The error rests in deciding that the difference between what is observed and what is expected is due to chance, when it is not. Type II errors, also referred to as **beta errors,** are symbolized by $\beta$.

Table 7.2 illustrates the relationship of the two types of errors. The column headings of the table show the decision that *was* made, whereas the row titles show the decision that *should have been* made. The body of the table also indicates the decisions that are correct and those that are in error.

The difficulty is that there is no way of knowing whether you have made the correct decision. The only way you can be certain is to know the actual values for the population, which usually are unknown. Indeed, that is what you are trying to estimate with your sample.

In our example, we decided to test $H_0$ at $\alpha = .05$. The two-tailed probability associated with our $Z = 2.06$ was .0394, which is more extreme than .05, so we rejected $H_0$. We concluded that the difference in the mean age of the sample and the expected age for the population was too great to be due to chance. However, there is a risk that the conclusion is wrong because there is a chance (or probability) of observing a sample outcome as extreme as 68.3 even if the population mean is 66.9. The Z score of 2.06 has a two-tailed probability of .0394, which is less than our level of significance, .05. The value also informs us that 3.94% of sample

TABLE 7.2    **Type I and Type II Errors for the Null Hypothesis**

|  | $H_0$ Rejected | $H_0$ Accepted |
|---|---|---|
| $H_0$ should be accepted | Type I ($\alpha$) error | Correct decision |
| $H_0$ should be rejected | Correct decision | Type II ($\beta$) error |

outcomes can result in Z scores as large or larger than 2.06 when the population mean actually is 66.9. Nevertheless, we decided to risk a Type I error at the .05 level and concluded that a difference so great that it occurred 5% or less of the time was not due to chance.

Our decision to reject $H_0$ exposed us to the risk of a Type I error. In fact, every time $H_0$ is rejected, there is a risk of the Type I error because extreme outcomes have some probability of happening by chance. The risk of a Type I error is equal to the level of significance, $\alpha$, because $H_0$ is rejected only when the sample statistic is in the region of rejection established by $\alpha$.

Although you can never be certain whether a decision is correct, you can *minimize* the risk of being wrong. When the level of significance is .05, only the 5% most extreme outcomes will lead to the rejection of $H_0$, and a Type I error is risked only 5% of the time. Given that the risk of a Type I error is equal to $\alpha$, it can be reduced simply by moving the level of significance out farther on the tail of the curve. If $\alpha$ = .02, there is only a 2% chance of a Type I error, and if $\alpha$ = .01, the chance is reduced to 1%.

Whereas moving the level of significance farther out on the tail *decreases* the risk of a Type I error, it *increases* the risk of a Type II error. Type II errors occur when $H_0$ should be rejected but is accepted. Thus, a more extreme level of significance makes it more difficult to reject $H_0$, thereby increasing the risk of a Type II error.

A Type II error consists of failing to recognize differences that are significant, that is, differences that are not due to chance but that are real differences. If we had set our level of significance at $\alpha$ = .01, according to Table 7.1 a Z score of 2.58 or larger would have been required to reject $H_0$. Our Z = 2.06, and at the .01 level of significance we would have accepted $H_0$ and risked the error of concluding that the population age did not differ from 66.9 when it actually does. However, if there is no sampling error and our sample result of 68.3 is actually correct, the appropriate conclusion is that the population age is not equal to 66.9.

The character of a Type II error can be illustrated with another example. Suppose that I invite you to engage in a coin-tossing game in which I win with heads and you win with tails. Before beginning, we decide to test the fairness of the coin by tossing it 30 times to make sure that it comes out about half heads and half tails. If the outcome were 25 heads and 5 tails, you might insist on using another coin because the large difference between what you expected and observed seems too great to be due to chance. The outcome suggests that, in the long run, there is a good possibility that heads will come up more often than tails. However, if the outcome of the 30 tosses is 16 heads and 14 tails, you would be less likely to question the fairness of the coin because the difference between what you expect and what you observe is small. You would likely conclude that the small difference is due to chance, but that conclusion could be wrong! If the coin is slightly biased in favor of heads, so slight that it favors heads by only 16 to 14 tails out of 30 tosses, and if the slight difference is consistent, you will lose in the long run. The risk of a Type II error consists of ignoring real and persistent differences, assuming that the differences are due to chance when in fact they are real. This is most likely to happen when the difference between what is observed and what is expected is small.

Avoiding a Type II error depends on distinguishing significant differences, whether large or small, that are consistent. Of course, it is difficult to distinguish between a real and a chance difference, especially when the difference is small. You are less likely to make a Type II error (i.e., to accept $H_0$) when you have a large difference because it is so far out on the tails of the distribution.

The means for guarding against a Type II error go beyond the considerations of an introductory text such as this one, but it is helpful to have a conceptual perspective of the problem. The risk of a Type II error is a function of the *power* of a sample statistic. A powerful statistic is one that makes it possible to distinguish small but persistent differences; that is, it allows you to reject $H_0$ even when the difference between what is observed and what is expected is small. At least three factors bear on the power of a statistic:[3]

1.  The level of significance is important. An extreme level of significance, .01, as opposed to .05, makes it more difficult to reject $H_0$, thus increasing the risk of a Type II error. A less extreme level of significance, .10 rather than .05 or .01, decreases the risk of a Type II error, leading to the conclusion that a difference is real and not due to chance.
2.  The reliability of the sample is important. A reliable sample is one with relatively little variation. Recall from Chapter 6 that the standard error provides us with a measure of sampling variability. Generally, large samples result in smaller standard errors; thus, variables with larger amounts of variation in the population should be addressed with larger samples. That will increase the accuracy of the sample estimate and provide protection against a Type II error.
3.  The size of the difference between the observed outcome and the expected outcome is important. If the difference is large (e.g., 28 heads out of 30 tosses), the risk of concluding that there is a difference is fairly safe and the risk of a Type II error small. However, when differences are small (e.g., 13 or 14 heads out of 30 tosses), the risk of a Type II error increases because it seems appropriate to conclude that no difference exists when really it might.

---

[3] For a detailed discussion of the concept of power in statistical testing, see Jacob Cohen, *Statistical Power Analysis for the Behavioral Sciences* (Hillsdale, N.J.: Lawrence Erlbaum Associates, 1988).

Although it might be an oversimplification to say so, a sample statistic is powerful, and a Type II error is minimized to the extent that the level of significance is not too extreme for the problem at hand; the sample is large relative to the standard error, and the difference between what is expected and what is observed is fairly large.

The trade-offs between a Type I and a Type II error have real implications in the world of everyday research. Generally, under laboratory and experimental conditions, the goal is to guard against a Type I error. In such settings, researchers want to avoid making the claim of a new discovery unless great certainty exists that the finding is real. This means that more extreme levels of significance are used. Type I errors are also of concern if the research has serious or life-threatening implications. Thus, high levels of certainty, such as .01, .001, and even .0001, are required to minimize the potential of negative effects in life-and-death decisions. For example, the risk of negative reactions to a new drug must be minimized, and the primary concern is to avoid a Type I error.

In other situations, such as evaluations of social interventions, the risk of a Type II error may be of greater concern. Using extreme levels of significance to judge whether a social intervention has an effect might result in the discontinuation of activities that have some good effects, although not dramatic ones. Social interventions are focused often on relatively intractable and complicated social problems, and to expect dramatic results (i.e., huge differences) might be looking for miracles. Expecting small differences from such interventions might be more realistic. Under these conditions, levels of significance such as .05, .10, or even .15 might be more appropriate. However, you must remember that in using less extreme levels of significance, the likelihood of the differences being due to chance increases.

Hypothesis testing is further illustrated with one-sample tests for three types of situations: Student's $t$ test, for comparing sample outcomes with known or expected population parameters; the standard-error-of-proportions test; and the chi-square test. All these are used to compare observed sample outcomes with expected or known population parameters.

## STUDENT'S t TEST: ONE SAMPLE

### Description

Student's $t$ test is used to determine the fit between $\overline{X}$ and $\mu$ when the variance of the population, $\sigma$, is unknown and $\dfrac{s}{\sqrt{n-1}}$ rather than $\dfrac{\sigma}{\sqrt{n}}$ must be used to estimate the standard error. The test statistic is calculated using the following formula:

$$t = \frac{\overline{X} - \mu}{\dfrac{s}{\sqrt{n-1}}} \tag{7.2}$$

where          $\overline{X}$ = the observed sample mean

$\mu$ = the known or expected population mean

$s$ = the standard deviation of the sample

$\dfrac{s}{\sqrt{n-1}}$ = the standard error of the mean, $\sigma_{\bar{x}}$

As in the case of the standard-error-of-the-mean test, the $t$ test is based on a ratio. The Student's $t$ is the ratio of the difference between the sample mean and the population mean *to* the standard error of the mean. Conceptually, it is the same model as the standard-error-of-the-mean test. It is equal to

$$\frac{\text{Observed mean} - \text{Expected mean}}{\text{Standard error}}$$

For the test statistic to be significant, the difference between the sample mean and the population mean in the numerator must be so large that it exceeds the variation expected for the variable, which is given by the standard error in the denominator.

Both null and directional hypotheses can be tested with Student's $t$ test. The general form of the hypotheses is the same as for the standard-error-of-the-mean test:

$H_0$: $\mu$ = some specified parameter
$H_1$: $\mu$ < or $\mu$ > some specified parameter

## Example 7.2

City Hall of Metrocity was criticized because the city had a higher rate of serious crimes over the years than was true for the nation. Information on violent crimes showed that over the past 20 years the city had an average of 399.40 violent crimes per 100,000 inhabitants with a standard deviation of 8.93. The national average over the same time period was 394.82. City Hall responded that although the rate was somewhat higher for Metrocity than the nation, the difference was not significant but due to chance variation. The goodness of fit between Metrocity and the national average was tested to settle the matter. The hypotheses are

$H_0$: $\mu$ = 394.82     The population mean does not differ from 394.82.
$H_1$: $\mu$ > 394.82     The population mean is greater than 394.82.

The null hypothesis states that the population mean is equal to (or does not differ from) the expected value of 394.82. The directional hypothesis indicates that if the nation is like Metrocity, the population mean is greater than 394.82. In both cases the hypotheses are statements about the population parameter and will be tested at the .05 level of significance.

In summary, the data are

$n = 20$
$\mu = 394.82$
$\overline{X} = 399.40$
$s = 8.93$
$\alpha = .05$

According to Formula 7.2, the test statistic is

$$t = \frac{399.40 - 394.82}{8.93/\sqrt{20-1}}$$

$$= \frac{4.58}{8.93/4.36}$$

$$= \frac{4.58}{2.05}$$

$$= 2.234$$

The test statistic for Student's $t$ is evaluated using the $t$ distribution. Gosset's formulation that $\dfrac{s}{\sqrt{n-1}}$ provides a good estimate of $\dfrac{\sigma}{\sqrt{n}}$ is accompanied by a distribution of $t$ values. Like the normal probability distribution, the distribution of $t$ values makes it possible to determine the probability of any $t$ score. However, whereas the Z distribution has a single bell-shaped form, $t$ values are represented by a family of distributions that vary, depending on the size of the sample. This means that the probability of $t$ values is adjusted according to sample size.

Sample size is taken into account using the **degrees of freedom** of a distribution, symbolized by df. The degrees of freedom for a given distribution are equal to the number of values that are free to vary in that distribution without changing the sum of the distribution. Suppose that you have a distribution of five values and you know that the sum of the distribution equals 90. If you assign four of the five values—15, 20, 25, and 20—the fifth value is not free to vary but must be equal to what is needed to achieve the sum of 90. Given the four values, 15 + 20 + 25 + 20 = 80, and the sum 90, the fifth value must equal 10. The point is that only four of the five values in the distribution are free to vary. Once you assign four values, the fifth must be whatever it needs to be to produce the sum of 90. In general, the degrees of freedom for the distribution of a single variable (a univariate distribution) is equal to $n - 1$.

The practical implication of using degrees of freedom is that reducing the sample size by 1 increases the size of the standard error term in the denominator, with the net effect of a smaller $t$ value. Using $n - 1$ has the greatest effect on small samples, so it guards against underestimating the standard error, which would result in an inflated $t$ value when small samples are used.

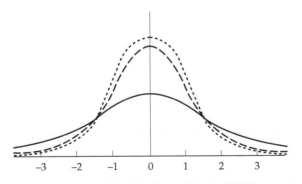

**FIGURE 7.7** *t* **Distribution: df = Solid Line = 2; Broken Line = 12; Dashed Line = 120**

The exact form of the distribution of *t* values changes with the degrees of freedom and sample size. When *n* and df are small, the distribution is flatter and the tails thicker, or farther from the abscissa. As *n* and its related degrees of freedom become large, the distribution approaches that of the normal curve. Figure 7.7 shows the form of the distribution for df = 2, 12, and 120. When df becomes larger than 120, the *t* distribution becomes indistinguishable from the normal probability distribution.

The *t* distribution is presented in Table B.3 in Appendix B. The left-hand column contains the degrees of freedom, whereas the column heads contain selected levels of significance for one- and two-tailed tests. The decision rule for the table is as follows: If the computed *t* value is equal to or larger than the table value at the intersect of the appropriate degrees of freedom and level of significance, reject the null hypothesis and accept the directional hypothesis. In our example, the sample of 20 years of serious crime rates resulted in the test statistic, *t* = 2.234. The degrees of freedom are df = *n* − 1 = 20 − 1 = 19. Given our level of significance at α = .05, the value in Table B.3 at the intersect of df = 19 and .05 is 2.093. Our test statistic of 2.234 is larger than 2.093, so the null hypothesis is rejected and the directional hypothesis accepted. The results indicate that Metrocity's violent crime rate of 399.40 is not a good fit to the national average of 394.82. The difference between the two is not due to chance but suggests that Metrocity has a higher serious crime rate than the nation as a whole.

However, we are soon reminded of the potential for error in making decisions about hypotheses. By rejecting $H_0$, we risk a Type I error; that is, we risk concluding that a real difference exists in serious crime rates between Metrocity and the nation when the difference may be due only to chance variation in sampling results. If we had set our level of significance at α = .01, with 19 degrees of freedom, a test statistic of 2.861 would be required to reject $H_0$. Given our *t* = 2.234, we could not reject $H_0$, and at the .01 level of significance we would avoid the Type I error. However, by avoiding the Type I error, we risk a Type II error, which consists of failing to recognize a difference when there is one. Given our example, it seems reasonable to accept the risk of a Type I error at $\alpha = .05$ and conclude that City Hall of Metrocity should be concerned about the city's high rate of violent crimes.

If you examine Table B.3 in Appendix B, you will find that for a given level of significance (e.g., .05), as the degrees of freedom increase, the table value at the intersect decreases. Thus, when df = 2, the value at the intersect is 4.303, and to reject the null hypothesis, the test statistic must be equal to or greater than 4.303. When df = 12, the value at the intersect is 2.179; when df = 28, the value is 2.048; and when df > 120, the table value is 1.96. The 1.96 value corresponds to the Z value for a two-tailed probability of .05 showing that the $t$ distribution approximates the normal curve when $n \geq 120$.

## Summary

Student's $t$ test is used to test the fit of an observed sample mean to a population mean when the population variance, $\sigma$, is unknown and only the variance of the sample, $s$, is available. Because the $t$ distribution is adjusted for sample size through the use of degrees of freedom, the $t$ test can be used for very small samples. The $t$ test requires the following:

1. The variable must be an interval measure.
2. The form of the distribution of the variable in the population must be normal.
3. The test can be used for small samples.

# THE STANDARD-ERROR-OF-PROPORTIONS TEST: ONE SAMPLE

## Description

The standard-error-of-proportions test is an extension of the binomial discussed in Chapter 5. It is used to evaluate the fit of a sample proportion to a population proportion. The test is an approximation to the normal distribution and is used as an alternative to the binomial test when $np$ and $nq \geq 10$. The test statistic is a Z score derived by calculating the ratio of the difference between the sample and population proportion *to* the standard error of proportions. The test is based on the same conceptual model as the standard-error-of-the-mean test and Student's $t$:

$$\frac{\text{Observed sample proportion} - \text{Expected population proportion}}{\text{Standard error of the proportion}}$$

A significant result occurs when the difference between the observed sample proportion and the expected population proportion exceeds what would be expected, given the variation of the measure in the population as estimated by the standard error for a proportion.

The test is based on the assumption that the distribution of the variable is binomial and that, given the statistic is a Z score, the distribution must approximate a normal form, which is the case when $np$ and $nq \geq 10$. The formula is as follows:

$$Z = \frac{p - P}{\sqrt{PQ/n}} \qquad (7.3)$$

where     $p - P$ = the difference between the sample and population proportions

                $P$ = the proportion of one of the binomial outcomes in the population

         $\sqrt{PQ/n}$ = standard error of the proportion

              $Q = 1 - P$, the proportion of the other binomial outcome in the population

The test can be used for both the null and the directional hypotheses, which take the form of

$H_0$: $P$ = some specified proportion
$H_1$: $P <$ or $P >$ some specified proportion

## Example 7.3

The State Department of Mental Health deinstitutionalized 1,500 mental health patients. It was expected that 25% would return for further inpatient care within one year of deinstitutionalization. A random sample of 200 patients was followed to evaluate the return rate during the first year. It was found that 32% returned for inpatient treatment. Did the 32% represent a good fit to the expectation that 25% of the population would return? The fit between the observed and the expected proportion will be tested at $\alpha = .05$. The data are

    $n = 200$
    $p = .32$
    $P = .25$
    $Q = .75 \ (1 - P)$
    $\alpha = .05$

The hypotheses consist of statements about the expected population parameter:

$H_0$: $P = .25$       The population proportion does not differ from .25.
$H_1$: $P > .25$       The population proportion is greater than .25.

According to Formula 7.3, the test statistic is

$$Z = \frac{.32 - .25}{\sqrt{(.25)(.75)/200}}$$

$$= \frac{.07}{\sqrt{.00094}}$$

$$= \frac{.07}{.031}$$

$$= 2.26$$

The Z score is evaluated using Table B.1 in Appendix B. We know that for $\alpha$ = .05, a Z score of 1.96 or greater is required to reject the null hypothesis and accept the directional hypothesis. The Z score of 2.26 is greater than 1.96, enabling us to reject $H_0$ and accept $H_1$. The exact probability of Z = 2.26 for a two-tailed probability is given in column C of Table B.1 (.0238); column B shows that the one-tailed probability is .0119. It can be concluded that more patients returned for inpatient services during the first year than expected.

## Summary

The standard-error-of-proportions test is used to evaluate the fit of an observed sample proportion to an expected population proportion. As an extension of the binomial test, it represents a good approximation to the normal distribution when both $np$ and $nq \geq 10$. As such, it is a powerful alternative to Student's $t$ test.[4] In sum, the standard-error-of-proportions test is used for dichotomous nominal measures and used when both $np$ and $nq \geq 10$.

# CHI-SQUARE: A ONE-SAMPLE TEST FOR NOMINAL DATA

## Description

The chi-square test ($\chi^2$) is used to evaluate whether a distribution of observations on a nominal measure fits some expected distribution for the population. The chi-square test is an extension of the binomial test (used for dichotomous measures) to multinomial measures. In using the binomial test, we evaluate the probability of a particular set of observed $p$ and $q$ outcomes against some expectation for the population. For example, if the expectation for the population is that $P = Q$, the observed $p$ outcomes should be approximately equal to $q$ outcomes. If not, the

---

[4] The power of a test relates to sample size and the capacity to identify small but significant differences. A powerful test is more likely to detect differences with a smaller sample than a less powerful one. Although the discussion of power goes beyond an introductory text such as this one, it is important to have a sense of the relative power of various tests. The criterion is the $t$ test, which generally has the greatest power, but its use is restricted to interval measures that are normally distributed. Less powerful alternatives must be used when the assumptions for the $t$ test are not met.

observed outcomes are not a good fit to the population expectation. However, the binomial is limited in that it can be used only for dichotomous nominal measures.

The chi-square test makes it possible to evaluate the probability of outcomes for multinomial categories. It is based on the ratio of the difference between the observed distribution of a sample across nominal categories and the expected distribution for the population *to* the expected variation across the categories. Again, the same conceptual model is used:

$$\frac{\text{Observed distribution} - \text{Expected distribution}}{\text{Expected variation}}$$

The formula for chi-square is

$$\chi^2 = \sum_{i=1}^{k} \frac{\left(O_i - E_i\right)^2}{E_i} \tag{7.4}$$

where     $O_i$ = the observed frequency for a given category

$E_i$ = the expected frequency for the category

The formula shows that the test statistic is obtained by squaring the difference between the sample observation and the population expectation for each scale category and dividing the squared difference by the number expected for the category. Then the resulting values for each category are summed to obtain the chi-square value.

The chi-square test is distribution free, meaning that it makes no assumptions about the form or shape of the distribution. It is somewhat restrictive in terms of sample size in that none of the categories can have expected frequencies equal to zero and no more than 20% of the categories can have expectations less than 5. The test also assumes that each observation is independent, meaning that each sample member can contribute to one and only one category of the measure. Chi-square can be used only to test the null hypothesis. Given that the underlying measurement is nominal and that the categories have no inherent sense of direction or order, a directional hypothesis is not possible. The general form of the null hypothesis is

$H_0$: The observed distribution of the sample across the scale categories
       does not differ from the expected.

## Example 7.4

Six social science departments at State University had faculties of about equal size (Table 7.3). The departments decided to collaborate in developing a behavioral research center. It was assumed that equal numbers of faculty would participate from each of the six departments. The table shows the number of faculty participating from each of the departments at the beginning of the third year of the venture.

TABLE 7.3   Participation in the Behavioral Science Center

| Department | Observed | Expected |
|---|---|---|
| Anthropology | 12 | 12 |
| Economics | 6 | 12 |
| Political science | 9 | 12 |
| Psychology | 10 | 12 |
| Social psychology | 19 | 12 |
| Sociology | 16 | 12 |
| | 72 | 72 |

The null hypothesis for chi-square is a statement about the general form of the distribution of observations across the scale categories. In the example, we assume that equal numbers of faculty from the various departments would participate in the behavioral science center. Thus, the null hypothesis is

$H_0$:   There is no difference in the participation of faculty from various departments in the behavioral science center.

Given the assumption that departments will be equally represented, it is expected that about $72/6 = 12$ members will participate from each department. Table 7.3 shows that there is some variation between what was observed and what was expected. Of course, the variation could be due to chance. We assess the hypothesis at $\alpha = .05$.

Table 7.4 provides a format for calculating the chi-square statistic. Column 1 shows the department categories; column $O_i$ is the observed number of faculty actually participating from each department; column $E_i$ shows the expected number, which is 12; $O_i - E_i$ shows the difference between what was expected and observed for each department; $(O_i - E_i)^2$ is the differences squared; $(O_i - E_i)^2/E_i$ is the squared difference divided by the expectation for each department; and the sum of the latter is the chi-square statistic. Table 7.4 shows that $\chi^2 = 9.49$.

The test statistic, $\chi^2 = 9.49$, is interpreted using the chi-square distribution shown in Table B.4 in Appendix B. Like Student's $t$, chi-square is a family of distributions based on sample size and the associated degrees of freedom. The degrees of freedom for chi-square equals $k - 1$, where $k$ refers to the number of categories in the nominal scale. In our example, the scale had six categories, so df $= 6 - 1 = 5$.

Table B.4 contains the degrees of freedom in the left-hand column and the levels of significance in the column heads. The test statistic is compared to the value at the intersect of the appropriate degrees of freedom and level of significance. The decision rule for Table B.4 is as follows: If the computed $\chi^2$ value is greater than the table value, reject $H_0$. Given the decision to test $H_0$ at $\alpha = .05$ and df $= 5$, our test statistic must exceed the table value of 11.07 in order to reject $H_0$. Our $\chi^2 = 9.49$ is less than 11.07, so $H_0$ cannot be rejected. The conclusion is that the variation in participation between the departments is due to chance and that the differences are not significant.

TABLE 7.4  **Participation in the Behavioral Science Center: Format for Calculating Chi-Square**

| Department | $O_i$ | $E_i$ | $O_i - E_i$ | $(O_i - E_i)^2$ | $(O_i - E_i)^2/E_i$ |
|---|---|---|---|---|---|
| Anthropology | 12 | 12 | 0.00 | 0 | 0.00 |
| Economics | 6 | 12 | −6.00 | 36 | 3.00 |
| Political science | 9 | 12 | −3.00 | 9 | .75 |
| Psychology | 10 | 12 | −2.00 | 4 | .33 |
| Social psychology | 19 | 12 | 7.00 | 49 | 4.08 |
| Sociology | 16 | 12 | 4.00 | 16 | 1.33 |
|  | 72 |  |  |  | $\chi^2 = 9.49$ |

## Summary

The chi-square test is used to assess the goodness of fit of a nominal measure with more than two categories. Although the test is useful for nominal measures, the value of $\chi^2$ is sensitive to sample size. Cautions have already been noted for small samples so that none of the scale categories can have 0 and no more than 20% can have less than five expected entries. In addition, the test is affected by large samples. Table 7.5 illustrates the problem by presenting two samples of different size but with identical proportions in the categories. Although sample A has 30 members and sample B has 90, the expected cells for each of the samples contain one-third of the sample members. Thus, the proportion expected for each scale category is identical for the two samples. However, in the case of sample A with 30 members, $\chi^2 = 5.0$, and with df = 2 it is not significant at $\alpha = .05$. Sample B, with 90 members, has a $\chi^2 = 15.0$, which is significant at the .05 level.

TABLE 7.5  **Sample Size and Chi-Square**

| Scale Category | $O_i$ | $E_i$ | $(O_i - E_i)^2/E_i$ |
|---|---|---|---|
| **Sample A ($n = 30$)** | | | |
| 1 | 5 | 10 | 2.5 |
| 2 | 10 | 10 | 0 |
| 3 | 15 | 10 | 2.5 |
|  | 30 |  | $\chi^2 = 5.0$ |
| **Sample B ($n = 90$)** | | | |
| 1 | 15 | 30 | 7.5 |
| 2 | 30 | 30 | 0 |
| 3 | 45 | 30 | 7.5 |
|  | 90 |  | $\chi^2 = 15.0$ |

The greater likelihood of significant outcomes with larger samples is in keeping with the logic of statistical testing. Differences are more likely to be significant with large samples than with small ones. This is true because the size of the difference is divided by the estimate of the standard error, and the larger the sample, the smaller the standard error and the more likely a significant difference. Carrying the logic to an extreme, if a sample is so large that it includes the entire population, any difference, however small, is significant; it is real. Thus, all test statistics are affected by sample size, but in the case of $\chi^2$ the relationship is somewhat more exaggerated. The point is that statistically significant findings must always be evaluated in terms of the substantive meaning of the size of the difference. In sum, the requirements for $\chi^2$ are as follows:

1. The minimum sample size must be such that no scale categories have zero entries and no more than 20% have less than five.
2. The distribution of the variable in the population across the scale categories must be specified.
3. The test provides for only a two-tailed test of significance.

## COMPUTER EXERCISES: SOME SUGGESTIONS

Learning to use software to test hypotheses is central to an introductory statistics course. Initial exercises on hypothesis testing also provide the opportunity to interpret printouts related to tests of significance. Although working the problem sets at the end of the chapter requires the use of statistical tables showing the probabilities of outcomes, a computer printout can not only provide the test statistic but also the exact level of its probability.

One way to develop exercises for one-sample tests is to draw a sample from the data set and then test the differences between the sample statistics and the data set where the total data set is the population. The exercise should include tests for interval, dichotomous, and multi-categorical nominal data. It is also important to write up the results, including a statement of the hypothesis and interpretation of the results. The exercises will provide an opportunity to examine the printout for Student's *t* test, the standard-error-of-proportions test, and chi-square.

## CHAPTER SUMMARY

Hypotheses are the axis around which scientific decision making revolves. They are statements that organize and specify presumed relationships in the world of observation. This chapter has reviewed the way in which hypotheses are used in social research. It is important to remember that they are statements about population parameters evaluated with sample statistics. Whereas the null hypothesis proposes that no difference exists between a population expectation and a sample statistic, the directional hypothesis both states that a difference does exist and indicates the direction of that difference.

Decisions about hypotheses are based on the use of levels of significance, which specify the point at which the difference between an expected population parameter and an observed sample statistic is too great to be due to chance. Chance differences are those that reflect random variation in sample outcomes. Two errors can be made in rejecting or accepting a hypothesis. Type I errors consist of rejecting $H_0$ when it should be accepted, whereas Type II errors involve accepting $H_0$ when it should be rejected. The two errors are not independent. In minimizing one you increase the hazard of the other. The only real safeguard for minimizing either error is to use sampling methods that provide good representations of the population and samples of a size commensurate with the standard error of the measurements.

Hypothesis testing was illustrated with four examples. The first, the standard-error-of-the-mean test, is used to evaluate the difference between an observed sample mean and an expected population mean when the standard deviation of the population is known. The second, Student's $t$ test, is used for comparing sample and population means when only the standard deviation of the sample is available. The third, the standard-error-of-proportions test, is used to evaluate hypotheses related to observed sample proportions and expected population proportions. The fourth, chi-square, is used for nominal measures with more than two categories. The four statistical tests in this chapter are known as one-sample tests because they evaluate the tenability of a population parameter on the basis of information from a sample. In the next two chapters, hypothesis testing is illustrated for two-sample tests, which are used to evaluate the similarity between two population parameters.

## KEY TERMS

**alpha error**   Rejecting the null hypothesis when it should be accepted; also known as a Type I error.

**beta error**   Accepting the null hypothesis when it should be rejected; also known as a Type II error.

**chi-square test**   A test used to evaluate the significance of the goodness of fit of multiple nominal categories.

**criterion of falsifiability**   Things can be proven false, but it is difficult if not impossible to prove things true.

**critical region**   The area of the curve defined by the level of significance that leads to the rejection of the null hypothesis and the acceptance of the directional hypothesis.

**degrees of freedom**   For a univariate distribution, the number of values that can vary in the distribution while maintaining the sum of the distribution.

**directional hypothesis**   A hypothesis that states the direction of the difference, such as less than or greater than.

**hypothesis**   An assertion subject to verification.

**level of significance**   The level of probability at which sample results are no longer seen as due to chance variation in sampling outcomes.

**null hypothesis**   The statement of "no difference" from what is expected for a population.

**one-tailed test**   A test focusing on the left or right tail of the distribution.

**region of acceptance**   The area of the normal curve defined by the level of significance for accepting the directional hypothesis.

**region of rejection**   The area of the normal curve defined by the level of significance in which the null hypothesis is rejected.

**standard-error-of-the-mean test**   A test used to evaluate the fit between a sample and a population mean. The standard deviation for the population must be known.

**standard-error-of-proportions test**   A test used to determine whether the sample proportion verifies a known or expected population proportion.

**statistical hypothesis**   A statement about a population parameter that can be verified with a sample statistic.

**Student's *t* test**   A test used to assess the difference between a sample and population mean when only the standard deviation of the sample is available.

**two-tailed test**   A test of the null hypothesis that is nondirectional and includes both the left and right tails of the distribution.

**Type I error**   Rejecting the null hypothesis as false when it should be accepted; also known as the alpha error.

**Type II error**   Accepting the null hypothesis as true when it should be rejected as false; also known as the beta error.

## *SYMBOLS*

| | |
|---|---|
| $\alpha$ | The level of significance |
| $\alpha$ error | Alpha (Type I) error |
| $\beta$ error | Beta (Type II) error |
| df | Degrees of freedom |
| $H_0$ | Null hypothesis |
| $H_1$ | Directional hypothesis |
| $P, Q$ | Population proportions for a dichotomous measure |
| $p, q$ | Sample proportions for a dichotomous measure |
| $t$ | Student's $t$ statistic |
| $\chi^2$ | Chi-square statistic |

## FORMULAS

$$Z = \frac{\overline{X} - \mu}{\sigma / \sqrt{n}}$$    Standard-error-of-the-mean test

$$t = \frac{\overline{X} - \mu}{s / \sqrt{n - 1}}$$    Student's $t$ test

$$Z = \frac{p - P}{\sqrt{PQ / n}}$$    Standard-error-of-proportions test

$$\chi^2 = \sum_{i=1}^{k} \frac{\left(O_i - E_i\right)^2}{E_i}$$    Chi-square test

## EXERCISES

1. What implications does the criterion of falsifiability have for testing the null and the directional hypotheses?

2. Use the diagram of the normal curve to illustrate the critical region for testing $H_0$ at $\alpha = .05$.

3. Use the diagram of the normal curve to illustrate the critical region for testing $H_0$ at $\alpha = .01$.

4. Use the diagram of the normal curve to illustrate the critical region for testing a directional hypothesis at $\alpha = .05$.

5. What proportion of the area of the normal curve is in the critical region for $Z = \pm 2.38$?

6. What proportion of the area of the normal curve is in the critical region for $Z = +2.38$?

7. What proportion of the area of the normal curve is in the critical region for $Z = \pm 1.93$?

8. What proportion of the area of the normal curve is in the critical region for $Z = -2.46$?

9. What proportion of the area of the normal curve is in the critical region for $Z = +1.72$?

10. A sample of 75 members was selected and found to have a mean test score of 120. The population mean was known to be 122, and the population standard deviation was 15.

    a. Which test is appropriate for evaluating the goodness of fit between the sample and population means?
    b. State a null hypothesis.
    c. If appropriate, state a directional hypothesis.
    d. What is the value of the test statistic?

**e.** What is your decision regarding $H_0$ at $\alpha = .05$?

**f.** If appropriate, what do you do with $H_1$ at $\alpha = .05$?

**g.** What can you say about the goodness of fit?

**h.** What was the risk of a Type I error?

11. The sample in exercise 10 was increased to 300 members, and the result of the test was a mean score of 120. The population mean and standard deviation remained at 122 and 15, respectively.

   **a.** Which test is appropriate for evaluating the goodness of fit between the sample and the population means?

   **b.** State a null hypothesis.

   **c.** If appropriate, state a directional hypothesis.

   **d.** What is the value of the test statistic?

   **e.** How do the conclusions to this exercise compare to those for exercise 10? Explain your conclusion.

12. The income of a sample of 25 individuals was $29,000 with a sample standard deviation of $370. The average income for the population was known to be $29,126. Was the sample a good fit to the population with respect to income?

   **a.** Which test is appropriate for the problem?

   **b.** State a null hypothesis.

   **c.** If appropriate, state a directional hypothesis.

   **d.** What is the value of the test statistic?

   **e.** What do you do with $H_0$ at $\alpha = .05$?

   **f.** What do you do with $H_1$ at $\alpha = .05$?

   **g.** What can you say about the goodness of fit?

   **h.** What was the risk of a Type I error?

13. Another sample was drawn, but this time it was increased to 50 members. Again the sample standard deviation was $370. The sample mean was $29,000, and that of the population $29,126. Test the same hypotheses as in exercise 12 using the same level of significance.

   **a.** What is the value of the test statistic?

   **b.** Is the conclusion about the goodness of fit the same as for the smaller sample in exercise 12? Explain the reasons for your conclusion.

14. Using the same data as in exercise 13, test $H_0$ at the .01 level of significance.

   **a.** What implications do the two levels of significance in exercises 12 and 13 have for a Type I error?

   **b.** What implications do they have for a Type II error?

15. It was found that a proportion of .40 women were among all the applicants for jobs at a high-tech firm. An examination of a sample of 65 applicants who were hired indicated that .27 were women. Did the proportion of women who were hired represent a good fit to the proportion of women who applied?

   **a.** Which test is appropriate to evaluate the fit between the proportion of all women applicants and those who were successful?

   **b.** State a null hypothesis.

   **c.** If appropriate, state a directional hypothesis.

**d.** What is the value of the test statistic?

**e.** What would you do with the null hypothesis at .05?

**f.** If appropriate, what would you do with the directional hypothesis at .05?

**g.** What are your conclusions?

16. A sample was drawn from a community with four active political parties. There was a longstanding belief that members of any of the four parties had an equal opportunity to be elected. A sample of 180 members showed that there were 49 Democrats, 61 Independents, 31 Republicans, and 39 Socialists.

   **a.** Which test is appropriate to test the goodness of fit between the sample results and the assumption of equality across the four parties?

   **b.** State a null hypothesis.

   **c.** If appropriate, state a directional hypothesis.

   **d.** What is the value of the test statistic?

   **e.** How many degrees of freedom does the distribution have?

   **f.** At what level of probability can the null hypothesis be rejected?

   **g.** If appropriate, at what level of probability can the directional hypothesis be accepted?

# 8

# COMPARING TWO CONTINUOUS MEASURES

## *Parametric Tests*

In Chapter 7, we found that one-sample tests make it possible to assess whether an observed sample statistic fits a known or expected population parameter. The tests included the standard-error-of-the-mean test and Student's *t* test, both of which are used for interval measures. They also included the standard-error-of-proportions test for dichotomous data and the chi-square test for nominal measures.

The tests of significance discussed in this chapter are used to determine whether two samples represent similar populations. The principle underlying the calculations for two-sample tests is similar to that of one-sample tests in that they are ratios of observed differences to expected differences. Thus, the numerator represents the observed difference between two samples, whereas the denominator is the standard error or expected variation for the variable in the populations represented by the two samples. Recall that the standard error is an estimate of the variability of a measure in the population. If the observed difference between the two samples is greater than expected, given the standard error, the difference is statistically significant. Before considering examples of two-sample tests, let's review the situations under which populations are compared.

## GROUP COMPARISONS

### *Types of Comparisons*

Comparisons of two or more groups usually occur in two situations. First, samples from *two different* populations can be compared to determine whether the distribution of a variable is similar in the two populations. Suppose you want to know whether white and nonwhite populations differ in their perception of the fairness of the legal system. Typically, you would select two samples, one representing nonwhites and another whites, and then compare their views on the legal system. If you find that nonwhites are more skeptical of the fairness of the legal system, you can conclude that the two populations differ.

Remember that sample comparisons are based on statistical inference. The real purpose of comparing two samples is to draw inferences about differences between the populations they represent. Thus, using appropriate sampling procedures that maximize representation of the populations is essential.

Second, samples from the *same* population may be compared. Such comparisons often arise when one sample is exposed to a special treatment or experience (the experimental group) and then compared to a sample without the special treatment (the control group) to determine whether the special treatment makes a difference. Suppose that you want to evaluate the effect of exposing whites to the information on differential treatment accorded to nonwhites and whites by the legal system. You could select a sample of whites, randomly assign them to two groups, one exposed to information (the experimental group) and the other not (the control group). You could then determine whether exposure to information made a difference in the perception of fairness for the two groups.

The goal is to compare two similar samples to determine the effect of exposure to information. The concern is that the two samples be as similar as possible except for the exposure experience. Selecting one sample and randomly assigning the sample members to experimental and control groups maximizes the likelihood that the two groups are similar at the outset and that any difference in their perception of the legal system should be due to the impact of the information on the experimental group.

The goal in the first example is to determine whether two populations differ, whereas in the second it is to assess the influence of some effect using an experimental and control group representing the same population. In the former case, differences between the two samples are presumed to derive from differences in their respective populations, whereas in the latter they are assumed to result from the experimental effect.

## Independent Samples and Dependent Samples

Comparisons of two samples raise an important issue: that of **independent samples** and **dependent samples.** Independent samples are those in which the selection of the members of one sample has no influence on the selection of the members of the other sample. Dependent samples are those in which the selection of members for one sample determines the characteristics of the members for the other sample.

Whether samples are selected from different or the same populations, their independence is a function of the strategy used for sample selection. Figure 8.1 illustrates the conditions under which independent samples can occur. Samples selected randomly from two populations are independent unless effort is made to match sample members from one population to another. For example, the random

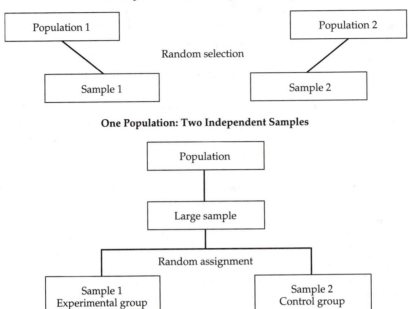

**FIGURE 8.1    Two Independent Samples**

selection of Smith from the first population has no influence on the random selection of Jones from the second population.

If a sample is randomly selected from the one population and then the selected members are randomly allocated to two groups (an experimental and a control group), the two groups are independent in that the characteristics of the members of one group do not determine those of the members of the other, as shown in the lower segment of Figure 8.1. The process of **random assignment** to the two groups avoids dependence between the two samples.

Figure 8.2 shows conditions for creating dependent samples. In the case of two different populations, shown in the upper segment of the figure, if Smith is selected from the first population and then effort is made to select a member from the second population whose characteristics match Smith, the two samples are dependent. In this case, the characteristics of the members of one group determine those of the other.

Dependent samples can also be created by selecting members from a single population and matching the characteristics of the two samples, as shown in the center segment of Figure 8.2. This is a **matched sample.** Matching the two samples ensures that they are similar, except for the experimental difference introduced by researchers. However, matching is problematic in that there is no way to know the variables on which individuals should be matched to produce similar samples. Even more important, there is no way to know whether the variables on which

**Two Populations: Two Dependent Samples**

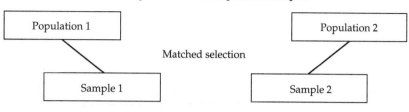

Matched selection

**One Population: Two Dependent Samples**

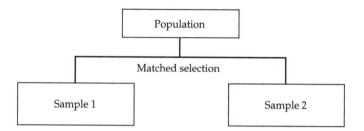

Matched selection

**One Population: Two Dependent Samples, Before-After Design**

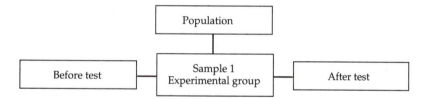

**FIGURE 8.2   Dependent Samples**

they are matched are most relevant to the population difference or experimental effect being studied. The most important characteristics for evaluating the experimental effect might be overlooked or cannot be measured. Moreover, it is difficult to match two or more individuals on more than a few variables, so matching can be done only in terms of a very limited number of characteristics. It might be that a large number of characteristics are relevant to the experimental effect.

In addition, dependent samples can be created from **before–after research designs,** in which a single sample is measured on some dimension *before* some intervention or experience (the pretest) and then measured on the same dimension *after* the intervention (the posttest). The pretest and posttest scores are then compared to determine the effect of the intervention. The advantage of this procedure is that unless extraneous events influence the subjects between the before-and-after measures, all differences in individual characteristics are controlled, and a strong case is made for the before-and-after difference being due to the intervention.

The designs discussed here provide a general framework for illustrating the different designs that influence the selection of statistical tests. The subject of research design is more complex than is suggested here and serves as a course in its own right.

## *Parametric and Nonparametric Tests*

Recall from Chapter 3 that distributions of continuous variables are often represented by the mean. Moreover, means derived from continuous measures can be evaluated using the model of the standard normal curve. Thus, differences between continuous variables can be tested by comparing their means. Because these tests focus on a specific parameter of the population, the mean, they are referred to as **parametric tests.** The use of parametric tests is restrictive because such tests are predicated on the assumption that the distribution of the variable in the population approximates that of the normal distribution.

Discrete data are evaluated using different statistical models because discrete measures fail to meet the assumptions of parametric tests. We know from Chapter 3 that it is inappropriate to use the mean to represent the distributions of nominal measures because the categories of the nominal scales have no inherent order. Comparisons of discrete measures cannot be based on the mean. Rather, techniques have been developed that are designed to identify differences in the general form or shape of distributions. These are referred to as **nonparametric tests,** and they are uniquely suited for ordinal and nominal data and are sensitive only to whether the form or shape of two distributions differs.

Whereas parametric tests assume that the distribution of the variable is normal in form, nonparametric tests make no assumptions about the form of the distribution. Further, discrete measures are made up of relatively limited scale categories, and their distributions are not likely to approximate a normal form. Thus, nonparametric tests are also referred to as **distribution-free tests;** that is, they are free of assumptions about the form of their distributions.

Generally, it is inappropriate to use parametric tests to evaluate data generated with ordinal or nominal measures.[1] However, it is permissible to use tests designed for discrete measures to analyze continuous ones, and sometimes this is necessary because interval data fail to meet other test criteria. For example, a continuous variable might not be normally distributed, in which case a nonparametric (distribution-free) test is more appropriate. However, nonparametric tests should be used for continuous data only when necessary, as they are less sensitive to differences than are their parametric alternatives.

In summary, when comparing two populations, you need to know whether the two samples representing the populations are independent or dependent and whether the measurement is continuous or discrete. All the statistical tests con-

---

[1] Under certain conditions, this rule can be violated for ordinal measures without doing injustice to the meaning of the measurement. Specific consideration of these conditions is beyond the scope of an introductory text such as this one.

sidered in this chapter are parametric in that they are based on specific population parameters. Three tests are presented for two independent samples: Student's *t* test for two samples with equal variances, Student's *t* test for samples with unequal variances, and the two-independent-proportions test. In addition, Student's *t* test using two dependent samples is considered.

## TWO INDEPENDENT SAMPLES FOR INTERVAL MEASURES

### Student's t Test for Two Independent Samples with Equal Variances

#### Description

Student's *t* test for comparing two samples is an extension of the one-sample Student's *t* discussed in Chapter 7. As in one-sample tests, the calculation is based on a ratio, but for two samples it is based on the ratio of the difference between the two sample means *to* their combined standard error terms, referred to as the **standard error of the difference.** Formula 8.1 illustrates the character of the ratio for the *t* test:[2]

$$t = \frac{\overline{X}_1 - \overline{X}_2}{s_{\overline{X}_1 - \overline{X}_2}}$$  (8.1)

where     $s_{\overline{X}_1 - \overline{X}_2}$ = the standard error of the difference

Formula 8.2 shows the expanded form of the equation. The denominator in Formula 8.2 provides a **pooled estimate** of the standard error for the two samples. The pooled estimate is appropriate only if the variances of the variable in the two populations are approximately equal. In addition to the assumption of equal variances, the *t* test requires that the variable be an interval measure and normally distributed in the two populations.

The computational formula is

$$t = \frac{\overline{X}_1 - \overline{X}_2}{\sqrt{\dfrac{(n_1 - 1)s_1^2 + (n_2 - 1)s_2^2}{n_1 + n_2 - 2}} \sqrt{\dfrac{n_1 + n_2}{n_1 n_2}}}$$  (8.2)

The rationale for the test is that if the difference between the two population means, as estimated by $\overline{X}_1$ and $\overline{X}_2$, is in keeping with the expected variation of the variable, it is concluded that the variable is similarly distributed in the two

---

[2] The formula can be written $[(\overline{X}_1 - \overline{X}_2) - (\mu_1 - \mu_2)]/(s_{\overline{X}_1 - \overline{X}_2})$. This form provides an explicit statement of the null hypothesis: There is no difference between the observed sample values of $\overline{X}_1 - \overline{X}_2$ and the expected population values of $\mu_1 - \mu_2$. Given the expectation of the null hypothesis that $\mu_1 - \mu_2 = 0$, the expression becomes $(\overline{X}_1 - \overline{X}_2) - 0$, and the numerator becomes $\overline{X}_1 - \overline{X}_2$, as shown in Formula 8.1.

populations. The phrase "is in keeping with the expected variation" is key in that "what is expected" is defined by the estimate of the standard error for the two samples. The standard error indicates how much variation the variables have in their respective populations, and if the difference between the means does not exceed that variation, the two populations are similar on the measure.

The estimate of the standard error in the denominator is contained in the first square-root expression. The second square-root expression consisting of $\sqrt{\dfrac{n_1 + n_2}{n_1 n_2}}$ is an added correction for sample size. This correction is used because small samples might underestimate the variances in the two populations. When sample sizes are small, the correction affects the solution in that it increases the size of the denominator and makes it more difficult to derive a test statistic that enables the rejection of $H_0$.

Like those for one-sample tests, hypotheses for two-sample tests are statements about population parameters that are tested with data from samples representing the populations and take the following forms:

$H_0: \mu_1 = \mu_2$ The mean for population 1 equals the mean for population 2.
$H_1: \mu_1 > \mu_2$ The mean for population 1 is greater than the mean for population 2.

or

$H_1: \mu_1 < \mu_2$ The mean for population 1 is less than the mean for population 2.

Decisions regarding the hypotheses are made using the distribution of $t$ values shown in Table B.3 in Appendix B. The degrees of freedom are based on the size of the two samples and equal $n_1 + n_2 - 2$, or 1 degree of freedom for each sample.

### Example 8.1

A researcher investigated the correspondence between literacy and alcoholism. The alcoholism rates of a sample of 31 low-literacy and 37 high-literacy communities were compared. The data in Table 8.1 indicate that the low-literacy communities had an average alcoholism rate of 6.115 per 100 residents, whereas high-literacy communities had a rate of 5.436. The variances of the two samples are not

**TABLE 8.1   Literacy and Alcoholism in Selected Communities**

| Alcoholism Rates per 100 Residents | |
|---|---|
| **Low Literacy** | **High Literacy** |
| $n_1 = 31$ | $n_2 = 37$ |
| $\bar{X}_1 = 6.115$ | $\bar{X}_2 = 5.436$ |
| $s_1^2 = 2.012$ | $s_2^2 = 1.566$ |

equal and might suggest that the populations differ in the variance of their alcoholism rates. The similarity, or homogeneity, of the variances must be checked.

### Homogeneity of Variances

While the variances of the two samples in our example are not equal, the difference might be a function of sampling variation, and the variances in their populations might in fact be equal. A simple test for the homogeneity of variances, the **Levene test,** shown in Formula 8.3, is used to evaluate homogeneity:

$$F = \frac{s_1^2 \, (\text{larger variance})}{s_2^2 \, (\text{smaller variance})} \qquad (8.3)$$

The test statistic is an F ratio, which is interpreted using Table B.7 in Appendix B. The test is two tailed because the concern is whether the variances differ in any way. Applied to our example, we find

$$F = \frac{2.012}{1.566} = 1.28$$

According to Table B.7 in Appendix B, the top row contains the degrees of freedom for the numerator and the left-hand column the degrees of freedom for the denominator. The decision rule is that if the test statistic is equal to or larger than the value at the intersect of the two degrees of freedom, reject $H_0$. The rejection of $H_0$ leads to the conclusion that the two variances differ more than would be expected by chance. Note that two values appear at the intersect in Table B.7. The number in light type is for the .05 level and the one in bold type for the .01 level of significance.

The degrees of freedom for our numerator are $n_1 - 1 = 31 - 1 = 30$ and for the denominator $n_2 - 1 = 37 - 1 = 36$. The value at the intersect of 30 and 36 for .05 (light type) is 1.78. Our test statistic of 1.28 does not equal or exceed that of 1.78, so the null hypothesis is accepted, and it is concluded that the difference between the two variances is due to chance.

Given that the variances are homogeneous, Formula 8.2 is appropriate for evaluating the difference between the two means. The hypotheses that will be tested at the .05 level of significance are

$H_0: \mu_1 = \mu_2$ The mean of population 1 equals that of population 2.

$H_1: \mu_1 > \mu_2$ The mean of population 1 is greater than that of population 2.

The computation of the test statistic, using Formula 8.2, is

$$t = \frac{\overline{X}_1 - \overline{X}_2}{\sqrt{\dfrac{(n_1 - 1)s_1^2 + (n_2 - 1)s_2^2}{n_1 + n_2 - 2}} \; \sqrt{\dfrac{n_1 + n_2}{n_1 n_2}}}$$

$$t = \frac{6.115 - 5.436}{\sqrt{\dfrac{(31 - 1)(2.012) + (37 - 1)(1.566)}{(31 + 37 - 2)}} \; \sqrt{\dfrac{31 + 37}{(31)(37)}}}$$

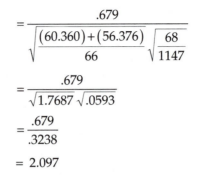

$$= \frac{.679}{\sqrt{\dfrac{(60.360)+(56.376)}{66}} \ \sqrt{\dfrac{68}{1147}}}$$

$$= \frac{.679}{\sqrt{1.7687}\ \sqrt{.0593}}$$

$$= \frac{.679}{.3238}$$

$$= 2.097$$

Given the test statistic of 2.097, the decision on the hypotheses is made using Table B.3 in Appendix B for Student's $t$ values. Each sample has $n - 1$ degrees of freedom, so for a two-sample $t$ test, df $= n_1 + n_2 - 2 = 31 + 37 - 2 = 66$. Given that the table does not show 66 degrees of freedom, it is appropriate to use the nearest, and preferably lesser, degrees of freedom. The value appearing at the intersect of 60 degrees of freedom and $\alpha = .05$ is 2.000.[3] Our test statistic of 2.097 is larger, so $H_0$ is rejected and $H_1$ accepted. There is a significant difference in the alcoholism rates of the two communities in that low-literacy communities have a higher rate.

### Summary
Student's $t$ test for the difference between the means of two independent populations with homogeneous variances is somewhat restrictive. The following criteria must be met:

1. The variable must be an interval measure.
2. The variances must be equal for the two populations.
3. The variable is assumed to be normally distributed in the two populations.
4. Given Student's estimate of the standard error, the test can be used for small samples.

A real advantage of the two-sample $t$ test is that it can be used for very small samples. Note that Table B.3 in Appendix B has $t$ values for as few as 1 degree of freedom. However, as sample size declines, the required test statistic for rejecting $H_0$ increases dramatically, making it difficult to reject $H_0$ with small samples. This means that, with small samples, $H_0$ can be rejected only when very large differences are observed.

The foregoing $t$ test is appropriate only when the variances of the two populations are homogeneous. The following example illustrates an alternative $t$ test when **unequal variances** are encountered.

---

[3] Using the nearest lesser degrees of freedom is a conservative estimate for rejecting $H_0$. The value for df $= 66$ would actually be less than 2.000, making it easier to reject $H_0$.

## Student's t *Test for Two Independent Samples with Unequal Variances*

In the previous example, the variances of the two samples were approximately equal, so the variances in Formula 8.2 were pooled to provide the standard error of the difference. However, when the variances are unequal, the estimate for the standard error of the difference must be adjusted to prevent large differences between sample variances from distorting the estimate of the difference between the means. Formula 8.4 provides an unpooled estimate of the standard error of the difference by using the sum of the individual estimates for the standard error:

$$t = \frac{\overline{X}_1 - \overline{X}_2}{\sqrt{\dfrac{s_1^2}{n_1 - 1} + \dfrac{s_2^2}{n_2 - 1}}} \tag{8.4}$$

Thus, the formula for the *t* test changes, as does the degrees of freedom associated with the statistic, as shown in the following formula:

$$\mathrm{df} = \frac{\left(\dfrac{s_1^2}{n_1} + \dfrac{s_2^2}{n_2}\right)^2}{\dfrac{\left(\dfrac{s_1^2}{n_1}\right)^2}{n_1 - 1} + \dfrac{\left(\dfrac{s_2^2}{n_2}\right)^2}{n_2 - 1}} \tag{8.5}$$

The degrees of freedom resulting from Formula 8.5 are more conservative in that they are less than you would get using the pooled estimate. Fewer degrees of freedom makes it more difficult to reject $H_0$. The logic in making it more difficult to reject $H_0$ is to avoid confounding the difference between variances with the difference between the means of the two samples.

### Example 8.2

The application of Formulas 8.4 and 8.5 can be illustrated using the preceding example of alcoholism rates. However, in this case, assume that the mean rates of alcoholism are the same but that the variance of low-literacy communities increases to 2.853 and that of high-literacy communities remains unchanged at 1.566. The hypotheses are the same as in Example 8.1 and will be tested at the .05 level of significance.

Testing for the homogeneity of variances using Formula 8.3, we find

$$F = \frac{2.853}{1.566} = 1.82$$

Table B.7 in Appendix B shows that with 30 degrees of freedom in the numerator and 36 degrees of freedom in the denominator, any value greater than 1.78 is significant at the .05 level. Our F = 1.82, so we must conclude that the two variances are unequal, and the test statistic and degrees of freedom should be determined using Formulas 8.4 and 8.5. Applying Formula 8.4, we find that the *t* value is

$$t = \frac{\overline{X}_1 - \overline{X}_2}{\sqrt{\dfrac{s_1^2}{n_1 - 1} + \dfrac{s_2^2}{n_2 - 1}}}$$

$$= \frac{6.115 - 5.436}{\sqrt{\dfrac{2.853}{31 - 1} + \dfrac{1.566}{37 - 1}}}$$

$$= \frac{.679}{\sqrt{.0951 + .0435}}$$

$$= \frac{.679}{.3723}$$

$$= 1.824$$

The *t* value, using the unpooled estimate, is equal to 1.824, which is less than the value of 2.097, which was attained using the pooled estimate. Recall that in calculating the pooled estimate, the difference between the means was the same, .697, but here one of the variances was changed, resulting in a significant difference between the variances. As a consequence, the unpooled estimate was used, resulting in a lower *t* value because of the change in the denominator. A smaller *t* value makes it more difficult to reject $H_0$.

The degrees of freedom for the unpooled estimate are determined using Formula 8.5, with the following results:

$$df = \frac{\left(\dfrac{s_1^2}{n_1} + \dfrac{s_2^2}{n_2}\right)^2}{\dfrac{\left(\dfrac{s_1^2}{n_1}\right)^2}{n_1 - 1} + \dfrac{\left(\dfrac{s_2^2}{n_2}\right)^2}{n_2 - 1}}$$

$$df = \frac{\left(\dfrac{2.853}{31} + \dfrac{1.566}{37}\right)^2}{\dfrac{\left(\dfrac{2.853}{31}\right)^2}{31 - 1} + \dfrac{\left(\dfrac{1.566}{37}\right)^2}{37 - 1}}$$

$$= \frac{(.0920 + .0423)^2}{\dfrac{(.0920)^2}{30} + \dfrac{(.0423)^2}{36}}$$

$$= \frac{.1343^2}{.00028 + .00005}$$

$$= \frac{.01804}{.00033}$$

$$= 54.67$$

The effect of using Formula 8.5 is to reduce the degrees of freedom to about 55, which is less than the degrees of freedom for the pooled estimate, 66. The lesser degrees of freedom increases the difficulty in rejecting $H_0$. The values for $t$ in Table B.3 in Appendix B show that a test statistic with 66 degrees of freedom requires a value of about 2.000 to reject $H_0$ at the .05 level of significance, whereas one with 55 degrees of freedom requires a value somewhere between 2.000 and 2.021 to reject $H_0$.

For our example of unequal variances, $t = 1.824$ is less than the table value of 2.000 to 2.021, so $H_0$ cannot be rejected. This is in contrast to the $t$ test for equal variances, in which the null hypothesis was rejected even though the difference in the two means was the same. The change in the decision is due to the large difference in variances between the two samples. The difference between the means is not sufficient, given the large difference in variances, to result in a significant test statistic at the .05 level.

### *An Alternative*

There is a less cumbersome method for evaluating the difference between two means with unequal variances. Rather than use the degrees of freedom shown in Formula 8.5, you can calculate $t$ value limits for evaluating the significance of the test statistic with the following formula:[4]

$$\text{Reject } H_0 \text{ if } t' > \frac{+\left(t_1 W_1 + t_2 W_2\right)}{W_1 + W_2} \tag{8.6}$$

$$\text{or if } t' < \frac{-\left(t_1 W_1 + t_2 W_2\right)}{W_1 + W_2}$$

where     $t' = $ the estimated $t$ limit

$t_1 = $ the table value of $t$ for $n_1 - 1$ degrees of freedom for the selected level of significance

$t_2 = $ the table value of $t$ for $n_2 - 1$ degrees of freedom for the selected level of significance

$$W_1 = \frac{s_1^2}{n_1} \text{ and } W_2 = \frac{s_2^2}{n_2}$$

[4] See Mark L. Berenson and David M. Levine, *Basic Business Statistics: Concepts and Applications* (Englewood Cliffs, N.J.: Prentice-Hall, 1992), pp. 432–33.

Applied to our example, the results are

$$t_1 = n_1 - 1 = 31 - 1 = 30; \text{ for } \alpha = .05, t_1 = 2.042$$

$$t_2 = n_2 - 1 = 37 - 1 = 36; \text{ for } \alpha = .05, t_2 = 2.032$$

$$W_1 = \frac{s_1^2}{n_1} = \frac{2.853}{31} = .0920$$

$$W_2 = \frac{s_2^2}{n_2} = \frac{1.566}{37} = .0423$$

and

$$\frac{\left(t_1 W_1 + t_2 W_2\right)}{W_1 + W_2} = \frac{(2.042)(.0920) + (2.032)(.0423)}{.0920 + .0423}$$

$$= \frac{.1879 + .0860}{.1343}$$

$$= 2.039$$

To reject $H_0$, you must have a positive or negative $t$ value that is greater than 2.039. Our $t = 1.824$ is not greater than 2.039, so $H_0$ is accepted. The result leads us to the same conclusion as Formula 8.5.

### Summary
The $t$ test for two independent samples with unequal variances is based on the same assumptions about the distribution of the variables as the test for equal variances, except that the variances of the variable in the two populations need not be homogeneous. The assumptions are as follows:

1. The variable is an interval measure.
2. The variable is normally distributed in the population.
3. The test can be used for small samples.

## Student's t Test and Explained Variance

Student's $t$ test for the difference between two means makes it possible to determine whether the null or directional hypothesis should be accepted or rejected at a particular level of significance. If the results are such that $H_0$ is rejected, we conclude that the difference between the two means exceeds the expectations established by our level of significance, and the directional hypothesis is accepted. Such conclusions are important to research, but you can gather additional information about the relationship between two measurements by looking at the amount of variation that one variable accounts for in another.

In Example 8.1, we examined samples representing two populations, one with low literacy and the other high, and compared their rates of alcoholism. Using the test of significance for homogeneous variances, we concluded that the mean alcoholism rates for the low-literacy communities were greater than for high-literacy ones. It would be interesting to know the extent to which the variation in alcoholism rates is associated with low and high literacy. The *strength of the association* can be assessed with a statistic known as omega squared, $\omega^2$, which is given in the following formula:

$$\omega^2 = \frac{t^2 - 1}{t^2 + n_1 + n_2 - 1} \tag{8.7}$$

The formula is based on the *t* test value and the size of the two samples. Applying the formula to the data from our example with homogeneous variances, we find

$$= \frac{2.097^2 - 1}{2.097^2 + 31 + 37 - 1}$$

$$= \frac{4.397 - 1}{4.397 + 31 + 37 - 1}$$

$$= \frac{3.397}{71.397}$$

$$= .0476$$

The solution shows that the proportion of variance explained in alcoholism rates by the differences between low and high literacy communities is .0476. It is more common to express the results in terms of the percent of explained variance or as 4.76 percent of the variance in alcoholism rates is explained by literacy. While the difference is significant at the .05 level, literacy does not account for very much of the variance in alcoholism rates, only 4.76 percent. Presumably, if other variables related to drinking were included in the analysis, a higher percentage of the variance would be explained.

# TWO INDEPENDENT SAMPLES
# WITH DICHOTOMOUS MEASURES

## Two-Independent-Proportions Test

### Description

The **two-independent-proportions test** is used to determine whether a dichotomous variable is distributed similarly in two populations. The test compares the distribution of the proportion of cases for two samples across the categories of a dichotomous scale. The test requires that both samples have 30 or more members. The resulting statistic is a Z score.

The test statistic is based on the ratio of the difference between the two sample proportions to the standard error of the two proportions, as shown in the following formula:

$$Z = \frac{p_1 - p_2}{\sigma_{p_1 - p_2}}$$ (8.8)

where     $\sigma_{p_1 - p_2}$ = estimate of the standard error

$$= \sqrt{\frac{p_1 q_1}{n_1} + \frac{p_2 q_2}{n_2}}$$

The calculation formula is

$$Z = \frac{p_1 - p_2}{\sqrt{\dfrac{p_1 q_1}{n_1} + \dfrac{p_2 q_2}{n_2}}}$$ (8.9)

If the two samples are of unequal size, the estimate of the standard error in the denominator must be based on a weighted average. The formula for the weighted average is

$$Z = \frac{p_1 - p_2}{\sqrt{p_e q_e \left( \dfrac{n_1 + n_2}{n_1 n_2} \right)}}$$ (8.10)

where $p_e$ and $q_e$ are calculated with

$$p_e = \frac{n_1 p_1 + n_2 p_2}{n_1 + n_2}$$ (8.11)

and

$$q_e = 1 - p_e$$ (8.12)

The two-independent-proportions test can be used to evaluate both nondirectional and directional hypotheses. The general forms of the hypotheses are

$H_0: P_1 = P_2$     The proportion for population 1 equals that of population 2.

$H_1: P_1 > P_2$     The proportion for population 1 is greater than that of population 2.

or

$H_1: P_1 < P_2$     The proportion for population 1 is less than that of population 2.

Note that the hypotheses use $P$ to indicate that they are statements about population proportions.

**TABLE 8.2   Insured and Noninsured: Advance of Illness**

| Stage of Illness | Insurance Status | |
| --- | --- | --- |
| | Uninsured | Insured |
| More advanced | 24 ($p_1$ = .65) | 18 ($p_2$ = .42) |
| Less advanced | 13 ($q_1$ = .35) | 25 ($q_2$ = .58) |
| Total | 37 | 43 |

**Example 8.3**

The stage of illness for a population of insured individuals on first being diagnosed with a serious illness was compared to that of a similar group of individuals who did not have insurance. Both groups were classified as in a more advanced stage or a less advanced stage of illness at first diagnosis. Table 8.2 shows the resulting data.

The following hypotheses are tested at the .05 level of significance:

$H_0: P_1 = P_2$:    There is no difference in the proportion of individuals with more advanced illness on first diagnosis for uninsured and insured.

$H_1: P_1 > P_2$:    A greater proportion of the uninsured are likely to be at a more advanced stage of illness on first diagnosis than the insured.

Formula 8.10 is used because the sample of uninsured, 37, is unequal to that of the insured, 43:

$$Z = \frac{p_1 - p_2}{\sqrt{p_e q_e \left( \frac{n_1 + n_2}{n_1 n_2} \right)}} \qquad \textbf{(8.10)}$$

Before using Formula 8.10, we must determine the values of $p_e$ and $q_e$ using the following formulas:

$$p_e = \frac{n_1 p_1 + n_2 p_2}{n_1 + n_2} \qquad \textbf{(8.11)}$$

$$= \frac{(37)(.65) + (43)(.42)}{37 + 43}$$

$$= \frac{24.05 + 18.06}{80}$$

$$= \frac{42.11}{80}$$

$$= .526$$

$$q_e = 1 - p_e \tag{8.12}$$

$$= 1.000 - .526$$

$$= .474$$

Given that $p_e$ and $q_e$ are known, the Z score can be calculated using the following formula:

$$Z = \frac{p_1 - p_2}{\sqrt{p_e q_e \left( \dfrac{n_1 + n_2}{n_1 n_2} \right)}} \tag{8.10}$$

$$Z = \frac{.65 - .42}{\sqrt{(.526)(.474)\left( \dfrac{37 + 43}{(37)(43)} \right)}}$$

$$= \frac{.23}{\sqrt{(.249)\left( \dfrac{80}{1{,}591} \right)}}$$

$$= \frac{.23}{\sqrt{(.249)(.050)}}$$

$$= \frac{.23}{.112}$$

$$Z = 2.05$$

The test statistic, Z = 2.05, is larger than the Z score of 1.96 associated with the .05 level of significance, so the null hypothesis can be rejected and the directional hypothesis accepted. Table B.1 in Appendix B shows that Z = 2.05 has a one-tailed significance of .02 (column B) and a two-tailed significance of .04 (column C). There appears to be an association between insurance and the severity of illness on first diagnosis. Those who come for treatment without health insurance are likely to be at a more advanced stage of illness.

### Summary

The standard error of the difference between two independent proportions is the most powerful statistic for comparing dichotomous measures representing two independent populations. The test is somewhat restrictive in that both samples must be larger than 30 if the normal distribution is to be used for interpreting the probability of the Z score. However, it is possible to apply the test to smaller samples and use the table of probabilities used for $t$ values, given in Table B.3 in Appendix B. In doing so, you must follow the procedures used to interpret a $t$ score. For our example, the test statistic 2.05 would be the $t$ value and df = $n_1 + n_2 - 2$, which for our example is

37 + 43 − 2 = 78. The nearest lower degrees of freedom in Table B.3 is 60, which requires a *t* value larger than 2.000 to reject $H_0$. Our test statistic of 2.05 is larger, so we can reject the null hypothesis and accept the directional hypothesis. Using the *t* distribution leads us to the same conclusions as the Z score. In summary, the two-sample-independent-proportions test can be used under the following conditions:

1. The two samples are independent.
2. The measure is dichotomous.
3. When both $n_1$ and $n_2$ are equal to or larger than 30, the distribution of Z values is used; if the samples are less than 30, the *t* distribution is used.

## COMPARING TWO DEPENDENT SAMPLES WITH INTERVAL MEASURES

### Student's t Test for Paired Comparisons

In the preceding, Formulas 8.1 and 8.4 were used to compare two independent samples. They were independent because the members of one sample had no influence on the membership of the other. However, frequently samples are dependent in that the members of one sample can be matched to those of another, or a measure can be taken on a sample before and after some event, and the before-and after-measures compared. Under either of these conditions, the two measures that we want to compare are not independent because whoever is matched with someone who scores low is also likely to score low, and those who score low on the before measure are most likely to do so on the after measure. Even under these conditions, we can determine whether a significant difference exists between matched groups. The calculations take into account the dependence of the two measures.

Student's *t* test has been adapted to evaluate the differences between two dependent measures. The logic underlying the distribution of the differences is based on the central limit theorem in that the sampling distribution of the means of the differences assumes a normal form. The *t* distribution, which can be used for small samples, evaluates the probability of the test statistic. The test statistic is based on the ratio of the mean difference *to* the standard error of the difference, $\sigma_d$, as shown in the following formula:

$$t = \frac{\bar{d}}{\sigma_d} \qquad (8.13)$$

where $\bar{d}$ = the mean difference between the before-and-after scores

$$\sigma_d = \sqrt{\frac{\Sigma d^2 - \dfrac{(\Sigma d)^2}{N}}{(N)(N-1)}} = \text{the standard error of the difference}$$

The complete formula for calculating Student's $t$ value is

$$t = \frac{\bar{d}}{\sqrt{\dfrac{\Sigma d^2 - \dfrac{(\Sigma d)^2}{N}}{(N)(N-1)}}} \tag{8.14}$$

This formula shows that the standard error of the difference, $\sigma_d$, is estimated using a formula similar in structure to the sums-of-squares approach used to compute variance in Formula 3.13 in Chapter 3. The uppercase $N$ is used in the formula because it refers to the number of differences between paired observations rather than the total number of observations. The general forms of the hypotheses are

$H_0$: $\delta = 0$     The difference in the before-and-after scores equals zero.
$H_1$: $\delta > 0$     The difference in the before-and-after scores is greater than zero.

or

$\delta < 0$     The difference in the before-and-after scores is less than zero.

Note that the symbol delta, $\delta$, is used because the hypotheses refer to the population. The $t$ statistic resulting from Formula 8.15 is evaluated using the $t$ distribution where df $= N - 1$, or the number of difference scores less 1. The uppercase $N$ indicates that the degrees of freedom refer to the number of before-and-after differences.

### Example 8.4

Fifteen individuals were given a test on self-esteem before and after participating in a course intended to enhance self-esteem. The results are shown in Table 8.3. The concern is whether the course increased self-esteem. We will test the null hypothesis at $\alpha = .05$. The hypotheses are

$H_0$: $\delta = 0$     There is no difference in self-esteem before and after participating in the course.
$H_0$: $\delta > 1$     Self-esteem will increase after participating in the course.

According to Formula 8.14 and the data in Table 8.3, the test statistic is

$$t = \frac{1.4}{\sqrt{\dfrac{145 - \dfrac{21^2}{15}}{15(15-1)}}}$$

$$= \frac{1.4}{\sqrt{\dfrac{115.6}{210}}}$$

$$= \frac{1.4}{\sqrt{.5505}}$$

$$= \frac{1.4}{.742}$$

$$= 1.887$$

The degrees of freedom are $N - 1 = 15 - 1 = 14$. According to the distribution of $t$ values in Table B.3 in Appendix B, the value for df = 14 at $\alpha = .05$ is 2.145. Our test statistic, $t = 1.887$, is less than 2.145, so $H_0$ cannot be rejected. Table B.3 shows that the two-tailed probability is somewhere between .05 and .10. A test of the null hypothesis indicates that exposure to the course did not have a significant effect on the self-esteem of participants as measured by the test.

If we had decided to test the research or directional hypothesis first, our decision would be different. The directional hypothesis is

$H_1: \delta > 0$     Self-esteem will increase after participating in the course.

The direction of the hypothesis is determined by the sign of the summed differences, shown in column $d$ in Table 8.3. In our example, if it is expected that the sum of the differences with positive signs is greater than those with negative signs, $H_1: \delta > 0$ is used. If the sum of the differences is expected to have a negative sign, $H_1: \delta < 0$ would have been used. Table B.3 in Appendix B shows that for

**TABLE 8.3   Change in Self-Esteem**

| Individual | Before | After | $d$ | $d^2$ |
|---|---|---|---|---|
| 1 | 90 | 93 | −3 | 9 |
| 2 | 91 | 90 | 1 | 1 |
| 3 | 93 | 89 | 4 | 16 |
| 4 | 89 | 88 | 1 | 1 |
| 5 | 85 | 88 | −3 | 9 |
| 6 | 89 | 86 | 3 | 9 |
| 7 | 83 | 84 | −1 | 1 |
| 8 | 88 | 83 | 5 | 25 |
| 9 | 84 | 83 | 1 | 1 |
| 10 | 82 | 80 | 2 | 4 |
| 11 | 83 | 77 | 6 | 36 |
| 12 | 81 | 76 | 5 | 25 |
| 13 | 72 | 74 | −2 | 4 |
| 14 | 70 | 70 | 0 | 0 |
| 15 | 71 | 69 | 2 | 4 |
| | | | $\Sigma d = 21$ | $\Sigma d^2 = 145$ |
| | | | $\bar{d} = 1.4$ | |

$t = 1.887$, we can accept the directional hypothesis at the .05 level of significance and conclude that the exposure made a difference. There is an advantage to having sufficient information to state the direction of the difference. Given that the research hypothesis states the direction of the difference, the region of acceptance, .05, is on one tail. For the null hypothesis, the area of .05 must be split between the left tail, .025, and the right, .025. Thus, the directional hypothesis is easier to accept at the same level of significance than it is to reject the null hypothesis.

### Summary
The $t$ test for two dependent samples is the most powerful alternative for dependent samples. However, to apply the test, the following assumptions must be met:

1. The variables must be interval measures.
2. The distribution of the differences must be normal in form.
3. Given the $t$ statistic, it can be applied to small samples.

## COMPUTER EXERCISES: SOME SUGGESTIONS

The statistical tests discussed in this chapter represent those most frequently used in social research, particularly Student's $t$ test for two group comparisons. You may use your software package to practice each of the techniques discussed in the chapter. Your data set should contain continuous variables appropriate for Student's $t$. Begin by selecting continuous variables that make for interesting comparisons, being sure to check the character of the distribution of each variable. The basic descriptors, including the mean, variance, skewness, and kurtosis, will give you information on the shape of the distribution of the variables. Your software may contain a statistical test for normality, which will indicate whether your variables meet the assumption of a normal distribution. You can also use the graphics of your software to print out a frequency polygon for each variable. The graph will give you a good sense of the form of the distribution.

Then you can use the $t$ test to see whether the means represented by two samples differ. Your software will provide $t$ values for independent and dependent samples. You can also select dichotomous variables and use the two-independent-proportions test. It is important to study the printout and understand all the information given for each test. Remember that the results of the tests of significance will include the exact probabilities of the test statistics for both one- and two-tailed hypotheses.

## CHAPTER SUMMARY

The purpose of this chapter was to discuss methods for evaluating the difference between two populations on continuous measures. Four different tests were presented. The first test evaluated two independent samples on interval measures with equal or homogeneous variances. The second compared independent interval measures with unequal variances. The third was used for two independent proportions for dichotomous measures. The fourth was a *t* test for comparing two dependent samples on an interval measure. Each test makes it possible to evaluate differences between two continuous measures for data collected under different conditions.

In Chapter 9 we will examine additional methods for comparing two populations, but the focus will be on discrete variables, including both ordinal and nominal levels of measurement.

## KEY TERMS

**before–after research design**  A design in which measurements are taken before and after a sample is exposed to some intervention or experience.

**dependent sample**  Two or more samples are dependent if the selection of the members of one sample influences the membership of the other.

**distribution-free tests**  Tests that make no assumptions about the shape or form of the distribution of the variable in the population.

**independent sample**  Two or more samples are independent if the selection of the members of one sample has no influence on that of the other.

**Levene test**  A method for determining the homogeneity of two variances.

**matched samples**  A design in which the members of one sample are matched with the members of another sample on variables relevant to the research concern.

**nonparametric tests**  Statistical tests for hypotheses that are statements about the general form of a discrete distribution.

**parametric tests**  Statistical tests for hypotheses that are statements about specific population parameters based on continuous measures.

**pooled estimate**  An estimate of the standard error in which the variances for samples are combined.

**random assignment**  Any procedure in which members are assigned to two or more groups using a random process such as random numbers tables or a systematic procedure such as assigning every other member to two groups.

**standard error of the difference**  Another term for the combined standard errors when testing for the difference between two means.

**Student's *t* test: two samples, equal variances**  A procedure for comparing two population means using independent samples with approximately equal variances.

**Student's *t* test: two samples, unequal variances**  A procedure for comparing two population means using independent samples with unequal variances.

**Student's *t* test: paired comparisons**   A procedure for comparing two population means using dependent samples.

**two-independent-proportions test**   A test for assessing whether two independent populations have the same proportion of observations in the categories of a dichotomous scale.

**unequal variances**   Variances for two samples that are so unequal that the difference is significant, i.e., not due to sampling variations.

## SYMBOLS

$p_e$          The estimate of $p$ when two samples of unequal size are compared

$q_e$          The estimate of $q$ when two samples of unequal size are compared

$\delta$          The before and after difference for a population.

## FORMULAS

$$t = \frac{\overline{X}_1 - \overline{X}_2}{\sqrt{\dfrac{(n_1 - 1)s_1^2 + (n_2 - 1)s_2^2}{n_1 + n_2 - 2}} \sqrt{\dfrac{n_1 + n_2}{n_1 n_2}}}$$

Student's *t* test for two independent samples, equal variances

$$df = n_1 + n_2 - 2$$

Degrees of freedom for Student's *t* two-independent-samples test

$$t = \frac{\overline{X}_1 - \overline{X}_2}{\sqrt{\dfrac{s_1^2}{n_1 - 1} + \dfrac{s_2^2}{n_2 - 1}}}$$

Student's *t* test for two independent samples, unequal variances

$$df = \frac{\left(\dfrac{s_1^2}{n_1} + \dfrac{s_2^2}{n_2}\right)^2}{\dfrac{\left(\dfrac{s_1^2}{n_1}\right)^2}{n_1 - 1} + \dfrac{\left(\dfrac{s_2^2}{n_2}\right)^2}{n_2 - 1}}$$

Degrees of freedom for Student's *t*, two independent samples, unequal variances

Reject $H_0$ if $t' > \dfrac{+(t_1 W_1 + t_2 W_2)}{W_1 + W_2}$

or if $t' < \dfrac{-(t_1 W_1 + t_2 W_2)}{W_1 + W_2}$

Alternate to df for unequal variances

$$Z = \frac{p_1 - p_2}{\sqrt{\dfrac{p_1 q_1}{n_1} + \dfrac{p_2 q_2}{n_2}}}$$

Difference between two independent proportions, equal size samples

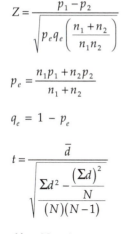

$$Z = \frac{p_1 - p_2}{\sqrt{p_e q_e \left( \frac{n_1 + n_2}{n_1 n_2} \right)}}$$

Difference between two independent proportions, unequal size samples

$$p_e = \frac{n_1 p_1 + n_2 p_2}{n_1 + n_2}$$

Weighted estimate for $p$ with unequal size samples

$$q_e = 1 - p_e$$

Weighted estimate for $q$ with unequal size samples

$$t = \frac{\overline{d}}{\sqrt{\frac{\Sigma d^2 - \frac{(\Sigma d)^2}{N}}{(N)(N-1)}}}$$

Student's $t$ test for dependent samples

$$df = N - 1$$

Degrees of freedom for two dependent samples

## EXERCISES

1. An employer was concerned about the potential differences in absenteeism rates between a group of closely supervised employees and a group not closely supervised. The sample of closely supervised employees, $n_1 = 64$, had a mean absenteeism rate of 19.9 days per year with a variance of 3.4. The less supervised group, $n_2 = 60$, had a mean of 20.6 absent days per year with a variance of 3.7. The variances were approximately equal.

   a. Which test is appropriate for evaluating the difference between the two means?
   b. State a null hypothesis.
   c. If appropriate, state a directional hypothesis.
   d. What is the value of the test statistic?
   e. What are the degrees of freedom?
   f. Can you reject the null hypothesis at the .05 level of significance?
   g. If appropriate, at what level of significance can you accept the directional hypothesis?
   h. What would you tell the employer about the difference in absenteeism rates of closely supervised and less closely supervised employees?

2. Assume that the same data were observed, except that $n_1 = 10$ and $n_2 = 9$. The variances are approximately equal.

   a. Which test is appropriate for the data?
   b. State a null hypothesis.
   c. If appropriate, state a directional hypothesis.
   d. What is the value of the test statistic?
   e. What are the degrees of freedom?
   f. Can you reject the null hypothesis at the .05 level of significance?
   g. Can you accept the directional hypothesis at the .025 level of significance?
   h. Explain the difference between the results in exercises 1 and 2.

3. The average number of complaints filed in profit and nonprofit hospitals was compared. The profit hospitals, $n_1 = 27$, had a mean number of 58.7 complaints with a variance of 6.3. The nonprofits, $n_2 = 30$, had a mean number of 56.6 complaints with a variance of 12.9.

    **a.** What is the F statistic for the homogeneity of the variances?
    **b.** Is the F statistic significant at the .05 level?
    **c.** Which test is appropriate to evaluate the difference between the means?
    **d.** State a null hypothesis.
    **e.** If appropriate, state a directional hypothesis.
    **f.** What is the value of the test statistic?
    **g.** How many degrees of freedom are there?
    **h.** Can you reject the null hypothesis at the .05 level of significance?
    **i.** If appropriate, can you accept the directional hypothesis at the .05 level of significance?
    **j.** What conclusions can you draw about the difference in the number of complaints in the two types of hospitals?

4. The mean number of prenatal clinic visits made by a sample of 16 lower-income females was 5.75 with a variance of .5. A sample of 20 middle-income females had a mean of 6.30 visits with a variance of .7.

    **a.** Which test is appropriate to evaluate the difference between the means?
    **b.** State a null hypothesis.
    **c.** If appropriate, state a directional hypothesis.
    **d.** What is the value of the test statistic?
    **e.** Can you reject the null hypothesis at the .05 level of significance?
    **f.** If appropriate, can you accept the directional hypothesis at the .05 level of significance?
    **g.** What conclusions can you draw about the difference in prenatal clinic visits for the two income groups?

5. A critic was concerned with the confidence that could be attached to the means of the two samples of prenatal clinic users in exercise 4.

    **a.** What would be the standard error of the mean for $n_1$?
    **b.** What would the confidence limits be if you wanted to be 95% confident of including your mean for $n_1$?
    **c.** What would be the standard error of the mean for $n_2$?
    **d.** What would the confidence limits be if you wanted to be 95% confident of including your mean for $n_2$?
    **e.** Which of the two sample means provides the most precise estimate of its population?

6. A researcher compared a sample of male and female offenders sentenced for similar illegal drug-related charges. The samples were independent. The offenders were categorized as receiving hard or soft sentences. The results were as follows:

| | **Gender of Offender** | |
| --- | --- | --- |
| **Sentence** | **Female** | **Male** |
| Soft | 15 ($p_1 = .38$) | 25 ($p_2 = .59$) |
| Hard | 24 ($q_1 = .62$) | 17 ($q_2 = .41$) |

    **a.** Which test is most appropriate for the data?
    **b.** State a null hypothesis.
    **c.** If appropriate, state a directional hypothesis.
    **d.** What is the value of the test statistic?
    **e.** Can you reject the null hypothesis at the .05 level of significance?
    **f.** If appropriate, at what level of significance can you accept the directional hypothesis?
    **g.** What conclusions can you draw about the differences in gender and soft and hard sentences?

**7.** An experiment was conducted in which two matched groups of individuals were compared on their tolerance of ethnic differences. The data are shown below. Group 1 was exposed to a series of informational seminars intended to foster appreciation of ethnic variations. Group 2 received no such exposure. The groups consisted of 18 matched individuals. The test scores were such that high scores indicated more tolerance.

### Ethnic Tolerance: Matched Comparisons

| Matched Pairs | Group 1, Training | Group 2, No Training |
|:---:|:---:|:---:|
| 1 | 99 | 98 |
| 2 | 97 | 96 |
| 3 | 96 | 94 |
| 4 | 96 | 93 |
| 5 | 95 | 94 |
| 6 | 92 | 94 |
| 7 | 90 | 88 |
| 8 | 89 | 93 |
| 9 | 89 | 90 |
| 10 | 87 | 83 |
| 11 | 87 | 86 |
| 12 | 86 | 88 |
| 13 | 86 | 83 |
| 14 | 84 | 80 |
| 15 | 82 | 79 |
| 16 | 81 | 76 |
| 17 | 80 | 81 |
| 18 | 76 | 73 |

    **a.** What test would be appropriate for the data?
    **b.** State a null hypothesis.
    **c.** If appropriate, state a directional hypothesis.
    **d.** What is the value of the test statistic?
    **e.** How many degrees of freedom does the distribution have?
    **f.** Can you reject the null hypothesis at the .05 level of significance?

**g.** If you rejected the null hypothesis, what would be the character of your risk for error?

**h.** If appropriate, at what level of significance can you accept the directional hypothesis?

**i.** If you accept the directional hypothesis, what would be the character of your risk for error?

**j.** Given the risks involved in making a decision, what would you say about the effect of the training, and how would you justify your answer?

# 9

# COMPARING TWO DISCRETE MEASURES

## *Nonparametric Tests*

The statistical tests discussed in Chapter 8 are used to compare the distributions of variables in two populations. However, the use of the tests is restricted to variables that are interval or dichotomous and represent normal or binomial distributions. Many variables of interest to researchers are best typified with discrete measures that are either ordinal or nominal. In addition, continuous measures do not always represent normal distributions. Still, it is important to be able to compare the distributions of such variables.

The tests presented in this chapter are *nonparametric* and *distribution free*. Parametric tests evaluate differences by comparing specific population parameters; that is, the hypotheses are focused on specific numbers, usually $\mu$, describing the population. **Nonparametric tests** assess whether the general forms of two or more distributions differ. It was also pointed out in Chapter 8 that **distribution-free tests** are less restrictive than parametric tests because they make no requirements about the distribution of the variable in the population.

An important consideration in using nonparametric tests is their *power*, where the **power of a test** is defined as its capacity to avoid a Type II error. Recall that a Type II error, $\beta$, is that of not rejecting $H_0$ when it should be rejected; it is the failure to recognize small but consistent differences. A powerful test is one that is sensitive to small but significant differences.

In contrast, a Type I error, $\alpha$, is that of rejecting $H_0$ when it should be accepted. It consists of concluding there is a real difference when it is only a chance difference because of sampling variation. Recall that a Type I error can be minimized by increasing the level of significance, $\alpha$, which makes it more difficult to reject $H_0$. If $H_0$ is not rejected, a Type I error cannot occur. The problem is that, by avoiding a Type I error, you risk a Type II error. In Chapter 7 it was pointed out that avoiding the risk of a Type II error depends on a number of factors, including the level of significance, the size of the sample, the reliability of the sample, and the size of the difference between what is observed and what is expected. The risk of a Type II error is minimized to the extent that a statistical test has the power to distinguish a false null hypothesis. This power is related to the probability of a Type II error and is defined as power $= 1 - \beta$.

The procedures for calculating the power of a test go beyond the scope of an introductory statistics text.[1] However, it is important to distinguish the power of different tests, which is also referred to as the *efficiency* of tests because it relates to sample size. More efficient tests lead to correct decisions with smaller samples than do less efficient tests. The standard against which nonparametric tests are evaluated is Student's *t* test. Comparisons may be made in terms of percentages, so a test may be described as 95% as efficient or powerful as Student's *t*, which means that for a nonparametric test to be as powerful as the *t* test, sample size must be increased by 5%. This is based on the logic that, all other things being equal, you are more likely to make the correct decision with a large sample than with a small one.[2] It also agrees with the general logic that large samples are more likely to produce accurate estimates of population parameters than are small samples.

This chapter presents tests for comparing two populations under four different conditions: two independent ordinal measures, two dependent ordinal measures, two independent nominal measures, and two dependent nominal measures. As in Chapter 8, the presentation of tests for the different situations is organized around a description of the statistic, an example illustrating its application, and a summary of the characteristics and requirements of the test.

## COMPARING TWO INDEPENDENT SAMPLES: ORDINAL MEASURES

### The Mann-Whitney U Test

#### Description

The **Mann-Whitney U test** is the most powerful alternative to Student's *t* test for comparing two independent samples and is the best choice when an interval measure fails to meet the requirements for Student's *t*. Usually, the Mann-Whitney U test is used when the distribution of an interval variable fails to approximate a normal distribution. The procedure involves combining the interval scores of the two samples to form a single distribution, then the combined interval scores are assigned ranks from the lowest to the highest value. The ranks for the observations of each sample are identified and summed, then the sums of the ranks for the two distributions are compared. The assumption is that if the two samples are

---

[1] An illustration of the calculation of power is available in Richard P. Runyon and Audrey Haber, *Fundamentals of Behavioral Statistics* (New York: McGraw-Hill, 1991), pp. 451–64.

[2] See Sidney Siegel, *Nonparametric Statistics for Social Scientists* (New York: McGraw-Hill, 1956), pp. 8–14, 20–21.

from similar populations, the ranks should be randomly distributed across the two samples and they should have approximately equal sums of ranks. The Mann-Whitney U test can also be used for original ordinal measures with a large number of ranks. The test is sensitive to differences in the central tendencies of two distributions, making it a logical alternative to Student's $t$ test, which is based on the differences between means.

The U statistic for two groups is determined using the following two formulas:

$$U = n_1 n_2 + \frac{n_1 (n_1 + 1)}{2} - R_1 \tag{9.1}$$

$$U' = n_1 n_2 + \frac{n_2 (n_2 + 1)}{2} - R_2 \tag{9.2}$$

where     $n_1$ = the size of the first sample

$n_2$ = the size of the second sample

$R_1$ = the sum of the ranks for $n_1$

$R_2$ = the sum of the ranks for $n_2$

U = the smaller value

U' = the larger value

The calculations can be simplified somewhat after solving for Formula 9.1 by solving for the second value, using the following formula rather than Formula 9.2:

$$U' = n_1 n_2 - U \tag{9.3}$$

### Mann-Whitney U and Small Samples

When neither $n_1$ nor $n_2$ is greater than 20, a table is available that shows selected probabilities for U values (see Table B.5 in Appendix B). The use of the table is illustrated with the following example.

### Example 9.1: Neither $n_1$ nor $n_2$ > 20

The job satisfaction of older and younger workers was evaluated using a scale of interval scores shown in Table 9.1. A high score indicated greater job satisfaction. Although job satisfaction is an interval measure, assume that the distribution failed to meet the assumptions of a normal scale and so the $t$ test could not be used. The Mann-Whitney U test requires combining the scores of older and younger workers and ranking the combined distributions, as shown in Table 9.1. The ranks are assigned so the highest score in either of the distributions receives rank 1 (99), the second highest receives rank 2 (98), and so on through rank 29. Scores can be tied, as is true for the score of 90 in Table 9.1. In the case of tied scores, the ranks are averaged. The two scores of 90 would receive ranks 7 and 8, but given that the scores are tied, the average of the two ranks is assigned, 7 + 8/ 2 = 7.5.

**TABLE 9.1  Job Satisfaction of Older and Younger Workers**

| Older Workers ($n_1 = 15$) | | Younger Workers ($n_2 = 14$) | |
|---|---|---|---|
| Score | Rank | Score | Rank |
| 94 | 5 | 99 | 1 |
| 92 | 6 | 98 | 2 |
| 90 | 7.5 | 97 | 3 |
| 87 | 11 | 95 | 4 |
| 79 | 14 | 90 | 7.5 |
| 74 | 17 | 89 | 9 |
| 70 | 20 | 88 | 10 |
| 66 | 22 | 81 | 12 |
| 65 | 23 | 80 | 13 |
| 63 | 24 | 77 | 15 |
| 62 | 25 | 76 | 16 |
| 61 | 26 | 73 | 18 |
| 60 | 27 | 72 | 19 |
| 59 | 28 | 69 | 21 |
| 58 | 29 | | |
| | $R_1 = 284.5$ | | $R_2 = 150.5$ |

After the ranks are assigned, they are summed and the sums of the ranks for the two distributions compared. Formula 9.4 provides a check to ensure that the sums of the ranks for the two groups are correct:

$$R_1 + R_2 = \frac{N(N+1)}{2} \tag{9.4}$$

Applied to our example,

$$R_1 + R_2 = \frac{29(29+1)}{2} = \frac{870}{2} = 435$$

The result is the correct sum of all the ranks. The sum of the ranks for our two groups of workers agrees with the total: 284.5 + 150.5 = 435.

The focus of the statistical test is on the difference between the sum of the ranks for older workers, $R_1 = 284.5$, and the younger workers, $R_2 = 150.5$. The issue is whether the difference in the sum of the ranks is due to chance in sampling or is so large that older and younger workers represent different populations in terms of job satisfaction. The assumption is that if the two groups are similar, the ranks should be randomly distributed across the two groups and the sums approximately equal. The following hypotheses are tested at $\alpha = .05$:

$H_0$:     There is no difference in the job satisfaction of older and younger workers.

$H_1$:     Older workers are less satisfied with their jobs than younger workers.

The direction of $H_1$ is determined by the larger sum of the two ranks. In our example, low ranks represent greater satisfaction, whereas high ranks represent less satisfaction. Given that the sum of the ranks for older workers is larger, the hypothesis is that they are less satisfied. Using Formula 9.1, we find that the U statistic for the sample of older workers is

$$U = n_1 n_2 + \frac{n_1 (n_1 + 1)}{2} - R_1$$

$$U = (15)(14) + (15)(15 + 1)/2 - 284.5$$

$$= 210 + 120 - 284.5$$

$$= 45.5$$

Applying Formula 9.3, we find that the U statistic for the sample of younger workers is

$$U' = (15)(14) - 45.5$$

$$= 210 - 45.5$$

$$= 164.5$$

According to Table B.5 in Appendix B, when $n_1 = 15$ and $n_2 = 14$, the U value at .05 must be less than 59, and U' must be greater than 151 to reject $H_0$ and accept $H_1$. Our U value of 45.5 is less than 59, and the U' of 164.5 is greater than 144, enabling us to reject $H_0$ and accept $H_1$. The conclusion is that older workers are less satisfied with their jobs than are younger workers.

### Mann-Whitney U and Large Samples

As $n_1$ and $n_2$ increase, the distribution of the U statistic approaches normality, and a Z value can be calculated to test the significance of U. The size of each sample can be as small as 10 if there are no ties between the ranks of the two groups.[3] It has been suggested that sample size should be increased by one member for each tie.[4] A correction for ties is also available.

The assumption underlying the use of the normal distribution for testing the significance of the U statistic is that if repeated samples are drawn from two populations and their ranks on an interval measure compared, the distribution of U values will resemble that of a normal curve. And, as in the case of the sampling distribution of the means, given that we know that the form of the distribution of

---

[3] Ties within groups do not affect the statistic.

[4] J. Anthony Capon, *Elementary Statistics for the Social Sciences* (Belmont, Calif.: Wadsworth Publishing, 1988), pp. 239–40.

the U values is normal, the probability of any particular U value can be determined by transforming the statistic to a Z score, as shown in the following formula:

$$Z = \frac{U - \frac{n_1 n_2}{2}}{\sqrt{\frac{n_1 n_2 (n_1 + n_2 + 1)}{12}}}$$

(9.5)

where    $U - \dfrac{n_1 n_2}{2}$ = the difference between the observed U and the expected population value

$\sqrt{\dfrac{n_1 n_2 (n_1 + n_2 + 1)}{12}}$ = the standard error for the measurement in the two populations

More generally, Formula 9.5 shows that the Z value is a function of the ratio of the difference between the observed statistic and the expected population parameter *to* the standard error of U. Mann-Whitney U can be used to test both null and directional hypotheses. The test focuses on the central tendencies of the distributions, and the general forms of the hypotheses are

$H_0$:    There is no difference in distribution of the ranks across the two populations.

$H_1$:    The sum of the ranks of population 1 is greater than population 2, or depending on the direction of the difference, the sum of the ranks of population 1 is less than population 2.

### Correction for Ties

In the event of tied scores, a correction can be applied. The correction involves a T value that is based on the number of tied scores and is given by the following formula:

$$T = \Sigma \frac{t^3 - t}{12}$$

(9.6)

where    $t$ = the scores tied for a rank.

The formula directs you to cube the number of scores tied for a particular rank, subtract the number of ties for that score from the cubed value, and divide by 12. This is done for each set of tied scores, and the results are summed. Suppose that two scores are tied for rank 5, four for rank 9, three for rank 14, and two for rank 16. According to the formula, the number of scores tied for each rank is cubed and then the number of tied scores is subtracted from the cubed value, and the difference divided by 12. The results for each set of ties are summed, and the sum is the T value.

$$T = \frac{2^3 - 2}{12} + \frac{4^3 - 4}{12} + \frac{3^3 - 3}{12} + \frac{2^3 - 2}{12}$$

$$= \frac{8 - 2}{12} + \frac{64 - 4}{12} + \frac{27 - 3}{12} + \frac{8 - 2}{12}$$

$$= .5 + 5 + 2 + .5 = 8$$

The T value is then used to correct the estimate of the standard error in the calculation of the Z score, as shown in the following formula:

$$Z = \frac{U - \frac{n_1 n_2}{2}}{\sqrt{\left(\frac{n_1 n_2}{N(N-1)}\right)\left(\frac{N^3 - N}{12} - T\right)}} \tag{9.7}$$

where $N$ is the sum of $n_1$ and $n_2$.

The following example illustrates the application of Formula 9.5 using the standard Z score.

### Example 9.2: When $n_1$ and $n_2$ > 20 or Smaller If No Ties

In the previous example of job satisfaction for older and younger workers, the data consist of ranks assigned to two samples, $n_1 = 15$ and $n_2 = 14$, as shown in Table 9.1. Given that only one tie occurs in the example, it is unnecessary to use the correction for ties, and the Z-score Formula 9.5 can be used to evaluate the data. From Example 9.1, we know that U = 45.5. The null and directional hypotheses are tested at $\alpha = .05$:

$H_0$:   There is no difference in the sums of the ranks for the two populations.

$H_1$:   The sum of the ranks in population 1 is greater than population 2.

Using Formula 9.5, we find the following:

$$Z = \frac{U - \frac{n_1 n_2}{2}}{\sqrt{\frac{n_1 n_2 (n_1 + n_2 + 1)}{12}}}$$

$$= \frac{45.5 - \frac{(15)(14)}{2}}{\sqrt{\frac{(15)(14)(15 + 14 + 1)}{12}}}$$

$$= \frac{45.5 - 105}{\sqrt{525}}$$

$$= \frac{-59.5}{22.9129}$$

$$= -2.60$$

The Z value is interpreted using Table B.1 in Appendix B: $Z = -2.60$ is greater than the $Z = \pm 1.96$ required for $\alpha = .05$, enabling us to reject the null hypothesis and accept the directional hypothesis. In fact, the exact probability of $Z = -2.60$, one tailed, is .0047 and two tailed, .0094, as shown in columns B and C of Table B.1.

### Summary

The Mann-Whitney U test is the most powerful alternative to Student's $t$ test, with an efficiency of 95%. Thus, its ability to distinguish a false $H_0$ is comparable to that of Student's $t$ if the sample size is increased by 5%. The test is especially useful for comparing two interval distributions that fail to meet the assumptions for using the $t$ test. The continuous nature of interval measures reduces the likelihood of ties, and even when limited ties occur, the correction factor can be used. In summary, the Mann-Whitney U test is characterized by the following:

1. It is sensitive to differences in the central tendencies of distributions.
2. It requires no assumptions about the form of the distribution of the variable.
3. It uses a correction when there are multiple tied ranks across the samples.
4. It requires that the two samples are independent.

## COMPARING TWO DEPENDENT SAMPLES: ORDINAL MEASURES

### The Wilcoxon Matched Pairs, Signed Ranks Test

#### Description

The **Wilcoxon matched pairs, signed ranks test** is used to determine whether two dependent samples represent similar populations. The dependent samples can be either matched or consist of comparisons of before and after measures for one sample. Although the Wilcoxon test is based on an ordinal statistic, it assumes that the original measure is interval. However, the test statistic is based on the ranked differences between the interval measures of paired members of the two samples and thus is an ordinal test. The test is used as an alternative to Student's $t$ test for dependent samples when the distributional assumptions of the $t$ test are not met. The test is especially useful because it takes into account the magnitude of the differences between the ranks because the ranks are based on the size of the differences in the original interval measures. The Wilcoxon test can be used for both null and directional hypotheses.

The test statistic is symbolized by T, where T equals the sum of the signed ranks ( + or − ) with the least sum. If the number of pairs is small, $N \leq 25$. Table

B.6 in Appendix B provides the probabilities associated with various T values. If $N > 25$, the distribution of T values approximates a normal distribution, and a Z score can be calculated, as shown in the following formula:

$$Z = \frac{T - \dfrac{N(N+1)}{4}}{\sqrt{\dfrac{N(N+1)(2N+1)}{24}}}$$ (9.8)

where $\quad T - \dfrac{N(N+1)}{4}$ = the difference between the signed ranks with the least sum and the expected difference in the population

$\sqrt{\dfrac{N(N+1)(2N+1)}{24}}$ = the standard error of the difference in the two populations

The probability of T is a function of the ratio of the difference between the observed T value and the expected population mean *to* the standard error of T.

### Example 9.3

A random sample of 25 junior high school students were provided with intensive exposure to the workings of the criminal justice system. Their attitudes toward the system were tested prior to and following the exposure. The test was scored so that a negative difference score indicated a gain in positive attitudes and a positive score a loss in positive attitudes. The results of the pretest and posttest scores are presented in Table 9.2.

The columns in Table 9.2 illustrate the application of the Wilcoxon test. The first column shows the individuals; columns 2 and 3 show each individual's pre- and posttest scores; column 4 shows the difference (*d*) between the pretest and posttest scores; and column 5 shows the rank assigned to the absolute differences in column 4. For example, three individuals have a difference of 1 (individual 8 has –1, individual 12 has +1, and individual 21 has –1), so each is given the average of the first three ranks, $1 + 2 + 3/3 = 2$. Next, the sign of the difference is assigned to each rank. Column 6 shows the least sum of the signed ranks. In the case of our example, the differences with the + sign have the least sum, 66.5, and this is the T value. The hypotheses tested at $\alpha = .01$ are

$H_0$:   Exposure to the criminal justice system has no effect on attitudes.
$H_1$:   Exposure to the criminal justice system increased positive attitudes.

The direction of $H_1$ is determined by the meaning of the sign of the sums in the example. In our case, the sum of the negative signs exceeds that of the positive signs, indicating that more individuals had higher posttest scores and a gain in positive attitudes toward the criminal justice system. The smaller sum of positive signs, T value 66.5, indicates that fewer individuals became more negative as a result of the exposure. Using the *sum of the ranks* makes the test sensitive to the size of the difference in changes from the pretest to the posttest.

**TABLE 9.2     Exposure to the Criminal Justice System and Attitudes**

| Individual | Pretest Score | Posttest Score | Difference (d) | Signed Rank of d | Least Sum of Signed Ranks |
|---|---|---|---|---|---|
| 1 | 75 | 88 | −13 | −21 | |
| 2 | 74 | 85 | −11 | −18 | |
| 3 | 77 | 84 | −7 | −11.5 | |
| 4 | 74 | 83 | −9 | −14.5 | |
| 5 | 68 | 82 | −14 | −22 | |
| 6 | 76 | 81 | −5 | −8.5 | |
| 7 | 64 | 80 | −16 | −24 | |
| 8 | 78 | 79 | −1 | −2 | |
| 9 | 68 | 79 | −11 | −18 | |
| 10 | 75 | 78 | −3 | −5.5 | |
| 11 | 73 | 78 | −5 | −8.5 | |
| 12 | 78 | 77 | +1 | +2 | 2 |
| 13 | 59 | 76 | −17 | −25 | |
| 14 | 79 | 75 | +4 | +7 | 7 |
| 15 | 63 | 75 | −12 | −20 | |
| 16 | 59 | 74 | −15 | −23 | |
| 17 | 75 | 73 | +2 | +4 | 4 |
| 18 | 70 | 73 | −3 | −5.5 | |
| 19 | 61 | 72 | −11 | −18 | |
| 20 | 78 | 70 | +8 | +13 | 13 |
| 21 | 69 | 70 | −1 | −2 | |
| 22 | 63 | 70 | −7 | −11.5 | |
| 23 | 70 | 64 | +6 | +10 | 10 |
| 24 | 72 | 62 | +10 | +16 | 16 |
| 25 | 70 | 61 | +9 | +14.5 | 14.5 |
| | | | | | T = 66.5 |

The sample consists of 25 individuals, so the test statistic, T = 66.5, is evaluated using Table B.6 in Appendix B. The decision rule is as follows: If the T statistic is equal to or less than the table value, reject $H_0$ and accept $H_1$. In our example, where $N$ = 25, Table B.6 shows that to reject $H_0$ at $\alpha$ = .01, the T value must be less than or equal to 68. Our test statistic of 66.5 is less than 68, therefore we can reject $H_0$ and accept $H_1$ at the .01 level of significance. The results indicate that intensive exposure produced a more positive attitude toward the criminal justice system.

Given a sample size of 25, the same example can be used to illustrate the Z-score formula for assessing the significance of the differences. The hypotheses will be tested at the .01 level of significance. According to Formula 9.8, the result is

$$Z = \frac{66.5 - \frac{25(25+1)}{4}}{\sqrt{\frac{25(25+1)[2(25)+1]}{24}}}$$

$$= \frac{66.5 - \frac{650}{4}}{\sqrt{\frac{(650)(51)}{24}}}$$

$$= \frac{66.5 - 162.5}{\sqrt{1381.25}}$$

$$= \frac{-96}{37.165}$$

$$Z = -2.58$$

We know that the Z score associated with $\alpha = .01$ is 2.58. Our result of $Z = -2.58$ enables us to reject $H_0$ and accept $H_1$.

### Summary

The Wilcoxon test with 95% of the power of Student's *t* test is a good alternative to evaluate the similarity of two dependent measures. In summary, the test has the following characteristics:

1. It is used to compare the ranked differences between two dependent interval measures represented by the T statistic.
2. It can be used for very small samples.
3. It evaluates both the null and the directional hypotheses.
4. It is sensitive to the magnitude of the difference between measures.
5. It is used for two dependent measures.

## COMPARING TWO INDEPENDENT SAMPLES: NOMINAL MEASURES

### The Chi-Square Test

#### Description

We have already encountered the chi-square statistic for evaluating the goodness of fit between an observed sample statistic and a known or expected population parameter. The **chi-square two-sample test** also is useful for evaluating the contingencies between two populations on measures with multiple nominal categories, as shown in the upper portion of Table 9.3. It can also be used to compare more than two samples on measures with two or more nominal categories, as shown in the middle portion of Table 9.3. Moreover, chi-square can be used to evaluate the contingency between two or more nominal measures with two or more nominal categories, as shown in the lower portion of Table 9.3. Chi-square is also useful because it has no distributional restrictions and thus can be used in a wide variety of situations.

Like other statistical tests, the chi-square statistic is based on the difference between observed and expected frequencies. In the case of chi-square, the differences relate to the observed and expected frequencies for each cell of a contingency table. The expected frequencies are a function of marginal totals related to each cell in that they are the product of the row total times the column total divided by the total number of observations. The difference between

**TABLE 9.3    Application of Chi-Square to Contingencies**

| | Comparing Two Populations on a Nominal Measure | |
|---|---|---|
| **Nominal Categories** | **Sample 1** <br> **(Experimental Group)** | **Sample 2** <br> **(Control Group)** |
| 1 | | |
| 2 | | |
| 3 | | |
| . | | |
| . | | |
| . | | |

| | Comparing Multiple Populations on a Nominal Measure | | | |
|---|---|---|---|---|
| **Nominal Categories** | **Sample 1** | **Sample 2** | **Sample 3** | **Sample 4** |
| 1 | | | | |
| 2 | | | | |
| 3 | | | | |
| . | | | | |
| . | | | | |
| . | | | | |

| | Comparing Two Nominal Measures | | | |
|---|---|---|---|---|
| | | **Social Class** | | |
| **Political Preference** | **1** | **2** | **3** | **. . .** |
| 1 | | | | |
| 2 | | | | |
| 3 | | | | |
| . | | | | |
| . | | | | |
| . | | | | |

the observed and expected frequency for each cell is then evaluated using the following formula:

$$\chi^2 = \sum_{i=1}^{k} \frac{\left(O_i - E_i\right)^2}{E_i} \qquad (9.9)$$

This formula directs you to subtract the difference between the observed and expected value for each cell, square the difference, divide the squared value by the expected value, and sum the results for all of the cells. Given that chi-square is intended for nominal scales consisting of categorical measures that have no inherent direction (i.e., the order of the categories is arbitrary), it can be used only to test a null hypothesis, the general form of which is

$H_0$:    There is no difference in the observed and expected frequencies across the scale categories.

A more technical statement of the hypothesis would be as follows: There is no difference in the observed and expected frequencies, given the marginal column and row totals, of the scale categories. This is the case because the expected frequency for each cell is a function of its column and row totals. The procedures for calculating chi-square can be illustrated with examples. First we examine an application to two dichotomous nominal measures, then we consider an example for multiple categorical variables.

### Example 9.4: 2 × 2 Tables

Table 9.4 shows a typical contingency table for dichotomous measures. Usually, the tables are designed so that the columns of the table display the independent measure and the rows the dependent measure. Tables displaying two dichotomous measures are referred to as 2 × 2 tables because they consist of two columns and two rows. The entries in the cells of the table display the contingency between gender and smoking. Ten females smoke and 19 do not, and 18 males smoke and 12 do not. The totals of the columns and the rows, referred to as the *marginal totals,* show that there are 29 females, 30 males, 28 smokers, and 31 nonsmokers. Overall, the sample included 59 males and females, or 59 smokers and nonsmokers.

The chi-square statistic is based on the difference between the observed and expected frequencies of the cells. The observed frequencies relate to the sample

**TABLE 9.4   Gender of High School Smokers**

| Smoking | Female | Male | Subtotals |
|---|---|---|---|
| Smokers | 10 | 18 | 28 |
| Nonsmokers | 19 | 12 | 31 |
| Subtotal | 29 | 30 | 59 |

Note: The cells of contingency tables are labeled across the rows, beginning with *a* for the upper left-hand cell.

**TABLE 9.5    Gender of High School Smokers**

| Smoking | Female | Male | Subtotals |
|---|---|---|---|
| Smokers | 10 (13.76) | 18 (14.24) | 28 |
| Nonsmokers | 19 (15.24) | 12 (15.76) | 31 |
| Subtotal | 29 | 30 | 59 |

observations. The expected frequencies represent what is expected for each cell given its marginal column and row totals. The expectation for each cell is the product of the column and row total divided by the total number of observations. The expectations for the cells of Table 9.4 are

Cell a = smokers × females ÷ total = (28)(29)/59 = 13.76
Cell b = smokers × males ÷ total = (28)(30)/59 = 14.24
Cell c = nonsmokers × females ÷ total = (31)(29)/59 = 15.24
Cell d = nonsmokers × males ÷ total = (31)(30)/59 = 15.76

The observed and expected frequencies are displayed in Table 9.5. Note that the sum of the expected frequencies in the cells must equal the column and row totals. For a 2 × 2 table you only need to calculate one expected frequency; the remainder can be determined by subtracting it from the row and column totals for each cell. If you know that cell a = 13.76, cell b equals 28 − 13.76 = 14.24. This also shows that a 2 × 2 table has only 1 degree of freedom. Once the expected frequency is determined for one cell, the remainder are fixed by the column and row totals. The null hypothesis, which is tested at the .05 level of significance, is

$H_0$:    Female and male high schoolers do not differ in regard to smoking.

The chi-square value is determined by using Formula 9.9, which directs you to subtract the difference between the observed and expected frequency for each cell, square the difference, and divide the squared difference by the expected cell frequency. The results for each cell are then summed for the chi-square value. Conceptually, it represents the ratio of the difference between the observed and the expected frequencies *to* the expected frequency (the variation expected in the population). Table 9.6 illustrates the computation of chi-square. The chi-square value is 3.845. The probability of the test statistic is evaluated using the chi-square distribution in Table B.4 in Appendix B. Although we have already seen that the degrees of freedom for a 2 × 2 table are always 1, in general the degrees of freedom for a contingency table equal the number of columns minus 1 multiplied by the number of rows minus 1, or df = (c − 1)(r − 1), or for our example, (2 − 1)(2 − 1) = 1. According to Table B.4, to reject $H_0$ at the .05 level we need a $\chi^2$ greater than 3.84. The result of 3.845 enables us to reject the null hypothesis and conclude that high school females and males differ when it comes to smoking.

Only nondirectional hypotheses can be used for nominal variables because nominal measures do not consist of ordered categories. However, in the case of two dichotomous measures (2 × 2 tables), directionality can be inferred by exam-

**TABLE 9.6  Computation of Chi-Square for Gender and High School Smokers**

| Cell | $O_i$ | $E_i$ | $O_i - E_i$ | $(O_i - E_i)^2$ | $(O_i - E_i)^2/E_i$ |
|---|---|---|---|---|---|
| a | 10 | 13.76 | −3.76 | 14.138 | 1.027 |
| b | 18 | 14.24 | 3.76 | 14.138 | .993 |
| c | 19 | 15.24 | 3.76 | 14.138 | .928 |
| d | 12 | 15.76 | −3.76 | 14.138 | .897 |
| | | | | | 3.845 |

ining the diagonal cells. For example, in Table 9.5 the diagonal cells a and d show that fewer females and more males smoke, whereas diagonal cells b and c show that fewer males and more females are nonsmokers. Although a directional hypothesis cannot be tested explicitly for significance, we can discuss the difference in the distribution of females and males across the smoking and nonsmoking categories.

Chi-square tends to overestimate the association of measures in 2 × 2 tables when the number of observations is less than 75. To provide a more conservative estimate of the relationship, the Yates correction is used as shown in the following formula:

$$\chi^2 = \sum_{i=1}^{k} \frac{\left( \left| O_i - E_i \right| - .5 \right)^2}{E_i} \tag{9.10}$$

The correction consists of reducing the absolute value of the difference between $O_i$ and $E_i$ in each cell by a value of .5. The results for our example are shown in Table 9.7.

Using the Yates correction results in a smaller chi-square value, $\chi^2 = 2.892$, whereas without the correction it was 3.845. In our example, the difference in the two outcomes is large enough to change the decision regarding $H_0$. Recall that the $\chi^2$ value that is needed to reject $H_0$ at the .05 level had to be greater than or equal to 3.84. Given the Yates correction, our value of 2.892 is insufficient to reject $H_0$. The extent of the effect of the Yates correction is a function of sample size, or the

**TABLE 9.7  Computation of Chi-Square for Gender and High School Smokers**

| Cell | $O_i$ | $E_i$ | $O_i - E_i$ | $(O_i - E_i) - .5$ | $(O_i - E_i)^2$ | $(O_i - E_i)^2/E_i$ |
|---|---|---|---|---|---|---|
| a | 10 | 13.76 | −3.76 | −3.26 | 10.63 | .773 |
| b | 18 | 14.24 | 3.76 | 3.26 | 10.63 | .747 |
| c | 19 | 15.24 | 3.76 | −3.26 | 10.63 | .697 |
| d | 12 | 15.76 | −3.76 | 3.26 | 10.63 | .675 |
| | | | | | | 2.892 |

number of cases in each cell. As the size of the sample increases, the impact of reducing the difference between the observed and the expected value by .5 declines. The effect of the correction on small samples is to guard against a Type I error associated with rejecting the null hypothesis. Using the Yates correction reduces the chi-square value, making it more difficult to reject the null hypothesis and decreasing the risk of a Type I error. As a further precaution, the use of chi-square is limited to cases in which the expected frequencies for each cell must be equal to or greater than 5.

Whereas small samples are of concern in using chi-square, large samples also present a problem that is common to all tests of significance. As sample sizes increase and become very large, increasingly small differences are statistically significant because large samples reduce the standard error in the denominator. This is true for all statistical tests; it follows from the logic of statistical inference that as sample sizes get large relative to the population, increasingly smaller differences are significant. If the sample is so large that it includes the entire population, any difference is significant. This is appropriate because no matter how small it is, a difference in the population is real.

Remember, though, that a statistically significant difference does not imply substantive significance. Substantive differences are those that have meaning in terms of theoretical concerns or everyday affairs. In addition, there is a difference between statistical significance and the strength of the relationship, or association of two measures. Statistical techniques for evaluating the strength of associations are available. Recall that in discussing Student's *t* test in the preceding chapter we were able to calculate the percentage of explained variance for a dependent variable given an independent variable that indicated the strength of their relationship. Later chapters treat this matter in some detail. A number of techniques specifically designed to measure the strength of associations are considered in the final chapter.

It is also interesting to note that with 1 degree of freedom, the square root of $\chi^2$ is equal to the Z score. In our example of smokers, before using the Yates correction we had $\chi^2 = 3.845$, and using the chi-square table it was significant just at the .05 level of significance. The square root of the chi-square value is $\sqrt{3.845} = 1.96 = Z$, which has a probability of .05. Then we applied the Yates correction, $\chi^2 = 2.892$, and it failed to be significant at the .05 level. The probability was closer to the .10 level. The square root of the chi-square value is $\sqrt{2.892} = 1.70 = Z$, which has a probability of .089, again closer to the .10 level. The examples illustrate the correspondence between the square root of $\chi^2$ and the Z score.

### Example 9.5: *n* × *n* Tables

The use of chi-square for $n \times n$ tables is based on the same formula and procedures as those for 2 × 2 tables. Just as in the case of 2 × 2 tables, there are limits to the number of expected observations for each cell for $n \times n$ tables. The conservative rule is that no more than 20% of the cells can have expected frequencies less than 5.

**TABLE 9.8   Religious Affiliation and Political Preference**

| Political Preference | Religious Affiliation | | | | | |
|---|---|---|---|---|---|---|
| | Episcopal | Baptist | Catholic | Methodist | Unitarian | Subtotal |
| Democrat | a | b | c | d | e | |
| | 5 (10.68) | 12 (22.46) | 32 (27.62) | 22 (15.83) | 17 (11.41) | 88 |
| Republican | f | g | h | i | j | |
| | 19 (11.16) | 29 (23.48) | 24 (28.87) | 13 (16.55) | 7 (11.94) | 92 |
| Independent | k | l | m | n | o | |
| | 5 (7.16) | 20 (15.06) | 19 (18.51) | 8 (10.62) | 7 (7.65) | 59 |
| Subtotal | 29 | 61 | 75 | 43 | 31 | 239 |

Table 9.8 shows the contingency between religious affiliation and political preference. The cells of the table contain the observed and, in parentheses, the expected frequencies. For example, the observed frequency for cell a is 5, and the expected frequency is 10.68. The expected frequency was derived by dividing the product of the marginal totals of cell a by the total number of observations, or $29 \times 88/239 = 10.68$.

The following null hypothesis is tested at $\alpha = .01$.

$H_0$:   There is no relationship between religious affiliation and political preference.

Chi-square is calculated using Formula 9.9 and is shown in Table 9.9, where $\chi^2 = 27.148$. The degrees of freedom are df = $(c - 1)(r - 1)$ = $(5 - 1)(3 - 1) = 8$. According to Table B.4 in Appendix B, to reject $H_0$ at $\alpha = .01$ with 8 degrees of freedom, we need a $\chi^2$ greater than 20.09. Rounded to two decimals, our $\chi^2 = 27.15$ is greater than the table value of 20.09, so the null hypothesis is rejected. There is a relationship between religious affiliation and political preference. It is not possible to test a directional hypothesis, but an examination of Table 9.8 provides some sense of the relationship between religious affiliation and political preference.

### Summary
The chi-square statistic is perhaps one of the most widely used and popular tests in the social sciences. When appropriately applied, it is useful because it enables us to evaluate the observed and expected frequencies for nominal measures for which alternative statistics are not readily available. The statistic makes no assumptions about the distribution of the variable in the population. Its major limitation is related to sample size and the expected frequencies of the table cells. The power of the test is difficult to evaluate, and contrary to the other tests discussed thus far, no simple comparison of chi-square can be made to Student's *t* test. However, it often is the only suitable alternative available for testing the relationship

**TABLE 9.9    Calculation of Chi-Square: Religious Affiliation and Political Preference**

| Cell | $O_i$ | $E_i$ | $O_i - E_i$ | $(O_i - E_i)^2$ | $(O_i - E_i)^2/E_i$ |
|------|-------|-------|-------------|-----------------|---------------------|
| a | 5 | 10.68 | −5.68 | 32.262 | 3.021 |
| b | 12 | 22.46 | −10.46 | 109.412 | 4.871 |
| c | 32 | 27.62 | 4.38 | 19.184 | .695 |
| d | 22 | 15.83 | 6.17 | 38.069 | 2.405 |
| e | 17 | 11.41 | 5.59 | 31.248 | 2.739 |
| f | 19 | 11.16 | 7.84 | 61.466 | 5.508 |
| g | 29 | 23.48 | 5.52 | 30.407 | 1.298 |
| h | 24 | 28.87 | −4.87 | 23.717 | .821 |
| i | 13 | 16.55 | −3.55 | 12.603 | .761 |
| j | 7 | 11.94 | −4.94 | 24.404 | 2.043 |
| k | 5 | 7.16 | −2.16 | 4.666 | .652 |
| l | 20 | 15.06 | 4.94 | 24.404 | 1.620 |
| m | 19 | 18.51 | .49 | .240 | .013 |
| n | 8 | 10.62 | −2.62 | 6.864 | .646 |
| o | 7 | 7.65 | −.65 | .423 | .055 |
|   | 239 |       |             |                 | 27.148 |

between two nominal measures. In review, the major characteristics of the statistic are as follows:

1. It is used to test the relationship between two independent nominal measures.
2. There are no distributional requirements.
3. For a 2 × 2 table, no cell should have an expected frequency of less than 5.
4. The Yates correction should always be used for 2 × 2 tables when $n \le 75$.
5. An $n \times n$ table can have no more than 20% of the expected frequencies less than 5.
6. As $n$ becomes larger, it might not be appropriate to assume that a statistically significant chi-square is substantively significant. Techniques that measure the strength of associations should be considered in those instances.

# COMPARING TWO DEPENDENT SAMPLES: NOMINAL MEASURES

## McNemar's Test

### Description

**McNemar's test** is used to evaluate the relationship between two dependent nominal measures. The typical situation in which the test is applied is a pre–post or before–after design. The design is based on measures prior to some intervention

**TABLE 9.10**  **Format for a 2 × 2 Contingency Table for Dependent Measures**

| Before | After | |
|---|---|---|
| | Negative | Positive |
| Positive | a (+ to −) | b (+ to +) |
| Negative | c (− to −) | d (− to +) |

or event, and after the intervention, a postmeasure is taken. The pre–post measures of subjects are compared to assess whether the intervention produced a change.

The data format is a 2 × 2 contingency table designed to reflect changes in the a and d cells of the table, as shown in Table 9.10. Sample members in cell a represent those who were positive before the intervention but became negative afterward, those in cell d were negative before and became positive afterward, and cells b and c represent those who did not change. McNemar's test focuses on the cells that show change and is computed using the following formula:

$$\chi^2 = \frac{\left(|a-d|-1\right)^2}{a+d}$$

**(9.11)**

The resulting test statistic is a chi-square value with probabilities of outcomes displayed in Table B.4 in Appendix B. The numerator in the formula directs you to subtract 1 from the absolute difference between cells a and d, square the result, and divide it by a + d. McNemar's test is an explicit one-tailed test because it is based on the direction of the change in cells a and d. The directional hypothesis consists of a statement of the direction of change given the contents of cells a and d.

### Example 9.6

A sample of 34 community members were asked whether they favored handguns (the pretest measure) and then were exposed to a presentation on the role of handguns in violent episodes. After the presentation, they again were asked about whether they favored handguns (the posttest measure). The results are shown in Table 9.11. The directional hypothesis, based on a review of the members in cells a and d, is tested at the .05 level of significance:

$H_1$:     a > d: more community members favored handguns before the intervention than after.

**TABLE 9.11**  **Change in Opinion on Handguns**

| Before | After | |
|---|---|---|
| | Oppose | Favor |
| Favor | 14 | 7 |
| Oppose | 8 | 5 |

Applying Formula 9.11, we find

$$\chi^2 = \frac{\left(|14-5|-1\right)^2}{14+5}$$

$$= \frac{8^2}{19}$$

$$= 3.37$$

The chi-square statistic is evaluated using Table B.4 in Appendix B. However, the table displays two-tailed probabilities, whereas McNemar's test is a one-tailed test. Thus, the probabilities across the top of the table must be halved. A one-tailed probability for .05 is located in the column for .10 two-tailed probabilities. Recall that 2 × 2 contingency tables have 1 degree of freedom. Given that our test statistic of 3.37 is greater than the table value of 2.71 at the intersect of 1 degree of freedom and the .10 probability, we can accept the directional hypothesis at the .05 level of significance and conclude that the intervention increased the number of people opposing handguns.

McNemar's test is restricted to sample sizes in which ½(a + d) ≥ 5. However, even with samples as small as 6, it is equal in efficiency to the standard-error-of-proportions test. Thus, McNemar's test is a powerful one if the concern is to evaluate changes in cells a and d.

### Summary
McNemar's test can be summarized as follows:

1. It serves as an alternative to the proportions test for two dependent samples.
2. It makes no assumptions about the form of the distribution.
3. It can be used when ½(a + d) ≥ 5.

## COMPUTER EXERCISES: SOME SUGGESTIONS

Using your software for the statistical comparisons of two groups that you began in the previous chapter can be continued here. In Chapter 8 you compared continuous measures using Student's *t* test and the standard-error-of-proportions test. Here your concern is with comparing groups on discrete measures. The Mann-Whitney U and Wilcoxon matched pairs, signed ranks tests are frequently applied to interval measures that fail to meet the assumptions of a normal distribution. You may have encountered such variables in your computer exercises in Chapter 8, or you may find other interval measures that do not meet the assumptions of normality. Use your software to compare two independent and two dependent measures. The printout will provide you with the test statistics and their probabilities.

You should also select a group of nominal measures suitable for the 2 × 2 and *n* × *n* chi-square tests. The software should alert you if the expected cell frequencies fail to meet the criteria for the tests. It will also print out the table so you can see if the expected frequencies are adequate for using chi-square. In addition, you should select two dichotomous variables and use McNemar's test to evaluate their relationship. Remember that the 2 × 2 tables should be arranged so that cells a and d represent the change cells.

## CHAPTER SUMMARY

The purpose of this chapter was to familiarize you with statistical tests used to evaluate differences between two discrete measures. The common characteristic of these tests is that they are distribution free; that is, they do not require that the distribution of the variable assume a particular form, such as a normal distribution. In addition, they are nonparametric in that rather than test hypotheses that focus on a specific parameter of a population, such as $\mu$, they detect more general differences in the shape or form of two distributions. Tests were examined for the following situations:

1. Two independent samples, ordinal measures: Mann-Whitney U test
2. Two dependent samples, ordinal measures: Wilcoxon test
3. Two independent samples, nominal measures: chi-square two-sample test
4. Two dependent samples, nominal measures: McNemar's chi-square

Two-sample comparisons play an important role in social research, but research designs often involve more than two groups. Chapter 10 will consider statistical tests for models used to compare multiple samples or measures.

## KEY TERMS

**chi-square two-sample test**   A test used to evaluate whether two populations are similarly distributed across a set of nominal categories.

**distribution-free tests**   Tests that make no assumptions about the form of the distribution of a variable.

**Mann-Whitney U test**   A test comparing the sums of the ranks of two independent samples on an ordinal measure. The test is based on differences in the sums of the combined ranks of the two samples.

**McNemar's test**   A test used to compare two dependent samples on a dichotomous measure.

**nonparametric tests**   Tests that assess overall distributional differences rather than focusing on the difference between two specific parameters.

**power of a test**   The capacity of a test to avoid a Type II error.

**Wilcoxon matched pairs, signed ranks test**   A test for two dependent samples based on interval scores; the differences in the scores are ranked, and the resulting statistic is sensitive to both direction and magnitude of differences.

## SYMBOLS

| | |
|---|---|
| U | The Mann-Whitney U statistic for two independent samples |
| T | The Wilcoxon statistic for two dependent samples |
| $\chi^2$ | Tests that use the chi-square distribution |

## FORMULAS

$$Z = \frac{U - \frac{n_1 n_2}{2}}{\sqrt{\frac{n_1 n_2 (n_1 + n_2 + 1)}{12}}}$$     Mann-Whitney U test

$$Z = \frac{T - \frac{N(N+1)}{4}}{\sqrt{\frac{N(N+1)(2N+1)}{24}}}$$     Wilcoxon test for two dependent samples

$$\chi^2 = \sum_{i=1}^{k} \frac{\left(O_i - E_i\right)^2}{E_i}$$     Chi-square test

$$\chi^2 = \sum_{i=1}^{k} \frac{\left(|O_i - E_i| - .5\right)^2}{E_i}$$     Chi-square test with the Yates correction

$$\chi^2 = \frac{\left(|a - d| - 1\right)^2}{a + d}$$     McNemar's test

## EXERCISES

1. A sample of sophomores and juniors was compared on their performance in an introductory statistics course. The distributions of their performances failed to meet the requirements for the *t* test, but the researcher wanted to test the differences between the two groups. The data that were observed are shown on the next page.

   a. Which test would be most suitable for the data?
   b. State an appropriate null hypothesis.
   c. If appropriate, state a directional hypothesis.
   d. What is the value of the test statistic?
   e. Can you reject the null hypothesis at the .05 level of significance?

**f.** If appropriate, can you accept the directional hypothesis at the .05 level of significance?

**g.** What are your conclusions?

| Sophomores | Juniors |
|------------|---------|
| 98 | 100 |
| 97 | 99 |
| 95 | 97 |
| 92 | 96 |
| 89 | 94 |
| 87 | 93 |
| 83 | 91 |
| 82 | 90 |
| 81 | 88 |
| 80 | 86 |
| 78 | 85 |
| 77 | 84 |
| 75 |  |

**2.** Two independent samples of employees were ranked on the quality of their performances. The following data were observed:

*Group 1*  

$n_1 = 26$  
$R_1 = 604.5$

*Group 2*  

$n_2 = 37$  
$R_2 = 1411.5$

**a.** If the concern is in differences between the central tendencies of the distributions, which test would you use?

**b.** State an appropriate null hypothesis.

**c.** If appropriate, state a directional hypothesis.

**d.** What is the value of the test statistic?

**e.** Can you reject the null hypothesis at the .05 level of significance?

**f.** If appropriate, can you accept the directional hypothesis at the .05 level of significance?

**g.** What did you learn about the two groups?

**3.** A group of disabled persons was scored on a self-image test prior to and one month following a workshop on maximizing social participation. A high score indicated a more positive self-image and a low score a more negative self-image. The results are shown on the next page.

**a.** Which test would be most suitable for the data?

**b.** State an appropriate null hypothesis.

**c.** If appropriate, state a directional hypothesis.

**d.** What is the value of the test statistic?

**e.** Can you reject the null hypothesis at the .05 level of significance?

**f.** If appropriate, can you accept the directional hypothesis at the .05 level of significance?

**g.** What can you say about the workshop?

| Individual | Preworkshop | Postworkshop |
|:---:|:---:|:---:|
| 1 | 78 | 84 |
| 2 | 81 | 82 |
| 3 | 76 | 85 |
| 4 | 80 | 78 |
| 5 | 85 | 87 |
| 6 | 83 | 86 |
| 7 | 80 | 82 |
| 8 | 79 | 84 |
| 9 | 69 | 73 |
| 10 | 74 | 73 |

4. Following the results of the small sample in exercise 3, a larger sample of 58 disabled persons was involved in a similar workshop. The T value for the data is 487.25.

   a. Which test would be most appropriate for the data?
   b. State an appropriate null hypothesis.
   c. If appropriate, state a directional hypothesis.
   d. What is the value of the test statistic?
   e. Can you reject the null hypothesis at the .05 level of significance?
   f. If appropriate, can you accept the directional hypothesis at the .05 level of significance?
   g. What are your conclusions?

5. Commitment to the work ethic was evaluated for children of immigrants and nonimmigrants. It was found that in a sample of 28 immigrant children, 17 had a strong work ethic and 11 a weaker work ethic. In the sample of 33 nonimmigrant children, 12 had a strong work ethic and 21 had a weaker one.

   a. Which test would be most appropriate for the data?
   b. State an appropriate null hypothesis.
   c. If appropriate, state a directional hypothesis.
   d. What is the value of the test statistic?
   e. Can you reject the null hypothesis at the .01 level of significance?
   f. If appropriate, can you accept the directional hypothesis at the .01 level of significance?
   g. What are your conclusions?

6. Suppose that the study in exercise 5 was repeated except that the immigrant sample numbered 122 and the nonimmigrant 127. Further, assume that 70 of the immigrant children and 53 of the nonimmigrant children had a strong work ethic.

   a. What test would be most appropriate for the data?
   b. State an appropriate null hypothesis.
   c. If appropriate, state a directional hypothesis.
   d. What is the value of the test statistic?
   e. At what level can you reject the null hypothesis?
   f. If appropriate, at what level can you accept the directional hypothesis?
   g. What accounts for the difference in the outcome for exercises 5 and 6?
   h. How is the difference noted in question g relevant to Type I and Type II errors?

7. A survey was done to assess the differences in union support by police officers, firefighters, teachers, and street department workers. The following was observed:

| Union Support | Police | Firefighters | Teachers | Street Department Workers |
|---|---|---|---|---|
| Strong | 15 | 12 | 24 | 23 |
| Moderate | 22 | 17 | 15 | 12 |

   a. Which test would be most appropriate for the data?
   b. State an appropriate null hypothesis.
   c. If appropriate, state a directional hypothesis.
   d. What is the value of the test statistic?
   e. Can you reject the null hypothesis at the .05 level of significance?
   f. If appropriate, can you accept the directional hypothesis at the .05 level of significance?
   g. What are your conclusions?

8. A sample of community residents was questioned about their support of the local police prior to and following their citation for a traffic violation. The data were as follows:

| Before | After Positive | Negative |
|---|---|---|
| Negative | 3 | 6 |
| Positive | 5 | 12 |

   a. Which test would be most appropriate for the data?
   b. State an appropriate null hypothesis.
   c. If appropriate, state a directional hypothesis.
   d. What is the value of the test statistic?
   e. Can you reject the null hypothesis at the .05 level of significance?
   f. If appropriate, can you accept the directional hypothesis at the .05 level of significance?
   g. What are your conclusions?

# 10

# COMPARING MORE THAN TWO POPULATIONS

## *Analysis of Variance*

In Chapters 8 and 9, we considered statistical models for comparing two populations using continuous and discrete measures. Such comparisons play an important role in social research, but situations are often encountered in which more
than two groups are involved. Analysis of variance, usually referred to by the
acronym **ANOVA,** is one method for comparing more than two populations.

Models for ANOVA are constructed so that differences between the samples
represent the independent variable and the measure on which the samples are
compared the dependent variable. For example, suppose that you want to compare the rates of alcoholism among four different ethnic groups. The four ethnic
groups would be the independent variable of ethnicity and the rates of alcoholism
across the groups the dependent variable. The goal of the analysis is to determine
whether rates of alcoholism vary across the ethnic groups. If so, ethnicity would
be seen as explaining some of the variation in alcoholism rates.

ANOVA techniques are useful because they can be adapted to a wide variety
of theoretical models organized around independent and dependent variable relationships. The techniques are theory driven in that the relationships between independent and dependent measures are the result of theoretical speculation. For
example, the relationship between ethnic groups and alcoholism rates might be
predicated on the theory that cultural components of ethnic groups influence the
use of alcohol. We consider several basic ANOVA models. The first two are parametric because they focus on a comparison of population means. Both are based
on the assumption that the dependent measure is interval, its distribution is normal, and the variances of the populations are approximately equal. Recall that
these are the same assumptions that must be met to use Student's $t$ test to compare two samples. Parametric ANOVA techniques are an extension of Student's
$t$ test. The two parametric models considered in this chapter include one-way
ANOVA and two-way ANOVA.

In addition, we examine one nonparametric model, the Kruskal-Wallis one-way ANOVA. The test is used when the dependent measure is ordinal. It is a distribution free test because no assumptions are made about the distribution of the dependent variable.

# PARAMETRIC ANOVA MODELS

## One-Way ANOVA F Test

### Description

In that parametric ANOVA techniques are an extension of the Student's $t$ test, they are based on the same logic. Recall that Student's $t$ test evaluates the difference between two sample means, $\overline{X}_1$ and $\overline{X}_2$, by comparing the difference between the two means to the standard error of the difference of the two samples (review Formulas 8.1 and 8.2). The test statistic for comparing multiple means, the F ratio, is an extension of Student's $t$ test. It compares the variation between multiple sample means, $\overline{X}_1$, $\overline{X}_2$, . . . , $\overline{X}_k$, to the variation within the multiple samples. Conceptually, this is similar to the $t$ test, for it compares the differences between means to the differences expected within their populations, which is equivalent to the standard error. However, the methods for multiple-group comparisons are illustrated using variances rather than standard deviations, as was the case in Student's $t$ test. Thus, they are referred to as *analysis of variance techniques.*[1]

The goal of **one-way ANOVA** is to disaggregate or partition the total variance of all the groups, $s_T^2$, into that which is due to the variation between the groups, $s_B^2$, and the variation within the groups, $s_W^2$. The **between-groups variance,** $s_B^2$, is referred to as the **explained variance** because it is that portion of the total variance in the dependent variable (e.g., alcoholism) that is explained by the independent variable (e.g., ethnicity). It is the variation that is due to differences between the ethnic groups with respect to alcoholism.

The **within-groups variance,** $s_W^2$, is referred to as the **unexplained variance** in that it represents the variation of alcoholism rates within each ethnic group and is not a function of differences between the groups. It is the collected, or pooled, within-group variance across the groups. The within-group variance also can be thought of as random variation due to random sampling outcomes within the groups. To the extent that the variation between the ethnic groups is a greater proportion of the total variance in alcoholism than that within the groups, the theory that differences in alcoholism are a function of ethnic group membership is strengthened. The model is **theory driven** in that it is based on the theoretical notion that ethnic group membership explains variation in alcoholism rates.

The between-groups variation is also referred to as **information;** that is, it informs us about variation in alcoholism that is due to ethnic differences. Within-groups

---

[1] The solutions for analysis of variance can also be derived using standard deviations, but variances are typically used.

variation is referred to as **error variance,** or **noise.** It is noise or error because it is random variation in alcoholism within each of the ethnic groups; the source of the variation is unknown. It does not inform us about the source of differences in alcoholism. Within-groups variation is not helpful in disaggregating differences in the rates of alcoholism; it appears as random error in sampling.

The sum of the between- and within-groups variances equals the total variance of the dependent variable: $s_B^2 + s_W^2 = s_T^2$, as shown in Figure 10.1. The purpose of ANOVA is to disaggregate the total variance into that which is due to between- and within-groups variance.

As in the case of all the statistical models that we have considered thus far, ANOVA is organized around a ratio. Here, the ratio is that of the between-groups variance *to* the within-groups variance and provides the F statistic, as shown in the following formula:

$$F = \frac{s_B^2}{s_W^2} \tag{10.1}$$

The distribution of the F statistic, called **Fisher's F,** is a family of distributions associated with various degrees of freedom represented by the measures related to $s_B^2$ and $s_W^2$. Table B.7 in Appendix B provides the distribution of F values necessary to reject $H_0$ at the .05 and .01 levels of significance. Specific directions for use of the table will be given in the example that follows.

The F distribution is based on the assumption that the dependent variable is an interval measure and represents a normal distribution. Further, the samples must be independent and the variances of the samples approximately equal. The assumption of equal variances is referred to as *homogeneity of variances,* or **homoscedasticity** (similarity of scatter). It guards against concluding that there are differences between the means of groups when the real difference is in their variances.

The F statistic is used to test the null hypothesis that the means of the populations represented by the samples are equal: $\mu_1 = \mu_2 = \mu_3 = \ldots = \mu_k$. If the null hypothesis is accepted, the conclusion is that the differences between the groups, $s_B^2$ (e.g., ethnicity), is not significant and any differences are due to chance variability in sampling. However, if $s_B^2$ is significantly greater than $s_W^2$, it indicates that a por-

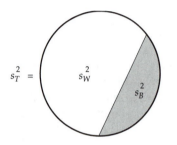

**FIGURE 10.1   Components of Variance**

tion of the total variance, $s_T^2$ is not due to sampling variability but to the independent variable (e.g., ethnicity), and $H_0$ must be rejected. The differences between the groups can be pinpointed more closely by testing for the location of the differences between samples. In terms of our example, this will enable you to determine whether alcoholism rates differ between all the ethnic groups or just some of them.

You might ask, Given that the data requirements are the same as for Student's $t$ test, why not use the $t$ test on pairs of samples to locate differences and avoid the calculation of ANOVA? This is not done for at least three reasons. First, if the intent is to test a theory, and the theory involves the effect of multiple groups on a dependent measure, the proper procedure is to use a multivariate model that tests the theory at hand. Second, the use of paired $t$ tests, especially if the number of groups is large, increases the risk of a Type I error. If you test $H_0$ at $\alpha = .05$, 5% of all paired $t$ tests will lead to the rejection of $H_0$, and each rejection represents the risk of a Type I error. The more pairs tested, the more likely a significant difference between two groups will be found and the more likely a Type I error will occur. ANOVA represents only one test, so a Type I error has only one opportunity to occur.

Third, unless all the samples are the same size, you need a procedure for weighting comparisons to ensure that the results are not due to differences in the size of the two groups being compared.

### Example 10.1

Three samples of 9 members each were selected representing urban, suburban, and rural residents to evaluate their perceptions of family integrity. Family integrity was measured using an interval scale,[2] shown in Table 10.1. In our example, the

**TABLE 10.1  Urban, Suburban, and Rural Perceptions of Family Integrity**

| Urban ($X_1$) | Suburban ($X_2$) | Rural ($X_3$) |
|:---:|:---:|:---:|
| 9 | 4 | 10 |
| 2 | 10 | 15 |
| 4 | 13 | 7 |
| 7 | 9 | 12 |
| 11 | 3 | 6 |
| 3 | 9 | 8 |
| 1 | 12 | 14 |
| 8 | 4 | 7 |
| 3 | 7 | 5 |
| 48 | 71 | 84 |
| $\bar{X}_1 = 5.33$ | $\bar{X}_2 = 7.89$ | $\bar{X}_3 = 9.33$ |

[2] Sample sizes of 9 members are small but are used here for convenience in illustrating ANOVA. To ensure that the assumption of normality is met, $n \geq 30$.

dependent variable is the score on perception of family integrity; the independent variable is place of residence, whether urban, suburban, or rural. The intent is to test a theory that place of residence determines perceptions of family integrity. If so, the variation in perceptions of family integrity between the places of residence should be significantly larger than the variation within places of residence.

Two things are apparent when you examine the data. First, there is variation in the perception scores within each of the groups. For example, one urban resident has a score as low as 1 on perception of family integrity and another a score as high as 11. Suburban residents have scores that range from 3 to 13, and rural dwellers range from 5 to 15. Second, there is variation between the three groups. This is clear from the differences in their means, ranging from a low of 5.33 for urban residents to a high of 9.33 for rural residents. The question is, Does the variation between the groups exceed what you would expect, given the variation within each of the groups? If so, the theory that place of residence influences perceptions of family integrity is supported. If not, the data fail to support the theory. The null hypothesis to be tested is

$$H_0: \mu_1 = \mu_2 = \mu_3$$

which states that the means of the three populations represented by the three samples of residents do not differ in their perceptions of family integrity. The null hypothesis is based on the assumption that the differences in the means are simply a function of random sampling variation. The F statistic will be used to determine whether the observed variation between the three groups is greater than you would expect, given the variation within the groups.

The F statistic is equal to the ratio of the between-groups variance *to* the within-groups variance. We begin the procedure by calculating sums of squares, SS, for the **total variance,** the within-groups sums of squares, and the between-groups sums of squares.

Formula 10.2 shows the total sums of the squares for the three distributions (note the similarity of the formula with the one used for the sums of squares for variance in Chapter 3, Formula 3.15):

$$SS_T = \Sigma X_i^2 - \frac{\left(\Sigma X_i\right)^2}{N} \tag{10.2}$$

where    $SS_T$ = total sums of squares

$\Sigma X_i^2$ = the sum of individual squared scores of all the groups

$\dfrac{\left(\Sigma X_i\right)^2}{N}$ = the sum of the scores of all the groups squared divided by the total number of observations

The within-groups sums of squares is determined with the following formula:

$$SS_W = \Sigma X_i^2 - \Sigma \frac{\left(\Sigma X_k\right)^2}{n_k} \tag{10.3}$$

where     $SS_W$ = the within-groups sums of squares

$\sum X_i^2$ = the sum of the squared raw scores of all the groups

$\sum \dfrac{\left(\sum X_k\right)^2}{n_k}$ = the expression $(\sum X_k)^2$ directs you to sum the scores of each sample and square the sums. Then divide each squared sample sum by the number of members in the sample, $n_k$, and total the results for all the samples.

The between-groups sums of squares is

$$SS_B = \sum \frac{\left(\sum X_k\right)^2}{n_k} - \frac{\left(\sum X_i\right)^2}{N} \tag{10.4}$$

Both terms in Formula 10.4 have been defined previously in Formulas 10.2 and 10.3. The first term is in Formula 10.3 and the second term in Formula 10.2. The between-groups sums of squares is equal to the difference between the average of the group sums squared and the average of the individual sums squared. Formulas have been given for the total and the between and within sums of squares, but given that $SS_T = SS_B + SS_W$, it is necessary only to solve for any two of the sums of squares; the third can be derived by subtraction or addition.

Table 10.2 shows the various sums and sums of squares necessary to calculate the three sums of squares. For purposes of illustration, all three formulas for sums of squares are completed, beginning with the total sums of squares.

**TABLE 10.2   Urban, Suburban, and Rural Perceptions of Family Integrity**

| Urban ($n = 9$) | | Suburban ($n = 9$) | | Rural ($n = 9$) | | |
|---|---|---|---|---|---|---|
| $X_1$ | $X_1^2$ | $X_2$ | $X_2^2$ | $X_3$ | $X_3^2$ | |
| 9 | 81 | 4 | 16 | 10 | 100 | |
| 2 | 4 | 10 | 100 | 15 | 225 | |
| 4 | 16 | 13 | 169 | 7 | 49 | |
| 7 | 49 | 9 | 81 | 12 | 144 | |
| 11 | 121 | 3 | 9 | 6 | 36 | |
| 3 | 9 | 9 | 81 | 8 | 64 | |
| 1 | 1 | 12 | 144 | 14 | 196 | |
| 8 | 64 | 4 | 16 | 7 | 49 | |
| 3 | 9 | 7 | 49 | 5 | 25 | |
| $\sum X_1 = 48$ | | $\sum X_2 = 71$ | | $\sum X_3 = 84$ | | $\sum X_i = 203$ |
| | $\sum X_1^2 = 354$ | | $\sum X_2^2 = 665$ | | $\sum X_3^2 = 888$ | $\sum X_3 = 1{,}907$ |

Using Formula 10.2, we find that the total sums of squares is[3]

$$SS_T = \Sigma X_i^2 - \frac{\left(\Sigma X_i\right)^2}{N}$$

$$= 1907 - \frac{203^2}{27}$$

$$= 1907 - \frac{41,209}{27}$$

$$= 1907 - 1526.259$$

$$= 380.741$$

Using Formula 10.3, we find that the within-groups sums of squares is

$$SS_W = \Sigma X_i^2 - \Sigma \frac{\left(\Sigma X_k\right)^2}{n_k}$$

$$= 1907 - \frac{48^2}{9} + \frac{71^2}{9} + \frac{84^2}{9}$$

$$= 1907 - 256 + 560.111 + 784$$

$$= 1907 - 1600.111$$

$$= 306.889$$

Using Formula 10.4, we find that the between-groups sums of squares is

$$SS_B = \Sigma \frac{\left(\Sigma X_k\right)^2}{n_k} - \frac{\left(\Sigma X_i\right)^2}{N}$$

$$= \frac{48^2}{9} + \frac{71^2}{9} + \frac{84^2}{9} - \frac{203^2}{27}$$

$$= 1600.111 - 1526.259$$

$$= 73.852$$

Note that $SS_B + SS_W = SS_T = 73.852 + 306.889 = 380.741$, showing that the sums of squares for between and within groups equals the total sums of squares.

Once the sums of squares have been determined, the between- and within-groups variances are obtained by dividing the sums of squares by their respective degrees of freedom. The between-groups variance is

$$s_B^2 = \frac{SS_B}{k-1} \tag{10.5}$$

---

[3] It is not necessary to calculate the total groups value, but it has been done here to illustrate that the within and between sums of the squares equal the total sums of the squares.

where $k - 1$ equals the number of groups representing the independent variable with $3 - 1$ degrees of freedom. The distribution of the group means was used to calculate the between-groups sums of squares in Formula 10.4. The between-groups variance is

$$s_B^2 = \frac{73.852}{3-1}$$

$$= 36.926$$

The within-groups variance is

$$s_W^2 = \frac{SS_W}{N-k} \qquad (10.6)$$

where $N - k$ equals the number of members in the three combined groups, $N$, less 1 degree of freedom for each group, $k$:

$$s_W^2 = \frac{306.889}{27-3}$$

$$= 12.787$$

The F ratio is then determined using Formula 10.1:

$$F = \frac{s_B^2}{s_W^2}$$

$$= \frac{36.926}{12.787}$$

$$= 2.89$$

The results of the calculations for one-way ANOVA are summarized in Table 10.3, which shows the sums of squares, the degrees of freedom, the variances, and the F ratio.

The probability for the F statistic is given in Table B.7 in Appendix B. The table provides values for $\alpha = .05$ (lightface type) and $\alpha = .01$ (boldface type). The degrees of freedom for the numerator of the F ratio (between-groups variance) are given across the top of the table and those for the denominator (within-groups variance) in the left-hand column. The decision rule is as follows: If the observed

**TABLE 10.3    Table of One-Way ANOVA Results**

|  | SS | df | $s^2$ | F |
|---|---|---|---|---|
| Between groups | 73.852 | $k - 1 = 2$ | 36.926 | 2.89 |
| Within groups | 306.889 | $N - k = 24$ | 12.787 |  |
| Total | 380.741 |  |  |  |

F ratio is equal to or larger than the table value, reject the null hypothesis: $\mu_1 = \mu_2 = \mu_3$.

The null hypothesis, that residents from urban, suburban, and rural communities do not differ in their perceptions of family integrity, is tested at $\alpha = .05$. The numerator for our F ratio has df $= 3 - 1 = 2$ and the denominator df $= 27 - 3 = 24$. The table value at the intersect of 2 and 24 degrees of freedom is 3.40. Our F ratio is 2.89, which is less than 3.40, so $H_0$ cannot be rejected. We must conclude that the differences between the group means are due to random sampling variation and do not exceed what you would expect by chance. The independent variable, place of residence, does not account for a significant portion of the variance in the dependent variable of perceptions of family integrity.

You can think of the F ratio as composed of information (the numerator $s_B^2$) and error, or noise (the denominator, $s_W^2$). The F ratio is significant if the ratio of the information to the error is large enough to be more than a chance difference. The results for our example are such that the information was insufficient to overwhelm the error, so we cannot conclude that place of residence accounts for a significant portion of the variance in perceptions of family integrity. The theory, intending to explain variation in perceptions of family integrity using place of residence, is not supported, and the attempt to improve knowledge about the source of variation in perceptions of family integrity was not successful.

### Summary

The purpose of one-way ANOVA is to determine whether an independent variable explains a significant proportion of the variation in a dependent variable. Inasmuch as the F statistic is an extension of Student's *t* test, it is the most powerful technique for comparing the means of more than two populations. However, its use is restricted to the following situations:

1. When the dependent variable represents an interval measure.
2. When the dependent variable is normally distributed in the populations represented by the samples.
3. When the variances of the samples are approximately equal or homogeneous.
4. When the samples are selected independently.
5. The independent variable can be categorical or discrete.

## Two-Way ANOVA F Test

### Description

Like one-way ANOVA, the goal of **two-way ANOVA** is to disaggregate the sources of variance in the dependent variable. However, two-way models examine the effects of two independent variables on the dependent measure. Assume, for example, that we added a second independent variable to our previous model, level of participation in extended family activities, by dividing our samples into members with low, medium, and high participation rates. Our model would then consist of two independent variables, place of residence and level of participation, and the dependent variable, perceptions of family integrity.

Some additional vocabulary is helpful for understanding discussions of two-way ANOVA. When more than one independent variable is involved, the model is referred to as a **factorial design,** and the independent variables are referred to as the **factors.** The independent variables also are known as the *main effects* because the effects of those variables on the dependent variable are of interest to the researcher. The addition of the second independent variable represents a more complex theory in that it involves the use of two independent concepts to explain the variation of a dependent one. The model can also improve the potential for understanding the variation of the dependent variable in that it may be simplistic to think that a significant proportion of something as complex as perceptions of family integrity can be explained by a single variable. Even the use of two independent variables might seem modest for constructing an explanation, but it is an advance over a single-variable model. There also are ANOVA models that can consider more than two independent effects, but they go beyond the goals of an introductory text. However, understanding the two-way ANOVA model provides substantial insight into the conceptual workings of more complicated ones.

The introduction of the second variable complicates the ANOVA model in that the between-groups variance must be disaggregated into the variance that is due to the first independent effect, in our example place of residence, and the second independent effect, level of participation in extended family activities. In addition, there is a potential third source of variance due to interaction between the two independent variables. This is **interaction variance.** Interaction can be thought of as variation that occurs because one independent variable influences or changes the effect of the second independent variable. For example, interaction would be present if place of residence influenced the level of participation in extended family activities and changed its effect on perceptions of family integrity. Thus, two-way ANOVA considers three possible sources of influence on the dependent measure.

The components of variance in a two-way model are illustrated in Figure 10.2. The area of the circle represents the total variance of the dependent variable. The darkened portion of the area is the within-groups variance, or the variance that is not explained by the independent variables or by interaction. It is the random variation within each of the subgroups. The white portion of the circle is the variance explained by the two main effects and interaction. A theory is powerful to the extent that the main effects explain a significant proportion of the variance in the dependent variable.

### Example 10.2

Table 10.4 presents the data on perceptions of family integrity cross-classified by place of residence and level of participation in extended family activities. The means for the three areas of residence are dissimilar, as are those for the three levels of participation in extended family activities. The question is whether the

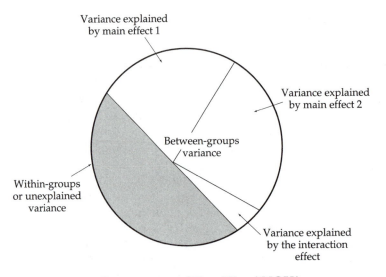

**FIGURE 10.2   Components of Two-Way ANOVA**

**TABLE 10.4   Perceptions of Family Integrity: Place of Residence and Participation in Extended Family Activities**

| Participation in Family Activities | Place of Residence | | | Factor 2 Sums and Means |
|---|---|---|---|---|
| | Urban ($X_1$) | Suburban ($X_2$) | Rural ($X_3$) | |
| High ($X_A$) | 9 | 12 | 14 | |
| | 11 | 9 | 15 | |
| | $\dfrac{7}{27}$ | $\dfrac{13}{34}$ | $\dfrac{12}{41}$ | $\Sigma X_A = 102$ |
| | | | | $\overline{X}_A = 11.33$ |
| Medium ($X_B$) | 8 | 9 | 10 | |
| | 4 | 10 | 8 | |
| | $\dfrac{3}{15}$ | $\dfrac{7}{26}$ | $\dfrac{7}{25}$ | $\Sigma X_B = 66$ |
| | | | | $\overline{X}_B = 7.33$ |
| Low ($X_C$) | 3 | 4 | 5 | |
| | 2 | 3 | 7 | |
| | $\dfrac{1}{6}$ | $\dfrac{4}{11}$ | $\dfrac{6}{18}$ | $\Sigma X_C = 35$ |
| | | | | $\overline{X}_C = 3.89$ |
| | $\Sigma X_1 = 48$ | $\Sigma X_2 = 71$ | $\Sigma X_3 = 84$ | |
| | $\overline{X}_1 = 5.33$ | $\overline{X}_2 = 7.89$ | $\overline{X}_3 = 9.33$ | |

variation between the means of the groups related to either factor is greater than expected given the variation within the groups. The null hypotheses tested with two-way ANOVA include one for each main effect and one for interaction:

$H_0$:    There is no difference between place of residence and perception of family integrity.

$H_0$:    There is no difference between level of participation in extended family activities and family integrity.

$H_0$:    There is no interaction between place of residence and level of participation in extended family activities.

Each hypothesis is tested with an F ratio. The general forms of the ratios are

$$F = \frac{s_1^2}{s_W} = \frac{\text{Between-groups variance : factor 1}}{\text{Within-groups variance}} \qquad \textbf{(10.7)}$$

$$F = \frac{s_2^2}{s_W} = \frac{\text{Between-groups variance : factor 2}}{\text{Within-groups variance}} \qquad \textbf{(10.8)}$$

$$F = \frac{s_{1.2}^2}{s_W} = \frac{\text{Interaction variance}}{\text{Within-groups variance}} \qquad \textbf{(10.9)}$$

As in one-way ANOVA, we begin by calculating the sums of squares. Six different sums of squares are calculated. They include the total sums of squares, the total within-groups sums of squares, the total between-groups sums of squares, the sums of squares for factors 1 and 2, and the interaction sums of squares. The formulas and calculation of the six sums of squares are illustrated using the data presented in Table 10.5. The data on the dependent variable are the same as they were for one-way ANOVA except that in the one-way model it is cross-classified by one factor, place of residence, and in the two-way model by the second factor, participation in extended family activities.

## Calculating the Sums of Squares

### Total Sums of Squares

The total sums of squares, $SS_T$, for two-way ANOVA is the same as for one-way in that it represents the total variance for the data set. Formula 10.2 is used to calculate the total sums of squares:

$$SS_T = \Sigma X_i^2 - \frac{\left(\Sigma X_i\right)^2}{N}$$

**TABLE 10.5    Perceptions of Family Integrity: Residence ($k$ Groups) and Participation ($j$ Groups)**

| Participation ($j$) | Urban $X_1$ | Urban $X_1^2$ | Suburban $X_2$ | Suburban $X_2^2$ | Rural $X_3$ | Rural $X_3^2$ | Sums |
|---|---|---|---|---|---|---|---|
| High ($X_A$) | 9 | 81 | 12 | 144 | 14 | 196 | |
| | 11 | 121 | 9 | 81 | 15 | 225 | |
| | 7 | 49 | 13 | 169 | 12 | 144 | $\Sigma X_A = 102$ |
| | 27 | 251 | 34 | 394 | 41 | 565 | $\Sigma X_A^2 = 1{,}210$ |
| Medium ($X_B$) | 8 | 64 | 9 | 81 | 10 | 100 | |
| | 4 | 16 | 10 | 100 | 8 | 64 | |
| | 3 | 9 | 7 | 49 | 7 | 49 | $\Sigma X_B = 66$ |
| | 15 | 89 | 26 | 230 | 25 | 213 | $\Sigma X_B^2 = 532$ |
| Low ($X_C$) | 3 | 9 | 4 | 16 | 5 | 25 | |
| | 2 | 4 | 3 | 9 | 7 | 49 | |
| | 1 | 1 | 4 | 16 | 6 | 36 | $\Sigma X_C = 35$ |
| | 6 | 14 | 11 | 41 | 18 | 110 | $\Sigma X_C^2 = 165$ |
| Sums | $\Sigma X_1 = 48$ | | $\Sigma X_2 = 71$ | | $\Sigma X_3 = 84$ | | $\Sigma X_i = 203$ |
| | | $\Sigma X_1^2 = 354$ | | $\Sigma X_2^2 = 665$ | | $\Sigma X_3^2 = 888$ | $\Sigma X_i^2 = 1{,}907$ |

The subscript $i$ in the formula refers to the 27 individual scores. The $N$ indicates that the calculations include the total set of observations. The results are

$$SS_T = 1907 - \frac{203^2}{27}$$

$$= 1907 - 1526.259$$

$$= 380.741$$

Note that cross-classifying the data by a second independent variable does not affect the total sums of squares. The result of 380.741 is the same total sums of squares that was found for one-way ANOVA.

### Within-Groups Sums of Squares

The within-groups sums of squares, $SS_W$, relates to all the subgroups resulting from cross-classifying the dependent variable by the two independent variables. The within-groups sums of squares is a pooled sum relating to the variation of the scores within each of the subgroups. In our example, each of the two factors contains three categories, so the within-groups sums of squares includes $3 \times 3 = 9$

subgroups, as shown in Table 10.5. Formula 10.10 is used to calculate the within-groups sums of squares:

$$SS_W = \Sigma X_i^2 - \Sigma \frac{\left(\Sigma X_m\right)^2}{n_m} \qquad (10.10)$$

where $\Sigma X_i^2$ is the sum of all the squared raw scores, and the subscript $m$ refers to the 9 subgroups. The result is

$$SS_W = 1907 - \frac{27^2}{3} + \frac{34^2}{3} + \frac{41^2}{3} + \frac{15^2}{3} + \frac{26^2}{3} + \frac{25^2}{3} + \frac{6^2}{3} + \frac{11^2}{3} + \frac{18^2}{3}$$

$$= 1907 - (243 + 385.333 + 560.333 + 75 + 225.333 + 208.333 + 12 + 40.333 + 108)$$

$$= 1907 - 1857.665$$

$$= 49.335$$

### Total Between-Groups Sums of Squares

The total between-groups sums of squares, $SS_B$, is the between-groups sums of squares for all groups created by the two independent variables. In our example, the total between-groups sums of squares for the 9 subgroups is calculated with the following formula:

$$SS_B = \Sigma \frac{\left(\Sigma X_m\right)^2}{n_m} - \frac{\left(\Sigma X_i\right)^2}{N} \qquad (10.11)$$

Note the parallel between Formula 10.11 and Formula 10.4, which is used to calculate the $SS_B$ in one-way ANOVA. The first term in the formula appears in Formula 10.4, except that the subscript was $k$ rather than the $m$ used in Formula 10.11. Subscript $k$ refers to the subgroups created by one independent variable, whereas $m$ refers to the subgroups created by two independent variables. The second term in Formula 10.11 is identical to that in Formula 10.2 in that it relates to all the groups combined. Both formulas represent the difference between the sums of squares of subgroups and the total sum squared. Applied to the data, we find

$$SS_B = \left[\frac{27^2}{3} + \frac{34^2}{3} + \frac{41^2}{3} + \frac{15^2}{3} + \frac{26^2}{3} + \frac{25^2}{3} + \frac{6^2}{3} + \frac{11^2}{3} + \frac{18^2}{3}\right] - \left[\frac{203^2}{27}\right]$$

$$= 1857.665 - 1526.259$$

$$= 331.406$$

At this point, the between, within, and total sums of squares have been calculated. The results show that $SS_B + SS_W = SS_T = 331.406 + 49.335 = 380.741$. Recall that $SS_B$ represents the sums of squares between the groups and provides information on differences between the groups, whereas $SS_W$ is the sums of squares within the groups and represents the pooled variation within the groups. Together they equal the total sums of squares for the 27 scores. Now $SS_B$, the total information, must be disaggregated to find out how much of the information is due to each of the two independent factors: place of residence and family participation. It is also necessary to determine whether interaction exists between the two independent effects.

### Factor 1 Sums of Squares

The sums of squares for factor 1, $SS_1$, is the sums of squares between the groups created by the categories of the first independent variable, place of residence. In Table 10.5 it relates to the sums of the columns, which represents individuals from urban, suburban, or rural residences. The formula for $SS_1$ is

$$SS_1 = \sum \frac{\left(\sum X_k\right)^2}{n_k} - \frac{\left(\sum X_i\right)^2}{N} \tag{10.12}$$

The subscript $k$ for $X_k$ and $n_k$ refers to the first independent variable and designates place of residence. The solution is

$$SS_1 = \frac{48^2}{9} + \frac{71^2}{9} + \frac{84^2}{9} - \frac{203^2}{27}$$

$$= (256 + 560.111 + 784) - 1526.259$$

$$= 1600.111 - 1526.259$$

$$= 73.852$$

The value of 73.852 is the same as found with Formula 10.4 for place of residence in the one-way ANOVA. It is not altered by the addition of the second variable in the two-way model. The value of 73.852 represents the independent relationship of place of residence to perceptions of family integrity.

### Factor 2 Sums of Squares

The sums of squares for factor 2, $SS_2$, is the between-groups sums of squares for the subgroups created by the categories of the second variable: participation in extended family activities. It is represented by the rows in Table 10.5. The formula for the sums of the subgroups in the rows is

$$SS_2 = \sum \frac{\left(\sum X_j\right)^2}{n_j} - \frac{\left(\sum X_i\right)^2}{N} \tag{10.13}$$

The subscript $j$ for $X_j$ and $n_j$ refers to the second independent factor and designates participation in extended family activities. The solution is

$$SS_2 = \frac{102^2}{9} + \frac{66^2}{9} + \frac{35^2}{9} - \frac{203^2}{27}$$

$$= 1156 + 484 + 136.111 - 1526.259$$

$$= 1776.111 - 1526.259$$

$$= 249.852$$

The value of 249.852 represents the information gained about perceptions of family integrity by adding the variable of participation in extended family activities to the model. It represents the independent effect of participation on perceptions of family integrity.

### Interaction Sums of Squares

The interaction sums of squares, $SS_{1.2}$, is the between-groups sums of squares not attributable to the independent effects of $SS_1$ and $SS_2$. Conceptually, it represents potential interaction between the two independent variables in that they may influence each other's effect on the dependent variable. Computationally, it is the remainder when $SS_1$ and $SS_2$ are subtracted from $SS_B$, as shown in the following formula:

$$SS_{1.2} = SS_B - SS_1 - SS_2 \qquad\qquad (10.14)$$

Applied to our data, we find

$$SS_{1.2} = 331.406 - 73.852 - 249.852$$
$$= 7.702$$

## Calculating the Variances

Once we know the sums of squares, we can derive the variance for each component of the model by dividing the sums of squares by their respective degrees of freedom. The variances that are of interest in evaluating the model are the within-groups, factor 1, factor 2, and interaction variances.

### Within-Groups Variance

Within-groups variance is the random variation of values within each of the groups in the model. It is variation within each of the 9 subgroups that is unexplained by the two main effects. The within-groups variance is given in the following formula:

$$s_W^2 = \frac{SS_W}{N - kj} \qquad\qquad (10.15)$$

$$= \frac{49.335}{18}$$

$$= 2.741$$

The degrees of freedom equals $N - kj$, which is the total number of observations, $N = 27$, minus the product of the number of categories in the first factor, $k = 3$, and in the second factor, $j = 3$. More simply, 1 degree of freedom for each of the 9 subgroups is subtracted from the total number of observations. Thus, the degrees of freedom are $N - kj = 27 - (3)(3) = 18$.

The addition of the second independent variable had a significant effect on the within-groups, or error variance. Recall that when only one independent variable was used, the error variance, given in Formula 10.6, was 12.787. Adding the second independent variable reduced it to 2.741. Lower error variance increases the likelihood of the significance of this independent variable.

### Factor 1 Variance

This represents the amount of variance in the dependent variable accounted for by factor 1. In our example, it is the variation in perceptions of family integrity that is accounted for by place of residence. The degrees of freedom associated with factor 1 are the number of residential categories, $k$, minus 1, or $k - 1 = 3 - 1 = 2$. The variance for factor 1 is

$$s_1^2 = \frac{SS_1}{k-1} \tag{10.16}$$

$$= \frac{73.852}{2}$$

$$= 36.926$$

### Factor 2 Variance

This is the variance in the dependent variable associated with factor 2: participation in extended family activities. The degrees of freedom for factor 2 equal the number of categories for participation, $j - 1 = 3 - 1 = 2$. The variance for factor 2 is

$$s_2^2 = \frac{SS_2}{j-1} \tag{10.17}$$

$$= \frac{249.852}{2}$$

$$= 124.926$$

### Interaction Variance

Interaction variance relates to the potential influence of the two factors on each other. The degrees of freedom for interaction equals the product of the degrees of freedom for the two factors, $(k - 1)(j - 1) = (3 - 1)(3 - 1) = 4$.

$$s_{1.2}^2 = \frac{SS_{1.2}}{(k-1)(j-1)} \tag{10.18}$$

$$= \frac{7.702}{4}$$

$$= 1.925$$

Table 10.6 summarizes the results of the two-way ANOVA. The first column defines the contents of the rows. The second column contains the sums of the squares. The between-groups sums of squares and the within-groups sums of squares equal the total sums of squares: $331.406 + 49.335 = 380.741$. The values

**TABLE 10.6   Results for Two-Way ANOVA**

|  | SS | df | $s^2$ | F |
|---|---|---|---|---|
| Between factor 1 | (73.852) | $k - 1 = 3 - 1 = 2$ | $s_1^2 = 36.926$ | 13.472 |
| Between factor 2 | (249.852) | $j - 1 = 3 - 1 = 2$ | $s_2^2 = 124.926$ | 45.578 |
| Interaction | (7.702) | $(k - 1)(j - 1) = 2 \times 2 = 4$ | $s_{1.2}^2 = 1.925$ | .702 |
| Between groups | 331.406 |  |  |  |
| Within groups | 49.335 | $N - kj = 27 - 9 = 18$ | $s_W^2 = 2.741$ |  |
| Total SS | 380.741 |  |  |  |

in parentheses in the column are the between-groups sums of squares disaggregated into factor 1, factor 2, and interaction sums of squares, 73.852 + 249.852 + 7.702 = 331.406, which totals the between-groups sums of squares. The third column shows the degrees of freedom associated with the two factors, interaction, and within-groups variance, whereas the fourth column shows their variances. The variances are used to test the null hypothesis using the F ratio.

### Testing the Hypothesis

The interaction hypothesis must be tested first because if it is significant it would indicate that the two factors are not independent, and their relationship to the dependent measure of perception of family integrity is confounded. The hypothesis is

$H_0$:   There is no interaction between place of residence and level of participation.

The F statistic for interaction is equal to the ratio of the interaction variance to the within-groups variance.

$$F_{1.2} = \frac{s_{1.2}^2}{s_W^2} \qquad (10.19)$$

$$= \frac{1.925}{2.741}$$

$$= .702$$

The significance of the statistic is evaluated using the F distribution in Table B.7 in Appendix B. The rows across the top of the table contain the degrees of freedom for interaction, and the left-hand column contains the degrees of freedom for within-groups variance. There are 4 degrees of freedom for interaction and 18 for the within-groups variance (see Table 10.6). The value at the intersect of 4 and 18 at $\alpha = .05$ is 2.93. Our computed value of .702 is less than 2.93, so $H_0$ is accepted. We can conclude that there is no interaction between place of residence and level of participation in extended family activities.

The hypotheses related to the two main effects can now be tested. The hypothesis for the first main effect is

$H_0$:   There is no relationship between place of residence and
        perceptions of family integrity.

The hypothesis is tested using the F ratio of the variance for factor 1 to the within-groups variance:

$$F_1 = \frac{s_1^2}{s_W^2}$$                   (10.20)

$$= \frac{36.926}{2.741}$$

$$= 13.472$$

Again, the statistic is evaluated using Table B.7 in Appendix B. There are 2 degrees of freedom for factor 1 in the numerator and 18 for the within-groups variance. The table value at the intersect of df = 2 and 18 at $\alpha$ = .05 is 3.55. The F value for factor 1, 13.472, is larger than the table value of 3.55, so the null hypothesis is rejected. We can conclude that perceptions of family integrity differ significantly, given place of residence.

The null hypothesis for factor 2 is as follows: There is no difference between the level of participation in extended family activities and perceptions of family integrity. The appropriate F ratio is

$$F_2 = \frac{s_2^2}{s_W^2}$$                   (10.21)

$$= \frac{124.926}{2.741}$$

$$= 45.577$$

There are 2 degrees of freedom for factor 2 and 18 for the within-groups variance. The table value for df = 2 and 18 at the .05 level is 3.55. Our value of 45.577 is much larger, so the null hypothesis is rejected. We can conclude that level of participation accounts for a significant proportion of the variance in perception of family integrity. The general conclusion is that both place of residence and participation in extended family activities have a significant effect on perceptions of family integrity.

The application of one- and two-way ANOVA to our example also illustrates that when only one independent variable, place of residence, was used to explain the variation in perception of family integrity, the results were not significant. The variance explained by place of residence, 36.926, was insufficient to overwhelm the error variance of 12.787 in the one-way ANOVA. The differences between the urban, suburban, and rural groups were not sufficient to overwhelm the differences within the groups. However, when the second independent variable, participation in extended family activities, was added to the model, the conclusion about the effect of place of residence was reversed. The reversal is due to the addition of the second independent variable, which accounted for additional variation in perceptions of family integrity and thereby reduced the within-groups variance from 12.787 in one-way ANOVA to 2.741 in two-way ANOVA. Of course, such a reversal will occur only if the second variable explains a significant amount of the variation in the dependent measure, as was the case in our model.

The introduction of the second independent variable can also confound the results if it interacts significantly with the first independent variable. The two-way model assumes that the two variables are independent in their effects on the dependent measure. In our model, this means that place of residence (whether it be urban, suburban, or rural) and participation in extended family activities (high, medium, or low) do not interact to produce a unique relationship with the dependent measure. For example, suburban residence could interact uniquely with medium participation in family activities, influencing the relationship with the dependent variable. Interaction means that the categories of the independent variables do not have a consistent directional influence on the dependent measure.

Given that the independent variables are found to be significant and the null hypothesis rejected, the relationship of the individual categories of the independent measures can be evaluated using the **Bonferroni method,** which adjusts for number of groups, level of significance, and differences in sample sizes.[4] Other techniques are available, but a discussion of these methods is beyond the scope of this text.

### *Summary*

The assumptions and requirements for two-way ANOVA are the same as those for one-way models:

1. The dependent variable must be an interval measure.
2. The dependent variable must be normally distributed in the populations represented by the samples.
3. The variances of the samples must be approximately equal or homogeneous.
4. The samples must be independent of each other.
5. The independent variables can be categorical or discrete.

There are situations in which the dependent variable does not meet the requirements of the F distribution. An alternative, the Kruskal-Wallis one-way ANOVA based on the chi-square distribution, is considered next.

---

[4] For a more complete discussion, see Marija J. Norusis, *SPSS 7.5 Guide to Data Analysis* (Englewood Cliffs, N.J.: Prentice-Hall, 1997).

# NONPARAMETRIC ANOVA

## Kruskal-Wallis One-Way ANOVA

### Description

The **Kruskal-Wallis one-way ANOVA** is used to assess whether more than two independent groups differ with respect to an ordinal dependent measure. The test serves as an alternative to parametric ANOVA when the dependent measure fails to meet the assumptions of the F test. As in the F test, the Kruskal-Wallis test treats the categories of the independent variable as group differences. It evaluates whether the variation of the ranks between the groups significantly exceeds the variation of the ranks within the groups. The technique takes into account groups of different sizes. The test statistic, evaluated using the chi-square distribution, symbolized by H, is

$$H = \frac{12}{N(N+1)} \sum_{i=1}^{n} \frac{R_j^2}{n_j} - 3(N+1) \tag{10.22}$$

where    $N$ = the total number of observations

$n_j$ = the number of observations for the categories of the independent variable

$R_j^2$ = the squared sum of the ranks for each category

The test requires only that the dependent measure be ordinal. The general form of the null hypothesis tested by the H statistic is

$H_0$:    There is no difference in the distribution of the ranks of the dependent measure across the groups representing the independent measure.

### Example 10.3

Fifty-six workers in eight different service branches of a social service agency were ranked in terms of the satisfaction of their clients, as shown in Table 10.7. The individual with the highest satisfaction score from clients received a rank of 1. The workers are ranked 1 through $n$ across the service categories, $S_1, S_2 \ldots S_k$. The worker with the highest rank, 1, is in the first service category, ranks 2 and 3 are in the seventh category, and so on. Overall, 56 workers were ranked across eight service categories. The example shows that the number of members in the categories of the independent variable need not be equal; for example, service category $S_1$ has 10 workers, $S_2$ has 8 workers, and so on. The null hypothesis for the example is

$H_0$:    There is no difference in the ranks of satisfaction across the service categories.

**TABLE 10.7   Service Categories and Rank of Client Satisfaction**

| | | | Satisfaction Rank | | | | |
|---|---|---|---|---|---|---|---|
| $S_1$ | $S_2$ | $S_3$ | $S_4$ | $S_5$ | $S_6$ | $S_7$ | $S_8$ |
| 9 | 52 | 45 | 44 | 22 | 36 | 21 | 18 |
| 27 | 29 | 54 | 47 | 23 | 33 | 13 | 15 |
| 48 | 40 | 25 | 38 | 32 | 17 | 12 | 34 |
| 39 | 53 | 35 | 31 | 7 | 37 | 20 | 4 |
| 56 | 14 | 41 | 49 | 8 | | 2 | |
| 6 | 16 | 46 | 19 | 11 | | 3 | |
| 55 | 10 | 30 | 24 | | | | |
| 50 | 5 | 51 | 28 | | | | |
| 26 | | 42 | | | | | |
| 1 | | 43 | | | | | |
| 317 | 219 | 412 | 280 | 103 | 123 | 71 | 71 |

Applying Formula 10.22, we find that the test statistic is

$$H = \frac{12}{56(56+1)}\left[\frac{317^2}{10} + \frac{219^2}{8} + \frac{412^2}{10} + \frac{280^2}{8} + \frac{103^2}{6} + \frac{123^2}{4} + \frac{71^2}{6} + \frac{71^2}{4}\right] - \left[3(56+1)\right]$$

$$= \frac{12}{3192}\left[50{,}469.26\right] - 171$$

$$= 189.734 - 171$$

$$= 18.73$$

The H statistic is interpreted using the chi-square distribution in Table B.4 in Appendix B. The df $= k - 1$, where $k$ is the number of groups represented by the independent measure. There are eight service categories, so df $= 8 - 1 = 7$. If $H_0$ is tested at $\alpha = .01$, we find the table value for df $= 8$ to be 18.48. Our test statistic of 18.73 is greater than 18.48, so the null hypothesis can be rejected, and we can conclude that client satisfaction is not equally distributed across the eight service groups.

### Summary
The Kruskal-Wallis one-way ANOVA is a good alternative to the F test when the dependent variable is ordinal. It can also be used for interval measures that fail to meet the assumption of the F test by ordinalizing the interval scores. The test is about 95% as efficient as F but is less restrictive. It requires only the following:

1. The observations can be ranked across the groups.
2. The categories are independent.

As with other rank tests, tied scores can present a problem. In using Kruskal-Wallis, if the scores within or between the groups are tied, the average of the tied ranks can be assigned. However, if more than 25% of the scores are tied, special procedures for dealing with multiple ties must be used.[5]

## COMPUTER EXERCISES: SOME SUGGESTIONS

It is clear from the discussion of ANOVA models that, although hand calculations are important for understanding the technique, having a computer do the calculations is a real advantage. Take some time to select variables from your computer data set that represent an interesting conceptual model. Then locate a continuous variable that meets the criteria for the dependent variable in an ANOVA model, as well as several discrete or categorical measures that serve as independent variables. Ideally, you need a group of variables that make up an interesting conceptual model. The printout will not only provide the F ratios and their level of significance, but depending on the software package, will also indicate whether the groups have homogeneous variances.

If your F ratio is significant and there is no interaction between your independent measures, you may be ready for the challenge of doing two group comparisons using the Bonferroni method. The software guide should provide sufficient information for you to interpret the results. You should also select an ordinal measure, or ordinalize an interval measure, and using one categorical measure, apply the Kruskal-Wallis one-way ANOVA. The printout will provide the test statistic and its probability.

## CHAPTER SUMMARY

This chapter has presented three statistical models that can be used to compare more than two samples or measures. One-way ANOVA determines whether one categorical measure, the independent variable, accounts for a significant proportion of the variance in a dependent interval variable. The F test is used to determine the significance of the ratio of the between- to the within-groups variance.

Two-way ANOVA, a factorial design, examines the effect of two independent categorical measures on a dependent interval variable. The two independent variables or factors are tested to determine whether they account for significant variance in the dependent variable. The model actually provides three F ratios, one for each of the two main effects, or independent variables, and a third for interaction.

In addition, the Kruskal-Wallis one-way model for independent groups was reviewed. It provides an alternative for comparing multiple groups when the

---

[5] The procedure involves a correction for tied scores and is discussed in Sidney Siegel, *Nonparametric Statistics for the Behavioral Sciences* (New York: McGraw-Hill, 1956), pp. 184–93.

dependent variable is ordinal and fails to meet the distributional requirements for the F test. Although the Kruskal-Wallis test is not as efficient as the F test, given the lack of stringent assumptions, it is a useful alternative.

## KEY TERMS

**ANOVA**   An acronym for "analysis of variance."

**between-groups variance**   The variance between two or more groups; also called *information* in that the variance is due to differences between groups.

**Bonferroni method**   A technique for evaluating the difference between pairs of groups in ANOVA.

**error variance**   A synonym for *within-groups variance* or *random variation.*

**explained variance**   The variance in the dependent measure explained by differences between groups; also known as between-groups variance.

**factor**   An independent variable in ANOVA.

**factorial design**   An ANOVA design that evaluates the relationship of two or more independent variables to a dependent variable.

**Fisher's F**   A statistic used to test the significance of the amount of variance that an independent variable(s) explains in the dependent variable. In ANOVA, it is the ratio of the explained to the unexplained variance.

**homoscedasticity**   The assumption that samples or measures have similar variances.

**information**   In ANOVA, the between-groups variance provides information on the source of variation in the dependent measure.

**interaction variance**   Variance due to the interaction between two or more independent measures.

**Kruskal-Wallis one-way ANOVA**   An ANOVA test for evaluating the effect of an independent variable on an ordinal, dependent one.

**noise**   In ANOVA, noise is another term for error variance. It is variation from undetermined sources.

**one-way ANOVA**   A technique for evaluating the effect of one independent measure on a dependent one.

**theory driven**   Statistical methods that are organized around theoretical speculations.

**total variance**   The sum of the explained and unexplained variance in a dependent measure.

**two-way ANOVA**   A technique for evaluating the variance of a dependent variable explained by two independent variables.

**unexplained variance**   The variation within groups; it is referred to as *error* in that it represents random error in measurement.

within-groups variance    The variation within groups; it is the unexplained variance in the dependent variable.

## SYMBOLS

| | |
|---|---|
| F | Fisher's F statistic |
| $F_1$ | The F statistic for factor 1 in a two-way ANOVA |
| $F_2$ | The F statistic for factor 2 in a two-way ANOVA |
| $F_{1.2}$ | The F statistic for interaction between factor 1 and factor 2 |
| H | The symbol for the Kruskal-Wallis one-way ANOVA |
| $SS_T$ | Total sums of squares |
| $SS_B$ | Sums of squares for between groups |
| $SS_W$ | Sums of squares for within groups |
| $SS_1$ | Sums of squares for factor 1 in a two-way ANOVA |
| $SS_2$ | Sums of squares for factor 2 in a two-way ANOVA |
| $SS_{1.2}$ | Sums of squares for the interaction of two independent variables |
| $s_B^2$ | Between-groups variance |
| $s_W^2$ | Within-groups variance |
| $s_1^2$ | Variance of factor 1 in a two-way ANOVA |
| $s_2^2$ | Variance of factor 2 in a two-way ANOVA |
| $s_{1.2}^2$ | Variance for the interaction of factor 1 and factor 2 in a two-way ANOVA |

## FORMULAS

$$F = \frac{s_B^2}{s_W^2}$$    F statistic

$$SS_T = \Sigma X_i^2 - \frac{\left(\Sigma X_i\right)^2}{N}$$    Total sums of squares

$$SS_W = \Sigma X_i^2 - \Sigma \frac{\left(\Sigma X_k\right)^2}{n_k}$$    Within-groups sums of squares

$$SS_B = \Sigma \frac{\left(\Sigma X_k\right)^2}{n_k} - \frac{\left(\Sigma X_i\right)^2}{N}$$    Between-groups sums of squares

$$s_B^2 = \frac{SS_B}{k-1}$$    Between-groups variance, one-way ANOVA

$$s_W^2 = \frac{SS_W}{N-k}$$      Within-groups variance, one-way ANOVA

$$SS_W = \Sigma X_i^2 - \Sigma \frac{\left(\Sigma X_m\right)^2}{n_m}$$      Within-groups sums of squares, two-way ANOVA

$$SS_B = \Sigma \frac{\left(\Sigma X_k\right)^2}{n_k} - \frac{\left(\Sigma X_i\right)^2}{N}$$      Total between-groups sums of squares, two-way ANOVA

$$SS_1 = \Sigma \frac{\left(\Sigma X_k\right)^2}{n_k} - \frac{\left(\Sigma X_i\right)^2}{N}$$      Factor 1 sums of squares, two-way ANOVA

$$SS_2 = \Sigma \frac{\left(\Sigma X_j\right)^2}{n_j} - \frac{\left(\Sigma X_i\right)^2}{N}$$      Factor 2 sums of squares, two-way ANOVA

$$SS_{1.2} = SS_B - SS_1 - SS_2$$      Interaction sums of squares, two-way ANOVA

$$s_W^2 = \frac{SS_W}{N-kj}$$      Within-groups variance, two-way ANOVA

$$s_1^2 = \frac{SS_1}{k-1}$$      Factor 1 variance, two-way ANOVA

$$s_2^2 = \frac{SS_2}{j-1}$$      Factor 2 variance, two-way ANOVA

$$s_{1.2}^2 = \frac{SS_{1.2}}{(k-1)(j-1)}$$      Interaction variance, two-way ANOVA

$$F_{1.2} = \frac{s_{1.2}^2}{s_W^2}$$      F statistic for interaction, two-way ANOVA

$$F_1 = \frac{s_1^2}{s_W^2}$$      F statistic for factor 1, two-way ANOVA

$$F_2 = \frac{s_2^2}{s_W^2}$$      F statistic for factor 2, two-way ANOVA

$$H = \frac{12}{N(N+1)} \sum_{i=1}^{n} \frac{R_j^2}{n_j} - 3(N+1)$$      Kruskal-Wallis one-way ANOVA

## EXERCISES

1. Samples of 12 members, each representing three unions, were tested with respect to their union loyalty. The test had a potential range of scores from 1 to 100, with 100

reflecting the greatest loyalty. The data that were observed are shown in the table below. Use ANOVA to test whether the differences in union loyalty between the three unions are significant at $\alpha = .01$.

| Autoworkers ($X_1$) | Teamsters ($X_2$) | Garment Workers ($X_3$) |
|:---:|:---:|:---:|
| 45 | 45 | 30 |
| 20 | 35 | 70 |
| 7 | 20 | 25 |
| 25 | 60 | 40 |
| 15 | 15 | 75 |
| 55 | 45 | 50 |
| 10 | 65 | 35 |
| 35 | 20 | 60 |
| 5 | 40 | 45 |
| 40 | 15 | 65 |
| 15 | 50 | 25 |
| 40 | 55 | 35 |

**a.** State the appropriate hypothesis for the F test.
**b.** What is the sum for each of the three distributions?
**c.** What is the total sums of squares, $SS_T$?
**d.** What is the within-groups sums of squares, $SS_W$?
**e.** What is the between-groups sums of squares, $SS_B$?
**f.** What is the within-groups degrees of freedom?
**g.** What is the between-groups degrees of freedom?
**h.** What is the within-groups variance?
**i.** What is the between-groups variance?
**j.** What is the F value?
**k.** What is your decision regarding the null hypothesis at the .01 level of significance?
**l.** Construct a table, such as Table 10.3, showing the results of your analysis.

**2.** A second independent variable was added to the data in exercise 1 so that union members were cross-classified by length of tenure in the union. They were grouped into the categories of Newcomers, Middle-Agers, and Old-Timers. The following data were observed:

|  | **Autoworkers** | **Teamsters** | **Garment Workers** |
|---|:---:|:---:|:---:|
| Newcomers | 45 | 60 | 70 |
|  | 55 | 45 | 75 |
|  | 35 | 65 | 60 |
|  | 40 | 55 | 65 |
| Middle-Agers | 40 | 45 | 50 |
|  | 20 | 50 | 40 |
|  | 15 | 35 | 35 |
|  | 25 | 40 | 45 |
| Old-Timers | 15 | 20 | 25 |
|  | 10 | 15 | 35 |
|  | 5 | 20 | 30 |
|  | 7 | 15 | 25 |

**a.** State the appropriate hypotheses for two-way ANOVA.
**b.** What is the sum of each of the union groups?
**c.** What is the sum of each of the tenure groups?
**d.** What is the total sums of squares?
**e.** What is the within-groups sums of squares?
**f.** What is the total between-groups sums of squares?
**g.** What is the sums of squares for factor 1?
**h.** What is the sums of squares for factor 2?
**i.** What is the sums of squares for interaction?
**j.** What is the within-groups variance?
**k.** What is the variance for interaction?
**l.** What is the variance for factor 1?
**m.** What is the variance for factor 2?
**n.** What is the F statistic for interaction?
**o.** Is the interaction term significant at the .01 level of significance?
**p.** What is the F statistic for factor 1?
**q.** Can you reject the null hypothesis for factor 1 at the .01 level of significance?
**r.** What is the F statistic for factor 2?
**s.** Can you reject the null hypothesis for factor 2 at the .01 level of significance?
**t.** Prepare a table similar to Table 10.6 showing your results.
**u.** What conclusions can you draw from the analysis?

3. Police officers from five precincts were ranked on an overall performance scale, 1 being the highest rank. The purpose was to determine the relationship between performance and precinct. The following was observed:

**Precinct**

| A | B | C | D | E |
|---|---|---|---|---|
| 9 | 12 | 5 | 18 | 11 |
| 20 | 17 | 23 | 3 | 8 |
| 27 | 29 | 15 | 24 | 21 |
| 2 | 4 | 38 | 6 | 31 |
| 19 | 16 | 25 | 34 | 14 |
| 30 | 28 | 37 | 41 | 32 |
| 40 | 33 | 35 | 10 | 22 |
| 39 | 26 | 43 | 44 | 7 |
| 42 | | 1 | 36 | 13 |
| 45 | | | | |

**a.** Which test is appropriate for the data?
**b.** State the appropriate hypothesis.
**c.** Calculate the test statistic.
**d.** How many degrees of freedom are involved?
**e.** What distribution is used to test the significance of the statistic?
**f.** What conclusions can you draw?

# 11

# LINEAR REGRESSION AND CORRELATION

In 1885, Francis Galton published a paper on the correspondence between the heights of fathers and sons. He concluded that there was a general tendency for the heights of offspring to *regress toward the population mean;* that is, the sons of tall men regress toward the population mean by being somewhat shorter than their fathers, and the sons of short men regress by being somewhat taller than their fathers. Galton's data indicated that the best prediction of a son's height was a value somewhere between that of his father and that of the general population mean. He titled his paper "Regression Towards Mediocrity in Hereditary Status" because he felt that the findings illustrated a more general hereditary tendency of regression toward mediocrity.[1]

Although Galton's substantive arguments regarding the regression toward mediocrity are not of concern here, the method he developed to explain the relationship between the heights of fathers and sons has come to play a key role in statistical analysis.

The method is known as **regression analysis** because of Galton's original concept of "regression to mediocrity." The technique is used to determine the value of a **dependent variable,** $Y$, that is likely to be associated with the value of an **independent variable,** $X$. Or, from another perspective, it indicates the changes in $Y$ that are likely to occur with changes in $X$. A contemporary of Galton's, Karl Pearson, developed a further elaboration of the method called **correlation analysis.** Regression analysis is used to determine the change in $Y$ that is associated with a change in $X$, whereas correlation analysis summarizes the strength of the association between two variables.

---

[1] "Regression towards Mediocrity in Hereditary Status" appeared in 1885 in the *Journal of the Anthropological Institute.*

# REGRESSION ANALYSIS

## *The Scattergram and Least Squares Method*

Suppose that you are interested in the extent to which income is a predictor of job satisfaction and that the data shown in Table 11.1 are available. A cursory examination of the data indicates that there is some correspondence between hourly income and job satisfaction; higher hourly wages tend to correspond with higher job satisfaction.

However, the correspondence is not true for everyone. Alan has the highest hourly wage, $10.50, and the highest job satisfaction score, 94; Beth has the second-highest wage but not the second-highest job satisfaction; and the worker with the lowest wage, Lily, does not have the lowest job satisfaction score.

A better perspective of the relationship between wages and job satisfaction can be gained with a graphic display in which the independent variable, $X$, hourly wage, appears on the horizontal axis and the dependent variable, $Y$, job satisfaction, on the vertical axis. Such a display is called a **bivariate scattergram** because it shows the joint distribution of two variables. The data points in the body of the graph represent the association between each individual's hourly wage and their satisfaction score, as shown in Figure 11.1. For example, the data point in the upper right-hand corner shows Alan's wage, $10.50, and his job satisfaction score, 94. The data point in the lower left-hand corner is Kermit's wage, $4.50, and job satisfaction score, 74.

Visual inspection of the scattergram indicates that the body of data points is generally distributed so that as wages increase so does job satisfaction. However,

**TABLE 11.1   Income and Job Satisfaction**

| Worker | Hourly Income (X) | Job Satisfaction (Y) |
|--------|-------------------|----------------------|
| Alan | 10.50 | 94 |
| Beth | 9.50 | 89 |
| Carl | 9.00 | 91 |
| Doris | 8.25 | 90 |
| Earl | 8.00 | 84 |
| Francis | 7.50 | 92 |
| Gary | 6.25 | 86 |
| Helen | 6.00 | 81 |
| Ivan | 5.75 | 86 |
| Jill | 5.50 | 82 |
| Kermit | 4.50 | 74 |
| Lily | 4.25 | 81 |

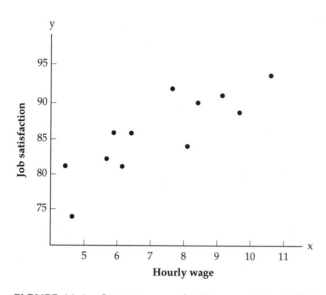

**FIGURE 11.1    Scattergram of Wages and Job Satisfaction**

the relationship is not perfect because the data points are somewhat scattered across the plane. If the correspondence were perfect—that is, if for every unit increase in income there was a unit increase in job satisfaction—the data points would represent a straight line, such as that shown in Figure 11.2. Changes in $Y$ would take place at a constant rate with changes in $X$. For example, in Figure 11.2, a change in $X$ from 4.5 to 5.0 (a unit of .5) is associated with a change in $Y$ from 72.5 to 75 (a unit of 2.5), and a change in $X$ from 5.0 to 5.5 corresponds to a change in $Y$ from 75 to 77.5. Thus, for each unit change in $X$ of .5, there is a unit change in $Y$ of 2.5.

As you might suspect, perfect relationships are rarely encountered in research. The more usual observation is like the data portrayed in Figure 11.1, where $Y$ tends to change with changes in $X$, but not consistently. For example, Francis has the second-highest job satisfaction score, but five other workers have higher hourly salaries. Because the correspondence is not perfect, it would be helpful to be able to derive a value that characterizes the extent to which changes in $Y$ are associated with changes in $X$ for a particular set of observations. The method for such a description was developed by Adrian Legendre, who in 1806 published an article describing the "least squares method."[2]

The **least squares** method is a procedure whereby the association between $X$ and $Y$ is represented by a straight best fitting line drawn through the center of the scatter of data points. The line is referred to as the *line of best fit* because it takes the most central path through the scatter of points. As such, the sum of the

---

[2]Adrian L. Legendre, *Nouvelles methodes pour lat determination des cometes* (Paris, 1806).

squared distances of the data points above and below the **line of best fit** equals the least squares, which is a minimum value:

$$\text{Best fitting line (regression line)} = \Sigma \text{ residuals}^2 = \text{Minimum} \qquad \textbf{(11.1)}$$

The common term for the best fitting line is the **regression line.** The distances between the regression line and the data points are referred to as the **residuals;** they are the differences between the line of best fit and the data points. Figure 11.3 shows the regression line for the scattergram of the data in Table 11.1. The broken lines between the data points and the regression line are the residuals. The regression line represents the **prediction for** $Y$ values, symbolized by $\hat{Y}$. The point at which the residual lines touch the regression line represents the predicted value, $\hat{Y}$, for job satisfaction given a specific hourly wage.

The sum of the squared differences between the observed $Y$ values and the predicted $\hat{Y}$ values equals a minimum, as shown in the following formula:

$$\text{Regression line} = \Sigma(Y - \hat{Y})^2 = \Sigma \text{ residuals}^2 = \text{Minimum} \qquad \textbf{(11.2)}$$

Thus, any number other than $\hat{Y}$ subtracted from the $Y$ values and squared will result in a larger sum. The regression line for a bivariate scattergram plays a role directly parallel to that of the mean for a univariate distribution. Recall that the mean has two properties: the sum of the differences around the mean equals zero, and the sum of the squared differences around the mean equals a minimum value. The sum of the residuals has similar properties. The sum of the residuals above and below the regression line equals zero in that the best fitting line is one that is equidistant from the data points above and below it, and the squared residuals around the regression line equals a minimum value. Just as the mean represents the point of balance for a univariate

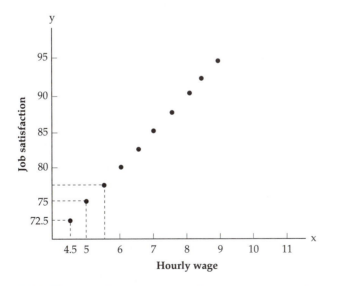

**FIGURE 11.2**  **Scattergram of Perfect Correspondence**

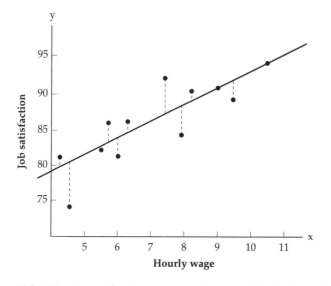

**FIGURE 11.3   The Regression Line for Job Satisfaction on Wages**

distribution, so the regression line represents the point of balance for a bivariate distribution.

The regression line makes it possible to predict the most likely $Y$ value associated with a given value of $X$. In our example, if the hourly wages of individuals are known, their job satisfaction scores can be predicted. Here again the role of the regression line is analogous to that of the mean because the mean represents the best guess or prediction for any score in a distribution. Recall the example of the census tracts and poverty rates for the two communities in Chapter 3. Each had a mean of 21.7 poor households per 100 over a sample of 10 census tracts. The best guess for poor households for any tract is 21.7. Similarly, in regression, the assumption is that the best guess for any job satisfaction score is based on hourly wage.

However, remember that one community, Urbanville, had low variation in its sample of scores; the poverty rates did not deviate much from the mean of 21.7 in any of the 10 census tracts. Thus, Urbanville's mean provides a relatively accurate estimate of poverty rates for its census tracts. Central City represents a different situation because there was more variation over its 10 census tracts. As a result, the mean is a less reliable predictor for Central City. We will see that regression lines also provide more or less reliable predictions, depending on the amount of variation (scatter) in the distribution of bivariate data points. Also, like the mean, although the regression line *always* represents the point of balance, some regression lines are better than others in providing a basis for prediction.

Simple regression analysis assumes that a straight line is a good representation of the scatter of data points, but not all bivariate distributions can be represented by a straight line. Figure 11.4 shows three different scattergrams. The regression line for graph (*a*) in Figure 11.4 is a straight line and represents a good

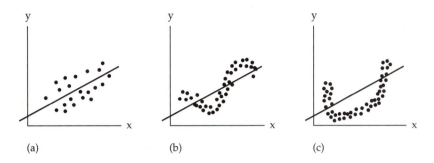

**FIGURE 11.4    Three Patterns of Scattergrams**

fit to the data points because they are scattered linearly. Only scattergrams that have a linear pattern are suitable for straight-line or **linear regression**.[3] The scattergrams for graphs (*b*) and (*c*) in Figure 11.4 are not well represented by a straight line. The **curvilinear data** in (*b*) and the U-shaped scatter in (*c*) are such that most of the data points are far removed from the straight regression line.

The relationship between independent and dependent variables can be either positive or negative. The example used in this chapter concerns a positive relationship between *X* and *Y*; as wages increase, so does job satisfaction. **Negative relationships,** or inverse relationships, are also likely and are equally important. For example, there is a negative relationship between the body's motor skills and blood-alcohol level. **Positive relationships** are characterized by lines that extend from the lower left-hand corner of the plane to the upper right-hand one, as shown in graph (*a*) in Figure 11.5. Negative relationships result in lines that extend from the upper left-hand corner to the lower right-hand one, as shown in graph (*b*) in Figure 11.5.

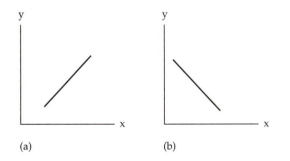

**FIGURE 11.5    Positive and Negative Regression Lines**

---

[3] Models are available for fitting lines to curvilinear data, but their consideration is beyond the scope of this text. For a discussion of three curvilinear models, including the power curve, the exponential curve, and the logarithmic curve, see Allen L. Edwards, *Statistical Methods* (New York: Holt, Rinehart and Winston, 1967), pp. 85–93.

It would not be practical to draw a straight line mechanically, by trial and error, through a scatter of points that meets the best fit criteria of the $\Sigma$ residuals$^2$ = minimum. Fortunately, the solution can be derived mathematically using the following formula:

$$\hat{Y} = a + bX \tag{11.3}$$

where    $\hat{Y}$ = the predicted value for the dependent variable, $Y$, given a value of the independent variable, $X$

$a$ = the $Y$ intercept, which is the value of $\hat{Y}$ when $X = 0$

$b$ = the regression coefficient indicating the amount of change in $Y$ given a unit change in $X$

$X$ = the value of the independent variable

The value $b$, the **regression coefficient,** represents the predicted change, $\hat{Y}$, given a unit change in $X$, whereas $a$ is the value for $Y$ when $X = 0$. When predicting $Y$ (the dependent variable) from $X$ (the independent variable), the notation for the **slope of the line** is $b_{YX}$, and the value is determined using the following formula:

$$b_{YX} = \frac{\Sigma(X - \overline{X})(Y - \overline{Y})}{\Sigma(X - \overline{X})^2} \tag{11.4}$$

An examination of Formula 11.4 shows that $b_{YX}$ is the ratio of the joint variation of $X$ and $Y$ around their respective means, $\Sigma(X - \overline{X})(Y - \overline{Y})$, to the sum of the squared variation of $X$ around its mean, $\Sigma(X - \overline{X})^2$. In other words, it is the ratio of the joint variation of the independent and dependent variables *to* the variation of the independent variable.

Formula 11.4 would be tedious to apply and can be more easily calculated using the sums of raw scores:

$$b_{YX} = \frac{\Sigma XY - \dfrac{\Sigma X \Sigma Y}{N}}{\Sigma X^2 - \dfrac{(\Sigma X)^2}{N}} \tag{11.5}$$

where    $N$ = the number of bivariate data points

The value of **intercept** $a_{YX}$, which is the value of the dependent variable, $Y$, when the independent variable $X$ = zero, is given by

$$a_{YX} = \overline{Y} - b_{YX}\overline{X} \tag{11.6}$$

As in Formula 11.4, the calculation of Formula 11.6 would be time consuming, and the solution can be more easily derived by using the sums of the scores:

$$a_{YX} = \frac{\Sigma Y - b_{YX}\Sigma X}{N} \tag{11.7}$$

Once we know the values for $b_{YX}$ and $a_{YX}$, we can determine the value of $\hat{Y}$ associated with any value of X. For example, if $b_{YX} = 3$ and $a_{YX} = 2$, the $\hat{Y}$ for any X value is given by Formula 11.3:

$$\hat{Y} = a + bX$$

for X = 0,

$$\hat{Y} = 2 + 3\,(0) = 2$$

for X = 1

$$\hat{Y} = 2 + 3\,(1) = 5$$

for X = 2

$$\hat{Y} = 2 + 3\,(2) = 8$$

for X = 7

$$\hat{Y} = 2 + 3\,(7) = 23$$

Note that the change in $\hat{Y}$ is constant for a given unit change in X and is determined by the value of $b_{YX}$. In the example above, $b_{YX} = 3$, so the value of 3 is multiplied by the X value of concern. As we will see later, the predicted Y value is the average expectation for a given value of X.

Applied to the data on hourly income and job satisfaction, the solutions for $b_{YX}$ and $a_{YX}$ can be derived using Formulas 11.5 and 11.7 (Table 11.2 provides a summary of the values needed for the formulas):

$$b_{YX} = \frac{\Sigma XY - \dfrac{\Sigma X \Sigma Y}{N}}{\Sigma X^2 - \dfrac{(\Sigma X)^2}{N}}$$

$$= \frac{7402.25 - \dfrac{(85)(1030)}{12}}{646.49 - \dfrac{(85)^2}{12}}$$

$$= \frac{7402.25 - 7295.833}{646.49 - 602.083}$$

$$= \frac{106.417}{44.407}$$

$$b_{YX} = 2.396$$

The value of the intercept is derived from Formula 11.7:

$$a_{YX} = \frac{\Sigma Y - b_{YX}\Sigma X}{N}$$

$$= \frac{1030-(2.396)(85)}{12}$$

$$= \frac{1030-203.66}{12}$$

$$= \frac{826.34}{12}$$

$$a_{YX} = 68.86$$

The regression coefficient is $b_{YX} = 2.396$, and the $Y$ intercept is $a_{YX} = 68.86$. The two values can be used to graph the regression line in the scattergram. You can begin by solving for the value of $\hat{Y}$ when $X = 0$. Using the $a_{YX}$ and $b_{YX}$ values, we find that the solution is given by the following formula:

$$\hat{Y} = a_{YX} + b_{YX}X \qquad (11.8)$$

$$= 68.86 + 2.396\,(0) = 68.86$$

which equals the intercept. Solving for $\hat{Y}$ for any other value of $X$ provides us with two points that can be used to locate the regression line. For example, let $X = 10$. Then

$$\hat{Y} = 68.86 + 2.396\,(10)$$

$$= 68.86 + 23.96 = 92.82$$

Placing a ruler at $\hat{Y} = 68.86$ and $X = 0$ and at $\hat{Y} = 92.82$ and $X = 10$, the best fitting line can be drawn as shown in Figure 11.6. The regression line is a best fit in that the sum of the squared distances (the residuals) of the data points above and

**TABLE 11.2   Income and Job Satisfaction**

| Worker | Income (X) | Satisfaction (Y) | $X^2$ | $Y^2$ | $XY$ |
|--------|-----------|------------------|-------|-------|------|
| Alan | 10.50 | 94 | 110.25 | 8836 | 987.00 |
| Beth | 9.50 | 89 | 90.25 | 7921 | 845.50 |
| Carl | 9.00 | 91 | 81.00 | 8281 | 819.00 |
| Doris | 8.25 | 90 | 68.06 | 8100 | 742.50 |
| Earl | 8.00 | 84 | 64.00 | 7056 | 672.00 |
| Francis | 7.50 | 92 | 56.25 | 8464 | 690.00 |
| Gary | 6.25 | 86 | 39.06 | 7396 | 537.50 |
| Helen | 6.00 | 81 | 36.00 | 6561 | 486.00 |
| Ivan | 5.75 | 86 | 33.06 | 7396 | 494.50 |
| Jill | 5.50 | 82 | 30.25 | 6724 | 451.00 |
| Kermit | 4.50 | 74 | 20.25 | 5476 | 333.00 |
| Lily | 4.25 | 81 | 18.06 | 6561 | 344.25 |
|  | 85.00 | 1030 | 646.49 | 88,772 | 7402.25 |

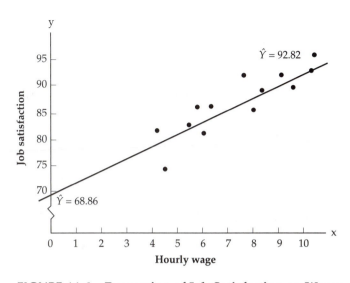

**FIGURE 11.6   Regression of Job Satisfaction on Wages**
Note: The break in the line of the y-axis indicates that Y should have
extended from 70 to 0, but the graph has been truncated to save space.

below the line is equal to a minimum value. Although the regression line passes
through the exact center of the data points, the data points are not on the regression line. The regression line represents the *prediction* for Y given an X value. Like
the mean, the regression line is the estimate of least error in the long run. Using
the regression line value will result in less error in estimating Y for a given X than
any other value. For example, the following $\hat{Y}$ values are associated with X:

If X = 1, then

$\hat{Y} = 68.86 + 2.396 \, (1)$

$= 68.86 + 2.396$

$= 71.26$, which is the average expectation for Y when X = 1

If X = 2, then

$\hat{Y} = 68.86 + 2.396 \, (2)$

$= 68.86 + 4.792$

$= 73.65$, which is the average expectation for Y when X = 2

If X = 5, then

$\hat{Y} = 68.86 + 2.396 \, (5)$

$= 68.86 + 11.980$

$= 80.84$, which is the average expectation for Y when X = 5

If $X = 12$, then

$\hat{Y} = 68.86 + 2.396\ (12)$

$= 68.86 + 28.752$

$= 97.61$, which is the average expectation for $Y$ when $X = 12$

In our example, none of the observed data points actually rest on the regression line, although theoretically they could. Thus, the regression line represents the average expected $Y$ value for each $X$ value. If wages are $5.00 per hour, on the average, job satisfaction will be 80.84, and if wages are increased to $12.00 per hour, the average job satisfaction value is estimated to be 97.61. The accuracy of the estimate of $Y$ depends on the goodness of fit of the regression line to the data points. Some regression lines represent better fits to data sets than others, so the accuracy of estimates also varies. Because regression lines vary in the accuracy of their predictions, an estimate of the amount of error associated with a particular regression line is needed. The *standard error of the estimate* is used to assess the goodness of fit of a regression line.

## The Standard Error of the Estimate

In stating the expected values for $Y$ given an $X$ value, it is always appropriate to modify the statement with the phrase "on the average." This is true because the predicted $\hat{Y}$ is not necessarily the observed $Y$ value associated with an $X$ value. It is an estimate and, as such, is a value expected on the average. As stated earlier, it is analogous to using the mean to predict the values of a distribution. Although the mean serves as a best guess for any value, there is error in the estimate, but the mean is the estimate with the least error.

The likelihood of error in a regression prediction can be illustrated using the example of hourly wages and job satisfaction. Given our regression solution, if $X$ = $6.00, the predicted level of job satisfaction is $\hat{Y} = 68.86 + 2.396\ (6) = 83.24$. However, in our example the actual job satisfaction value associated with $X = \$6.00$ was 81, as shown in Table 11.2. The difference between what is predicted and what is actually observed is the error (residual) associated with the prediction. It is the difference between 81, the observed value associated with $X = \$6.00$, and the predicted value, 83.24.

The error in prediction using the regression line is comparable to the error in using the mean as an estimate for a distribution of scores. We know that the sum of the differences around the mean equals zero. Some scores in the distribution are higher than the mean and others lower, but the differences between the scores above and below the mean balance out and equal zero, $\Sigma(X - \overline{X}) = 0$. The estimates provided by regression lines have the same property. The differences above and below the regression line, as measured by the residuals, equal zero.

The fact that the sum of the differences between the estimated and the observed values equals zero is simply another way of saying that the regression line passes through the exact center of the data points. However, some regression lines represent a better fit than others. This is true because in some cases the data points are all very close to the regression line, representing a good fit, whereas in other cases the data points are further removed, representing a less good fit.

Figure 11.7 illustrates the difference in the accuracy of two regression lines. A relatively inaccurate line is characterized by graph (*a*) in Figure 11.7, in which the data points are further removed from the regression line. A more accurate line is shown in graph (*b*), where the data points are very close to the line. In both cases, the regression lines are best fitting lines so that the sum of the residuals above and below the lines equals zero.

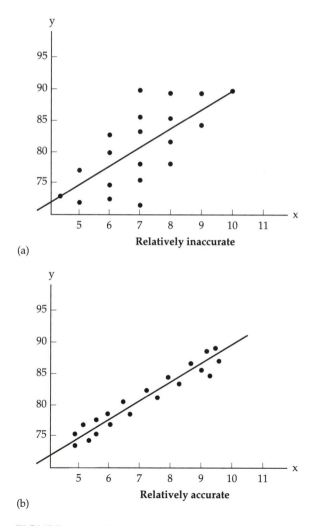

**FIGURE 11.7   Two Best Fitting Lines**

In the case of the mean, the standard deviation is used to represent the amount of error or variance around the mean. Similarly, the accuracy of the regression line is represented with a value known as the **standard error of the estimate,** which is simply the standard deviation of the observed values around the regression line. The difference between the predicted and the observed values is referred to as the **residual variance.** The formula for the standard error of the estimate is

$$s_{YX} = \sqrt{\frac{\Sigma\left(Y - \hat{Y}\right)^2}{N - 2}}$$     **(11.9)**

where     $s_{YX}$ = the symbol for the standard error of predicting $Y$ from $X$

$Y$ = the observed value of the dependent variable

$\hat{Y}$ = the predicted value for a given value of the independent variable, $X$

The formula is parallel to that used for the standard deviation, which you will recall is

$$s = \sqrt{\frac{\Sigma\left(X - \overline{X}\right)^2}{n - 1}}$$

The denominator in Formula 11.9 is $N - 2$ because the number of observations refers to two measures, the bivariate data points. Applying Formula 11.9 to the data on wages and job satisfaction shown in Table 11.3, the standard error of the estimate is

$$s_{YX} = \sqrt{\frac{108.68}{12 - 2}}$$

$$= \sqrt{10.868}$$

$$= 3.30$$

Not only is the standard error of the estimate analogous to the standard deviation, but the variance of the distribution of the $Y$ values around $\hat{Y}$ can also be calculated using the following formula:

$$s_{YX}^2 = \frac{\Sigma\left(Y - \hat{Y}\right)^2}{N - 2}$$     **(11.10)**

$$= \frac{108.68}{12 - 2}$$

$$= 10.868$$

The use of Formula 11.9 is tedious in that each $\hat{Y}$ value must be calculated to derive the $Y - \hat{Y}$ distribution. An alternative method, given in Formula 11.11, circumvents these lengthy calculations:

$$s_{YX} = \sqrt{\frac{\Sigma Y^2 - a_{YX}\Sigma Y - b_{YX}\Sigma XY}{N-2}}$$     **(11.11)**

where     $\Sigma Y^2$ = the sum of the squared $Y$ values

$a_{YX}\Sigma Y$ = the value of the intercept, $a$, times the sum of the $Y$ values

$b_{YX}\Sigma XY$ = the value of the slope, $b$, times the sum of the products of $X$ and $Y$

The values for our example are given in Table 11.2, and the solution, given rounding errors, is very close to that derived from Formula 11.9:

$$s_{YX} = \sqrt{\frac{88,772 - 68.86(1030) - 2.396(7402.25)}{12-2}}$$

$$= \sqrt{\frac{88,772 - 70,925.80 - 17,735.79}{10}}$$

$$= \sqrt{\frac{110.41}{10}}$$

$$= 3.32$$

The size of the standard error of the estimate is a function of the distance between the estimates of $\hat{Y}$ and the observed $Y$ values, or the *size of the residuals*. A large standard error of the estimate indicates that the observed $Y$ values are further removed from the regression line, so the regression line is less representative

**TABLE 11.3  Observed and Estimated Values of Job Satisfaction Based on Wages**

| $X$ | $Y$ | $\hat{Y}$ | $Y - \hat{Y}$ | $(Y - \hat{Y})^2$ |
|---|---|---|---|---|
| 10.50 | 94 | 94.02 | −.02 | .00 |
| 9.50 | 89 | 91.62 | −2.62 | 6.86 |
| 9.00 | 91 | 90.42 | .58 | .34 |
| 8.25 | 90 | 88.63 | 1.37 | 1.88 |
| 8.00 | 84 | 88.03 | −4.03 | 16.24 |
| 7.50 | 92 | 86.83 | 5.17 | 26.73 |
| 6.25 | 86 | 83.84 | 2.16 | 4.67 |
| 6.00 | 81 | 83.24 | −2.24 | 5.02 |
| 5.75 | 86 | 82.64 | 3.36 | 11.29 |
| 5.50 | 82 | 82.04 | −.04 | .00 |
| 4.50 | 74 | 79.64 | −5.64 | 31.81 |
| 4.25 | 81 | 79.04 | 1.96 | 3.84 |
| | | | | 108.68 |

of the distribution of observed $Y$ values. A small standard error means that the regression line is a good representation of the $Y$ values.

The regression line represents the average, or mean, expected value for $Y$ associated with a particular $X$. Moreover, because data are ordinarily taken from samples, it is assumed that repeated samples drawn from the same population will produce $\hat{Y}$ values that differ somewhat, given the variation from one sample to another. If a large number of samples are drawn, the distribution of $\hat{Y}$ values associated with a specific $X$ value will represent a normal distribution. The assumption that the $\hat{Y}$ values are normally distributed around a given $X$ value is based on the same assumption of sampling variation and the central limit theorem that apply to the standard error of the mean. The distribution of the $\hat{Y}$ estimates around the $X$ values is shown in Figure 11.8.

The figure shows that each $X$ value has an associated theoretical distribution of $\hat{Y}$ values. To the extent that the original measure is normally distributed, the $\hat{Y}$ values will be normally distributed with the mean resting on the regression line. The assumption of normality is usually justified on the basis of sample size, where the number of bivariate observations is greater than or equal to 30.

Our example has fewer than 30 observations, but for purposes of illustration the requirement will be ignored. Consider the case in which $Y = 84$ and $X = \$8.00$. The assumption is that the value of 84 is a function of sampling variability, but the mean expectation for the predicted $Y$ value associated with $X = \$8.00$ is 88.03 (see Table 11.3). Given that the distribution of potential $\hat{Y}$ values is normal in form, about 68% of all predictions should fall ±1.00 standard deviation units above and below the mean of 88.03, 95% should be ±2.00, and 99% should be ±3.00.

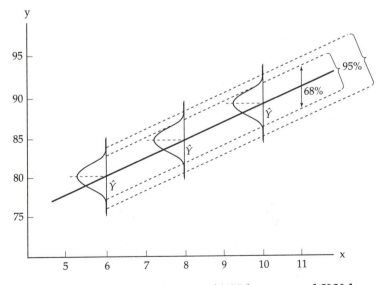

**FIGURE 11.8    The Distribution of $Y$ Values around $X$ Values**

## Some Applications Using the Standard Error of the Estimate

Given that the original variables are normally distributed, information about the theoretical distribution of the $\hat{Y}$ values provided by the standard error of the estimate make it possible to determine the probability of observing a particular $Y$ value given a value of $X$. The probability is based on the normal probability distribution and is derived using the following formula:

$$Z_{\hat{Y}X} = \frac{Y - \hat{Y}}{s_{YX}} \qquad (11.12)$$

where $Y$ = the value for which a probability is desired

$\hat{Y}$ = the predicted value for the $X$ value of concern

$s_{YX}$ = the standard error of the estimate

This formula represents the ratio of the difference between $Y - \hat{Y}$ *to* the standard error of the estimate, $s_{YX}$. For example, if you want to determine the probability of observing a job satisfaction score of 89 or greater for an individual with an hourly wage of $9.50, you determine the predicted $Y$ for the hourly wage of $9.50, which in our example is 91.62 (see Table 11.3); the answer is

$$Z_{89.\$9.50} = \frac{89 - 91.62}{3.32}$$

$$= \frac{-2.62}{3.32}$$

$$= -.79$$

According to column B of Table B.1 in Appendix B, $Z = -.79$ has a probability equal to or greater than .2148. You would expect a job satisfaction score of 89 or greater given an income of $9.50 about 21.48% or less of the time. The probability of a job satisfaction score of 89 or greater is quite different with an hourly rate of $4.25 (the job satisfaction score associated with $4.25 is 79.04; see Table 11.3), as shown here:

$$Z_{89.\$4.25} = \frac{89 - 79.04}{3.32}$$

$$= \frac{9.96}{3.32} = 3.00$$

The probability associated with $Z = 3.00$ is equal to or less than .0013. You would expect someone earning $4.25 to have a job satisfaction score as high as 89 only slightly more than one-tenth of 1% of the time (not a very likely occurrence).

It is also possible to construct confidence limits around $\hat{Y}$ if the measure is normally distributed. The confidence limits around a prediction are given in the following formula:

$$CL_{\hat{Y}X} = \hat{Y} - Zs_{YX} \text{ to } \hat{Y} + Zs_{YX} \tag{11.13}$$

Note the similarity between this formula and that used for interval estimates around the mean in Chapter 6. As in the case of interval estimates around the mean, the intervals around a prediction value represent the boundaries within which the true population prediction is likely to be located. The 95% level of confidence for $X = \$9.50$ and its predicted value, $\hat{Y} = 91.62$, would be as follows:

$$CL_{91.62,\$9.50} = 91.62 - 1.96 \ (3.32) \text{ to } 91.62 + 1.96 \ (3.32)$$

$$= 91.62 - 6.507 \text{ to } 91.62 + 6.507$$

$$= 85.11 \text{ to } 98.13$$

The confidence limits inform us that the limits of 85.11 to 98.13 given an income of \$9.50 per hour will include the real population mean for $\hat{Y}$, job satisfaction, 95% of the time. Five percent of the time the true population mean would lie beyond the limits of 85.11 to 98.13. Whereas we can be confident at the 95% level that the limits include the true population mean, we lack precision in that the limits are quite broad. The width of the limits is a function of the standard error of the estimate, which was quite large due to our small sample, $N = 12$.

The assumption that the $Y$ values are normally distributed around $\hat{Y}$ is justified only if samples are large (i.e., $\geq 30$). Our example of wages and job satisfaction consists of only 12 observations, so using Formula 11.13 to determine confidence limits is inappropriate. The example was used only to illustrate the use of $Z$ scores in creating confidence limits. If the number of observations is less than 30, Student's $t$ distribution can be used as an alternative. Recall that although Student's $t$ assumes that the distribution of the variable in the population is normal, it can be used with small samples, such as in our example. The formula for confidence limits using Student's $t$ distribution is

$$CL_{\hat{Y}X} = \hat{Y} - ts_{YX} \text{ to } \hat{Y} + ts_{YX} \tag{11.14}$$

To apply Formula 11.14, we must identify the Student's $t$ value associated with the specified level of confidence. For example, the $t$ value for the 95% confidence level for a sample of 12 is found in the distribution of $t$ values in Table B.3 in Appendix B. The degrees of freedom associated with a bivariate distribution are $N - 2$, 1 degree of freedom, for each of the two distributions of $X$ and $Y$. The degrees of freedom for our example would be $12 - 2 = 10$, and the $t$ value associated with 95% confidence levels is found at the intersect of df = 10 and $\alpha = .05$. Table B.3 shows the value to be $t = 2.228$. The 95% confidence limits for $X = \$9.50$ and $\hat{Y} = 91.62$ are

$$CL_{91.62,\$9.50} = 91.62 - 2.228 \ (3.32) \text{ to } 91.62 + 2.228 \ (3.32)$$

$$= 91.62 - 7.397 \text{ to } 91.62 + 7.397$$

$$= 84.22 \text{ to } 99.02$$

Notice that the 95% confidence limits resulting from Student's $t$ distribution are somewhat wider and less precise than those found using the Z distribution. The difference comes about because the $t$ distribution compensates for sample size and the increased likelihood of error in the estimates associated with small samples. The level of confidence remains unchanged at 95%, but some precision is sacrificed in using the $t$ distribution because of the small sample.

## Testing the Significance of the Regression Coefficient, b

The significance of the **regression coefficient,** $b$, can also be tested using Student's $t$ distribution. However, when testing significance, the issue is generalizing the sample results to a population. This means that the sample must be selected to represent the population. In addition, other distributional assumptions must be met. These are as follows:

1. A straight line is an appropriate description of the relationship of $Y$ and $X$ in the population. This is referred to as the assumption of **rectilinearity.**
2. For each $X$ value, there is a distribution of $Y$ values in the population, and those distributions are normal in form. The assumption is illustrated in Figure 11.8.
3. The distributions of $Y$ values in the population associated with each $X$ value have similar scatters. This is called **homoscedasticity.** This assumption is similar to that made for the similarity of group variances for ANOVA.
4. The $Y$ values are independent; that is, one $Y$ value associated with $X$ does not influence that of another $Y$ value.

The $t$ statistic is given in the following formula:

$$t = \frac{b - \beta}{s_b}$$
(11.15)

where     $b$ = the value of the slope, or the regression coefficient

$\beta$ = the expected value of the regression coefficient for the population

$s_b$ = the **standard error of b,** which is calculated using Formula 11.16

$$s_b = \frac{s_{YX}}{\sqrt{\Sigma X^2 - \dfrac{(\Sigma X)^2}{N}}}$$
(11.16)

where          $s_{YX}$ = the standard error of the estimate

$\sqrt{\Sigma X^2 - \dfrac{(\Sigma X)^2}{N}}$ = the standard deviation of the independent variable

Given our example, $s_{YX} = 3.32$ (see Formula 11.11) and from Table 11.2, we find the values for

$$\sqrt{\Sigma X^2 - \frac{(\Sigma X)^2}{N}} = \sqrt{646.49 - \frac{(85)^2}{12}}$$

Then, using Formula 11.16, we find

$$s_b = \frac{3.32}{\sqrt{646.49 - \frac{(85)^2}{12}}} = \frac{3.32}{\sqrt{44.4067}} = \frac{3.32}{6.6638} = .4982$$

The significance of the regression coefficient of 2.396 can be tested using Formula 11.15. The null hypothesis would be that the coefficient in the population, $\beta = 0$, and it is tested using our sample coefficient, $b = 2.396$. Using Formula 11.15, we find that Student's $t$ statistic is

$$t = \frac{b - \beta}{s_b}$$

$$= \frac{2.396 - 0}{.4982}$$

$$t = 4.809$$

The degrees of freedom are $N - 2 = 12 - 2 = 10$. With 10 degrees of freedom, the null hypothesis can be rejected at .05 with a $t$ value greater than 2.228. Our test statistic of 4.809 enables us to reject the null hypothesis and accept the directional hypothesis. The conclusion is that there is a relationship between hourly wages and job satisfaction that cannot be accounted for by random variation.

## The Regression of X on Y

Regression analysis was illustrated in the preceding example by using $Y$ as the dependent variable. The same procedure could be used to derive a best fitting line using $X$ as the dependent variable. In terms of our example, this means that job satisfaction, $Y$, can be used to predict hourly wages, $X$. The underlying argument is that more satisfied workers are likely to end up with higher wages. The calculations are the same as when $Y$ was treated as the dependent variable except that the $X$ and $Y$ values are transposed, as shown in the following formulas:

$$b_{XY} = \frac{\Sigma YX - \dfrac{\Sigma Y \Sigma X}{N}}{\Sigma Y^2 - \dfrac{\Sigma(Y)^2}{N}} \tag{11.17}$$

$$a_{XY} = \frac{\Sigma X - b_{XY} \Sigma Y}{N} \tag{11.18}$$

Applied to the data in Table 11.2, the solutions are

$$b_{XY} = \frac{7402.25 - \dfrac{(1030)(85)}{12}}{88,772 - \dfrac{(1030)^2}{12}}$$

$$= \frac{7402.25 - 7295.83}{88,772 - 88,408.33}$$

$$= \frac{106.42}{363.67}$$

$$b_{XY} = .2926$$

$$a_{XY} = \frac{85 - (.2926)(1030)}{12}$$

$$= \frac{85 - 301.378}{12}$$

$$= \frac{-216.378}{12} = -18.03$$

The $b_{XY}$ and $a_{XY}$ values can then be used to predict wages, $X$, given a particular job satisfaction score, $Y$. For example, the values predicted for $X$ when $Y = 94$ would be

$$\hat{X} = a_{XY} + b_{XY}Y \qquad\qquad \textbf{(11.19)}$$

$$= -18.03 + .2926 \,(94)$$

$$= 9.47$$

And, when $Y = 81$, $X$ would equal

$$\hat{X} = -18.03 + .2926 \,(81)$$

$$= 5.67$$

Figure 11.9 illustrates the best fitting line for the regression of $X$ on $Y$, wages on job satisfaction. As in the case of $Y$, the line represents the most central path through the data points. However, in this case the $\Sigma$ residuals$^2$ = minimum is determined by the horizontal distances of the data points from the regression line, as shown in Figure 11.9. The residuals for the regression of $Y$ on $X$ are measured vertically. The $Y$ on $X$ regression line is referred to as the vertical, and the $X$ on $Y$ is the horizontal regression line.

As in the case of the regression of $Y$ on $X$, we could calculate the standard error of the estimate for the regression of $X$ on $Y$ and use the results to construct confidence limits around our predictions of $X$. You might find this a helpful exercise using the example of job satisfaction and hourly income.

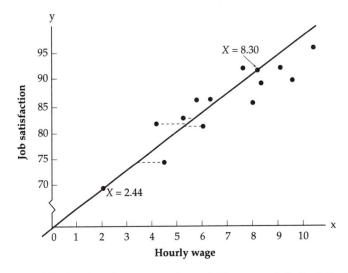

**FIGURE 11.9   The Regression of Wages on Job Satisfaction**

## CORRELATION

Regression analysis is a prediction method that makes it possible to predict the value of a dependent variable that is likely to be associated with the value of an independent variable. However, often the interest is in evaluating the extent or strength of the *association* between $X$ and $Y$. The **correlation coefficient** provides such a measure.

The correlation coefficient is the geometric mean of the slopes of the two lines, which is the square root of the slopes of the two regression lines, $b_{YX}$ and $b_{XY}$, as shown in the following formula:

$$r = \sqrt{b_{YX}b_{XY}} \tag{11.20}$$

The correlation coefficient for our example is

$$r = \sqrt{(2.396)(.2926)}$$
$$= \sqrt{.7011}$$
$$= .8373$$

Symbolized by $r$, the correlation coefficient has values that are standardized on a scale of −1.00 to +1.00. A value of .00 indicates that there is no association or relationship between the values of the two variables. A value of +1.00 indicates a perfect positive association **(positive correlation)** and −1.00 a perfect negative, or inverse association **(negative correlation)**. A perfect positive association occurs when a unit increase in $X$ is associated with a unit increase in $Y$ (or a unit decrease in $X$ is associated with a unit decrease in $Y$). An inverse relationship is such that a unit increase in $X$ is associated with a unit decrease in $Y$ (or a unit decrease in $X$

is associated with a unit increase in $Y$). Figure 11.10 illustrates both high and low positive and negative relationships using scattergrams. When the correlation value is high, whether positive or negative, the scatter of points appears as an elongated ellipse, as in graphs (*a*) and (*b*), and when it is low the pattern approaches that of a circle, as in graphs (*c*) and (*d*).

Figure 11.11 provides a geometric illustration of correlation. It combines the graph of the regression of $Y$ on $X$ and of $X$ on $Y$. The two broken lines in Figure 11.11 show that the two regression lines intersect at the point opposite $\overline{Y} = 85.83$ and the $\overline{X} = 7.08$.[4] The correlation coefficient can be thought of as a summary of the prediction of $Y$ given $X$ and of $X$ given $Y$. The size of the coefficient is a function of the angle of the intersect of the two regression lines opposite the point of origin of $X$ and $Y$. Figure 11.11 shows that the two regression lines for our data are quite close together, in keeping with the high correlation value of .8373.

Figure 11.12 illustrates the position of the two regression lines for different levels of correlation. In the case of a high positive correlation, the lines rise from the lower-left to the upper-right corner of the plane, as in graph (*a*). When the correlation is negative, the lines begin at the upper left and descend to the lower

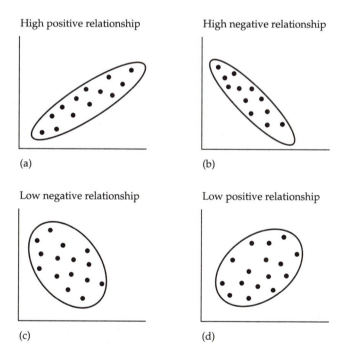

High positive relationship     High negative relationship

(a)     (b)

Low negative relationship     Low positive relationship

(c)     (d)

**FIGURE 11.10**   **Patterns of Correlation**

[4] The mean for $Y$ is found by dividing the sum of the $Y$ values, 1,030, by the number of $Y$ values, 12, which equals 85.83. Mean $\overline{X}$ is the sum of the $X$ values, 85, divided by the number of $X$ values, 12, which equals 7.08.

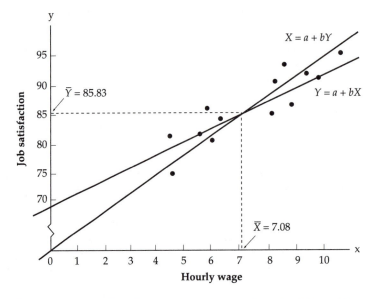

**FIGURE 11.11    The Regression of Y on X and of X on Y**

right, as in graph (*c*). As the two regression lines move closer together, the correlation coefficient approaches ±1.00, as shown in graphs (*b*) and (*d*). When the two lines are superimposed, the correlation is perfect, as in graphs (*b*) and (*d*). As the two lines move farther apart, the strength of the association weakens, and when they are perpendicular, as in graph (*e*), the correlation coefficient becomes zero, and the relationship between the two measures is random.

The correlation coefficient also can be represented as the ratio of the *covariance* (joint variation) of X and Y *to* the product of the standard deviations of X and Y, as shown in the following formula:

$$r = \frac{\dfrac{\Sigma\left(X - \overline{X}\right)\left(Y - \overline{Y}\right)}{N-1}}{\sqrt{\dfrac{\Sigma\left(X - \overline{X}\right)^2}{n-1}}\sqrt{\dfrac{\Sigma\left(Y - \overline{Y}\right)^2}{n-1}}} \qquad (11.21)$$

Because the coefficient is based on the products of the differences around the mean, it may be referred to as the **product moment correlation coefficient.** It also is described as **Pearson's r,** after its founder, Sir Karl Pearson. It would be quite cumbersome to use Formula 11.21 to calculate *r*. The solution can be more easily determined using the sums of the raw scores:

$$r = \frac{N\Sigma XY - \Sigma X \Sigma Y}{\sqrt{\left[N\Sigma X^2 - \left(\Sigma X\right)^2\right]\left[N\Sigma Y^2 - \left(\Sigma Y\right)^2\right]}} \qquad (11.22)$$

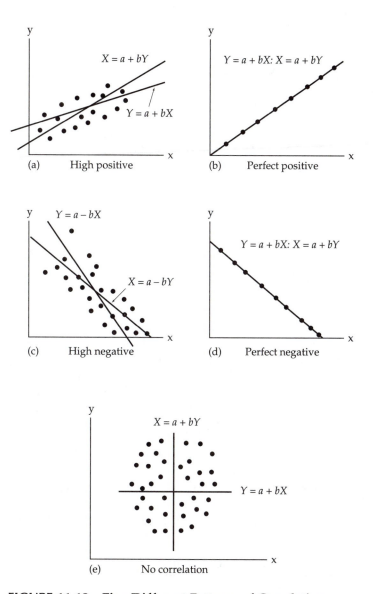

**FIGURE 11.12   Five Different Patterns of Correlation**

Applied to the data on hourly wages and job satisfaction shown in Table 11.2, the solution is

$$r = \frac{12(7402.25) - 85(1030)}{\sqrt{\left[12(646.49) - (85)^2\right]\left[12(88772) - (1030)^2\right]}}$$

$$= \frac{(88,827.00) - (87,550.00)}{\sqrt{\left[(7757.88) - (7225.00)\right]\left[(1,065,264.00) - (1,060,900.00)\right]}}$$

$$= \frac{1277}{\sqrt{(532.88)(4364)}}$$

$$= \frac{1277}{\sqrt{2,325,488.32}}$$

$$= \frac{1277}{1524.9552}$$

$$= .8374$$

The solution of $r = .8374$, given rounding errors, is very close to that derived using the square root of the products of the two slopes (Formula 11.20), which was .8373.

Although no hard and fast rules exist for interpreting the meaning of a specific correlation value, some rules of thumb for the meaning of different correlation coefficients can be useful. Table 11.4 presents some guidelines for interpreting correlation values, but as with all rules of thumb, you must use these guidelines with caution. You must also remember that the meaning of a correlation value is, to some extent, a function of the issue at hand. Thus, if theoretical expectations are that no correlation should be present, a smaller value might be of greater interest than if a correlation is expected.

Like regression analysis, Pearson's correlation coefficient assumes that the scatter of bivariate data points for the $X$ and $Y$ variables forms a linear pattern. This is referred to as the assumption of rectilinearity, which simply means that the

**TABLE 11.4   Interpreting Correlation Coefficients**

| *r* Value | Level of Association |
|---|---|
| .75 to 1.00 | Very high positive |
| .50 to .74 | High positive |
| .25 to .49 | Moderate positive |
| .00 to .24 | Low positive |
| .00 to −.24 | Low negative |
| −.25 to −.49 | Moderate negative |
| −.50 to −.74 | High negative |
| −.75 to −1.00 | Very high negative |

scatter plot can be represented with a straight line. If the assumption of **linear correlation** is violated, the $r$ value will be underestimated.

## Regression, Correlation, and Analysis of Variance

Measures of regression and correlation can also be interpreted in terms of the concept of ANOVA, discussed in Chapter 10. Recall that the relationship between two variables can be described in terms of the variance that they share. The total variance of two variables can be decomposed into explained variance and error variance (unexplained variance). Explained variance is the portion of the total variance that is accounted for by the association of the two variables, and unexplained variance is that due to random fluctuations of sample values.

The concepts can be illustrated using the example of regression, where $Y$, job satisfaction, is the dependent variable and $X$, hourly wages, the independent variable. The data and summary calculations are shown in Table 11.5. The total variance is the average of the sum of the squared differences between the observed $Y$ values and the mean of $Y$ and is calculated by

$$\text{Total variance} = \frac{\Sigma(\text{observed } Y - \text{mean } Y)^2}{N-2} \tag{11.23}$$

$$= \frac{\Sigma(Y - \bar{Y})^2}{N-2}$$

The value for the expression in the numerator, 363.68, is the sum of the third column from the left in Table 11.5.

**TABLE 11.5   Job Satisfaction as a Function of Hourly Wages**

| $Y$ | $Y - \bar{Y}$ | $(Y - \bar{Y})^2$ | $\hat{Y}$ | $\hat{Y} - \bar{Y}$ | $(\hat{Y} - \bar{Y})^2$ | $Y - \hat{Y}$ | $(Y - \hat{Y})^2$ |
|---|---|---|---|---|---|---|---|
| 94 | 8.17 | 66.75 | 94.02 | 8.19 | 67.08 | −.02 | .00 |
| 89 | 3.17 | 10.05 | 91.62 | 5.79 | 33.52 | −2.62 | 6.86 |
| 91 | 5.17 | 26.73 | 90.42 | 4.59 | 21.07 | .58 | .34 |
| 90 | 4.17 | 17.39 | 88.63 | 2.80 | 7.84 | 1.37 | 1.88 |
| 84 | −1.83 | 3.35 | 88.03 | 2.20 | 4.84 | −4.03 | 16.24 |
| 92 | 6.17 | 38.07 | 86.83 | 1.00 | 1.00 | 5.17 | 26.73 |
| 86 | .17 | .03 | 83.84 | −1.99 | 3.96 | 2.16 | 4.67 |
| 81 | −4.83 | 23.33 | 83.24 | −2.59 | 6.71 | −2.24 | 5.02 |
| 86 | .17 | .03 | 82.64 | −3.19 | 10.18 | 3.36 | 11.29 |
| 82 | −3.83 | 14.67 | 82.04 | −3.79 | 14.36 | −.04 | .00 |
| 74 | −11.83 | 139.95 | 79.64 | −6.19 | 38.32 | −5.64 | 31.81 |
| 81 | 4.83 | 23.33 | 79.04 | −6.79 | 46.10 | 1.96 | 3.84 |
| 1030 | | 363.68 | | | 254.98 | | 108.68 |
| $\bar{Y} = 85.83$ | | | | | | | |

$$\text{Total variance} = \frac{363.68}{12-2}$$

$$= 36.37$$

The explained variance is the average of the sum of the squared differences between the predicted value, $\hat{Y}$, and the mean, $\overline{Y}$. It represents the proportion of the variation in $Y$, the dependent variable, that is associated with $X$, the independent variable, and is calculated by

$$\text{Explained variance} = \frac{\Sigma\left(\text{predicted } Y - \text{mean } Y\right)^2}{N-2} \qquad \textbf{(11.24)}$$

$$= \frac{\Sigma\left(Y - \hat{Y}\right)^2}{N-2}$$

$$= \frac{254.98}{12-2}$$

$$= 25.50$$

The error variance is the average of the sums of the squared differences between the observed $Y$ values and the predicted values, $\hat{Y}$. It represents the variation in $Y$ that is not associated with $X$ and is due to random variation in sampling outcomes:

$$\text{Error variance} = \frac{\Sigma\left(\text{observed } Y - \text{predicted } Y\right)^2}{N-2} \qquad \textbf{(11.25)}$$

$$= \frac{\Sigma\left(Y - \hat{Y}\right)^2}{N-2}$$

$$= \frac{108.68}{12-2}$$

$$= 10.87$$

The proportion of variance in $Y$ that is associated with $X$, symbolized by $r^2$, equals the ratio of the explained variance to the total variance and is determined using the following formula:

$$r^2 = \frac{\dfrac{\Sigma\left(\hat{Y} - \overline{Y}\right)^2}{N-2}}{\dfrac{\Sigma\left(Y - \overline{Y}\right)^2}{N-2}} \qquad \textbf{(11.26)}$$

The solution for our example is

$$= \frac{25.50}{36.37}$$

$$= .7011$$

The solution could also have been derived by using the ratio of the sums of the squared deviations:

$$r^2 = \frac{\Sigma(\hat{Y} - \bar{Y})^2}{\Sigma(Y - \bar{Y})^2} \tag{11.27}$$

$$= \frac{254.98}{363.68}$$

$$= .7011$$

Further, $r^2$ could have been determined simply by squaring the correlation coefficient, $r$. Recall that $r = .8373$, so $.8373^2 = .7011$. The value $r^2$ is referred to as the **coefficient of determination** because it represents the variance determined by the association of $X$ and $Y$. The formula for the coefficient of determination is as follows:

$$\text{Coefficient of determination} = r^2 \tag{11.28}$$

In our example, 70.11% of the variation in job satisfaction and wages is determined by their association. The coefficient of determination thus represents the variance that $X$ and $Y$ have in common. The coefficient of determination, $r^2$, is also known as a measure of the proportional reduction in error (PRE). It represents the proportional reduction in error that is achieved in estimating the values for $X$ and $Y$ by taking their association into account (Chapter 12 gives special attention to the concept of PRE).

The remainder of the total variation, $1.0000 - .7011 = .2989$, is known as the **coefficient of nondetermination.** It represents the variance in $X$ and $Y$ that remains unaccounted for by their association. In our example, 29.89% of the variance in job satisfaction and hourly wages is due to other factors. More generally, the coefficient of nondetermination is as follows:

$$\text{Coefficient of nondetermination} = 1 - r^2 \tag{11.29}$$

## Testing the Significance of r

Usually, correlation coefficients are based on data derived from samples, and it is important to determine whether the sample statistic is a chance occurrence or a statistically significant outcome. The significance of a correlation coefficient can be tested using Student's $t$ distribution, the use of which is based on the same assumptions about the data as the $t$ test for the significance of the regression coefficient. Given these assumptions, the significance of $r$ is tested using the following formula:

$$t = r\sqrt{\frac{N-2}{1-r^2}} \qquad \text{(11.30)}$$

For our example, the test determines whether the sample estimate of $r = .8373$ is a chance occurrence or is so far out on the tail of the distribution that it is not likely due to chance, indicating that there is a real relationship between $X$ and $Y$ in the population. The general form of the hypotheses tested is

$H_0$:  $\rho = 0$
$H_1$:  $\rho > 0$ or $\rho < 0$

The symbol $\rho$ is used to represent the population parameter for $r$. For our example, the null hypothesis would be $H_0$: $\rho = 0$; that is, there is no association between $X$ and $Y$. The directional hypothesis is $H_1 : \rho > 0$; that is, there is a positive association between $X$ and $Y$. The direction of the hypothesis indicates that $Y$ increases with increases in $X$. If we test $H_0$ at $\alpha = .01$, the solution is

$$t = .8373\sqrt{\frac{12-2}{1-.8373^2}}$$

$$= 4.84$$

The distribution of Student's $t$ values in Table B.3 in Appendix B shows that with $N - 2 = 12 - 2 = 10$ degrees of freedom, a $t$ value of 3.169 or greater is needed to reject the null hypothesis at $\alpha = .01$. Our $t = 4.84$ allows us to reject the null hypothesis and accept the directional one. We conclude that the association between $X$ and $Y$ is not due to chance sampling results but represents a real association that would be repeated if additional samples were drawn from the population. Table B.8 in Appendix B also contains critical values for assessing the significance of selected correlation coefficients. The decision rule for Table B.8 is as follows: If the computed $r$ value is equal to or larger than the table value, reject the null hypothesis and accept the directional hypothesis. The table confirms that the $r$ value for our example is significant beyond the .01 level.

The significance of $r$ also can be evaluated using the F distribution in Table B.7 in Appendix B. We already reviewed the relationship of correlation to ANOVA. The significance of $r$ is tested using the ratio of the explained variance to the unexplained variance, as was done in ANOVA. Taking the degrees of freedom into account, we find that the F ratio is

$$F = \frac{r^2}{1-r^2}(N-2) \qquad \text{(11.31)}$$

$$= \frac{.8373^2}{1-.8373^2}(12-2)$$

$$= \frac{.7011}{1-.7011}(10)$$

$$= 23.45$$

The F statistic is evaluated where the degrees of freedom for the explained variance equals 1 (across the top of Table B.7 in Appendix B), and the unexplained variance has $N - 2 = 12 - 2 = 10$ degrees of freedom. The value at the intersect of 1 and 10 degrees of freedom for $\alpha = .01$ is 10.04. Our value of 23.45 allows us to reject the null hypothesis.

When using $r$ to draw inferences from samples to populations, we must know whether a particular sample, $r$, is significant. The foregoing tests of significance provide that information. We have already found that tests of significance are sensitive to sample size, and this is in keeping with the logic of statistical inference. Large sample estimates of population parameters are less likely to err than are small sample estimates. However, in some cases the sensitivity is greater. For example, in discussing chi-square, we found that even moderately large samples tended to result in significant outcomes. The same problem attends significance tests for correlation coefficients. Very small coefficients will be significant with relatively small samples. Although significance means that the statistic is not a chance occurrence, it does not mean that the relationship is substantively significant (important). Substantive significance is always a matter of the issue of concern and depends on the theoretical and practical context.

## The Standard Error of r and Confidence Limits

As in the case of other statistical summaries of relationships, if $r$ is based on a sample, it is likely to vary somewhat from sample to sample, with greater variation in the $r$ values when small samples are used. An estimate of the error likely for an $r$ value based on a given sample size can be evaluated by calculating the **standard error of $r$** and using it to create confidence limits. The estimate of the standard error is determined as follows:

$$\sigma_z = \sqrt{\frac{1}{N-3}} \qquad \text{(11.32)}$$

The standard error for our example is

$$\sigma_z = \sqrt{\frac{1}{12-3}}$$

$$= .3333$$

The value of $\sigma_z$ can then be used to construct confidence limits, which show how precise an estimate the sample $r$ is of the real population value. First, however, the $r$ value, which does not come from a normal distribution, must be normalized using a new distribution, symbolized by a lowercase $z$ (not to be confused with the Z score). The conversion is made by using Table B.9 in Appendix B. To convert $r = .8373$ to $z$, locate the observed $r$ value in the table margins. The first two digits, .83, are found in the left-hand column and the third, 7, in the row across the top of the table. The $z$ value at the intersect of .83 and 7 is 1.2111. The value of 1.2111 represents the normalized coefficient for $r = .837$ and can be used to construct confidence limits using the following formula:

$$CL = z - Z\sigma_z \text{ to } z + Z\sigma_z \qquad (11.33)$$

The Z value relates to the Z score for a given level of confidence.

Assume that you want to set confidence limits for $r = .837$ at the .05 level of significance. Using the $z$ value to represent $r$, we find that the results are

$$CL = 1.2111 - 1.96\,(.3333) \text{ to } 1.2111 + 1.96\,(.3333)$$

$$= 1.2111 - .6533 \text{ to } 1.2111 + .6533$$

$$= .5578 \text{ to } 1.8644$$

The $z$ values for the confidence limits must then be converted back to $r$ values using Table B.9 in Appendix B. The $z$ values are restored to $r$ values by locating the $z$ value in the body of the table and identifying the associated $r$ value in the column and row margins of the table. The lower-limit value of .5578 is equivalent to $r = .506$ and the upper-limit value of 1.8644 equivalent to $r = .953$. Thus, the 95% confidence limits around $r = .837$ range from .506 to .953. This means that 95% of the time we would expect to include the real population value for the association of income and job satisfaction between the limits of .506 and .953. Note that the confidence limits are not symmetrical around the original correlation coefficient. The upper limit of .953 is .116 units above the coefficient of .837, but the lower limit of .506 is .331 units below .837. The only case in which symmetry occurs is when $r = 0$. As $r$ approaches +1.00, the limits become more skewed toward the upper limit, and as $r$ approaches –1.00, they become more skewed toward the lower limit.

The confidence limits of .506 to .953 are not very precise, as they indicate that the real population value could vary considerably from $r = .837$. Our previous use of confidence limits indicates that the width (precision) of the limits is a function of the standard error, in this case, $\sigma_z$, which in turn is affected by sample size. The larger the sample, the lower the standard error and the more precise the confidence limits. Our example consisted of a very small sample, $N = 12$, which accounts for the imprecision of the confidence limits.

Suppose that our example had consisted of 103 bivariate observations rather than 12 and that $r$ remained at .837. The standard error would then be

$$\sigma_z = \sqrt{\frac{1}{103 - 3}}$$

$$= .10$$

And the 95% confidence limits would be

$$CL = 1.2111 - 1.96 \, (.10) \text{ to } 1.2111 + 1.96 \, (.10)$$

$$= 1.2111 - .196 \text{ to } 1.2111 + .196$$

$$= 1.0151 \text{ to } 1.4071$$

And converting the $z$ values to $r$, we find the confidence limits to be

$$= .767 \text{ to } .886$$

The larger sample provides narrower confidence limits, indicating that the sample statistic of $r = .837$ is a relatively precise estimate of the association between wages and job satisfaction in the population.

## COMPUTER EXERCISES: SOME SUGGESTIONS

Regression and correlation are two of the most frequently used techniques in data analysis. Computer exercises are helpful in understanding the application and interpretation of these procedures. It is important that you identify at least two interval variables that are normally distributed. A relatively large sample, 60 or more, of paired observations (e.g., individuals with scores on both interval measures) would be helpful. After checking the distributions of the variables across your sample, create a contingency table showing the bivariate distribution. You will get a sense of the relationship between the two variables by the pattern of the bivariate data points. The computer can also create a best fitting line for your data and give the solutions for the slope of the line and the intercept. You can then predict various values for the dependent variable, using the independent.

The software program will provide the standard error of the estimate so that you can establish confidence limits around predicted dependent values. You can also test for the significance of the slope of the line, $b_{YX}$. It will be interesting to switch the roles of the dependent and independent variables and plot the regression of $X$ on $Y$. You may repeat all the calculations completed for the regression of $Y$ on $X$ as well as test the significance of $b_{XY}$.

Correlation analysis is also possible using the software. You can test the significance of the correlation coefficient, and depending on the software, the printout may contain the F statistic and its level of significance. In addition, you may calculate the standard error for $r$ and construct confidence limits around your correlation coefficient. After becoming familiar with the printout, you will find that a great deal of information on the association between two interval measures is readily available.

## CHAPTER SUMMARY

The purpose of this chapter was to familiarize you with the concepts of regression and correlation analysis. Regression is a useful means for summarizing the changes in a dependent variable given independent variable values. Based on the least squares method, the regression line provides an estimate of the $Y$ value that is expected for a specific value of $X$. In our example, we were able to predict the level of job satisfaction for a particular hourly wage.

However, we also found that some regression lines are better than others. Although the mathematical model always provides the best fitting line, if the data points are far removed from the line, the estimated $Y$ value for a given value of $X$ can vary considerably from one observation to another. The standard error of the estimate is useful for assessing the accuracy of the regression line.

The coefficient of determination, $r^2$, provides another perspective of the relationship between the two variables. Derived from regression, it estimates the amount of total variation shared by $X$ and $Y$. The coefficient of nondetermination, $1 - r^2$, indicates how much of the variation is unexplained by the association of the two variables.

Correlation analysis is an extension of the regression concept. It provides a summary of the strength of the association between $X$ and $Y$. A widely used statistic, the correlation coefficient has values that range from –1.00 to +1.00. If the estimate of $r$ is based on a sample, confidence limits can be used to measure the precision of the statistic.

## KEY TERMS

**bivariate scattergram**   A graph displaying the joint distribution of two interval variables.

**coefficient of determination**   The amount of variance explained by the association of two variables.

**coefficient of nondetermination**   The variance unexplained by the association of two variables.

**correlation analysis**   A method for summarizing the strength of the association between two variables.

**correlation coefficient**   A coefficient summarizing the strength of the association between two variables.

**curvilinear data**   A bivariate data display that has a curved form rather than a straight line.

**dependent variable**   In regression analysis, the variable whose values are influenced by the independent variable.

**homoscedasticity**   The assumption that the scatter of the $Y$ values associated with $X$ values are approximately equal.

**independent variable**   In regression analysis, the variable that influences the value of the dependent variable.

**intercept**   The value of the dependent variable, $Y$, when the independent variable, $X = 0$.

**least squares**   A property of the best fitting line where the sum of the squared residuals is equal to the least value.

**line of best fit**   The line representing a point of balance for bivariate data where the sum of the residuals equals zero and the sum of the squared residuals equals a minimum value.

**linear correlation**   A correlation based on a pattern similar to an elongated ellipse or a straight line.

**linear regression**   A model based on the assumption that a straight line is the best representation for a bivariate scatter of data.

**negative correlation**   A correlation describing an inverse relationship; as the values of one variable increase, those of the other decrease.

**negative relationship**   In regression, the inverse relationship between the independent and dependent variables; as one increases, the other decreases.

**Pearson's *r***   A name for the linear correlation of two interval variables.

**positive correlation**   A correlation in which two variables are directly related; as the values of one increase, so do those of the other.

**positive relationship**   In regression, it means that if the independent variable increases, so does the dependent variable; if it decreases, the dependent variable also decreases.

**product moment correlation coefficient**   Another name for the linear correlation coefficient because the value is based on the cross-products of the differences around the means of two variables.

**prediction**   In regression analysis, the estimate for the dependent variable, $Y$, given a value of the independent variable, $X$.

**rectilinearity**   The assumption that a straight line represents the association between two variables.

**regression analysis**   A method for determining the value of a dependent variable given that of an independent variable.

**regression coefficient**   The value of the slope of the line describing the change in $Y$ given a unit change in $X$.

**regression line**   The line of best fit for a bivariate scattergram.

**residuals**   Lines representing the distance between observed bivariate data points and the best fitting line.

**residual variance**   The scatter or variance of the bivariate data points around the best fitting line.

**slope of the line**   The value representing the amount of change in $Y$ given a unit change in $X$.

**standard error of the estimate**   The standard deviation of the bivariate data points around the best fitting line.

**standard error of *b***   In regression analysis, the standard error of the slope of the regression line.

**standard error of *r***   The expected variation around the correlation coefficient of sample observations.

## SYMBOLS

| | |
|---|---|
| $X$ | Independent variable in regression analysis |
| $Y$ | Dependent variable in regression analysis |
| $\hat{Y}$ | Estimate for $Y$ given a value of $X$ |
| $a$ | The intercept; the value of $Y$ when $X = 0$ |
| $b$ | The slope of the line |
| $\beta$ | The expected value of the regression coefficient for the population |
| $b_{YX}$ | The slope of the line for the regression of $Y$ on $X$ |
| $a_{YX}$ | The intercept for the regression of $Y$ on $X$ |
| $s_{YX}$ | The standard error of the estimate |
| $s^2_{YX}$ | The variance for the regression of $Y$ on $X$ |
| $Z_{\hat{Y}X}$ | The Z score for $\hat{Y}$ on $X$ |
| $CL_{\hat{Y}X}$ | The confidence limits for a regression prediction |
| $r$ | The correlation coefficient |
| $\rho$ | The symbol for correlation coefficient of the population |
| $b_{XY}$ | The slope of the line for the regression of $X$ on $Y$ |
| $a_{XY}$ | The intercept for the regression of $X$ on $Y$ |
| $\hat{X}$ | The predicted value for $X$ given a value of $Y$ |
| $r^2$ | The coefficient of determination |
| $s_b$ | The standard error for a regression coefficient |
| $\sigma_z$ | The standard error for $r$ |

## FORMULAS

| | |
|---|---|
| Minimum $\Sigma$ residuals$^2$ | Best fitting line |
| $\Sigma(Y - \hat{Y})^2$ | Minimum $\Sigma$ residuals$^2$ |
| $\hat{Y} = a + bX$ | Equation for a straight line |

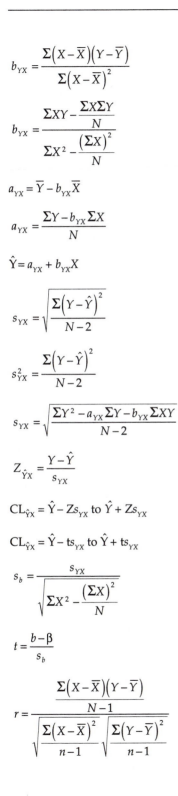

$$b_{YX} = \frac{\Sigma(X-\overline{X})(Y-\overline{Y})}{\Sigma(X-\overline{X})^2}$$     Slope of the line: difference around the means

$$b_{YX} = \frac{\Sigma XY - \dfrac{\Sigma X \Sigma Y}{N}}{\Sigma X^2 - \dfrac{(\Sigma X)^2}{N}}$$     Slope of the line: sums of squares for $Y$ on $X$

$$a_{YX} = \overline{Y} - b_{YX}\overline{X}$$     Intercept: difference around the means for $Y$ on $X$

$$a_{YX} = \frac{\Sigma Y - b_{YX}\Sigma X}{N}$$     Intercept: sums of squares for $Y$ on $X$

$$\hat{Y} = a_{YX} + b_{YX}X$$     Prediction for $Y$ given $X$

$$s_{YX} = \sqrt{\frac{\Sigma(Y-\hat{Y})^2}{N-2}}$$     Standard error of the estimate

$$s_{YX}^2 = \frac{\Sigma(Y-\hat{Y})^2}{N-2}$$     Residual variance

$$s_{YX} = \sqrt{\frac{\Sigma Y^2 - a_{YX}\Sigma Y - b_{YX}\Sigma XY}{N-2}}$$     Standard error of the estimate, alternative

$$Z_{\hat{Y}X} = \frac{Y-\hat{Y}}{s_{YX}}$$     Z score for $Y$ estimates

$$CL_{\hat{Y}X} = \hat{Y} - Zs_{YX} \text{ to } \hat{Y} + Zs_{YX}$$     Confidence limits for predicted $Y$ using $Z$ scores

$$CL_{\hat{Y}X} = \hat{Y} - ts_{YX} \text{ to } \hat{Y} + ts_{YX}$$     Confidence limits for predicted $Y$ using Student's $t$

$$s_b = \frac{s_{YX}}{\sqrt{\Sigma X^2 - \dfrac{(\Sigma X)^2}{N}}}$$     Standard error for a regression coefficient

$$t = \frac{b-\beta}{s_b}$$     Student's $t$ for a regression coefficient

$$r = \frac{\dfrac{\Sigma(X-\overline{X})(Y-\overline{Y})}{N-1}}{\sqrt{\dfrac{\Sigma(X-\overline{X})^2}{n-1}}\sqrt{\dfrac{\Sigma(Y-\overline{Y})^2}{n-1}}}$$     Correlation coefficient: differences around the means

$$r = \frac{N\Sigma XY - \Sigma X \Sigma Y}{\sqrt{\left[N\Sigma X^2 - (\Sigma X)^2\right]\left[N\Sigma Y^2 - (\Sigma Y)^2\right]}}$$

Correlation coefficient: sums of squares

$$b_{XY} = \frac{\Sigma YX - \dfrac{\Sigma Y \Sigma X}{N}}{\Sigma Y^2 - \dfrac{\Sigma (Y)^2}{N}}$$

Slope of the line for the regression of $X$ on $Y$

$$a_{XY} = \frac{\Sigma X - b_{XY}\Sigma Y}{N}$$

Intercept for the regression of $X$ on $Y$

$$\hat{X} = a_{XY} + b_{XY}Y$$

Prediction for $X$ on $Y$

$$r = \sqrt{b_{YX}b_{XY}}$$

Coefficient of correlation, square root of the products of the slopes

$$\frac{\Sigma(Y - \bar{Y})^2}{N-2}$$

Total variance for the dependent variable

$$\frac{\Sigma(\hat{Y} - \bar{Y})^2}{N-2}$$

Explained variance for the dependent variable

$$\frac{\Sigma(Y - \hat{Y})^2}{N-2}$$

Error variance for the dependent variable

$$r^2 = \frac{\dfrac{\Sigma(\hat{Y} - \bar{Y})^2}{N-2}}{\dfrac{\Sigma(Y - \bar{Y})^2}{N-2}}$$

The variance explained by the association of $X$ and $Y$

$$r^2 = \frac{\Sigma(\hat{Y} - \bar{Y})^2}{\Sigma(Y - \bar{Y})^2}$$

Variance explained by the association of $X$ and $Y$

$$t = r\sqrt{\frac{N-2}{1-r^2}}$$

$t$ test for the significance of a correlation coefficient

$$F = \frac{r^2}{1-r^2}(N-2)$$

F ratio for the coefficient of determination

$$\sigma_z = \sqrt{\frac{1}{N-3}}$$

Standard error for a correlation coefficient

$$CL = z - Z\sigma_z \text{ to } z + Z\sigma_z$$

Confidence limits for a correlation coefficient

# EXERCISES

1. A sample of 12 individuals was randomly selected and scored on a 10-point scale for health and on a similar scale for happiness. The concern was whether health predicted happiness. The data are presumed to be appropriate for regression analysis. The following was observed:

| Individual | Health | Happiness |
|---|---|---|
| A | 2 | 5 |
| B | 8 | 6 |
| C | 7 | 5 |
| D | 5 | 5 |
| E | 4 | 6 |
| F | 4 | 3 |
| G | 3 | 4 |
| H | 2 | 3 |
| I | 5 | 3 |
| J | 6 | 6 |
| K | 7 | 7 |
| L | 3 | 2 |

   a. What would be the general hypothesis regarding the two variables?
   b. Which is the dependent variable? Which is the independent variable?
   c. Draw a scattergram of the data.
   d. What is the value of the slope of the line?
   e. What is the value of the intercept?
   f. Given the slope and the intercept, solve for predicted $Y$ when $X = 0$, $X = 1$, $X = 2$, and $X = 10$.
   g. Using the predicted $Y$ values, draw the best fitting line on your scattergram.
   h. Calculate the standard error of the estimate for the data.
   i. Calculate the confidence limits at the 95% level for predicted $Y$ when $X = 6$ using Student's $t$ distribution.
   j. What would happen to the standard error of the estimate if the sample were increased to 102 but all other values remained the same?
   k. What would happen to the confidence limits with the increase in the sample to 102?
   l. What is the total variance for $Y$?
   m. What is the explained variance (between groups) for $Y$ given $X$?
   n. What is the unexplained variance (within groups) for $Y$ given $X$?
   o. Draw a scattergram illustrating the explained and unexplained variance.

2. Assume that the data for exercise 1 are appropriate for correlation analysis.

   a. What would the appropriate hypotheses be for the data?
   b. What is the value of $r$?
   c. Use two predicted $Y$ values using the slope and intercept values for predicting $Y$ from $X$ and two predicted $X$ values using the slope and intercept values for predicting $X$ from $Y$. Then draw a scattergram with the two regression lines.
   d. How would you describe the relationship between health and happiness?

  **e.** At what level is $r$ significant?

  **f.** What is the coefficient of determination, and what does it mean?

  **g.** What is the standard error for $r$?

  **h.** What would happen to the standard error if the sample were increased to 103 and all other values remained the same?

  **i.** Determine the 95% confidence limits for the original sample size (remember the $z$ transform).

  **j.** Determine the 95% confidence limits for a sample size of 103 (remember the $z$ transform).

  **k.** What can you say about the association between health and happiness?

# 12

# THE ASSOCIATION OF DISCRETE DATA

Chapter 11 introduced the concepts and methods of linear regression and correlation. Whereas regression summarizes the extent to which the value of the dependent variable can be predicted from that of an independent variable, correlation provides a more general summary of the association between variables. The discussion in Chapter 11 was limited to interval data. In this chapter the consideration of **association** is extended to discrete data (both ordinal and nominal) and to nonparametric tests of association. The concept of association, as used in statistical analysis, deserves more careful attention.

## *THE CONCEPT OF ASSOCIATION*

Chapter 2 introduced the idea of a contingency table. Recall that such tables are used to display the contingency (or association) of two or more variables by cross-classifying them. An important utility of contingency displays is that they assist in anticipating what the values will be for a dependent variable given those of an independent one. Suppose, for example, that the data in Chapter 11 on hourly wages and job satisfaction were simplified to dichotomous measures, as shown in Table 12.1. The table shows a perfect association between the two measures. All those with high wages are satisfied and those with low wages dissatisfied. This means that if you know that someone has high wages, you also know that they are satisfied. You can use wages to predict whether someone is satisfied or dissatisfied with their job.

Of course, very few associations are perfect. The more likely situation is the one encountered in the example from Chapter 11. The data indicated that although those with high hourly wages tended to be more satisfied with their jobs, this was not consistently true. Correlation provided a numerical description with the coefficient $r$ that summarized the strength of the association between the two measures.

The coefficient $r$ is limited to interval data, and if it is used to make generalizations to populations, the distributions involved must meet the assumptions

**TABLE 12.1   Hourly Wages and Job Satisfaction: Perfect Association**

|              | High Wages | Low Wages | Total |
|--------------|:----------:|:---------:|:-----:|
| Satisfied    | 50         | 0         | 50    |
| Dissatisfied | 0          | 50        | 50    |
| Total        | 50         | 50        | 100   |

outlined in Chapter 11. Not all distributions meet the criteria for the product moment correlation, so methods exist for testing the association of discrete measures that also provide coefficients that serve as indices of association. Some of these methods embody a measure of the **proportional reduction in error (PRE)** in predicting the value of a dependent variable from that of an independent variable. They indicate the extent to which the independent variable reduces the error in predicting the value of a dependent variable.[1] Other methods are less powerful in that they confirm only in a general sense whether two variables are associated. In the presentation of tests that follows, the distinction is made between PRE tests and tests that indicate only association.

The concept of PRE can be illustrated with the example of hourly wages and job satisfaction. Assume that the data are as shown in Table 12.2. The association is no longer perfect, as was the case in Table 12.1. Only 35 of the 50 with high wages are satisfied, and only 35 of those with low wages are dissatisfied. How much does knowledge about hourly wages improve our capacity to predict job satisfaction? You might be tempted to add the 35 satisfied individuals with high wages and the 35 dissatisfied ones with low wages and consider the sum to represent the successful predictions of job satisfaction. If the sum is divided by the total number of sample members, the following proportion is 35 + 35/100 = .70. The implication would be that given information on wages, job satisfaction can be predicted correctly 70% of the time.

However, that conclusion would give too much credit to the predictive power of hourly wage. After all, simply by guessing what the association might be,

**TABLE 12.2   Hourly Wages and Job Satisfaction: Imperfect Association**

|              | High Wages | Low Wages | Total |
|--------------|:----------:|:---------:|:-----:|
| Satisfied    | 35         | 15        | 50    |
| Dissatisfied | 15         | 35        | 50    |
| Total        | 50         | 50        | 100   |

[1] For a more detailed discussion of PRE, see John H. Mueller, Karl F. Schuessler, and Herbert L. Costner, *Statistical Reasoning in Sociology* (Boston: Houghton Mifflin, 1970), pp. 239–48.

without any information on wages, some of your guesses would be correct. Even if you made an extreme guess, such as that everyone is satisfied regardless of wage, you would be wrong only in half the cases because 50 out of 100 are satisfied, which is in keeping with your guess.

What is needed is a measure that shows the extent to which knowledge about the value of the independent variable improves the prediction of the value of the dependent variable *over a pure guess*. In our example, such a measure would show the extent to which information on hourly wages improves our prediction of who is satisfied over only guessing without any information on hourly wage, and PRE measures do just that: They indicate the extent to which information about the independent variable improves prediction of the dependent variable. They inform us of the proportional reduction in error over a guess. The general concept of PRE can be described as a function of the following ratio:

$$\frac{\text{Error using only the dependent variable} - \text{Error using the independent variable}}{\text{Error using only the dependent variable}}$$

where the error using only the dependent variable is equal to a guess that half are satisfied and half are dissatisfied. The error using the independent variable is the actual number of errors that occur by cross-classifying job satisfaction with hourly wages. These errors include the 15 who have high wages but are dissatisfied and the 15 who have low wages but are satisfied. The following formula provides a symbolic expression of the concept:

$$PRE = \frac{E_1 - E_2}{E_1} \tag{12.1}$$

$$PRE = \frac{50 - 30}{50}$$

$$= .40$$

Applied to the data in Table 12.2, PRE in predicting job satisfaction using hourly pay was improved by 40%. The PRE measure is also a measure of explained variance in that it is a measure of the variance in the dependent variable that is explained by the independent. The explained variance divided by the total variance indicates the proportion of variance explained by the independent variable. It can be represented as

$$r^2 = \frac{\text{Explained variance}}{\text{Total variance}} \tag{12.2}$$

In Chapter 11, $r^2$ was referred to as the coefficient of determination. Given that the explained variance equals the total variance minus the explained variance, the formula could have been written as

$$r^2 = \frac{\text{Total variance} - \text{Unexplained variance}}{\text{Total variance}} \tag{12.3}$$

The total variance is all the variation in the dependent variable, and the unexplained variance is the error that remains using the independent variable. Thus, $r^2$ is a PRE measure indicating the proportional reduction of error in predicting the dependent variable by using the independent one.

A second matter of importance in considering measures of association is the range of values taken by coefficients of different tests. Some statistical tests provide standardized coefficients that are easy to interpret and can be compared to other similar measures. Two types of value ranges occur (we have already encountered the first type in the discussion of correlation coefficients):

| Negative association | No association | Positive association |
|:---:|:---:|:---:|
| –1 | 0 | +1 |

Measures of association ranging in values from –1.00 to +1.00 are **directional coefficients** in that they consist of values above and below zero and indicate whether the association is positive or negative.

The second type of standard is based on a scale that extends from zero to one. This type is less sensitive than the first because it does not distinguish negative from positive associations; it is **nondirectional.** It provides only a measure of the strength of association, with values ranging from zero to one:

| No association | High association |
|:---:|:---:|
| 0 | +1 |

Several tests of association using each of the standards are discussed. They include tests for both ordinal data including Spearman's Rho and gamma, and for nominal data including lambda, phi-coefficient, and Cramer's V. The presentation of each technique is organized around a description of the method and its use, an illustration of the method with an example, and a summary of the test characteristics.

## THE ASSOCIATION OF ORDINAL MEASURES

### Spearman's Rho

#### Description

**Spearman's rho,** symbolized by $r_s$ and known also as a rank order correlation, is a PRE measure used to compare the ranks of individuals (or items) on two ordinal variables. A perfect positive association between the ranks occurs when rank 1 on one measure is associated with rank 1 on the second measure, rank 2 has that rank on both measures, and so on. A perfect positive association results in a value of +1.00. If the ranks are inverted so that the first rank on variable 1 is the last rank on variable 2, and the second rank on variable 1 is second to last on variable 2, and so on, the result is a value of –1.00. If the relationship between the two variables is random, the value approaches zero. The technique is based on a summary of the difference between the ranks of the two measures and is computed as follows:

$$r_s = 1 - \frac{6 \Sigma d_i^2}{N(N^2 - 1)} \tag{12.4}$$

where    $\Sigma d_i^2$ = the sum of the squared differences between the ranks

           $N$ = the number of paired ranks

Formula 12.4 is easy to apply but is sensitive to tied ranks; if ties are present, a better alternative is the sums-of-the-squares approach used for Pearson's $r$ and given in the following formula:

$$r_s = \frac{N \Sigma XY - \Sigma X \Sigma Y}{\sqrt{\left[ N \Sigma X^2 - (\Sigma X)^2 \right] \left[ N \Sigma Y^2 - (\Sigma Y^2) \right]}} \tag{12.5}$$

This provides a good estimate of $r_s$.

### Example 12.1

Fifteen cities were ranked on a cost-of-living index and a measure of the quality of the urban environment. Rank 1 represented the highest cost of living as well as the best environment. The data are shown in Table 12.3. The table indicates that city A and city B were tied for the highest rank in cost of living and received the average of the first two ranks, $1 + 2/2 = 3/2 = 1.5$. However, city A was ranked eleventh in quality of the environment and city B ninth. Using the summary data

**TABLE 12.3  Urban Cost of Living and Quality of Environment: Ranks of 15 Cities**

| City | Cost of Living (X) | Quality (Y) | Difference ($d_i$) | Squared Difference ($d_i^2$) | $X^2$ | $Y^2$ | XY |
|------|------|------|------|------|------|------|------|
| A | 1.50 | 11 | −9.5 | 90.25 | 2.25 | 121 | 16.50 |
| B | 1.50 | 9 | −7.5 | 56.25 | 2.25 | 81 | 13.50 |
| C | 3.0 | 6 | −3.0 | 9.00 | 9.00 | 36 | 18.00 |
| D | 5.0 | 2 | 3.0 | 9.00 | 25.00 | 4 | 10.00 |
| E | 5.0 | 2 | 3.0 | 9.00 | 25.00 | 4 | 10.00 |
| F | 5.0 | 2 | 3.0 | 9.00 | 25.00 | 4 | 10.00 |
| G | 7.0 | 4 | 3.0 | 9.00 | 49.00 | 16 | 28.00 |
| H | 8.0 | 5 | 3.0 | 9.00 | 64.00 | 25 | 40.00 |
| I | 11.0 | 7 | 4.0 | 16.00 | 121.00 | 49 | 77.00 |
| J | 11.0 | 8 | 3.0 | 9.00 | 121.00 | 64 | 88.00 |
| K | 11.0 | 10 | 1.0 | 1.00 | 121.00 | 100 | 110.00 |
| L | 11.0 | 15 | −4.0 | 16.00 | 121.00 | 225 | 165.00 |
| M | 11.0 | 14 | −3.0 | 9.00 | 121.00 | 196 | 154.00 |
| N | 14.5 | 12 | 2.5 | 6.25 | 210.25 | 144 | 174.00 |
| O | 14.5 | 13 | 1.5 | 2.25 | 210.25 | 169 | 188.50 |
|  | 120.00 | 120 |  | 260.00 | 1227.00 | 1238 | 1102.50 |

from Table 12.3 and Formula 12.4, we find that the estimate of association between the two variables is

$$r_s = 1 - \frac{6\Sigma d_i^2}{N(N^2 - 1)}$$

$$r_s = 1 - \frac{6(260)}{15(15^2 - 1)}$$

$$= 1 - \frac{1560}{3360}$$

$$= 1 - .4643$$

$$= .536$$

The coefficient of .536 shows a high positive correlation between the two variables, but because of the tied ranks, using Formula 12.4 might represent an overestimate of the association. Using Formula 12.5, we get a slightly different result:

$$r_s = \frac{N\Sigma XY - \Sigma X \Sigma Y}{\sqrt{\left[N\Sigma X^2 - (\Sigma X)^2\right]\left[N\Sigma Y^2 - (\Sigma Y^2)\right]}}$$

$$= \frac{15(1102.5) - 120(120)}{\sqrt{\left[15(1227) - 120^2\right]\left[15(1238) - 120^2\right]}}$$

$$= \frac{16,537.5 - 14,400}{\sqrt{[18,405 - 14,400][18,570 - 14,400]}}$$

$$= \frac{2137.50}{\sqrt{(4005)(4170)}}$$

$$= \frac{2137.50}{4086.67}$$

$$= .523$$

Using the sums-of-the-squares approach provides a somewhat more conservative estimate of the coefficient, .523, rather than .536. Formula 12.5 is intended for interval data, so when it is applied to ordinal measures it is only 91% as efficient as it is for interval measures. However, it is still a relatively powerful estimate of association, and if the sample size were increased by 9% it would be as powerful as if interval data were used.

Moreover, $r_s^2$ is a PRE measure indicating the percentage reduction in error attained by using the independent variable to estimate the values of the dependent variable. For our example, $r_s^2 = .523^2 = .2735$ means that 27.35% of the variation in the dependent variable, environmental quality, is explained by the rank that cities have on cost of living.

The significance of a Spearman's rho can also be evaluated using Student's $t$ distribution:

$$t = r_s \sqrt{\frac{N-2}{1-r_s^2}} \qquad (12.6)$$

where $N$ equals the pairs of ranks and df $= N - 2$. The test can be used for samples with as few as 10 paired ranks. The general forms of the hypotheses are

$H_0: \rho_s = 0$          There is no association between the ranks.
$H_1: \rho_s \geq 0$ or $\rho_s \leq 0$      There is a positive or negative association between the ranks.

For our example, the appropriate hypotheses would be

$H_0: \rho_s = 0$     There is no association between cost of living and quality of the environment.
$H_1: \rho_s > 0$     There is a positive association between cost of living and quality of the environment.

The $t$ value is

$$t = .523 \sqrt{\frac{15-2}{1-.523^2}}$$

$$= .523 \,(4.230)$$

$$= 2.21$$

Given $N - 2 = 15 - 2 = 13$ degrees of freedom, Table B.3 in Appendix B shows that the test statistic is significant beyond the .05 level. The association between cost of living and quality of the environment is significant, so we can reject $H_0$ and accept $H_1$.

### Summary
Spearman's coefficient of correlation measures the percentage reduction in error in predicting the value of a dependent ordinal variable using an independent ordinal measure. The coefficient has values ranging from $-1.00$ to $+1.00$ and so is directly comparable to Pearson's coefficient. Even with samples as small as 10, it is 91% as efficient as the more rigorous Pearson's coefficient. The only assumption that must be met to use Spearman's test is that the two variables represent an ordinal measure. Although Spearman's coefficient is a useful alternative, it is not appropriate for ordinal measures that consist of only a few categories, such as five- or seven-point ordinal scales, with multiple ties in each category. The gamma statistic, discussed next, is designed for such data.

## The Gamma Statistic

### Description

Spearman's rho assesses the association between ranks by focusing on the difference between individuals' ranks on the independent and dependent measures. Another approach to association is to examine the correspondence between two ranked variables by ordering the observations on the independent variable from rank 1 through $n$ and then evaluating the disorder of the ranks of the associated pairs on the dependent variable. This is the approach taken by the **gamma statistic,** which is based on the question, If the rank is known on the independent variable, can the rank of the dependent variable be predicted? The gamma statistic summarizes the **agreements** and **inversions** (disagreements) between the ranks:

$$\gamma = \frac{f_a - f_i}{f_a + f_i} \tag{12.7}$$

The formula can be translated as

$$\frac{\text{Number of agreements} - \text{Number of inversions}}{\text{Number of agreements} + \text{Number of inversions}}$$

Agreements occur when the rank of the dependent variable agrees with that of the independent, and an inversion takes place when the rank of the dependent variable is out of order with the rank of the independent variable. The computation has three possible outcomes: perfect agreement, +1.00, in which each pair has the same rank; perfect inversion, –1.00, in which the ranks are inverted (the first rank on variable 1 appears with the last rank on variable 2 and so on); or disorder (values between –1.00 and +1.00), in which there is a mixture of agreements and inversions. Gamma is also a PRE measure in that the resulting coefficient provides an estimate of the proportional reduction in error in estimating the value of the dependent variable using the independent variable.

### Example 12.2

A sample of 10 communities was ranked on their level of alcohol consumption and crime rates (rank 1 was the highest rate for both measures; see Table 12.4). Does knowledge about a community's rank on alcohol consumption improve prediction of rank on crime rate? If there is agreement between the ranks, high alcohol consumption will be associated with a high crime rate. If the ranks are inverted, high alcohol consumption will be associated with a low crime rate. To the extent that the ranks are disordered, knowledge about alcohol consumption will not improve predictions about crime rates.

The data in Table 12.4 present the communities ranked from 1 through 10 on alcohol consumption and their associated rank on crime rates. The agreement of the ranks, $f_a$, is determined by counting the number of larger ranks below each community's rank on crime rates. They are agreements if they go in the right direction of being larger ranks. The results for agreements are shown in the fourth

**TABLE 12.4    Alcohol Consumption and Crime Rates**

| Community | Alcohol Consumption | Crime Rate | $f_a$ | $f_i$ |
|-----------|---------------------|------------|-------|-------|
| A | 1 | 2 | 8 | 1 |
| B | 2 | 3 | 7 | 1 |
| C | 3 | 5 | 5 | 2 |
| D | 4 | 4 | 5 | 1 |
| E | 5 | 7 | 3 | 2 |
| F | 6 | 8 | 2 | 2 |
| G | 7 | 1 | 3 | 0 |
| H | 8 | 10 | 0 | 2 |
| I | 9 | 6 | 1 | 0 |
| J | 10 | 9 | 0 | 0 |
|   |    |   | 34 | 11 |

column, labeled $f_a$, in Table 12.4. Beginning with community A, which has rank 2 on crime rate, count the number of communities that have a higher rank on that measure. Eight communities below A have a rank higher than 2, seven communities below B have ranks higher than 3, five have ranks higher than that of community C, and so on. The sum of the ranks in agreement, 34, is shown under $f_a$.

The number of inversions, $f_i$, is counted similarly, except that the count is of the number of ranks that are inverted, that is, smaller than the preceding rank. Thus, community A, with rank 2, has only one community following it with a smaller rank; community B also has only one; community C has two with smaller ranks; and so on. The sum of the inverted ranks is 11, shown under $f_i$.

The results show that the sum of the ranks in agreement is 34 and that the sum of the inversions is 11. Note that the sum of $f_a$ and $f_i$ = 34 + 11 = 45, which equals the total number of pairs that can result from a sample of 10. The number of pairs of ranks can be determined by $n(n-1)/2$. For our example, it is $10(10-1)/2 = 90/2 = 45$. The total number of unique pairs of ranks that can be formed when $n = 10$ is 45. Once the agreements and inversions have been determined, gamma can be calculated with Formula 12.7:

$$\gamma = \frac{f_a - f_i}{f_a + f_i}$$

$$= \frac{34 - 11}{34 + 11}$$

$$= .511$$

The value of .511 indicates that using the rank on alcohol consumption for communities improves the capacity to predict their crime rates by about 51%.

Although the example illustrates the application of gamma, the data set does not have any ties, for which gamma is especially useful. Suppose that the same

**TABLE 12.5    Alcohol Consumption and Crime Rates**

| Crime Rate (Y) | Alcohol Consumption (X) | | | | Total |
|---|---|---|---|---|---|
| | **Very High** | **High** | **Low** | **Very Low** | **Total** |
| Very high | a    24 | b    14 | c    12 | d    4 | |
| High | e    17 | f    18 | g    22 | h    12 | |
| Low | i    7 | j    4 | k    11 | l    13 | |
| Very low | m    2 | n    6 | o    10 | p    15 | 191 |

variables were used with a larger sample, $n = 191$, and that the communities were ranked using the categories of very high, high, low, and very low. The results are shown in Table 12.5. As in the previous example, we must assess the number of agreements and inversions. However, the increase in sample size and the limited number of ordinal categories result in multiple ties, making the count somewhat more complicated. Thus, when $n = 191$, the possible pairs of observations are $n(n - 1)/2 = 191(191 - 1)/2 = 18,145$, a seemingly unmanageable number. However, for a data format like the one in Table 12.5, the number of agreements can be determined by observing the following procedures. Begin with the cell in the upper left-hand corner of the table, cell a. (For purposes of illustration, the cell labels are included in the table entries.) The number of observations in cell a is multiplied by the sum of observations in the row of cells below and to the right of cell a (do not count the observations in the cells in the same row and column as cell a). The result equals the number of agreements. The same is done for cell b and all other cells. The agreements for the ranks are determined as follows:

Cell a = 24[(18 + 22 + 12) + (4 + 11 + 13) + (6 + 10 + 15)]    =    2664

Cell b = 14[(22 + 12) + (11 + 13) + (10 + 15)]    =    1162

Cell c = 12(12 + 13 + 15)    =    480

Cell d = 4(0)    =    0

Cell e = 17[(4 + 11 + 13) + (6 + 10 + 15)]    =    1003

Cell f = 18[(11 + 13) + (10 + 15)]    =    882

Cell g = 22(13 + 15)    =    616

Cell h = 12(0)    =    0

Cell i = 7(6 + 10 + 15)    =    217

Cell j = 4(10 + 15)    =    100

Cell k = 11(15)    =    165

Cell l = 13(0)    =    0

$$f_a = 7289$$

Inversions are counted similarly, except that you begin with the upper right-hand cell, d, and move to the lower left-hand cell:

| | | |
|---|---|---:|
| Cell d = 4[(17 + 18 + 22) + (7 + 4 + 11) + (2 + 6 + 10)] | = | 388 |
| Cell c = 12[(17 + 18) + (7 + 4) + (2 + 6)] | = | 648 |
| Cell b = 14(17 + 7 + 2) | = | 364 |
| Cell a = 24(0) | = | 0 |
| Cell h = 12[(7 + 4 + 11) + (2 + 6 + 10)] | = | 480 |
| Cell g = 22[(7 + 4) + (2 + 6)] | = | 418 |
| Cell f = 18(7 + 2) | = | 162 |
| Cell e = 17(0) | = | 0 |
| Cell l = 13(2 + 6 + 10) | = | 234 |
| Cell k = 11(2 + 6) | = | 88 |
| Cell j = 4(2) | = | 8 |
| Cell i = 7(0) | = | 0 |
| | $f_i =$ | 2790 |

The agreements total 7,289 and the inversions 2,790. Recall that there were 18,145 possible pairs. The remainder, 18,145 – 7,289 – 2,790 = 8,066, represent tied pairs and are not included in the calculations. The improved ability to predict crime rates given knowledge about a community's rank on alcohol consumption is given by Formula 12.7:

$$\gamma = \frac{f_a - f_i}{f_a + f_i}$$

$$= \frac{7289 - 2790}{7289 + 2790}$$

$$= .4464$$

Gamma, as a PRE measure, enables us to conclude that we have gained 44.64% in our capacity to predict crime rates by using information on alcohol consumption. The significance of gamma can also be determined to assess whether the observed coefficient is significant or is only the result of sampling variation. The hypotheses take the same form as those for a correlation coefficient. The test is

$$Z = \gamma \sqrt{\frac{f_a - f_i}{n(1 - \gamma^2)}} \qquad \textbf{(12.8)}$$

$$= .4464 \sqrt{\frac{7289 - 2790}{191(1 - .4464^2)}}$$

$$= .4464\sqrt{29.4170}$$

$$= (.4464)(5.4237)$$

$$Z = 2.42$$

According to Table B.1 in Appendix B, a $Z = 2.42$ is significant beyond the .05 level, indicating that $H_0$ can be rejected and $H_1$ accepted. However, note that the test of significance can be used only if $n \geq 10$.

### Summary

Gamma is a useful nonparametric PRE measure for testing the association of an independent and a dependent variable. It provides direction for the potential values and can range from –1.00 to +1.00; it is used to compare ordinal measures, even with multiple tied ranks. The basic difference between Spearman's rho and the gamma test is that Spearman's evaluates the differences between paired ranks, whereas gamma focuses on the order of paired ranks.

# THE ASSOCIATION OF NOMINAL MEASURES

Evaluations of nominal scales present unique problems for analysis because the categories of the scales have no inherent order. The lack of a fixed order in the original measure means that resulting coefficients have no direction and, except in the case of dichotomous measures, are limited to values between zero and one. Further, some might be limited in their interpretation as a PRE measure. Nevertheless, they provide some assessment of the association between nominal measures.

Three techniques are presented for nominal measures. The first, lambda, has a PRE interpretation and can be applied to measures with multiple categories. The second, the phi coefficient, can sometimes be interpreted as a PRE measure, but it can be used only for dichotomous variables. The third, Cramer's V, is not a PRE measure but serves to evaluate the association of nominal scales with multiple categories.

## Lambda

### Description

**Lambda,** $\lambda$, is used to evaluate the association between two nominal variables from three different perspectives. First, $\lambda$ provides an estimate of the **symmetrical association** between two variables. In this case, neither variable is treated as independent or dependent. The coefficient represents the mutual association between the two variables. It is symmetrical in that the variable in the columns can be switched with that in the rows of the contingency table without affecting the value of $\lambda$.

The second measure, $\lambda_r$, treats the variable in the table rows as the dependent variable. The coefficient represents the PRE measure in predicting the dependent variable in the rows of the table, using the columns as the independent variable.

The third measure, $\lambda_c$, treats the variable in the columns as dependent and the row variable as independent. Both $\lambda_r$ and $\lambda_c$ are **asymmetrical tests of association** because the coefficient of one does not necessarily equal that of the other. The values for the measures of $\lambda$ range from 0 to 1.00 with 0 being no association and 1.00 perfect association. The formulas for each measure of lambda and their application are illustrated with an example.

### *Example 12.3*

Data on political party preference and religious affiliation are presented in Table 12.6. The formula for assessing the mutual association of the two nominal variables is

$$\lambda = \frac{\Sigma f_r + \Sigma f_c - \left(F_r + F_c\right)}{2n - \left(F_r + F_c\right)} \tag{12.9}$$

where $f_r$ = the largest frequency in each row of the table

$f_c$ = the largest frequency in each column of the table

$F_r$ = the largest marginal frequency for the rows

$F_c$ = the largest marginal frequency for the columns

$n$ = the sample size

Applied to the data in Table 12.6, we find

$$\lambda = \frac{\left(43 + 42\right) + \left(43 + 42 + 18\right) - \left(76 + 63\right)}{2\left(149\right) - \left(76 + 63\right)}$$

$$= \frac{188 - 139}{298 - 139}$$

$$= \frac{49}{159}$$

$$= .31$$

The coefficient suggests a moderate association between the two variables. It is a PRE measure, so we can conclude that using the two variables to estimate their association results in a 31% gain over simply guessing independently

**TABLE 12.6   Political Party Preference and Religious Affiliation**

| Religion | Democrat | Republican | Independent | Total |
|----------|----------|------------|-------------|-------|
| Catholic | 43 | 21 | 12 | 76 |
| Protestant | 13 | 42 | 18 | 73 |
| Total | 56 | 63 | 30 | 149 |

what the value of each variable might be. Treating religious affiliation as the dependent variable, we get the results given by the following formula:

$$\lambda_r = \frac{f_c - F_r}{n - F_r} \tag{12.10}$$

where   $f_c$ = the largest frequency in each column of the independent variable

$F_r$ = the largest marginal frequency for the rows

$n$ = the sample size

The result for predicting religious affiliation is

$$= \frac{(43 + 42 + 18) - 76}{149 - 76}$$

$$= \frac{103 - 76}{73}$$

$$= .37$$

The coefficient indicates that the error in predicting religious affiliation using knowledge of political party preference was reduced by 37%. We can also determine the improvement in error of predicting political party preference on the basis of knowledge of religious affiliation by using the following formula:

$$\lambda_c = \frac{f_r - F_c}{n - F_c} \tag{12.11}$$

where   $f_r$ = the largest frequency in each row of the independent variable

$F_c$ = the largest marginal total for the columns of the dependent variable

$n$ = the sample size

The results for predicting political party preference are

$$= \frac{(43 + 42) - 63}{149 - 63}$$

$$= \frac{85 - 63}{86}$$

$$= .26$$

The solution indicates that our prediction of political party preference is improved by 26% using information about religious affiliation, a gain somewhat less than when political party preference was treated as the independent variable. The symmetrical association, $\lambda$, given in Formula 12.9 can be derived by taking the average of $\lambda_r$ and $\lambda_c$:

$$\lambda = \frac{\lambda_r + \lambda_c}{2} \tag{12.12}$$

For our example we find the value found originally for $\lambda$.

$$= \frac{.37 + .26}{2}$$

$$= .31$$

### Summary

Lambda is a useful measure of association for nominal data. It can be used to evaluate the contingencies of two variables and makes no restrictive assumptions. A major advantage of the statistic is that it can be interpreted as a PRE measure that indicates the improvement of predicting one variable given the values of another.

## Phi Coefficient

### Description

The **phi coefficient,** $\phi$, is a statistical technique for evaluating the association between two dichotomous measures. Although the test is limited to $2 \times 2$ tables, the coefficient is a PRE value and is directional, ranging in values from $-1.00$ to $+1.00$. However, note that the maximum value of $\pm 1.00$ can be attained only when cells $a + b = c + d$ and $a + c = b + d$. If this criterion is not met, the maximum value will be somewhat less than $\pm 1.00$.

### Example 12.4

Data were gathered comparing the extent of student contact with tenured and non-tenured faculty, resulting in the outcomes shown in Table 12.7. The total sample consisted of 42 students. The phi coefficient is calculated by the following formula:

$$\phi = \frac{bc - ad}{\sqrt{(a+b)(c+d)(a+c)(b+d)}} \tag{12.13}$$

**TABLE 12.7   Student Contact with Tenured and Nontenured Faculty**

| Contact | Tenured | Nontenured | Total |
|---|---|---|---|
| Low contact | 13 | 7 | 20 |
| High contact | 6 | 16 | 22 |
| Total | 19 | 23 | 42 |

Applied to Table 12.7, the results are

$$\phi = \frac{(7)(6)-(13)(16)}{\sqrt{(13+7)(6+16)(13+6)(7+16)}}$$

$$= \frac{(42)-(208)}{\sqrt{(20)(22)(19)(23)}}$$

$$= \frac{-166}{\sqrt{192,280}}$$

$$= \frac{-166}{438.4974}$$

$$= -.3786$$

The coefficient indicates a moderate negative association between faculty tenure and student contact. Inspection of the $2 \times 2$ table shows that the tenured faculty have somewhat less contact than do the nontenured. To interpret the result as a PRE measure, we must square the phi coefficient. For our example, $\phi^2 = -.3786^2 = .1433$. The answer indicates that knowing the tenure status of faculty improves the capacity to predict student contact by 14.33%.

The statistical significance of $\phi$ can be tested with the chi-square distribution using the following formula:

$$\chi^2 = n \ \phi^2 \tag{12.14}$$

For our example, we find

$$\chi^2 = 42(.1433)$$

$$= 6.019$$

As is the case of all $2 \times 2$ contingency tables, df = 1, and according to Table B.4 in Appendix B, the null hypothesis can be rejected at the .02 level of significance.

### Summary
The phi coefficient is a useful PRE measure for a $2 \times 2$ contingency table. It takes values from $-1.00$ to $+1.00$ providing information on the direction of the association.

## Cramer's V

### Description

Although the phi coefficient is useful, it is limited to data represented by $2 \times 2$ contingency tables. **Cramer's V** is an alternative that can be used for $n \times n$ tables. It is somewhat limited in that it is not a PRE measure and the results can take values only from 0 to 1.00. Thus the statistic is nondirectional. Cramer's V is based on the chi-square value using the following formula:

$$V = \sqrt{\frac{\chi^2}{n(k-1)}} \qquad \text{(12.15)}$$

where     $\chi^2$ = the chi-square value for the data

        $n$ = the total number of observations

        $k$ = the number of rows or columns, whichever has the least number of cells

### Example 12.5

The relationship between employee work performance problems and their use of health services was evaluated. The data were based on 172 workers who displayed one of four primary performance problems at work and had access to three types of treatment programs (Table 12.8). For example, 27 workers who experienced problems with absenteeism used the cardiovascular program, and 24 workers who had difficulty relating to other workers used the alcohol treatment program.

     The first step in determining the V statistic is calculating the chi-square value for the data. The chi-square formula is

$$\chi^2 = \sum \frac{(O-E)^2}{E} \qquad \text{(12.16)}$$

The calculation of chi-square is shown in Table 12.9. Recall that the expected values for each cell are the product of the cell marginals divided by the total number of observations. The computation of the statistic is shown in Table 12.9, and the result is $\chi^2 = 27.93$. Once the chi-square value is known, the V statistic is determined using the following formula:

$$V = \sqrt{\frac{\chi^2}{n(k-1)}} \qquad \text{(12.17)}$$

$$V = \sqrt{\frac{27.93}{172(3-1)}}$$

**TABLE 12.8**    **Performance Problem and Type of Clinic Used**

| Type of Problem | Type of Clinic Used | | | |
| --- | --- | --- | --- | --- |
| | Cardiovascular | Mental Health | Alcoholism | Total |
| Absenteeism | 27 | 13 | 8 | 48 |
| Tardiness | 15 | 14 | 11 | 40 |
| Poor work | 15 | 12 | 14 | 41 |
| Problems with other workers | 3 | 16 | 24 | 43 |
| Total | 60 | 55 | 57 | 172 |

$$= \sqrt{\frac{27.93}{344}}$$

$$= \sqrt{.0812}$$

$$= .285$$

The test statistic of .285 is interpreted as any other coefficient of association. It suggests that there is a moderately low association between job performance problems and the types of clinics used by workers.

The significance of the V statistic is a function of the chi-square value. It is determined by evaluating the significance of $\chi^2 = 27.93$. The df $= (c - 1)(r - 1) = (3 - 1)(4 - 1) = 6$. According to Table B.4 in Appendix B, the statistic is significant beyond the .001 level, indicating that the results are not likely due to random variation in sampling outcomes.

### Summary

The utility of Cramer's V rests in its use for evaluating the association between nominal measures consisting of multiple categories. Although it does not provide a PRE measure and the results are nondirectional, it does provide information on the association of two nominal measures and the significance of the association. It is useful because few alternatives exist for evaluating the strength of the association of nominal data.

**TABLE 12.9   Calculation of Chi-Square for Table 12.8**

| Cell | $O$ | $E$ | $O - E$ | $(O - E)^2$ | $(O - E)^2/E$ |
| --- | --- | --- | --- | --- | --- |
| a | 27 | 16.74 | 10.26 | 105.27 | 6.29 |
| b | 13 | 15.35 | −2.35 | 5.52 | .36 |
| c | 8 | 15.91 | −7.91 | 62.57 | 3.93 |
| d | 15 | 13.95 | 1.05 | 1.10 | .08 |
| e | 14 | 12.79 | 1.21 | 1.46 | .11 |
| f | 11 | 13.26 | −2.26 | 5.11 | .39 |
| g | 15 | 14.30 | .70 | .49 | .03 |
| h | 12 | 13.11 | −1.11 | 1.23 | .09 |
| i | 14 | 13.59 | .41 | .17 | .01 |
| j | 3 | 15.00 | −12.00 | 144.00 | 9.60 |
| k | 16 | 13.75 | 2.25 | 5.06 | .37 |
| l | 24 | 14.25 | 9.75 | 95.06 | 6.67 |
| | | | | | 27.93 |

## COMPUTER EXERCISES: SOME SUGGESTIONS

The procedures in this chapter do not appear in all software packages. Your software guide should indicate whether all of these techniques are available under a section titled "Nonparametric Procedures" or in the index. For each test available, you must select variables that meet the criteria for the test. Thus, for Spearman's Rho, you need ordinal variables with many ranks, or you can select an interval variable and assign ranks to the values. Once you have established the proper data format for the technique, the software should provide the statistic and its level of significance. In your software you may also find tests of association that are not included in this text. Generally, they are not difficult to understand, and the software guide should provide sufficient information for using and interpreting new procedures.

## CHAPTER SUMMARY

The purpose of this chapter was to introduce methods for evaluating the association of ordinal and nominal measures. All the techniques presented can be seen as alternatives to Pearson's coefficient of correlation. Although Pearson's $r$ is the most efficient measure of association, it is based on rather restrictive assumptions about the level of measurement, the distribution of the variable in the population, a linear data pattern, and the homogeneity of the variance of the measures.

Much of the data of interest to social science fails to meet the rigid requirements of parametric regression and correlation techniques. As an alternative, nonparametric methods play an important role in statistical descriptions. Of greatest interest are measures of association that inform us of the proportional reduction of error in using one variable to estimate the values of another. These measures provide the same level of information as parametric ones. In the case of some data, such as nominal measures with multiple categories, simpler measures of association, such as Cramer's V, must suffice. In addition, some nonparametric alternatives provide standardized coefficients that take the same range of values as Pearson's correlation coefficient, and their interpretation is the same.

The measures considered in this chapter represent a sample of a much larger number of available nonparametric techniques. The conceptual introduction they provide should help you understand and apply various alternatives that are encountered in statistical computer software packages and the research literature.

## KEY TERMS

**agreements**   In gamma, the number of ranks that follow the same order for two measures.

**association**   The extent to which the values of two measures vary together.

**asymmetrical tests of association**   Tests that evaluate the influence of one measure (independent variable) on another (dependent variable).

**Cramer's V**   A statistic summarizing the association of two nominal variables with multiple categories. The values range from 0 to 1.00.

**directional coefficient**   A coefficient ranging from –1.00 to +1.00.

**gamma statistic**   A statistic summarizing the association of two ordinal measures. It is a PRE measure with values from –1.00 to +1.00.

**inversions**   In gamma, the number of ranks that are inverse in order for two measures.

**lambda**   A statistic summarizing the association between two nominal measures. It provides symmetrical and asymmetrical estimates of association ranging from 0 to 1.00 with a PRE interpretation.

**nondirectional coefficient**   A coefficient indicating the extent of association without specifying the direction. The values range from 0 to 1.00.

**phi coefficient**   A statistic summarizing the association between two dichotomous nominal measures with values ranging from –1.00 to +1.00 and a PRE interpretation.

**proportional reduction in error (PRE)**   The percentage gain realized in predicting the values of a dependent variable using an independent variable.

**Spearman's rho**   A statistic summarizing the association between two ordinal measures using the difference between the ranks with values ranging from –1.00 to +1.00 and a PRE interpretation.

**symmetrical association**   Measures of association that summarize the shared variation of two variables.

## SYMBOLS

| | |
|---|---|
| $r_s$ | Spearman's rho |
| PRE | Proportional reduction in error |
| $\gamma$ | The gamma statistic |
| $f_a$ | The number of agreements in gamma |
| $f_i$ | The number of inversions in gamma |
| $\lambda$ | Symmetrical lambda |
| $\lambda_r$ | Lambda using the table rows as the dependent variable |
| $\lambda_c$ | Lambda using the table columns as the dependent variable |
| $\phi$ | The phi coefficient |
| V | Cramer's V |

## FORMULAS

$$PRE = \frac{E_1 - E_2}{E_1}$$ 
Proportional reduction in error

$$r_s = 1 - \frac{6\Sigma d_i^2}{N(N^2 - 1)}$$ 
Spearman's rho

$$r_s = \frac{N\Sigma XY - \Sigma X\Sigma Y}{\sqrt{\left[N\Sigma X^2 - (\Sigma X)^2\right]\left[N\Sigma Y^2 - (\Sigma Y^2)\right]}}$$ 
Spearman's rho sums of squares

$$t = r_s \sqrt{\frac{N - 2}{1 - r_s^2}}$$ 
Test of significance for rho

$$\gamma = \frac{f_a - f_i}{f_a + f_i}$$ 
Gamma

$$Z = \gamma \sqrt{\frac{f_a - f_i}{n(1 - \gamma^2)}}$$ 
Test of significance for gamma

$$\lambda = \frac{\Sigma f_r + \Sigma f_c - (F_r + F_c)}{2n - (F_r + F_c)}$$ 
Test of symmetrical lambda

$$\lambda_r = \frac{f_c - F_r}{n - F_r}$$ 
Test for lambda, rows are dependent

$$\lambda_c = \frac{f_r - F_c}{n - F_c}$$ 
Test for lambda, columns are dependent

$$\lambda = \frac{\lambda_r + \lambda_c}{2}$$ 
Procedure for averaging lambda

$$\phi = \frac{bc - ad}{\sqrt{(a+b)(c+d)(a+c)(b+d)}}$$ 
Phi coefficient

$$\chi^2 = n\,\phi^2$$ 
Test of significance for the phi coefficient

$$V = \sqrt{\frac{\chi^2}{n(k-1)}}$$ 
Cramer's V

## EXERCISES

1. A sample of students was ranked on their social skills and academic success. The concern was whether social skills were associated with academic success. The following data were observed:

| Student | Rank on Academic Success | Rank on Social Skills |
|---|---|---|
| Amy | 1 | 5 |
| Bob | 2 | 3 |
| Carol | 3 | 4 |
| Dennis | 4 | 2 |
| Ellen | 5 | 7 |
| Frank | 6 | 1 |
| Gail | 7 | 9 |
| Henry | 8 | 13 |
| Inez | 9 | 8 |
| Jesse | 10 | 6 |
| Karen | 11 | 10 |
| Louis | 12 | 12 |
| Margo | 13 | 14 |
| Neil | 14 | 11 |
| Olive | 15 | 15 |

   a. Which test would be appropriate to evaluate the association?
   b. State the null hypothesis.
   c. If appropriate, state the directional hypothesis.
   d. What is the value of the test statistic?
   e. Can you reject $H_0$ at the .01 level of significance?
   f. If appropriate, can you accept the directional hypothesis?
   g. What can you say about the association between social skills and academic performance?
   h. Write a statement characterizing the association.

2. A sample of 12 neighborhoods was ranked in terms of median family income and percentage of individuals with some college education. A rank of 1 on income indicated the highest, while a rank of 1 on college indicated the highest percentage of those with some college. The particular research concern was in the order of the paired ranks. The data are shown on the following page.

   a. Which test would be appropriate to evaluate the association?
   b. State the null hypothesis.
   c. If appropriate, state the directional hypothesis.
   d. What is the value of the test statistic?
   e. Can you reject $H_0$ at the .05 level of significance?
   f. If appropriate, can you accept the directional hypothesis?
   g. What can you say about the association between income and some college?
   h. Write a statement characterizing the association.

| Neighborhood | Income | Some College |
|:---:|:---:|:---:|
| A | 1 | 11 |
| B | 2 | 10 |
| C | 3 | 12 |
| D | 4 | 8 |
| E | 5 | 9 |
| F | 6 | 1 |
| G | 7 | 5 |
| H | 8 | 7 |
| I | 9 | 2 |
| J | 10 | 3 |
| K | 11 | 6 |
| L | 12 | 4 |

3. Data were gathered from a sample of 266 individuals regarding their perceived level of stress and frequency of illness. The interest was in whether the paired ranks of the two variables were associated. The following data were observed:

| Frequency of Illness | Perceived Stress Level | | | | | Total |
|---|:---:|:---:|:---:|:---:|:---:|:---:|
| | **Very High** | **High** | **Average** | **Low** | **Very Low** | |
| Very frequent | 32 | 19 | 13 | 8 | 2 | |
| Frequent | 26 | 14 | 9 | 7 | 6 | |
| Occasional | 4 | 9 | 14 | 19 | 21 | |
| Seldom | 5 | 7 | 11 | 16 | 24 | |
| | | | | | | 266 |

    **a.** Which test would be appropriate to evaluate the association?
    **b.** State the null hypothesis.
    **c.** If appropriate, state the directional hypothesis.
    **d.** What is the value of the test statistic?
    **e.** Can you reject $H_0$ at the .05 level of significance?
    **f.** If appropriate, can you accept the directional hypothesis?
    **g.** What can you say about the association between frequency of illness and perceived level of stress?
    **h.** Write a statement characterizing the association.

4. The relationship between academic achievement and an optimistic versus pessimistic outlook among 116 students was evaluated. The following data were found:

| Outlook | Future Goals | | |
|---|:---:|:---:|:---:|
| | **Graduate Degree** | **College Degree** | **High School** |
| Optimistic | 37 | 18 | 6 |
| Pessimistic | 9 | 12 | 34 |

a. Which test would be appropriate to evaluate the association?
b. What is the symmetrical association between the measures?
c. What can you say about the association of the two variables?
d. What test is used if outlook is treated as the dependent variable?
e. What is the value of the statistic?
f. What can you say about the association, given the answer to question e?
g. What test is used if academic achievement is treated as the dependent variable?
h. What is the value of the statistic?
i. What can you say about the association, given the answer to question h?

5. Blue- and white-collar workers were compared on their support for environmental protection programs. The following data were observed:

| Program Support | Occupational Status | |
|---|---|---|
| | White Collar | Blue Collar |
| Strong support | 25 | 9 |
| Weak support | 10 | 26 |

a. Which is the best statistic for evaluating the association of the two measures?
b. What is the value of the statistic?
c. What can you say about the association?
d. Is the observed statistic likely to occur by chance at the .01 level of significance?
e. What percentage gain is there in explaining support for environmental programs using occupational status?

6. The religious and behavioral orientations of a sample of 111 individuals were evaluated with the following results:

| Behavioral Orientation | Religious Orientation | | |
|---|---|---|---|
| | Conservative | Moderate | Liberal |
| Permissive | 8 | 13 | 18 |
| Moderate | 11 | 15 | 9 |
| Authoritarian | 19 | 13 | 5 |

a. Which is the best statistic for evaluating the association of the two measures?
b. What is the value of the statistic?
c. What can you say about the association?
d. Is the observed statistic likely to occur by chance at the .05 level of significance?

# APPENDIX

# BASIC MATHEMATICAL PROCEDURES

The following discussion reviews some symbols commonly used in statistics, including rules that govern the use of signed numbers, exponents, squares and square roots, factorials, and a convention for rounding decimals.

## SOME BASIC SYMBOLS

You should be familiar with some basic symbols used in statistical work. Two such symbols are $n$ and $X$. The symbol $n$ is used to signify the number of members in a sample, whereas $X$ represents the score or value that a sample member has for a variable. If you were to describe the performance of a sample of 25 students on an exam, $n = 25$ represents the number of students in your sample and $X$ the exam score of a particular student. Whereas $n$ refers to the number of members in a *sample,* $N$ refers to the number of members in a *population.* In some cases, $N$ represents the number of members resulting from combining two or more samples.

The symbol $X$ frequently is used with a subscript $i$ and appears as $X_i$. The symbol $X_i$ refers to any one of a set of outcomes. The scores of specific students can be identified by using subscripts to represent individual students. A distribution of test scores could be presented as follows:

$$X_1 = 99$$
$$X_2 = 97$$
$$X_3 = 96$$
$$X_4 = 95$$
$$X_5 = 93$$

Where $X_1$ had a test score of 99, $X_2$ had a score of 97, and so on. Ordinarily, however, a distribution of sample outcomes is listed more simply, as

$$X$$

99

97

96

95

93

and it is understood that $X_1 = 99$, $X_2 = 97$, and so on. If a sample is described in terms of two variables (characteristics), the second variable can be designated with another symbol, such as $Y$. If you describe the students in terms of test scores, $X$, and IQ scores, $Y$, the data could be presented as

| X | Y |
|---|---|
| 99 | 118 |
| 97 | 121 |
| 96 | 119 |
| 95 | 127 |
| 93 | 122 |

Another frequently used symbol is the Greek letter sigma, $\Sigma$, which is called the *summation sign* and indicates that items to the right of $\Sigma$ are to be added. When combined with a variable $X$, the symbol indicates that the values of $X$ are to be summed. The symbol

$$\sum_{i=1}^{n} X_i$$

directs you to add the values observed for $X$. The symbol $i = 1$ below the sigma and the $n$ above it direct you to begin with the first value for $X_i$ in the distribution and sum all the values through $n$, or the last one. In reference to our example of test scores,

$$\sum_{i=1}^{n} X_i$$

is shorthand notation for $X_1 + X_2 + X_3 + X_4 + X_5$, which directs you to add the values $99 + 97 + 96 + 95 + 93 = 480$. The symbol can be specified to refer to a subset of the group of scores. For example,

$$\sum_{i=2}^{4} X_i$$

would direct you to add the exam scores of students 2 through 4, or 97 + 96 + 95 = 288.

Symbols are useful because they provide explicit instructions for the procedures used to solve equations. However, unnecessarily elaborate symbolizations can be confusing, and in many cases simplified forms are adequate. Thus, the symbol $\Sigma X_i$, without the notations above and below the sigma, is used in this text unless more elaborate notation is necessary to avoid confusion. Other symbols you should familiarize yourself with include the following:

= where a = b is read "a is equal to b"

≠ where a ≠ b is read "a is unequal to b"

≃ where a ≃ b is read "a is approximately equal to b"

\> where a > b is read "a is greater than b"

≥ where a ≥ b is read "a is greater than or equal to b"

\< where a < b is read "a is less than b"

≤ where a ≤ b is read "a is less than or equal to b"

c > a > b is read "a is less than c but greater than b"

## THE USE OF SIGNED NUMBERS

The rules governing basic arithmetic procedures with signed numbers for addition, subtraction, multiplication, and division are as follows:

*Addition Rule 1: Numbers with the same sign are summed and assigned the common sign.* Column A illustrates the rule for positively signed numbers and column B the rule for negatively signed numbers.

| A | B |
|---|---|
| +7 | –3 |
| +6 | –9 |
| +3 | –4 |
| +4 | –8 |
| +20 | –24 |

The sign for positive numbers is usually omitted in presentation, and it is understood that when no sign appears the number is positive. However, negatively signed numbers are always presented with the negative sign.

*Addition Rule 2: Numbers with unlike signs are summed by adding the positive and negative scores separately, and the difference between the two sums is given the sign of the largest of the two sums.* Column A illustrates the case when the sum is positive and column B when it is negative. In column A, the result, 7, is given a positive sign because the sum of the numbers with positive signs, 12, is larger than that with negative signs, 5. In column B, the sum of the negative numbers, 13, is larger than that of the positive signs, 7, so the result is −6.

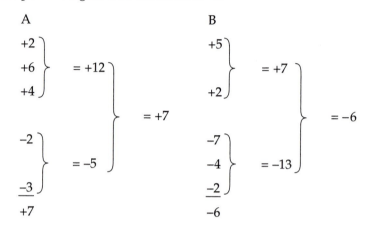

*Subtraction Rule: Two signed numbers are subtracted by changing the sign of the number to be subtracted and adding the two values. The sum is then signed using the rules for addition.* Formulas 1.1 through 1.6 illustrate the rule:

**1.1**  $(+5) - (+2) = (+5) + (-2) = +3$

**1.2**  $(+5) - (-2) = (+5) + (+2) = +7$

**1.3**  $(-5) - (+2) = (-5) + (-2) = -7$

**1.4**  $(-5) - (-2) = (-5) + (+2) = -3$

**1.5**  $(-3) - (+4) = (-3) + (-4) = -7$

**1.6**  $(-3) - (-4) = (-3) + (+4) = +1$

*Multiplication Rule 1: When multiplying two signed numbers, if the signs are alike, the result is always positive, but when the signs are unlike, the result is always negative.* Formulas 1.7 through 1.10 illustrate the rule:

**1.7**    $(+6) \times (+2) = +12$

**1.8**    $(-6) \times (-2) = +12$

**1.9**    $(-6) \times (+2) = -12$

**1.10**   $(+6) \times (-2) = -12$

*Multiplication Rule 2: When more than two numbers are multiplied, if the expression contains an even number of negatively signed values, the result is always positive, but if it contains an uneven number of negatively signed values, the result is negative.* Formulas 1.11 through 1.14 illustrate the rule.

**1.11**  $(+6) \times (+2) \times (-2) \times (-2) = +48$

**1.12**  $(-6) \times (+2) \times (+2) \times (-2) = +48$

**1.13**  $(-6) \times (+2) \times (+2) \times (+2) = -48$

**1.14**  $(-6) \times (-2) \times (-2) \times (-2) = -48$

*Division Rule: When dividing two signed numbers, if the signs are alike, the result is always positive, but when the signs are unlike, the result is always negative.* Formulas 1.15 through 1.18 illustrate the rule:

**1.15**  $(+6) \div (+2) = +3$

**1.16**  $(-6) \div (-2) = +3$

**1.17**  $(-6) \div (+2) = -3$

**1.18**  $(+6) \div (-2) = -3$

## EXPONENTS

An **exponent** indicates how often a number is used as a repeated factor. It is written above and to the right of the number. Thus, in the term $2^3$, the 3 indicates that the 2 is to be repeated three times as a factor, such that $2 \times 2 \times 2 = 8$. The result, 8, is referred to as the third power of 2. Additional examples are

$$3^2 = 3 \times 3 = 9$$

$$3^4 = 3 \times 3 \times 3 \times 3 = 81$$

$$4^3 = 4 \times 4 \times 4 = 64$$

$$10^5 = 10 \times 10 \times 10 \times 10 \times 10 = 100{,}000$$

## SQUARES AND SQUARE ROOTS

The **square** of a number is the product of multiplying that number by itself. Thus, the square of $4^2$ is $4 \times 4 = 16$. The square is also referred to as the *second power* of a number, so $4^2$ is the proper expression for the square of 4. The general symbol used for squares is $N^2$ or $n^2$.

The **square root** of a number is one of its two equal factors. Thus, the square root of 16 is 4 because 4 is one of its equal factors; that is, $4 \times 4 = 16$. The square root of a number can also be thought of as a number that, when multiplied by itself, is equal to the original number. The square root of 4 is 2 because $2 \times 2 = 4$, and the square root of 81 is 9 because $9 \times 9 = 81$. The symbol for square roots is $\sqrt{\phantom{x}}$ so that $\sqrt{4} = 2$.

Calculating square roots can be time consuming, especially if decimals are involved, but the advent of the pocket calculator with a square-root function has made it possible to determine the square root of any number with the push of a key.

## FACTORIALS

The symbol $n!$ is read "n factorial" and is referred to as the **factorial**. It represents the following product:

$$n! = 1 \times 2 \times 3 \times 4 \times . . . \times n$$

where $n$ refers to the number of observations. The following examples illustrate the factorial:

$$4! = 1 \times 2 \times 3 \times 4 = 24$$

$$2! = 1 \times 2 = 2$$

$$7! = 1 \times 2 \times 3 \times 4 \times 5 \times 6 \times 7 = 5,040$$

There is one exception; $0!$ is always treated as $1!$.

## ROUNDING DECIMALS

Computations frequently result in values that include decimals, and because the number of repeating decimals can be large, rules for rounding them are required. The convention for rounding used here is based on the following rules:

1. If the first digit to be dropped has a value from 0 to 4, it is dropped, and the preceding digit remains unchanged.
2. If the first digit to be dropped is a value greater than 5, it is dropped, and the preceding value is increased by 1.
3. If the first digit to be dropped is the value 5, it is the midpoint, and half the time the number that precedes it should remain the same and half the time it should be increased by 1. A convenient rule to remember is that if the preceding number is even, add 1; if it is odd, it remains the same.

In applying the rules to the value of 42.4734, suppose that you want to round the value to the second decimal. The first digit to be dropped is 3, which is in the range of 0 to 4, so you drop the digit and those following it, and the rounded value is reported as 42.47. In rounding the value 36.9573 to the second decimal, the first digit to be dropped is 7, which is greater than 5, so the preceding digit is increased by 1, and the rounded value is 36.96.

In rounding the value 2.734962 to the fourth decimal, the first digit to be dropped is 6, so you add 1 to the preceding digit, and the value becomes 2.7350. In rounding the value 2.465 to the second decimal, because the first value to be dropped is 5 and the preceding value, 6, is an even number, you add 1 for a rounded value of 2.47. In rounding the value 2.435, because the value 3 preceding the digit to be dropped, 5, is uneven, the value remains the same, and it is reported as 2.43.

The number of decimals that are reported is a matter of personal choice, but the *general principle of economy in reporting numbers* is a helpful guide. According to this principle, the number of reported digits should be no greater than necessary to provide an accurate understanding of the data given the original measurement and the purposes at hand. Moreover, the number of decimals reported should be a function of the precision of the original measure. More decimals are reported from very precise instruments of measurement than from less exact ones. The purpose at hand can also play a role in the decision. If the purpose requires more precision, more decimals should be used.

Another consideration is the *significance* of the last digit based on the assumption that only important digits should be reported. According to this rule, the number of digits reported is based on whether the value of the last reported digit changes the meaning or interpretation of the results. If it is unimportant to the interpretation, it should not be reported.

Always keep in mind that the purpose of numerical descriptions is to provide others with a clear understanding of what is occurring. Thus, numbers should never be reported for their own sake but only to the extent that they contribute to understanding the phenomena that you are trying to describe.

## APPENDIX SUMMARY

This appendix reviewed some basic symbols and mathematical procedures. You should review and practice each one, using the exercises to apply the concepts presented here.

## KEY TERMS

**exponent**   The power of a number or the number of times a factor is used.

**factorial**   Equal to $1 \times 2 \times 3 \times \ldots \times n$, symbolized by $n!$

**square**   The value of a number multiplied by itself, symbolized by $N^2$.

**square root**   One of the two equal factors of a number, symbolized by $\sqrt{N}$.

## SYMBOLS

| | |
|---|---|
| $n$ | Number of members in a sample |
| $N$ | Number of members in a population |
| $n!$ | Factorial |
| $\sqrt{\phantom{x}}$ | Square root |
| $X$ | A variable or a measured characteristic |
| $X_i$ | Any one value for a variable |
| $\Sigma$ | Summation |

$$\sum_{i=1}^{n} X_i$$  The symbol indicating that the values for a variable, $X$, should be summed beginning with the first and including all of the values

$=$  Equals

$\approx$  Approximately equals

$>$  Greater than

$\geq$  Greater than or equal to

$<$  Less than

$\leq$  Less than or equal to

## EXERCISES

**1.** Add the following numbers:

| a. | b. | c. | d. |
|---|---|---|---|
| +12 | +19 | −3 | +194 |
| +7 | +23 | +7 | −213 |
| +6 | −14 | −14 | −147 |
| −3 | −17 | −5 | +206 |
| −2 | −24 | +6 | −190 |

**2.** Subtract the following values:

| a. | b. | c. | d. | e. | f. | g. | h. |
|---|---|---|---|---|---|---|---|
| +12 | +7 | +9 | −13 | −9 | −15 | −2 | +6 |
| −3 | −2 | +6 | +3 | −3 | +12 | −1 | +3 |

**3.** Multiply the following values:

a. $+2 \times +4$    f. $+2 \times +3 \times -4$    j. $+5 \times +3 \times +2 \times -1$

b. $+9 \times -6$    g. $-2 \times +6 \times +2$    k. $+2 \times -2 \times +3 \times -1$

c. $+3 \times -14$    h. $-9 \times +3 \times -4$    l. $-7 \times -3 \times -2 \times +4$

d. $-7 \times 2$    i. $-3 \times -2 \times -4$    m. $-2 \times -6 \times -5 \times -8$

e. $-9 \times -2$

**4.** Divide the following:

| a. | b. | c. | d. | e. | f. | g. |
|---|---|---|---|---|---|---|
| +9 | +4 | −8 | −6 | −2 | +12 | +104 |
| +3 | −2 | +2 | −3 | −4 | −37 | −49 |

**5.** Evaluate the following exponents.

a. $4^2$    b. $3^5$    c. $8^3$    d. $9^2$    e. $7^4$    f. $2^{10}$    g. $12^3$    h. $15^4$    i. $3^7$

**6.** Evaluate the following factorials.

a. $2!$    b. $5!$    c. $6!$    d. $8!$    e. $11!$

**7.** Solve the following square roots using a pocket calculator.

a. $\sqrt{2}$    b. $\sqrt{7}$    c. $\sqrt{215}$    d. $\sqrt{31}$    e. $\sqrt{74}$    f. $\sqrt{91}$    g. $\sqrt{313}$    h. $\sqrt{1}$

**8.** Round the following values to the second decimal.

    **a.** 25.146      **b.** 6.087      **c.** 795.843      **d.** 1.99923      **e.** 8.6531

**9.** Round the following values to the third decimal.

    **a.** 9.7478      **b.** 784.7109      **c.** 2.4908      **d.** 32.9563      **e.** 9.99992

**10.** Round the following values to the fourth decimal.

    **a.** 3.519784      **b.** 26.377961      **c.** 13.823041      **d.** 10.600562      **e.** 8.139972

# APPENDIX B

# STATISTICAL TABLES

**TABLE B.1**  **Proportions of Area under the Normal Curve: Z Scores**

Table B.1 is used to assess the probabilities for interval variables that have been transformed to Z values. It is assumed that the variables are normally distributed. The table consists of five columns. Column A contains the Z score; column B contains the area of a value on the right *or* left tail of the distribution. They are referred to as the one-tailed probabilities. Column C contains the area of a value on the right *and* left tails of the distribution and is referred to as the two-tailed probability. Column D shows the area between a value and the mean on *either* the right or left side of the distribution. Column E shows the area between a value and the mean on the right *and* left side of the distribution. The areas of the curve related to each of the columns are shown below.

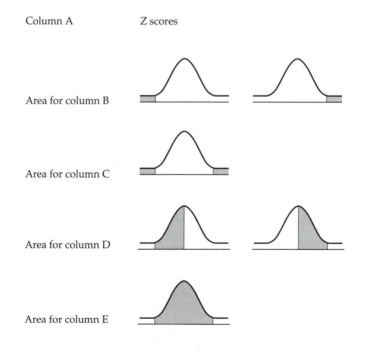

**TABLE B.1    Z Values from .00 to .35**

| A<br>Z scores | B<br>Area beyond<br>either ± Z<br>one tailed | C<br>Area beyond<br>both ± Z<br>two tailed | D<br>Area from mean to<br>either + or –Z | E<br>Area from mean<br>to + and –Z |
|---|---|---|---|---|
| 0.00 | .5000 | 1.0000 | .0000 | .0000 |
| 0.01 | .4960 | .9920 | .0040 | .0080 |
| 0.02 | .4920 | .9840 | .0080 | .0160 |
| 0.03 | .4880 | .9760 | .0120 | .0240 |
| 0.04 | .4840 | .9680 | .0160 | .0320 |
| 0.05 | .4801 | .9602 | .0199 | .0398 |
| 0.06 | .4761 | .9522 | .0239 | .0478 |
| 0.07 | .4721 | .9442 | .0279 | .0558 |
| 0.08 | .4681 | .9362 | .0319 | .0638 |
| 0.09 | .4641 | .9282 | .0359 | .0718 |
| 0.10 | .4602 | .9204 | .0398 | .0796 |
| 0.11 | .4562 | .9124 | .0438 | .0876 |
| 0.12 | .4522 | .9044 | .0478 | .0956 |
| 0.13 | .4483 | .8966 | .0517 | .1034 |
| 0.14 | .4443 | .8886 | .0557 | .1114 |
| 0.15 | .4404 | .8808 | .0596 | .1192 |
| 0.16 | .4364 | .8728 | .0636 | .1272 |
| 0.17 | .4325 | .8650 | .0675 | .1350 |
| 0.18 | .4286 | .8572 | .0714 | .1428 |
| 0.19 | .4247 | .8494 | .0753 | .1506 |
| 0.20 | .4207 | .8414 | .0793 | .1586 |
| 0.21 | .4168 | .8336 | .0832 | .1664 |
| 0.22 | .4129 | .8258 | .0871 | .1742 |
| 0.23 | .4090 | .8180 | .0910 | .1820 |
| 0.24 | .4052 | .8104 | .0948 | .1896 |
| 0.25 | .4013 | .8026 | .0987 | .1974 |
| 0.26 | .3974 | .7948 | .1026 | .2052 |
| 0.27 | .3936 | .7872 | .1064 | .2128 |
| 0.28 | .3897 | .7794 | .1103 | .2206 |
| 0.29 | .3859 | .7718 | .1141 | .2282 |
| 0.30 | .3821 | .7642 | .1179 | .2358 |
| 0.31 | .3783 | .7566 | .1217 | .2434 |
| 0.32 | .3745 | .7490 | .1255 | .2510 |
| 0.33 | .3707 | .7414 | .1293 | .2586 |
| 0.34 | .3669 | .7338 | .1331 | .2662 |
| 0.35 | .3632 | .7264 | .1368 | .2736 |

*Continued*

**TABLE B.1    Z Values from .36 to .70—*Continued***

| A<br><br>Z scores | B<br>Area beyond<br>either ± Z<br>one tailed | C<br>Area beyond<br>both ± Z<br>two tailed | D<br><br>Area from mean to<br>either + or –Z | E<br><br>Area from mean<br>to + and –Z |
|---|---|---|---|---|
| 0.36 | .3594 | .7188 | .1406 | .2812 |
| 0.37 | .3557 | .7114 | .1443 | .2886 |
| 0.38 | .3520 | .7040 | .1480 | .2960 |
| 0.39 | .3483 | .6966 | .1517 | .3034 |
| 0.40 | .3446 | .6892 | .1554 | .3108 |
| 0.41 | .3409 | .6818 | .1591 | .3182 |
| 0.42 | .3372 | .6744 | .1628 | .3256 |
| 0.43 | .3336 | .6672 | .1664 | .3328 |
| 0.44 | .3300 | .6600 | .1700 | .3400 |
| 0.45 | .3264 | .6528 | .1736 | .3472 |
| 0.46 | .3228 | .6456 | .1772 | .3544 |
| 0.47 | .3192 | .6384 | .1808 | .3616 |
| 0.48 | .3156 | .6312 | .1844 | .3688 |
| 0.49 | .3121 | .6242 | .1879 | .3758 |
| 0.50 | .3085 | .6170 | .1915 | .3830 |
| 0.51 | .3050 | .6100 | .1950 | .3900 |
| 0.52 | .3015 | .6030 | .1985 | .3970 |
| 0.53 | .2981 | .5962 | .2019 | .4038 |
| 0.54 | .2946 | .5892 | .2054 | .4108 |
| 0.55 | .2912 | .5824 | .2088 | .4176 |
| 0.56 | .2877 | .5754 | .2123 | .4246 |
| 0.57 | .2843 | .5686 | .2157 | .4314 |
| 0.58 | .2810 | .5620 | .2190 | .4380 |
| 0.59 | .2776 | .5552 | .2224 | .4448 |
| 0.60 | .2743 | .5486 | .2257 | .4514 |
| 0.61 | .2709 | .5418 | .2291 | .4582 |
| 0.62 | .2676 | .5352 | .2324 | .4648 |
| 0.63 | .2643 | .5286 | .2357 | .4714 |
| 0.64 | .2611 | .5222 | .2389 | .4778 |
| 0.65 | .2578 | .5156 | .2422 | .4844 |
| 0.66 | .2546 | .5092 | .2454 | .4908 |
| 0.67 | .2514 | .5028 | .2486 | .4972 |
| 0.68 | .2483 | .4966 | .2517 | .5034 |
| 0.69 | .2451 | .4902 | .2549 | .5098 |
| 0.70 | .2420 | .4840 | .2580 | .5160 |

**TABLE B.1  Z Values from .71 to 1.05—*Continued***

| A Z scores | B Area beyond either ± Z one tailed | C Area beyond both ± Z two tailed | D Area from mean to either + or −Z | E Area from mean to + and −Z |
|---|---|---|---|---|
| 0.71 | .2389 | .4778 | .2611 | .5222 |
| 0.72 | .2358 | .4716 | .2642 | .5284 |
| 0.73 | .2327 | .4654 | .2673 | .5346 |
| 0.74 | .2296 | .4592 | .2704 | .5408 |
| 0.75 | .2266 | .4532 | .2734 | .5468 |
| 0.76 | .2236 | .4472 | .2764 | .5528 |
| 0.77 | .2206 | .4412 | .2794 | .5588 |
| 0.78 | .2177 | .4354 | .2823 | .5646 |
| 0.79 | .2148 | .4296 | .2852 | .5704 |
| 0.80 | .2119 | .4238 | .2881 | .5762 |
| 0.81 | .2090 | .4180 | .2910 | .5820 |
| 0.82 | .2061 | .4122 | .2939 | .5878 |
| 0.83 | .2033 | .4066 | .2967 | .5934 |
| 0.84 | .2005 | .4010 | .2995 | .5990 |
| 0.85 | .1977 | .3954 | .3023 | .6046 |
| 0.86 | .1949 | .3898 | .3051 | .6102 |
| 0.87 | .1922 | .3844 | .3078 | .6156 |
| 0.88 | .1894 | .3788 | .3106 | .6212 |
| 0.89 | .1867 | .3734 | .3133 | .6266 |
| 0.90 | .1841 | .3682 | .3159 | .6318 |
| 0.91 | .1814 | .3628 | .3186 | .6372 |
| 0.92 | .1788 | .3576 | .3212 | .6424 |
| 0.93 | .1762 | .3524 | .3238 | .6476 |
| 0.94 | .1736 | .3472 | .3264 | .6528 |
| 0.95 | .1711 | .3422 | .3289 | .6578 |
| 0.96 | .1685 | .3370 | .3315 | .6630 |
| 0.97 | .1660 | .3320 | .3340 | .6680 |
| 0.98 | .1635 | .3270 | .3365 | .6730 |
| 0.99 | .1611 | .3222 | .3389 | .6778 |
| 1.00 | .1587 | .3174 | .3413 | .6826 |
| 1.01 | .1562 | .3124 | .3438 | .6876 |
| 1.02 | .1539 | .3078 | .3461 | .6922 |
| 1.03 | .1515 | .3030 | .3485 | .6970 |
| 1.04 | .1492 | .2984 | .3508 | .7016 |
| 1.05 | .1469 | .2938 | .3531 | .7062 |

*Continued*

**TABLE B.1**  Z Values from 1.06 to 1.40—*Continued*

| A Z scores | B Area beyond either ± Z one tailed | C Area beyond both ± Z two tailed | D Area from mean to either + or −Z | E Area from mean to + and −Z |
|---|---|---|---|---|
| 1.06 | .1446 | .2892 | .3554 | .7108 |
| 1.07 | .1423 | .2846 | .3577 | .7154 |
| 1.08 | .1401 | .2802 | .3599 | .7198 |
| 1.09 | .1379 | .2758 | .3621 | .7242 |
| 1.10 | .1357 | .2714 | .3643 | .7286 |
| 1.11 | .1335 | .2670 | .3665 | .7330 |
| 1.12 | .1314 | .2628 | .3686 | .7372 |
| 1.13 | .1292 | .2584 | .3708 | .7416 |
| 1.14 | .1271 | .2542 | .3729 | .7458 |
| 1.15 | .1251 | .2502 | .3749 | .7498 |
| 1.16 | .1230 | .2460 | .3770 | .7540 |
| 1.17 | .1210 | .2420 | .3790 | .7580 |
| 1.18 | .1190 | .2380 | .3810 | .7620 |
| 1.19 | .1170 | .2340 | .3830 | .7660 |
| 1.20 | .1151 | .2302 | .3849 | .7698 |
| 1.21 | .1131 | .2262 | .3869 | .7738 |
| 1.22 | .1112 | .2224 | .3888 | .7776 |
| 1.23 | .1093 | .2186 | .3907 | .7814 |
| 1.24 | .1075 | .2150 | .3925 | .7850 |
| 1.25 | .1056 | .2112 | .3944 | .7888 |
| 1.26 | .1038 | .2076 | .3962 | .7924 |
| 1.27 | .1020 | .2040 | .3980 | .7960 |
| 1.28 | .1003 | .2006 | .3997 | .7994 |
| 1.29 | .0985 | .1970 | .4015 | .8030 |
| 1.30 | .0968 | .1936 | .4032 | .8064 |
| 1.31 | .0951 | .1902 | .4049 | .8098 |
| 1.32 | .0934 | .1868 | .4066 | .8132 |
| 1.33 | .0918 | .1836 | .4082 | .8164 |
| 1.34 | .0901 | .1802 | .4099 | .8198 |
| 1.35 | .0885 | .1770 | .4115 | .8230 |
| 1.36 | .0869 | .1738 | .4131 | .8262 |
| 1.37 | .0853 | .1706 | .4147 | .8294 |
| 1.38 | .0838 | .1676 | .4162 | .8324 |
| 1.39 | .0823 | .1646 | .4177 | .8354 |
| 1.40 | .0808 | .1616 | .4192 | .8384 |

**TABLE B.1** Z Values from 1.41 to 1.75—*Continued*

| A<br>Z scores | B<br>Area beyond<br>either ± Z<br>one tailed | C<br>Area beyond<br>both ± Z<br>two tailed | D<br>Area from mean to<br>either + or −Z | E<br>Area from mean<br>to + and −Z |
|---|---|---|---|---|
| 1.41 | .0793 | .1586 | .4207 | .8414 |
| 1.42 | .0778 | .1556 | .4222 | .8444 |
| 1.43 | .0764 | .1528 | .4236 | .8472 |
| 1.44 | .0749 | .1498 | .4251 | .8502 |
| 1.45 | .0735 | .1470 | .4265 | .8530 |
| 1.46 | .0721 | .1442 | .4279 | .8558 |
| 1.47 | .0708 | .1416 | .4292 | .8584 |
| 1.48 | .0694 | .1388 | .4306 | .8612 |
| 1.49 | .0681 | .1362 | .4319 | .8638 |
| 1.50 | .0668 | .1336 | .4332 | .8664 |
| 1.51 | .0655 | .1310 | .4345 | .8690 |
| 1.52 | .0643 | .1286 | .4357 | .8714 |
| 1.53 | .0630 | .1260 | .4370 | .8740 |
| 1.54 | .0618 | .1236 | .4382 | .8764 |
| 1.55 | .0606 | .1212 | .4394 | .8788 |
| 1.56 | .0594 | .1188 | .4406 | .8812 |
| 1.57 | .0582 | .1164 | .4418 | .8836 |
| 1.58 | .0571 | .1142 | .4429 | .8858 |
| 1.59 | .0559 | .1118 | .4441 | .8882 |
| 1.60 | .0548 | .1096 | .4452 | .8904 |
| 1.61 | .0537 | .1074 | .4463 | .8926 |
| 1.62 | .0526 | .1052 | .4474 | .8948 |
| 1.63 | .0516 | .1032 | .4484 | .8968 |
| 1.64 | .0505 | .1010 | .4495 | .8990 |
| 1.65 | .0495 | .0990 | .4505 | .9010 |
| 1.66 | .0485 | .0970 | .4515 | .9030 |
| 1.67 | .0475 | .0950 | .4525 | .9050 |
| 1.68 | .0465 | .0930 | .4535 | .9070 |
| 1.69 | .0455 | .0910 | .4545 | .9090 |
| 1.70 | .0446 | .0892 | .4554 | .9108 |
| 1.71 | .0436 | .0872 | .4564 | .9128 |
| 1.72 | .0427 | .0854 | .4573 | .9146 |
| 1.73 | .0418 | .0836 | .4582 | .9164 |
| 1.74 | .0409 | .0818 | .4591 | .9182 |
| 1.75 | .0401 | .0802 | .4599 | .9198 |

*Continued*

**TABLE B.1    Z Values from 1.76 to 2.10—*Continued***

| A<br><br>Z scores | B<br>Area beyond<br>either ± Z<br>one tailed | C<br>Area beyond<br>both ± Z<br>two tailed | D<br><br>Area from mean to<br>either + or –Z | E<br><br>Area from mean<br>to + and –Z |
|---|---|---|---|---|
| 1.76 | .0392 | .0784 | .4608 | .9216 |
| 1.77 | .0384 | .0768 | .4616 | .9232 |
| 1.78 | .0375 | .0750 | .4625 | .9250 |
| 1.79 | .0367 | .0734 | .4633 | .9266 |
| 1.80 | .0359 | .0718 | .4641 | .9282 |
| 1.81 | .0351 | .0702 | .4649 | .9298 |
| 1.82 | .0344 | .0688 | .4656 | .9312 |
| 1.83 | .0336 | .0672 | .4664 | .9328 |
| 1.84 | .0329 | .0658 | .4671 | .9342 |
| 1.85 | .0322 | .0644 | .4678 | .9356 |
| 1.86 | .0314 | .0628 | .4686 | .9372 |
| 1.87 | .0307 | .0614 | .4693 | .9386 |
| 1.88 | .0301 | .0602 | .4699 | .9398 |
| 1.89 | .0294 | .0588 | .4706 | .9412 |
| 1.90 | .0287 | .0574 | .4713 | .9426 |
| 1.91 | .0281 | .0562 | .4719 | .9438 |
| 1.92 | .0274 | .0548 | .4726 | .9452 |
| 1.93 | .0268 | .0536 | .4732 | .9464 |
| 1.94 | .0262 | .0524 | .4738 | .9476 |
| 1.95 | .0256 | .0512 | .4744 | .9488 |
| 1.96 | .0250 | .0500 | .4750 | .9500 |
| 1.97 | .0244 | .0488 | .4756 | .9512 |
| 1.98 | .0239 | .0478 | .4761 | .9522 |
| 1.99 | .0233 | .0466 | .4767 | .9534 |
| 2.00 | .0228 | .0456 | .4772 | .9544 |
| 2.01 | .0222 | .0444 | .4778 | .9556 |
| 2.02 | .0217 | .0434 | .4783 | .9566 |
| 2.03 | .0212 | .0424 | .4788 | .9576 |
| 2.04 | .0207 | .0414 | .4793 | .9586 |
| 2.05 | .0202 | .0404 | .4798 | .9596 |
| 2.06 | .0197 | .0394 | .4803 | .9606 |
| 2.07 | .0192 | .0384 | .4808 | .9616 |
| 2.08 | .0188 | .0376 | .4812 | .9624 |
| 2.09 | .0183 | .0366 | .4817 | .9634 |
| 2.10 | .0179 | .0358 | .4821 | .9642 |

**TABLE B.1   Z Values from 2.11 to 2.45—*Continued***

| A  Z scores | B  Area beyond either ± Z one tailed | C  Area beyond both ± Z two tailed | D  Area from mean to either + or –Z | E  Area from mean to + and –Z |
|---|---|---|---|---|
| 2.11 | .0174 | .0348 | .4826 | .9652 |
| 2.12 | .0170 | .0340 | .4830 | .9660 |
| 2.13 | .0166 | .0332 | .4834 | .9668 |
| 2.14 | .0162 | .0324 | .4838 | .9676 |
| 2.15 | .0158 | .0316 | .4842 | .9684 |
| 2.16 | .0154 | .0308 | .4846 | .9692 |
| 2.17 | .0150 | .0300 | .4850 | .9700 |
| 2.18 | .0146 | .0292 | .4854 | .9708 |
| 2.19 | .0143 | .0286 | .4857 | .9714 |
| 2.20 | .0139 | .0278 | .4861 | .9722 |
| 2.21 | .0136 | .0272 | .4864 | .9728 |
| 2.22 | .0132 | .0264 | .4868 | .9736 |
| 2.23 | .0129 | .0258 | .4871 | .9742 |
| 2.24 | .0125 | .0250 | .4875 | .9750 |
| 2.25 | .0122 | .0244 | .4878 | .9756 |
| 2.26 | .0119 | .0238 | .4881 | .9762 |
| 2.27 | .0116 | .0232 | .4884 | .9768 |
| 2.28 | .0113 | .0226 | .4887 | .9774 |
| 2.29 | .0110 | .0220 | .4890 | .9780 |
| 2.30 | .0107 | .0214 | .4893 | .9786 |
| 2.31 | .0104 | .0208 | .4896 | .9792 |
| 2.32 | .0102 | .0204 | .4898 | .9796 |
| 2.33 | .0099 | .0198 | .4901 | .9802 |
| 2.34 | .0096 | .0192 | .4904 | .9808 |
| 2.35 | .0094 | .0188 | .4906 | .9812 |
| 2.36 | .0091 | .0182 | .4909 | .9818 |
| 2.37 | .0089 | .0178 | .4911 | .9822 |
| 2.38 | .0087 | .0174 | .4913 | .9826 |
| 2.39 | .0084 | .0168 | .4916 | .9832 |
| 2.40 | .0082 | .0164 | .4918 | .9836 |
| 2.41 | .0080 | .0160 | .4920 | .9840 |
| 2.42 | .0078 | .0156 | .4922 | .9844 |
| 2.43 | .0075 | .0150 | .4925 | .9850 |
| 2.44 | .0073 | .0146 | .4927 | .9854 |
| 2.45 | .0071 | .0142 | .4929 | .9858 |

*Continued*

**TABLE B.1    Z Values from 2.46 to 2.80—*Continued***

| A<br><br>Z scores | B<br>Area beyond<br>either ± Z<br>one tailed | C<br>Area beyond<br>both ± Z<br>two tailed | D<br><br>Area from mean to<br>either + or −Z | E<br><br>Area from mean<br>to + and −Z |
|---|---|---|---|---|
| 2.46 | .0069 | .0138 | .4931 | .9862 |
| 2.47 | .0068 | .0136 | .4932 | .9864 |
| 2.48 | .0066 | .0132 | .4934 | .9868 |
| 2.49 | .0064 | .0128 | .4936 | .9872 |
| 2.50 | .0062 | .0124 | .4938 | .9876 |
| 2.51 | .0060 | .0120 | .4940 | .9880 |
| 2.52 | .0059 | .0118 | .4941 | .9882 |
| 2.53 | .0057 | .0114 | .4943 | .9886 |
| 2.54 | .0055 | .0110 | .4945 | .9890 |
| 2.55 | .0054 | .0108 | .4946 | .9892 |
| 2.56 | .0052 | .0104 | .4948 | .9896 |
| 2.57 | .0051 | .0102 | .4949 | .9898 |
| 2.58 | .0049 | .0098 | .4951 | .9902 |
| 2.59 | .0048 | .0096 | .4952 | .9904 |
| 2.60 | .0047 | .0094 | .4953 | .9906 |
| 2.61 | .0045 | .0090 | .4955 | .9910 |
| 2.62 | .0044 | .0088 | .4956 | .9912 |
| 2.63 | .0043 | .0086 | .4957 | .9914 |
| 2.64 | .0041 | .0082 | .4959 | .9918 |
| 2.65 | .0040 | .0080 | .4960 | .9920 |
| 2.66 | .0039 | .0078 | .4961 | .9922 |
| 2.67 | .0038 | .0076 | .4962 | .9924 |
| 2.68 | .0037 | .0074 | .4963 | .9926 |
| 2.69 | .0036 | .0072 | .4964 | .9928 |
| 2.70 | .0035 | .0070 | .4965 | .9930 |
| 2.71 | .0034 | .0068 | .4966 | .9932 |
| 2.72 | .0033 | .0066 | .4967 | .9934 |
| 2.73 | .0032 | .0064 | .4968 | .9936 |
| 2.74 | .0031 | .0062 | .4969 | .9938 |
| 2.75 | .0030 | .0060 | .4970 | .9940 |
| 2.76 | .0029 | .0058 | .4971 | .9942 |
| 2.77 | .0028 | .0056 | .4972 | .9944 |
| 2.78 | .0027 | .0054 | .4973 | .9946 |
| 2.79 | .0026 | .0052 | .4974 | .9948 |
| 2.80 | .0026 | .0052 | .4974 | .9948 |

**TABLE B.1   Z Values from 2.81 to 3.15—***Continued*

| A<br><br>Z scores | B<br>Area beyond<br>either ± Z<br>one tailed | C<br>Area beyond<br>both ± Z<br>two tailed | D<br><br>Area from mean to<br>either + or –Z | E<br><br>Area from mean<br>to + and –Z |
|---|---|---|---|---|
| 2.81 | .0025 | .0050 | .4975 | .9950 |
| 2.82 | .0024 | .0048 | .4976 | .9952 |
| 2.83 | .0023 | .0046 | .4977 | .9954 |
| 2.84 | .0023 | .0046 | .4977 | .9954 |
| 2.85 | .0022 | .0044 | .4978 | .9956 |
| 2.86 | .0021 | .0042 | .4979 | .9958 |
| 2.87 | .0021 | .0042 | .4979 | .9958 |
| 2.88 | .0020 | .0040 | .4980 | .9960 |
| 2.89 | .0019 | .0038 | .4981 | .9962 |
| 2.90 | .0019 | .0038 | .4981 | .9962 |
| 2.91 | .0018 | .0036 | .4982 | .9964 |
| 2.92 | .0018 | .0036 | .4982 | .9964 |
| 2.93 | .0017 | .0034 | .4983 | .9966 |
| 2.94 | .0016 | .0032 | .4984 | .9968 |
| 2.95 | .0016 | .0032 | .4984 | .9968 |
| 2.96 | .0015 | .0030 | .4985 | .9970 |
| 2.97 | .0015 | .0030 | .4985 | .9970 |
| 2.98 | .0014 | .0028 | .4986 | .9972 |
| 2.99 | .0014 | .0028 | .4986 | .9972 |
| 3.00 | .0013 | .0026 | .4987 | .9974 |
| 3.01 | .0013 | .0026 | .4987 | .9974 |
| 3.02 | .0013 | .0026 | .4987 | .9974 |
| 3.03 | .0012 | .0024 | .4988 | .9976 |
| 3.04 | .0012 | .0024 | .4988 | .9976 |
| 3.05 | .0011 | .0022 | .4989 | .9978 |
| 3.06 | .0011 | .0022 | .4989 | .9978 |
| 3.07 | .0011 | .0022 | .4989 | .9978 |
| 3.08 | .0010 | .0020 | .4990 | .9980 |
| 3.09 | .0010 | .0020 | .4990 | .9980 |
| 3.10 | .0010 | .0020 | .4990 | .9980 |
| 3.11 | .0009 | .0018 | .4991 | .9982 |
| 3.12 | .0009 | .0018 | .4991 | .9982 |
| 3.13 | .0009 | .0018 | .4991 | .9982 |
| 3.14 | .0008 | .0016 | .4992 | .9984 |
| 3.15 | .0008 | .0016 | .4992 | .9984 |

*Continued*

**TABLE B.1    Z Values from 3.16 to 4.00—*Continued***

| A<br><br><br>Z scores | B<br>Area beyond<br>either ± Z<br>one tailed | C<br>Area beyond<br>both ± Z<br>two tailed | D<br><br>Area from mean to<br>either + or –Z | E<br><br>Area from mean<br>to + and –Z |
|---|---|---|---|---|
| 3.16 | .0008 | .0016 | .4992 | .9984 |
| 3.17 | .0008 | .0016 | .4992 | .9984 |
| 3.18 | .0007 | .0014 | .4993 | .9986 |
| 3.19 | .0007 | .0014 | .4993 | .9986 |
| 3.20 | .0007 | .0014 | .4993 | .9986 |
| 3.21 | .0007 | .0014 | .4993 | .9986 |
| 3.22 | .0006 | .0012 | .4494 | .9988 |
| 3.23 | .0006 | .0012 | .4494 | .9988 |
| 3.24 | .0006 | .0012 | .4494 | .9988 |
| 3.25 | .0006 | .0012 | .4494 | .9988 |
| 3.30 | .0005 | .0010 | .4995 | .9990 |
| 3.35 | .0004 | .0008 | .4996 | .9992 |
| 3.40 | .0003 | .0006 | .4997 | .9994 |
| 3.45 | .0003 | .0006 | .4997 | .9994 |
| 3.50 | .0002 | .0004 | .4998 | .9996 |
| 3.55 | .0002 | .0004 | .4998 | .9996 |
| 3.60 | .0002 | .0004 | .4998 | .9996 |
| 3.65 | .0001 | .0002 | .4999 | .9998 |
| 3.70 | .0001 | .0002 | .4999 | .9998 |
| 3.75 | .0001 | .0002 | .4999 | .9998 |
| 3.80 | .0001 | .0002 | .4999 | .9998 |
| 3.85 | .00006 | .00012 | .49994 | .99988 |
| 3.90 | .00005 | .00010 | .49995 | .99990 |
| 3.95 | .00004 | .00008 | .49996 | .99992 |
| 4.00 | .00003 | .00006 | .49997 | .99994 |

## TABLE B.2    Areas under the Binomial Curve

The left-hand column of the table, headed *n*, contains values representing different sample sizes, or the number of binomial trials. For example, the first page of the table contains values for samples of 2 through 7 members, and the largest sample value in the table is 15 on the final page of the table. The second column, headed *r*, is the number of occurrences of *p* outcomes in a trial (e.g., the number of heads in a series of coin tosses). The values across the top of the table, beginning with .05 and ending with .95, represent the probability, *p*, of the occurrence of *p* on a single trial. The body of the table contains the probability of an *r* outcome for *n* trials given the probability of *p* on a single trial. Thus, with a sample containing 8 trials and *p* = .5, the likelihood of an outcome of *r* = 7 is given at the intersect of *n* = 8, *r* = 7, which is .031.

| n | r | 0.05 | 0.1 | 0.2 | 0.3 | *p* 0.4 | 0.5 | 0.6 | 0.7 | 0.8 | 0.9 | 0.95 |
|---|---|------|-----|-----|-----|-----|-----|-----|-----|-----|-----|------|
| 2 | 0 | 0.902 | 0.810 | 0.640 | 0.490 | 0.360 | 0.250 | 0.160 | 0.090 | 0.040 | 0.010 | 0.002 |
|   | 1 | 0.095 | 0.180 | 0.320 | 0.420 | 0.480 | 0.500 | 0.480 | 0.420 | 0.320 | 0.180 | 0.095 |
|   | 2 | 0.002 | 0.010 | 0.040 | 0.090 | 0.160 | 0.250 | 0.360 | 0.490 | 0.640 | 0.810 | 0.902 |
| 3 | 0 | 0.857 | 0.729 | 0.512 | 0.343 | 0.216 | 0.125 | 0.064 | 0.027 | 0.008 | 0.001 | |
|   | 1 | 0.135 | 0.243 | 0.384 | 0.441 | 0.432 | 0.375 | 0.288 | 0.189 | 0.096 | 0.027 | 0.007 |
|   | 2 | 0.007 | 0.027 | 0.096 | 0.189 | 0.288 | 0.375 | 0.432 | 0.441 | 0.384 | 0.243 | 0.135 |
|   | 3 | | 0.001 | 0.008 | 0.027 | 0.064 | 0.125 | 0.216 | 0.343 | 0.512 | 0.729 | 0.857 |
| 4 | 0 | 0.815 | 0.656 | 0.410 | 0.240 | 0.130 | 0.062 | 0.026 | 0.008 | 0.002 | | |
|   | 1 | 0.171 | 0.292 | 0.410 | 0.412 | 0.346 | 0.250 | 0.154 | 0.076 | 0.026 | 0.004 | |
|   | 2 | 0.014 | 0.049 | 0.154 | 0.265 | 0.346 | 0.375 | 0.346 | 0.265 | 0.154 | 0.049 | 0.014 |
|   | 3 | | 0.004 | 0.026 | 0.076 | 0.154 | 0.250 | 0.346 | 0.412 | 0.410 | 0.292 | 0.171 |
|   | 4 | | | 0.002 | 0.008 | 0.026 | 0.062 | 0.130 | 0.240 | 0.410 | 0.656 | 0.815 |
| 5 | 0 | 0.774 | 0.590 | 0.328 | 0.168 | 0.078 | 0.031 | 0.010 | 0.002 | | | |
|   | 1 | 0.204 | 0.328 | 0.410 | 0.360 | 0.259 | 0.156 | 0.077 | 0.028 | 0.006 | | |
|   | 2 | 0.021 | 0.073 | 0.205 | 0.309 | 0.346 | 0.312 | 0.230 | 0.132 | 0.051 | 0.008 | 0.001 |
|   | 3 | 0.001 | 0.008 | 0.051 | 0.132 | 0.230 | 0.312 | 0.346 | 0.309 | 0.205 | 0.073 | 0.021 |
|   | 4 | | | 0.006 | 0.028 | 0.077 | 0.156 | 0.259 | 0.360 | 0.410 | 0.328 | 0.204 |
|   | 5 | | | | 0.002 | 0.010 | 0.031 | 0.078 | 0.168 | 0.328 | 0.590 | 0.774 |
| 6 | 0 | 0.735 | 0.531 | 0.262 | 0.118 | 0.047 | 0.016 | 0.004 | 0.001 | | | |
|   | 1 | 0.232 | 0.354 | 0.393 | 0.303 | 0.187 | 0.094 | 0.037 | 0.010 | 0.002 | | |
|   | 2 | 0.031 | 0.098 | 0.246 | 0.324 | 0.311 | 0.234 | 0.138 | 0.060 | 0.015 | 0.001 | |
|   | 3 | 0.002 | 0.015 | 0.082 | 0.185 | 0.276 | 0.312 | 0.276 | 0.185 | 0.082 | 0.015 | 0.002 |
|   | 4 | | 0.001 | 0.015 | 0.060 | 0.138 | 0.234 | 0.311 | 0.324 | 0.246 | 0.098 | 0.031 |
|   | 5 | | | 0.002 | 0.010 | 0.037 | 0.094 | 0.187 | 0.303 | 0.393 | 0.354 | 0.232 |
|   | 6 | | | | 0.001 | 0.004 | 0.016 | 0.047 | 0.118 | 0.262 | 0.531 | 0.735 |
| 7 | 0 | 0.698 | 0.478 | 0.210 | 0.082 | 0.028 | 0.008 | 0.002 | | | | |
|   | 1 | 0.257 | 0.372 | 0.367 | 0.247 | 0.131 | 0.055 | 0.017 | 0.004 | | | |
|   | 2 | 0.041 | 0.124 | 0.275 | 0.318 | 0.261 | 0.164 | 0.077 | 0.025 | 0.004 | | |
|   | 3 | 0.004 | 0.023 | 0.115 | 0.227 | 0.290 | 0.273 | 0.194 | 0.097 | 0.029 | 0.003 | |
|   | 4 | | 0.003 | 0.029 | 0.097 | 0.194 | 0.273 | 0.290 | 0.227 | 0.115 | 0.023 | 0.004 |

*Continued*

Source: John E. Freund and Richard Manning Smith, *Statistics: A First Course*, 4th ed. (Upper Saddle River, N.J.: Prentice-Hall, 1986), pp. 502–5. Adapted by permission.

## TABLE B.2   Areas under the Binomial Curve—*Continued*

| n | r | 0.05 | 0.1 | 0.2 | 0.3 | 0.4 | 0.5 | 0.6 | 0.7 | 0.8 | 0.9 | 0.95 |
|---|---|------|-----|-----|-----|-----|-----|-----|-----|-----|-----|------|
|   | 5 |  |  | 0.004 | 0.025 | 0.077 | 0.164 | 0.261 | 0.318 | 0.275 | 0.124 | 0.041 |
|   | 6 |  |  |  | 0.004 | 0.017 | 0.055 | 0.131 | 0.247 | 0.367 | 0.372 | 0.257 |
|   | 7 |  |  |  |  | 0.002 | 0.008 | 0.028 | 0.082 | 0.210 | 0.478 | 0.698 |
| 8 | 0 | 0.663 | 0.430 | 0.168 | 0.058 | 0.017 | 0.004 | 0.001 |  |  |  |  |
|   | 1 | 0.279 | 0.383 | 0.336 | 0.198 | 0.090 | 0.031 | 0.008 | 0.001 |  |  |  |
|   | 2 | 0.051 | 0.149 | 0.294 | 0.296 | 0.209 | 0.109 | 0.041 | 0.010 | 0.001 |  |  |
|   | 3 | 0.005 | 0.033 | 0.147 | 0.254 | 0.279 | 0.219 | 0.124 | 0.047 | 0.009 |  |  |
|   | 4 |  | 0.005 | 0.046 | 0.136 | 0.232 | 0.273 | 0.232 | 0.136 | 0.046 | 0.005 |  |
|   | 5 |  |  | 0.009 | 0.047 | 0.124 | 0.219 | 0.279 | 0.254 | 0.147 | 0.033 | 0.005 |
|   | 6 |  |  | 0.001 | 0.010 | 0.041 | 0.109 | 0.209 | 0.296 | 0.294 | 0.149 | 0.051 |
|   | 7 |  |  |  | 0.001 | 0.008 | 0.031 | 0.090 | 0.198 | 0.336 | 0.383 | 0.279 |
|   | 8 |  |  |  |  | 0.001 | 0.004 | 0.017 | 0.058 | 0.168 | 0.430 | 0.663 |
| 9 | 0 | 0.630 | 0.387 | 0.134 | 0.040 | 0.010 | 0.002 |  |  |  |  |  |
|   | 1 | 0.299 | 0.387 | 0.302 | 0.156 | 0.060 | 0.018 | 0.004 |  |  |  |  |
|   | 2 | 0.063 | 0.172 | 0.302 | 0.267 | 0.161 | 0.070 | 0.021 | 0.004 |  |  |  |
|   | 3 | 0.008 | 0.045 | 0.176 | 0.267 | 0.251 | 0.164 | 0.074 | 0.021 | 0.003 |  |  |
|   | 4 | 0.001 | 0.007 | 0.066 | 0.172 | 0.251 | 0.246 | 0.167 | 0.074 | 0.017 | 0.001 |  |
|   | 5 |  | 0.001 | 0.017 | 0.074 | 0.167 | 0.246 | 0.251 | 0.172 | 0.066 | 0.007 | 0.001 |
|   | 6 |  |  | 0.003 | 0.021 | 0.074 | 0.164 | 0.251 | 0.267 | 0.176 | 0.045 | 0.008 |
|   | 7 |  |  |  | 0.004 | 0.021 | 0.070 | 0.161 | 0.267 | 0.302 | 0.172 | 0.063 |
|   | 8 |  |  |  |  | 0.004 | 0.018 | 0.060 | 0.156 | 0.302 | 0.387 | 0.299 |
|   | 9 |  |  |  |  |  | 0.002 | 0.010 | 0.040 | 0.134 | 0.387 | 0.630 |
| 10 | 0 | 0.599 | 0.349 | 0.107 | 0.028 | 0.006 | 0.001 |  |  |  |  |  |
|   | 1 | 0.315 | 0.387 | 0.268 | 0.121 | 0.040 | 0.010 | 0.002 |  |  |  |  |
|   | 2 | 0.075 | 0.194 | 0.302 | 0.233 | 0.121 | 0.044 | 0.011 | 0.001 |  |  |  |
|   | 3 | 0.010 | 0.057 | 0.201 | 0.267 | 0.215 | 0.117 | 0.042 | 0.009 | 0.001 |  |  |
|   | 4 | 0.001 | 0.011 | 0.088 | 0.200 | 0.251 | 0.205 | 0.111 | 0.037 | 0.006 |  |  |
|   | 5 |  | 0.001 | 0.026 | 0.103 | 0.201 | 0.246 | 0.201 | 0.103 | 0.026 | 0.001 |  |
|   | 6 |  |  | 0.006 | 0.037 | 0.111 | 0.205 | 0.251 | 0.200 | 0.088 | 0.011 | 0.001 |
|   | 7 |  |  | 0.001 | 0.009 | 0.042 | 0.117 | 0.215 | 0.267 | 0.201 | 0.057 | 0.010 |
|   | 8 |  |  |  | 0.001 | 0.011 | 0.044 | 0.121 | 0.233 | 0.302 | 0.194 | 0.075 |
|   | 9 |  |  |  |  | 0.002 | 0.010 | 0.040 | 0.121 | 0.268 | 0.387 | 0.315 |
|   | 10 |  |  |  |  |  | 0.001 | 0.006 | 0.028 | 0.107 | 0.349 | 0.599 |

**TABLE B.2    Areas under the Binomial Curve—*Continued***

| n | r | 0.05 | 0.1 | 0.2 | 0.3 | 0.4 | 0.5 | 0.6 | 0.7 | 0.8 | 0.9 | 0.95 |
|---|---|------|-----|-----|-----|-----|-----|-----|-----|-----|-----|------|
| 11 | 0 | 0.569 | 0.314 | 0.086 | 0.020 | 0.004 | | | | | | |
| | 1 | 0.329 | 0.384 | 0.236 | 0.093 | 0.027 | 0.005 | 0.001 | | | | |
| | 2 | 0.087 | 0.213 | 0.295 | 0.200 | 0.089 | 0.027 | 0.005 | 0.001 | | | |
| | 3 | 0.014 | 0.071 | 0.221 | 0.257 | 0.177 | 0.081 | 0.023 | 0.004 | | | |
| | 4 | 0.001 | 0.016 | 0.111 | 0.220 | 0.236 | 0.161 | 0.070 | 0.017 | 0.002 | | |
| | 5 | | 0.002 | 0.039 | 0.132 | 0.221 | 0.226 | 0.147 | 0.057 | 0.010 | | |
| | 6 | | | 0.010 | 0.057 | 0.147 | 0.226 | 0.221 | 0.132 | 0.039 | 0.002 | |
| | 7 | | | 0.002 | 0.017 | 0.070 | 0.161 | 0.236 | 0.220 | 0.111 | 0.016 | 0.001 |
| | 8 | | | | 0.004 | 0.023 | 0.081 | 0.177 | 0.257 | 0.221 | 0.071 | 0.014 |
| | 9 | | | | 0.001 | 0.005 | 0.027 | 0.089 | 0.200 | 0.295 | 0.213 | 0.087 |
| | 10 | | | | | 0.001 | 0.005 | 0.027 | 0.093 | 0.236 | 0.384 | 0.329 |
| | 11 | | | | | | | 0.004 | 0.020 | 0.086 | 0.314 | 0.569 |
| 12 | 0 | 0.540 | 0.282 | 0.069 | 0.014 | 0.002 | | | | | | |
| | 1 | 0.341 | 0.377 | 0.206 | 0.071 | 0.017 | 0.003 | | | | | |
| | 2 | 0.099 | 0.230 | 0.283 | 0.168 | 0.064 | 0.016 | 0.002 | | | | |
| | 3 | 0.017 | 0.085 | 0.236 | 0.240 | 0.142 | 0.054 | 0.012 | 0.001 | | | |
| | 4 | 0.002 | 0.021 | 0.133 | 0.231 | 0.213 | 0.121 | 0.042 | 0.008 | 0.001 | | |
| | 5 | | 0.004 | 0.053 | 0.158 | 0.227 | 0.193 | 0.101 | 0.029 | 0.003 | | |
| | 6 | | | 0.016 | 0.079 | 0.177 | 0.226 | 0.177 | 0.079 | 0.016 | | |
| | 7 | | | 0.003 | 0.029 | 0.101 | 0.193 | 0.227 | 0.158 | 0.053 | 0.004 | |
| | 8 | | | 0.001 | 0.008 | 0.042 | 0.121 | 0.213 | 0.231 | 0.133 | 0.021 | 0.002 |
| | 9 | | | | 0.001 | 0.012 | 0.054 | 0.142 | 0.240 | 0.236 | 0.085 | 0.017 |
| | 10 | | | | | 0.002 | 0.016 | 0.064 | 0.168 | 0.283 | 0.230 | 0.099 |
| | 11 | | | | | | 0.003 | 0.017 | 0.071 | 0.206 | 0.377 | 0.341 |
| | 12 | | | | | | | 0.002 | 0.014 | 0.069 | 0.282 | 0.540 |
| 13 | 0 | 0.513 | 0.254 | 0.055 | 0.010 | 0.001 | | | | | | |
| | 1 | 0.351 | 0.367 | 0.179 | 0.054 | 0.011 | 0.002 | | | | | |
| | 2 | 0.111 | 0.245 | 0.268 | 0.139 | 0.045 | 0.010 | 0.001 | | | | |
| | 3 | 0.021 | 0.100 | 0.246 | 0.218 | 0.111 | 0.035 | 0.006 | 0.001 | | | |
| | 4 | 0.003 | 0.028 | 0.154 | 0.234 | 0.184 | 0.087 | 0.024 | 0.003 | | | |
| | 5 | | 0.006 | 0.069 | 0.180 | 0.221 | 0.157 | 0.066 | 0.014 | 0.001 | | |
| | 6 | | 0.001 | 0.023 | 0.103 | 0.197 | 0.209 | 0.131 | 0.044 | 0.006 | | |
| | 7 | | | 0.006 | 0.044 | 0.131 | 0.209 | 0.197 | 0.103 | 0.023 | 0.001 | |

*Continued*

**TABLE B.2    Areas under the Binomial Curve—*Continued***

| n | r | 0.05 | 0.1 | 0.2 | 0.3 | 0.4 | 0.5 | 0.6 | 0.7 | 0.8 | 0.9 | 0.95 |
|---|---|------|-----|-----|-----|-----|-----|-----|-----|-----|-----|------|
|  | 8 |  |  | 0.001 | 0.014 | 0.066 | 0.157 | 0.221 | 0.180 | 0.069 | 0.006 |  |
|  | 9 |  |  |  | 0.003 | 0.024 | 0.087 | 0.184 | 0.234 | 0.154 | 0.028 | 0.003 |
|  | 10 |  |  | 0.001 | 0.006 | 0.035 | 0.111 | 0.218 | 0.246 | 0.100 | 0.021 |  |
|  | 11 |  |  |  | 0.001 | 0.010 | 0.045 | 0.139 | 0.268 | 0.245 | 0.111 |  |
|  | 12 |  |  |  |  | 0.002 | 0.011 | 0.054 | 0.179 | 0.367 | 0.351 |  |
|  | 13 |  |  |  |  |  | 0.001 | 0.010 | 0.055 | 0.254 | 0.513 |  |
| 14 | 0 | 0.488 | 0.229 | 0.044 | 0.007 | 0.001 |  |  |  |  |  |  |
|  | 1 | 0.359 | 0.356 | 0.154 | 0.041 | 0.007 | 0.001 |  |  |  |  |  |
|  | 2 | 0.123 | 0.257 | 0.250 | 0.113 | 0.032 | 0.006 | 0.001 |  |  |  |  |
|  | 3 | 0.026 | 0.114 | 0.250 | 0.194 | 0.085 | 0.022 | 0.003 |  |  |  |  |
|  | 4 | 0.004 | 0.035 | 0.172 | 0.229 | 0.155 | 0.061 | 0.014 | 0.001 |  |  |  |
|  | 5 |  | 0.008 | 0.086 | 0.196 | 0.207 | 0.122 | 0.041 | 0.007 |  |  |  |
|  | 6 |  | 0.001 | 0.032 | 0.126 | 0.207 | 0.183 | 0.092 | 0.023 | 0.002 |  |  |
|  | 7 |  |  | 0.009 | 0.062 | 0.157 | 0.209 | 0.157 | 0.062 | 0.009 |  |  |
|  | 8 |  |  | 0.002 | 0.023 | 0.092 | 0.183 | 0.207 | 0.126 | 0.032 | 0.001 |  |
|  | 9 |  |  |  | 0.007 | 0.041 | 0.122 | 0.207 | 0.196 | 0.086 | 0.008 |  |
|  | 10 |  |  |  | 0.001 | 0.014 | 0.061 | 0.155 | 0.229 | 0.172 | 0.035 | 0.004 |
|  | 11 |  |  |  |  | 0.003 | 0.022 | 0.085 | 0.194 | 0.250 | 0.114 | 0.026 |
|  | 12 |  |  |  |  | 0.001 | 0.006 | 0.032 | 0.113 | 0.250 | 0.257 | 0.123 |
|  | 13 |  |  |  |  |  | 0.001 | 0.007 | 0.041 | 0.154 | 0.356 | 0.359 |
|  | 14 |  |  |  |  |  |  | 0.001 | 0.007 | 0.044 | 0.229 | 0.488 |
| 15 | 0 | 0.463 | 0.206 | 0.035 | 0.005 |  |  |  |  |  |  |  |
|  | 1 | 0.366 | 0.343 | 0.132 | 0.031 | 0.005 |  |  |  |  |  |  |
|  | 2 | 0.135 | 0.267 | 0.231 | 0.092 | 0.022 | 0.003 |  |  |  |  |  |
|  | 3 | 0.031 | 0.129 | 0.250 | 0.170 | 0.063 | 0.014 | 0.002 |  |  |  |  |
|  | 4 | 0.005 | 0.043 | 0.188 | 0.219 | 0.127 | 0.042 | 0.007 | 0.001 |  |  |  |
|  | 5 | 0.001 | 0.010 | 0.103 | 0.206 | 0.186 | 0.092 | 0.024 | 0.003 |  |  |  |
|  | 6 |  | 0.002 | 0.043 | 0.147 | 0.207 | 0.153 | 0.061 | 0.012 | 0.001 |  |  |
|  | 7 |  |  | 0.014 | 0.081 | 0.177 | 0.196 | 0.118 | 0.035 | 0.003 |  |  |
|  | 8 |  |  | 0.003 | 0.035 | 0.118 | 0.196 | 0.177 | 0.081 | 0.014 |  |  |
|  | 9 |  |  | 0.001 | 0.012 | 0.061 | 0.153 | 0.207 | 0.147 | 0.043 | 0.002 |  |
|  | 10 |  |  |  | 0.003 | 0.024 | 0.092 | 0.186 | 0.206 | 0.103 | 0.010 | 0.001 |
|  | 11 |  |  |  | 0.001 | 0.007 | 0.042 | 0.127 | 0.219 | 0.188 | 0.043 | 0.005 |
|  | 12 |  |  |  |  | 0.002 | 0.014 | 0.063 | 0.170 | 0.250 | 0.129 | 0.031 |
|  | 13 |  |  |  |  |  | 0.003 | 0.022 | 0.092 | 0.231 | 0.267 | 0.135 |
|  | 14 |  |  |  |  |  |  | 0.005 | 0.031 | 0.132 | 0.343 | 0.366 |
|  | 15 |  |  |  |  |  |  |  | 0.005 | 0.035 | 0.206 | 0.463 |

# TABLE B.3  Selected Probabilities Associated with Student's *t* Values

The degrees of freedom associated with sample size appear in the left-hand column and selected probabilities for one- and two-tailed tests across the top of the table. The decision rule is as follows: If the computed *t* value is equal to or larger than the value at the intersect of df and the selected probability, reject the null hypothesis and accept the directional hypothesis.

| df | Level of significance for one-tailed test | | | | | |
|---|---|---|---|---|---|---|
| | .10 | .05 | .025 | .01 | .005 | .0005 |
| | Level of significance for two-tailed test | | | | | |
| | .20 | .10 | .05 | .02 | .01 | .001 |
| 1 | 3.078 | 6.314 | 12.706 | 31.821 | 63.657 | 636.619 |
| 2 | 1.886 | 2.920 | 4.303 | 6.965 | 9.925 | 31.598 |
| 3 | 1.638 | 2.353 | 3.182 | 4.541 | 5.841 | 12.941 |
| 4 | 1.533 | 2.132 | 2.776 | 3.747 | 4.604 | 8.610 |
| 5 | 1.476 | 2.015 | 2.571 | 3.365 | 4.032 | 6.859 |
| 6 | 1.440 | 1.943 | 2.447 | 3.143 | 3.707 | 5.959 |
| 7 | 1.415 | 1.895 | 2.365 | 2.998 | 3.499 | 5.405 |
| 8 | 1.397 | 1.860 | 2.306 | 2.896 | 3.355 | 5.041 |
| 9 | 1.383 | 1.833 | 2.262 | 2.821 | 3.250 | 4.781 |
| 10 | 1.372 | 1.812 | 2.228 | 2.764 | 3.169 | 4.587 |
| 11 | 1.363 | 1.796 | 2.201 | 2.718 | 3.106 | 4.437 |
| 12 | 1.356 | 1.782 | 2.179 | 2.681 | 3.055 | 4.318 |
| 13 | 1.350 | 1.771 | 2.160 | 2.650 | 3.012 | 4.221 |
| 14 | 1.345 | 1.761 | 2.145 | 2.624 | 2.977 | 4.140 |
| 15 | 1.341 | 1.753 | 2.131 | 2.602 | 2.947 | 4.073 |
| 16 | 1.337 | 1.746 | 2.120 | 2.583 | 2.921 | 4.015 |
| 17 | 1.333 | 1.740 | 2.110 | 2.567 | 2.898 | 3.965 |
| 18 | 1.330 | 1.734 | 2.101 | 2.552 | 2.878 | 3.922 |
| 19 | 1.328 | 1.729 | 2.093 | 2.539 | 2.861 | 3.883 |
| 20 | 1.325 | 1.725 | 2.086 | 2.528 | 2.845 | 3.850 |
| 21 | 1.323 | 1.721 | 2.080 | 2.518 | 2.831 | 3.819 |
| 22 | 1.321 | 1.717 | 2.074 | 2.508 | 2.819 | 3.792 |
| 23 | 1.319 | 1.714 | 2.069 | 2.500 | 2.807 | 3.767 |
| 24 | 1.318 | 1.711 | 2.064 | 2.492 | 2.797 | 3.745 |
| 25 | 1.316 | 1.708 | 2.060 | 2.485 | 2.787 | 3.725 |
| 26 | 1.315 | 1.706 | 2.056 | 2.479 | 2.779 | 3.707 |
| 27 | 1.314 | 1.703 | 2.052 | 2.473 | 2.771 | 3.690 |
| 28 | 1.313 | 1.701 | 2.048 | 2.467 | 2.763 | 3.674 |
| 29 | 1.311 | 1.699 | 2.045 | 2.462 | 2.756 | 3.659 |
| 30 | 1.310 | 1.697 | 2.042 | 2.457 | 2.750 | 3.646 |
| 40 | 1.303 | 1.684 | 2.021 | 2.423 | 2.704 | 3.551 |
| 60 | 1.296 | 1.671 | 2.000 | 2.390 | 2.660 | 3.460 |
| 120 | 1.289 | 1.658 | 1.980 | 2.358 | 2.617 | 3.373 |
| ∞ | 1.282 | 1.645 | 1.960 | 2.326 | 2.576 | 3.291 |

Source: From Sir Ronald A. Fisher and Frank Yates, *Statistical Tables for Biological, Agricultural, and Medical Research* (London: Longman Group, 1979), table 3, p. 46. Reproduced by permission of Addison Wesley Longman Ltd.

## TABLE B.4    Critical Values of Chi-Square

The procedures for using Table B.4 are discussed in Chapter 7. The decision rule is as follows: If the computed $\chi^2$ value is equal to or larger than the table value, reject $H_0$ and accept $H_1$.

| df | .99 | .98 | .95 | .90 | .80 | .70 | .50 | .30 | .20 | .10 | .05 | .02 | .01 | .001 |
|---|---|---|---|---|---|---|---|---|---|---|---|---|---|---|
| | | | | | Probability under $H_0$ that $\chi^2 \geq$ chi square | | | | | | | | | |
| 1 | .00016 | .00063 | .0039 | .016 | .064 | .15 | .46 | 1.07 | 1.64 | 2.71 | 3.84 | 5.41 | 6.64 | 10.83 |
| 2 | .02 | .04 | .10 | .21 | .45 | .71 | 1.39 | 2.41 | 3.22 | 4.60 | 5.99 | 7.82 | 9.21 | 13.82 |
| 3 | .12 | .18 | .35 | .58 | 1.00 | 1.42 | 2.37 | 3.66 | 4.64 | 6.25 | 7.82 | 9.84 | 11.34 | 16.27 |
| 4 | .30 | .43 | .71 | 1.06 | 1.65 | 2.20 | 3.36 | 4.88 | 5.99 | 7.78 | 9.49 | 11.67 | 13.28 | 18.46 |
| 5 | .55 | .75 | 1.14 | 1.61 | 2.34 | 3.00 | 4.35 | 6.06 | 7.29 | 9.24 | 11.07 | 13.39 | 15.09 | 20.52 |
| 6 | .87 | 1.13 | 1.64 | 2.20 | 3.07 | 3.83 | 5.35 | 7.23 | 8.56 | 10.64 | 12.59 | 15.03 | 16.81 | 22.46 |
| 7 | 1.24 | 1.56 | 2.17 | 2.83 | 3.82 | 4.67 | 6.35 | 8.38 | 9.80 | 12.02 | 14.07 | 16.62 | 18.48 | 24.32 |
| 8 | 1.65 | 2.03 | 2.73 | 3.49 | 4.59 | 5.53 | 7.34 | 9.52 | 11.03 | 13.36 | 15.51 | 18.17 | 20.09 | 26.12 |
| 9 | 2.09 | 2.53 | 3.32 | 4.17 | 5.38 | 6.39 | 8.34 | 10.66 | 12.24 | 14.68 | 16.92 | 19.68 | 21.67 | 27.88 |
| 10 | 2.56 | 3.06 | 3.94 | 4.86 | 6.18 | 7.27 | 9.34 | 11.78 | 13.44 | 15.99 | 18.31 | 21.16 | 23.21 | 29.59 |
| 11 | 3.05 | 3.61 | 4.58 | 5.58 | 6.99 | 8.15 | 10.34 | 12.90 | 14.63 | 17.28 | 19.68 | 22.62 | 24.72 | 31.26 |
| 12 | 3.57 | 4.18 | 5.23 | 6.30 | 7.81 | 9.03 | 11.34 | 14.01 | 15.81 | 18.55 | 21.03 | 24.05 | 26.22 | 32.91 |
| 13 | 4.11 | 4.76 | 5.89 | 7.04 | 8.63 | 9.93 | 12.34 | 15.12 | 16.98 | 19.81 | 22.36 | 25.47 | 27.69 | 34.53 |
| 14 | 4.66 | 5.37 | 6.57 | 7.79 | 9.47 | 10.82 | 13.34 | 16.22 | 18.15 | 21.06 | 23.68 | 26.87 | 29.14 | 36.12 |
| 15 | 5.23 | 5.98 | 7.26 | 8.55 | 10.31 | 11.72 | 14.34 | 17.32 | 19.31 | 22.31 | 25.00 | 28.26 | 30.58 | 37.70 |
| 16 | 5.81 | 6.61 | 7.96 | 9.31 | 11.15 | 12.62 | 15.34 | 18.42 | 20.46 | 23.54 | 26.30 | 29.63 | 32.00 | 39.29 |
| 17 | 6.41 | 7.26 | 8.67 | 10.08 | 12.00 | 13.53 | 16.34 | 19.51 | 21.62 | 24.77 | 27.59 | 31.00 | 33.41 | 40.75 |
| 18 | 7.02 | 7.91 | 9.39 | 10.86 | 12.86 | 14.44 | 17.34 | 20.60 | 22.76 | 25.99 | 28.87 | 32.35 | 34.80 | 42.31 |
| 19 | 7.63 | 8.57 | 10.12 | 11.65 | 13.72 | 15.35 | 18.34 | 21.69 | 23.90 | 27.20 | 30.14 | 33.69 | 36.19 | 43.82 |
| 20 | 8.26 | 9.24 | 10.85 | 12.44 | 14.58 | 16.27 | 19.34 | 22.78 | 25.04 | 28.41 | 31.41 | 35.02 | 37.57 | 45.32 |
| 21 | 8.90 | 9.92 | 11.59 | 13.24 | 15.44 | 17.18 | 20.34 | 23.86 | 26.17 | 29.62 | 32.67 | 36.34 | 38.93 | 46.80 |
| 22 | 9.54 | 10.60 | 12.34 | 14.04 | 16.31 | 18.10 | 21.24 | 24.94 | 27.30 | 30.81 | 33.92 | 37.66 | 40.29 | 48.27 |
| 23 | 10.20 | 11.29 | 13.09 | 14.85 | 17.19 | 19.02 | 22.34 | 26.02 | 28.43 | 32.01 | 35.17 | 38.97 | 41.64 | 49.73 |
| 24 | 10.86 | 11.99 | 13.85 | 15.66 | 18.06 | 19.94 | 23.34 | 27.10 | 29.55 | 33.20 | 36.42 | 40.27 | 42.98 | 51.18 |
| 25 | 11.52 | 12.70 | 14.61 | 16.47 | 18.94 | 20.87 | 24.34 | 28.17 | 30.68 | 34.38 | 37.65 | 41.57 | 44.31 | 52.62 |
| 26 | 12.20 | 13.41 | 15.38 | 17.29 | 19.82 | 21.79 | 25.34 | 29.25 | 31.80 | 35.56 | 38.88 | 42.86 | 45.64 | 54.05 |
| 27 | 12.88 | 14.12 | 16.15 | 18.11 | 20.70 | 22.72 | 26.34 | 30.32 | 32.91 | 36.74 | 40.11 | 44.14 | 46.96 | 55.48 |
| 28 | 13.56 | 14.85 | 16.93 | 18.94 | 21.59 | 23.65 | 27.34 | 31.39 | 34.03 | 37.92 | 41.34 | 45.42 | 48.28 | 56.89 |
| 29 | 14.26 | 15.57 | 17.71 | 19.77 | 22.48 | 24.58 | 28.34 | 32.46 | 35.14 | 39.09 | 42.56 | 46.69 | 49.59 | 58.30 |
| 30 | 14.95 | 16.31 | 18.49 | 20.60 | 23.36 | 25.51 | 29.34 | 33.53 | 36.25 | 40.26 | 43.77 | 47.96 | 50.89 | 59.70 |

Source: From Sir Ronald A. Fisher and Frank Yates, *Statistical Tables for Biological, Agricultural, and Medical Research* (London: Longman Group, 1979), table 55, p. 47. Reproduced by permission of Addison Wesley Longman Ltd.

# TABLE B.5 Critical Values of Mann-Whitney U and U'

The procedures for using Table B.5 are discussed in Chapter 9. The decision rule is as follows: If the computed U is equal to or less than the smaller value *and* if the computed U' value is equal to or larger than the larger value at the intersect of $n_1$ and $n_2$, reject $H_0$. The direction of $H_1$ is determined by whether the computed value is less or greater than the two table values. (Dashes in the body of the table indicate that no decision is possible at the stated level of significance.)

## One-Tailed $\alpha = .005$, Two-Tailed $\alpha = .01$

Each cell shows the smaller value (U) over the larger value (U') as U/U'.

| $N_2$ \ $N_1$ | 1 | 2 | 3 | 4 | 5 | 6 | 7 | 8 | 9 | 10 | 11 | 12 | 13 | 14 | 15 | 16 | 17 | 18 | 19 | 20 |
|---|---|---|---|---|---|---|---|---|---|---|---|---|---|---|---|---|---|---|---|---|
| 1 | -- | -- | -- | -- | -- | -- | -- | -- | -- | -- | -- | -- | -- | -- | -- | -- | -- | -- | -- | -- |
| 2 | -- | -- | -- | -- | -- | -- | -- | -- | -- | -- | -- | -- | -- | -- | -- | -- | -- | -- | 0/38 | 0/40 |
| 3 | -- | -- | -- | -- | -- | -- | -- | -- | 0/27 | 0/30 | 0/33 | 1/35 | 1/38 | 1/41 | 2/43 | 2/46 | 2/49 | 2/52 | 3/54 | 3/57 |
| 4 | -- | -- | -- | -- | -- | 0/24 | 0/28 | 1/31 | 1/35 | 2/38 | 2/42 | 3/45 | 3/49 | 4/52 | 5/55 | 5/59 | 6/62 | 6/66 | 7/69 | 8/72 |
| 5 | -- | -- | -- | -- | 0/25 | 1/29 | 1/34 | 2/38 | 3/42 | 4/46 | 5/50 | 6/54 | 7/58 | 7/63 | 8/67 | 9/71 | 10/75 | 11/79 | 12/83 | 13/87 |
| 6 | -- | -- | -- | 0/24 | 1/29 | 2/34 | 3/39 | 4/44 | 5/49 | 6/54 | 7/59 | 9/63 | 10/68 | 11/73 | 12/78 | 13/83 | 15/87 | 16/92 | 17/97 | 18/102 |
| 7 | -- | -- | -- | 0/28 | 1/34 | 3/39 | 4/45 | 6/50 | 7/56 | 9/61 | 10/67 | 12/72 | 13/78 | 15/83 | 16/89 | 18/94 | 19/100 | 21/105 | 22/111 | 24/116 |
| 8 | -- | -- | -- | 1/31 | 2/38 | 4/44 | 6/50 | 7/57 | 9/63 | 11/69 | 13/75 | 15/81 | 17/87 | 18/94 | 20/100 | 22/106 | 24/112 | 26/118 | 28/124 | 30/130 |
| 9 | -- | -- | 0/27 | 1/35 | 3/42 | 5/49 | 7/56 | 9/63 | 11/70 | 13/77 | 16/83 | 18/90 | 20/97 | 22/104 | 24/111 | 27/117 | 29/124 | 31/131 | 33/138 | 36/144 |
| 10 | -- | -- | 0/30 | 2/38 | 4/46 | 6/54 | 9/61 | 11/69 | 13/77 | 16/84 | 18/92 | 21/99 | 24/106 | 26/114 | 29/121 | 31/129 | 34/136 | 37/143 | 39/151 | 42/158 |
| 11 | -- | -- | 0/33 | 2/42 | 5/50 | 7/59 | 10/67 | 13/75 | 16/83 | 18/92 | 21/100 | 24/108 | 27/116 | 30/124 | 33/132 | 36/140 | 39/148 | 42/156 | 45/164 | 48/172 |
| 12 | -- | -- | 1/35 | 3/45 | 6/54 | 9/63 | 12/72 | 15/81 | 18/90 | 21/99 | 24/108 | 27/117 | 31/125 | 34/134 | 37/143 | 41/151 | 44/160 | 47/169 | 51/177 | 54/186 |
| 13 | -- | -- | 1/38 | 3/49 | 7/58 | 10/68 | 13/78 | 17/87 | 20/97 | 24/106 | 27/116 | 31/125 | 34/135 | 38/144 | 42/153 | 45/163 | 49/172 | 53/181 | 56/191 | 60/200 |
| 14 | -- | -- | 1/41 | 4/52 | 7/63 | 11/73 | 15/83 | 18/94 | 22/104 | 26/114 | 30/124 | 34/134 | 38/144 | 42/154 | 46/164 | 50/174 | 54/184 | 58/194 | 63/203 | 67/213 |
| 15 | -- | -- | 2/43 | 5/55 | 8/67 | 12/78 | 16/89 | 20/100 | 24/111 | 29/121 | 33/132 | 37/143 | 42/153 | 46/164 | 51/174 | 55/185 | 60/195 | 64/206 | 69/216 | 73/227 |
| 16 | -- | -- | 2/46 | 5/59 | 9/71 | 13/83 | 18/94 | 22/106 | 27/117 | 31/129 | 36/140 | 41/151 | 45/163 | 50/174 | 55/185 | 60/196 | 65/207 | 70/218 | 74/230 | 79/241 |
| 17 | -- | -- | 2/49 | 6/62 | 10/75 | 15/87 | 19/100 | 24/112 | 29/124 | 34/136 | 39/148 | 44/160 | 49/172 | 54/184 | 60/195 | 65/207 | 70/219 | 75/231 | 81/242 | 86/254 |
| 18 | -- | -- | 2/52 | 6/66 | 11/79 | 16/92 | 21/105 | 26/118 | 31/131 | 37/143 | 42/156 | 47/169 | 53/181 | 58/194 | 64/206 | 70/218 | 75/231 | 81/243 | 87/255 | 92/268 |
| 19 | -- | 0/38 | 3/54 | 7/69 | 12/83 | 17/97 | 22/111 | 28/124 | 33/138 | 39/151 | 45/164 | 51/177 | 56/191 | 63/203 | 69/216 | 74/230 | 81/242 | 87/255 | 93/268 | 99/281 |
| 20 | -- | 0/40 | 3/57 | 8/72 | 13/87 | 18/102 | 24/116 | 30/130 | 36/144 | 42/158 | 48/172 | 54/186 | 60/200 | 67/213 | 73/227 | 79/241 | 86/254 | 92/268 | 99/281 | 105/295 |

Source: From Richard P. Runyon, Audrey Haber, David J. Pittenger, and Kay A. Coleman, *Fundamentals of Behavioral Statistics* (New York: McGraw-Hill, 1996), pp. 657–660.

*Continued*

## TABLE B.5   Critical Values of Mann-Whitney U and U'—*Continued*

### One-Tailed α = .01, Two-Tailed α = .02

Each cell lists U (upper) and U' (lower).

| N₂＼N₁ | 1 | 2 | 3 | 4 | 5 | 6 | 7 | 8 | 9 | 10 | 11 | 12 | 13 | 14 | 15 | 16 | 17 | 18 | 19 | 20 |
|---|---|---|---|---|---|---|---|---|---|---|---|---|---|---|---|---|---|---|---|---|
| 1 | -- | -- | -- | -- | -- | -- | -- | -- | -- | -- | -- | -- | -- | -- | -- | -- | -- | -- | -- | -- |
| 2 | -- | -- | -- | -- | -- | -- | -- | -- | -- | -- | -- | -- | 0/26 | 0/28 | 0/30 | 0/32 | 0/34 | 0/36 | 1/37 | 1/39 |
| 3 | -- | -- | -- | -- | -- | -- | 0/21 | 0/24 | 1/26 | 1/29 | 1/32 | 2/34 | 2/37 | 2/40 | 3/42 | 3/45 | 4/47 | 4/50 | 4/52 | 5/55 |
| 4 | -- | -- | -- | -- | 0/20 | 1/23 | 1/27 | 2/30 | 3/33 | 3/37 | 4/40 | 5/43 | 5/47 | 6/50 | 7/53 | 7/57 | 8/60 | 9/63 | 9/67 | 10/70 |
| 5 | -- | -- | -- | 0/20 | 1/24 | 2/28 | 3/32 | 4/36 | 5/40 | 6/44 | 7/48 | 8/52 | 9/56 | 10/60 | 11/64 | 12/68 | 13/72 | 14/76 | 15/80 | 16/84 |
| 6 | -- | -- | -- | 1/23 | 2/28 | 3/33 | 4/38 | 6/42 | 7/47 | 8/52 | 9/57 | 11/61 | 12/66 | 13/71 | 15/75 | 16/80 | 18/84 | 19/89 | 20/94 | 22/98 |
| 7 | -- | -- | 0/21 | 1/27 | 3/32 | 4/38 | 6/43 | 7/49 | 9/54 | 11/59 | 12/65 | 14/70 | 16/75 | 17/81 | 19/86 | 21/91 | 23/96 | 24/102 | 26/107 | 28/112 |
| 8 | -- | -- | 0/24 | 2/30 | 4/36 | 6/42 | 7/49 | 9/55 | 11/61 | 13/67 | 15/73 | 17/79 | 20/84 | 22/90 | 24/96 | 26/102 | 28/108 | 30/114 | 32/120 | 34/126 |
| 9 | -- | -- | 1/26 | 3/33 | 5/40 | 7/47 | 9/54 | 11/61 | 14/67 | 16/74 | 18/81 | 21/87 | 23/94 | 26/100 | 28/107 | 31/113 | 33/120 | 36/126 | 38/133 | 40/140 |
| 10 | -- | -- | 1/29 | 3/37 | 6/44 | 8/52 | 11/59 | 13/67 | 16/74 | 19/81 | 22/88 | 24/96 | 27/103 | 30/110 | 33/117 | 36/124 | 38/132 | 41/139 | 44/146 | 47/153 |
| 11 | -- | -- | 1/32 | 4/40 | 7/48 | 9/57 | 12/65 | 15/73 | 18/81 | 22/88 | 25/96 | 28/104 | 31/112 | 34/120 | 37/128 | 41/135 | 44/143 | 47/151 | 50/159 | 53/167 |
| 12 | -- | -- | 2/34 | 5/43 | 8/52 | 11/61 | 14/70 | 17/79 | 21/87 | 24/96 | 28/104 | 31/113 | 35/121 | 38/130 | 42/138 | 46/146 | 49/155 | 53/163 | 56/172 | 60/180 |
| 13 | -- | 0/26 | 2/37 | 5/47 | 9/56 | 12/66 | 16/75 | 20/84 | 23/94 | 27/103 | 31/112 | 35/121 | 39/130 | 43/139 | 47/148 | 51/157 | 55/166 | 59/175 | 63/184 | 67/193 |
| 14 | -- | 0/28 | 2/40 | 6/50 | 10/60 | 13/71 | 17/81 | 22/90 | 26/100 | 30/110 | 34/120 | 38/130 | 43/139 | 47/149 | 51/159 | 56/168 | 60/178 | 65/187 | 69/197 | 73/207 |
| 15 | -- | 0/30 | 3/42 | 7/53 | 11/64 | 15/75 | 19/86 | 24/96 | 28/107 | 33/117 | 37/128 | 42/138 | 47/148 | 51/159 | 56/169 | 61/179 | 66/189 | 70/200 | 75/210 | 80/220 |
| 16 | -- | 0/32 | 3/45 | 7/57 | 12/68 | 16/80 | 21/91 | 26/102 | 31/113 | 36/124 | 41/135 | 46/146 | 51/157 | 56/168 | 61/179 | 66/190 | 71/201 | 76/212 | 82/222 | 87/233 |
| 17 | -- | 0/34 | 4/47 | 8/60 | 13/72 | 18/84 | 23/96 | 28/108 | 33/120 | 38/132 | 44/143 | 49/155 | 55/166 | 60/178 | 66/189 | 71/201 | 77/212 | 82/224 | 88/235 | 93/247 |
| 18 | -- | 0/36 | 4/50 | 9/63 | 14/76 | 19/89 | 24/102 | 30/114 | 36/126 | 41/139 | 47/151 | 53/163 | 59/175 | 65/187 | 70/200 | 76/212 | 82/224 | 88/236 | 94/248 | 100/260 |
| 19 | -- | 1/37 | 4/53 | 9/67 | 15/80 | 20/94 | 26/107 | 32/120 | 38/133 | 44/146 | 50/159 | 56/172 | 63/184 | 69/197 | 75/210 | 82/222 | 88/235 | 94/248 | 101/260 | 107/273 |
| 20 | -- | 1/39 | 5/55 | 10/70 | 16/84 | 22/98 | 28/112 | 34/126 | 40/140 | 47/153 | 53/167 | 60/180 | 67/193 | 73/207 | 80/220 | 87/233 | 93/247 | 100/260 | 107/273 | 114/286 |

## TABLE B.5  Critical Values of Mann-Whitney U and U'—*Continued*

### One-Tailed α = .025, Two-Tailed α = .05

| $N_2$ \ $N_1$ | 1 | 2 | 3 | 4 | 5 | 6 | 7 | 8 | 9 | 10 | 11 | 12 | 13 | 14 | 15 | 16 | 17 | 18 | 19 | 20 |
|---|---|---|---|---|---|---|---|---|---|---|---|---|---|---|---|---|---|---|---|---|
| 1 | -- | -- | -- | -- | -- | -- | -- | -- | -- | -- | -- | -- | -- | -- | -- | -- | -- | -- | -- | -- |
| 2 | -- | -- | -- | -- | -- | -- | -- | 0 16 | 0 18 | 0 20 | 0 22 | 1 23 | 1 25 | 1 27 | 1 29 | 1 31 | 2 32 | 2 34 | 2 36 | 2 38 |
| 3 | -- | -- | -- | -- | 0 15 | 1 17 | 1 20 | 2 22 | 2 25 | 3 27 | 3 30 | 4 32 | 4 35 | 5 37 | 5 40 | 6 42 | 6 45 | 7 47 | 7 50 | 8 52 |
| 4 | -- | -- | -- | 0 16 | 1 19 | 2 22 | 3 25 | 4 28 | 4 32 | 5 35 | 6 38 | 7 41 | 8 44 | 9 47 | 10 50 | 11 53 | 11 57 | 12 60 | 13 63 | 13 67 |
| 5 | -- | -- | 0 15 | 1 19 | 2 23 | 3 27 | 5 30 | 6 34 | 7 38 | 8 42 | 9 46 | 11 49 | 12 53 | 13 57 | 14 61 | 15 65 | 17 68 | 18 72 | 19 76 | 20 80 |
| 6 | -- | -- | 1 17 | 2 22 | 3 27 | 5 31 | 6 36 | 8 40 | 10 44 | 11 49 | 13 53 | 14 58 | 16 62 | 17 67 | 19 71 | 21 75 | 22 80 | 24 84 | 25 89 | 27 93 |
| 7 | -- | -- | 1 20 | 3 25 | 5 30 | 6 36 | 8 41 | 10 46 | 12 51 | 14 56 | 16 61 | 18 66 | 20 71 | 22 76 | 24 81 | 26 86 | 28 91 | 30 96 | 32 101 | 34 106 |
| 8 | -- | 0 16 | 2 22 | 4 28 | 6 34 | 8 40 | 10 46 | 13 51 | 15 57 | 17 63 | 19 69 | 22 74 | 24 80 | 26 86 | 29 91 | 31 97 | 34 102 | 36 108 | 38 111 | 41 119 |
| 9 | -- | 0 18 | 2 25 | 4 32 | 7 38 | 10 44 | 12 51 | 15 57 | 17 64 | 20 70 | 23 76 | 26 82 | 28 89 | 31 95 | 34 101 | 37 107 | 39 114 | 42 120 | 45 126 | 48 132 |
| 10 | -- | 0 20 | 3 27 | 5 35 | 8 42 | 11 49 | 14 56 | 17 63 | 20 70 | 23 77 | 26 84 | 29 91 | 33 97 | 36 104 | 39 111 | 42 118 | 45 125 | 48 132 | 52 138 | 55 145 |
| 11 | -- | 0 22 | 3 30 | 6 38 | 9 46 | 13 53 | 16 61 | 19 69 | 23 76 | 26 84 | 30 91 | 33 99 | 37 106 | 40 114 | 44 121 | 47 129 | 51 136 | 55 143 | 58 151 | 62 158 |
| 12 | -- | 1 23 | 4 32 | 7 41 | 11 49 | 14 58 | 18 66 | 22 74 | 26 82 | 29 91 | 33 99 | 37 107 | 41 115 | 45 123 | 49 131 | 53 139 | 57 147 | 61 155 | 65 163 | 69 171 |
| 13 | -- | 1 25 | 4 35 | 8 44 | 12 53 | 16 62 | 20 71 | 24 80 | 28 89 | 33 97 | 37 106 | 41 115 | 45 124 | 50 132 | 54 141 | 59 149 | 63 158 | 67 167 | 72 175 | 76 184 |
| 14 | -- | 1 27 | 5 37 | 9 47 | 13 57 | 17 67 | 22 76 | 26 86 | 31 95 | 36 104 | 40 114 | 45 123 | 50 132 | 55 141 | 59 151 | 64 160 | 67 171 | 74 178 | 78 188 | 83 197 |
| 15 | -- | 1 29 | 5 40 | 10 50 | 14 61 | 19 71 | 24 81 | 29 91 | 34 101 | 39 111 | 44 121 | 49 131 | 54 141 | 59 151 | 64 161 | 70 170 | 75 180 | 80 190 | 85 200 | 90 210 |
| 16 | -- | 1 31 | 6 42 | 11 53 | 15 65 | 21 75 | 26 86 | 31 97 | 37 107 | 42 118 | 47 129 | 53 139 | 59 149 | 64 160 | 70 170 | 75 181 | 81 191 | 86 202 | 92 212 | 98 222 |
| 17 | -- | 2 32 | 6 45 | 11 57 | 17 68 | 22 80 | 28 91 | 34 102 | 39 114 | 45 125 | 51 136 | 57 147 | 63 158 | 67 171 | 75 180 | 81 191 | 87 202 | 93 213 | 99 224 | 105 235 |
| 18 | -- | 2 34 | 7 47 | 12 60 | 18 72 | 24 84 | 30 96 | 36 108 | 42 120 | 48 132 | 55 143 | 61 155 | 67 167 | 74 178 | 80 190 | 86 202 | 93 213 | 99 225 | 106 236 | 112 248 |
| 19 | -- | 2 36 | 7 50 | 13 63 | 19 76 | 25 89 | 32 101 | 38 111 | 45 126 | 52 138 | 58 151 | 65 163 | 72 175 | 78 188 | 85 200 | 92 212 | 99 224 | 106 236 | 113 248 | 119 261 |
| 20 | -- | 2 38 | 8 52 | 13 67 | 20 80 | 27 93 | 34 106 | 41 119 | 48 132 | 55 145 | 62 158 | 69 171 | 76 184 | 83 197 | 90 210 | 98 222 | 105 235 | 112 248 | 119 261 | 127 273 |

*Continued*

## TABLE B.5   Critical Values of Mann-Whitney U and U'—*Continued*

### One-Tailed $\alpha = .05$, Two-Tailed $\alpha = .10$

| $N_2$ \ $N_1$ | 1 | 2 | 3 | 4 | 5 | 6 | 7 | 8 | 9 | 10 | 11 | 12 | 13 | 14 | 15 | 16 | 17 | 18 | 19 | 20 |
|---|---|---|---|---|---|---|---|---|---|---|---|---|---|---|---|---|---|---|---|---|
| 1 | -- | -- | -- | -- | -- | -- | -- | -- | -- | -- | -- | -- | -- | -- | -- | -- | -- | -- | 0/19 | 0/20 |
| 2 | -- | -- | -- | -- | 0/10 | 0/12 | 0/14 | 1/15 | 1/17 | 1/19 | 1/21 | 2/22 | 2/24 | 2/26 | 3/27 | 3/29 | 3/31 | 4/32 | 4/34 | 4/36 |
| 3 | -- | -- | 0/9 | 0/12 | 1/14 | 2/16 | 2/19 | 3/21 | 3/24 | 4/26 | 5/28 | 5/31 | 6/33 | 7/35 | 7/38 | 8/40 | 9/42 | 9/45 | 10/47 | 11/49 |
| 4 | -- | -- | 0/12 | 1/15 | 2/18 | 3/21 | 4/24 | 5/27 | 6/30 | 7/33 | 8/36 | 9/39 | 10/42 | 11/45 | 12/48 | 14/50 | 15/53 | 16/56 | 17/59 | 18/62 |
| 5 | -- | 0/10 | 1/14 | 2/18 | 4/21 | 5/25 | 6/29 | 8/32 | 9/36 | 11/39 | 12/43 | 13/47 | 15/50 | 16/54 | 18/57 | 19/61 | 20/65 | 22/68 | 23/72 | 25/75 |
| 6 | -- | 0/12 | 2/16 | 3/21 | 5/25 | 7/29 | 8/34 | 10/38 | 12/42 | 14/46 | 16/50 | 17/55 | 19/59 | 21/63 | 23/67 | 25/71 | 26/76 | 28/80 | 30/84 | 32/88 |
| 7 | -- | 0/14 | 2/19 | 4/24 | 6/29 | 8/34 | 11/38 | 13/43 | 15/48 | 17/53 | 19/58 | 21/63 | 24/67 | 26/72 | 28/77 | 30/82 | 33/86 | 35/91 | 37/96 | 39/101 |
| 8 | -- | 1/15 | 3/21 | 5/27 | 8/32 | 10/38 | 13/43 | 15/49 | 18/54 | 20/60 | 23/65 | 26/70 | 28/76 | 31/81 | 33/87 | 36/92 | 39/97 | 41/103 | 44/108 | 47/113 |
| 9 | -- | 1/17 | 3/24 | 6/30 | 9/36 | 12/42 | 15/48 | 18/54 | 21/60 | 24/66 | 27/72 | 30/78 | 33/84 | 36/90 | 39/96 | 42/102 | 45/108 | 48/114 | 51/120 | 54/126 |
| 10 | -- | 1/19 | 4/26 | 7/33 | 11/39 | 14/46 | 17/53 | 20/60 | 24/66 | 27/73 | 31/79 | 34/86 | 37/93 | 41/99 | 44/106 | 48/112 | 51/119 | 55/125 | 58/132 | 62/138 |
| 11 | -- | 1/21 | 5/28 | 8/36 | 12/43 | 16/50 | 19/58 | 23/65 | 27/72 | 31/79 | 34/87 | 38/94 | 42/101 | 46/108 | 50/115 | 54/122 | 57/130 | 61/137 | 65/144 | 69/151 |
| 12 | -- | 2/22 | 5/31 | 9/39 | 13/47 | 17/55 | 21/63 | 26/70 | 30/78 | 34/86 | 38/94 | 42/102 | 47/109 | 51/117 | 55/125 | 60/132 | 64/140 | 68/148 | 72/156 | 77/163 |
| 13 | -- | 2/24 | 6/33 | 10/42 | 15/50 | 19/59 | 24/67 | 28/76 | 33/84 | 37/93 | 42/101 | 47/109 | 51/118 | 56/126 | 61/134 | 65/143 | 70/151 | 75/159 | 80/167 | 84/176 |
| 14 | -- | 2/26 | 7/35 | 11/45 | 16/54 | 21/63 | 26/72 | 31/81 | 36/90 | 41/99 | 46/108 | 51/117 | 56/126 | 61/135 | 66/144 | 71/153 | 77/161 | 82/170 | 87/179 | 92/188 |
| 15 | -- | 3/27 | 7/38 | 12/48 | 18/57 | 23/67 | 28/77 | 33/87 | 39/96 | 44/106 | 50/115 | 55/125 | 61/134 | 66/144 | 72/153 | 77/163 | 83/172 | 88/182 | 94/191 | 100/200 |
| 16 | -- | 3/29 | 8/40 | 14/50 | 19/61 | 25/71 | 30/82 | 36/92 | 42/102 | 48/112 | 54/122 | 60/132 | 65/143 | 71/153 | 77/163 | 83/173 | 89/183 | 95/193 | 101/203 | 107/213 |
| 17 | -- | 3/31 | 9/42 | 15/53 | 20/65 | 26/76 | 33/86 | 39/97 | 45/108 | 51/119 | 57/130 | 64/140 | 70/151 | 77/161 | 83/172 | 89/183 | 96/193 | 102/204 | 109/214 | 115/225 |
| 18 | -- | 4/32 | 9/45 | 16/56 | 22/68 | 28/80 | 35/91 | 41/103 | 48/114 | 55/123 | 61/137 | 68/148 | 75/159 | 82/170 | 88/182 | 95/193 | 102/204 | 109/215 | 116/226 | 123/237 |
| 19 | 0/19 | 4/34 | 10/47 | 17/59 | 23/72 | 30/84 | 37/96 | 44/108 | 51/120 | 58/132 | 65/144 | 72/156 | 80/167 | 87/179 | 94/191 | 101/203 | 109/214 | 116/226 | 123/238 | 130/250 |
| 20 | 0/20 | 4/36 | 11/49 | 18/62 | 25/75 | 32/88 | 39/101 | 47/113 | 54/126 | 62/138 | 69/151 | 77/163 | 84/176 | 92/188 | 100/200 | 107/213 | 115/225 | 123/237 | 130/250 | 138/262 |

**TABLE B.6 Critical Values of Wilcoxon T Statistic (One- and Two-Tailed Levels of Significance)**

The procedures for using Table B.6 are discussed in Chapter 9. The decision rule is as follows: If the computed T value is equal to or smaller than the table value at the intersect of $N$ and level of significance, reject $H_0$.

| | Level of significance for one-tailed test | | |
| | .025 | .01 | .005 |
| | Level of significance for two-tailed test | | |
| $N$ | .05 | .02 | .01 |
|---|---|---|---|
| 6 | 0 | — | — |
| 7 | 2 | 0 | — |
| 8 | 4 | 2 | 0 |
| 9 | 6 | 3 | 2 |
| 10 | 8 | 5 | 3 |
| 11 | 11 | 7 | 5 |
| 12 | 14 | 10 | 7 |
| 13 | 17 | 13 | 10 |
| 14 | 21 | 16 | 13 |
| 15 | 25 | 20 | 16 |
| 16 | 30 | 24 | 20 |
| 17 | 35 | 28 | 23 |
| 18 | 40 | 33 | 28 |
| 19 | 46 | 38 | 32 |
| 20 | 52 | 43 | 38 |
| 21 | 59 | 49 | 43 |
| 22 | 66 | 56 | 49 |
| 23 | 73 | 62 | 55 |
| 24 | 81 | 69 | 61 |
| 25 | 89 | 77 | 68 |

Source: From F. Wilcoxon, *Some Rapid Approximate Statistical Procedures* (New York: American Cyanamid Company, 1964), p. 28, as adapted in Sidney Siegel, *Nonparametric Statistics for the Behavioral Sciences* (New York: McGraw-Hill, 1956), p. 254.

**TABLE B.7   The Distribution of F (Two-Tailed Levels of Significance .05, light type, .01, bold type)**

The procedures for using Table B.10 are discussed in Chapters 8 and 10. The decision rule is as follows: If the F statistic is equal to or larger than the table value at the intersect of the two degrees of freedom, reject $H_0$.

$f_1$, Degrees of Freedom (for greater mean square)

| $f_2$ | 1 | 2 | 3 | 4 | 5 | 6 | 7 | 8 | 9 | 10 | 11 | 12 | 14 | 16 | 20 | 24 | 30 | 40 | 50 | 75 | 100 | 200 | 500 | ∞ |
|---|---|---|---|---|---|---|---|---|---|---|---|---|---|---|---|---|---|---|---|---|---|---|---|---|
| 1 | 161 / **4,052** | 200 / **4,999** | 216 / **5,403** | 225 / **5,625** | 230 / **5,764** | 234 / **5,859** | 237 / **5,928** | 239 / **5,981** | 241 / **6,022** | 242 / **6,056** | 243 / **6,082** | 244 / **6,106** | 245 / **6,142** | 246 / **6,169** | 248 / **6,208** | 249 / **6,234** | 250 / **6,261** | 251 / **6,286** | 252 / **6,302** | 253 / **6,323** | 253 / **6,334** | 254 / **6,352** | 254 / **6,361** | 254 / **6,366** |
| 2 | 18.51 / **98.49** | 19.00 / **99.00** | 19.16 / **99.17** | 19.25 / **99.25** | 19.30 / **99.30** | 19.33 / **99.33** | 19.36 / **99.36** | 19.37 / **99.37** | 19.38 / **99.39** | 19.39 / **99.40** | 19.40 / **99.41** | 19.41 / **99.42** | 19.42 / **99.43** | 19.43 / **99.44** | 19.44 / **99.45** | 19.45 / **99.46** | 19.46 / **99.47** | 19.47 / **99.48** | 19.47 / **99.48** | 19.48 / **99.49** | 19.49 / **99.49** | 19.49 / **99.49** | 19.50 / **99.50** | 19.50 / **99.50** |
| 3 | 10.13 / **34.12** | 9.55 / **30.82** | 9.28 / **29.46** | 9.12 / **28.71** | 9.01 / **28.24** | 8.94 / **27.91** | 8.88 / **27.67** | 8.84 / **27.49** | 8.81 / **27.34** | 8.78 / **27.23** | 8.76 / **27.13** | 8.74 / **27.05** | 8.71 / **26.92** | 8.69 / **26.83** | 8.66 / **26.69** | 8.64 / **26.60** | 8.62 / **26.50** | 8.60 / **26.41** | 8.58 / **26.35** | 8.57 / **26.27** | 8.56 / **26.23** | 8.54 / **26.18** | 8.54 / **26.14** | 8.53 / **26.12** |
| 4 | 7.71 / **21.20** | 6.94 / **18.00** | 6.59 / **16.69** | 6.39 / **15.98** | 6.26 / **15.52** | 6.16 / **15.21** | 6.09 / **14.98** | 6.04 / **14.80** | 6.00 / **14.66** | 5.96 / **14.54** | 5.93 / **14.45** | 5.91 / **14.37** | 5.87 / **14.24** | 5.84 / **14.15** | 5.80 / **14.02** | 5.77 / **13.93** | 5.74 / **13.83** | 5.71 / **13.74** | 5.70 / **13.69** | 5.68 / **13.61** | 5.66 / **13.57** | 5.65 / **13.52** | 5.64 / **13.48** | 5.63 / **13.46** |
| 5 | 6.61 / **16.26** | 5.79 / **13.27** | 5.41 / **12.06** | 5.19 / **11.39** | 5.05 / **10.97** | 4.95 / **10.67** | 4.88 / **10.45** | 4.82 / **10.29** | 4.78 / **10.15** | 4.74 / **10.05** | 4.70 / **9.96** | 4.68 / **9.89** | 4.64 / **9.77** | 4.60 / **9.68** | 4.56 / **9.55** | 4.53 / **9.47** | 4.50 / **9.38** | 4.46 / **9.29** | 4.44 / **9.24** | 4.42 / **9.17** | 4.40 / **9.13** | 4.38 / **9.07** | 4.37 / **9.04** | 4.36 / **9.02** |
| 6 | 5.99 / **13.74** | 5.14 / **10.92** | 4.76 / **9.78** | 4.53 / **9.15** | 4.39 / **8.75** | 4.28 / **8.47** | 4.21 / **8.26** | 4.15 / **8.10** | 4.10 / **7.98** | 4.06 / **7.87** | 4.03 / **7.79** | 4.00 / **7.72** | 3.96 / **7.60** | 3.92 / **7.52** | 3.87 / **7.39** | 3.84 / **7.31** | 3.81 / **7.23** | 3.77 / **7.14** | 3.75 / **7.09** | 3.72 / **7.02** | 3.71 / **6.99** | 3.69 / **6.94** | 3.68 / **6.90** | 3.67 / **6.88** |
| 7 | 5.59 / **12.25** | 4.74 / **9.55** | 4.35 / **8.45** | 4.12 / **7.85** | 3.97 / **7.46** | 3.87 / **7.19** | 3.79 / **7.00** | 3.73 / **6.84** | 3.68 / **6.71** | 3.63 / **6.62** | 3.60 / **6.54** | 3.57 / **6.47** | 3.52 / **6.35** | 3.49 / **6.27** | 3.44 / **6.15** | 3.41 / **6.07** | 3.38 / **5.98** | 3.34 / **5.90** | 3.32 / **5.85** | 3.29 / **5.78** | 3.28 / **5.75** | 3.25 / **5.70** | 3.24 / **5.67** | 3.23 / **5.65** |
| 8 | 5.32 / **11.26** | 4.46 / **8.65** | 4.07 / **7.59** | 3.84 / **7.01** | 3.69 / **6.63** | 3.58 / **6.37** | 3.50 / **6.19** | 3.44 / **6.03** | 3.39 / **5.91** | 3.34 / **5.82** | 3.31 / **5.74** | 3.28 / **5.67** | 3.23 / **5.56** | 3.20 / **5.48** | 3.15 / **5.36** | 3.12 / **5.28** | 3.08 / **5.20** | 3.05 / **5.11** | 3.03 / **5.06** | 3.00 / **5.00** | 2.98 / **4.96** | 2.96 / **4.91** | 2.94 / **4.88** | 2.93 / **4.86** |
| 9 | 5.12 / **10.56** | 4.26 / **8.02** | 3.86 / **6.99** | 3.63 / **6.42** | 3.48 / **6.06** | 3.37 / **5.80** | 3.29 / **5.62** | 3.23 / **5.47** | 3.18 / **5.35** | 3.13 / **5.26** | 3.10 / **5.18** | 3.07 / **5.11** | 3.02 / **5.00** | 2.98 / **4.92** | 2.93 / **4.80** | 2.90 / **4.73** | 2.86 / **4.64** | 2.82 / **4.56** | 2.80 / **4.51** | 2.77 / **4.45** | 2.76 / **4.41** | 2.73 / **4.36** | 2.72 / **4.33** | 2.71 / **4.31** |
| 10 | 4.96 / **10.04** | 4.10 / **7.56** | 3.71 / **6.55** | 3.48 / **5.99** | 3.33 / **5.64** | 3.22 / **5.39** | 3.14 / **5.21** | 3.07 / **5.06** | 3.02 / **4.95** | 2.97 / **4.85** | 2.94 / **4.78** | 2.91 / **4.71** | 2.86 / **4.60** | 2.82 / **4.52** | 2.77 / **4.41** | 2.74 / **4.33** | 2.70 / **4.25** | 2.67 / **4.17** | 2.64 / **4.12** | 2.61 / **4.05** | 2.59 / **4.01** | 2.56 / **3.96** | 2.55 / **3.93** | 2.54 / **3.91** |
| 11 | 4.84 / **9.65** | 3.98 / **7.20** | 3.59 / **6.22** | 3.36 / **5.67** | 3.20 / **5.32** | 3.09 / **5.07** | 3.01 / **4.88** | 2.95 / **4.74** | 2.90 / **4.63** | 2.86 / **4.54** | 2.82 / **4.46** | 2.79 / **4.40** | 2.74 / **4.29** | 2.70 / **4.21** | 2.65 / **4.10** | 2.61 / **4.02** | 2.57 / **3.94** | 2.53 / **3.86** | 2.50 / **3.80** | 2.47 / **3.74** | 2.45 / **3.70** | 2.42 / **3.66** | 2.41 / **3.62** | 2.40 / **3.60** |
| 12 | 4.75 / **9.33** | 3.88 / **6.93** | 3.49 / **5.95** | 3.26 / **5.41** | 3.11 / **5.06** | 3.00 / **4.82** | 2.92 / **4.65** | 2.85 / **4.50** | 2.80 / **4.39** | 2.76 / **4.30** | 2.72 / **4.22** | 2.69 / **4.16** | 2.64 / **4.05** | 2.60 / **3.98** | 2.54 / **3.86** | 2.50 / **3.78** | 2.46 / **3.70** | 2.42 / **3.61** | 2.40 / **3.56** | 2.36 / **3.49** | 2.35 / **3.46** | 2.32 / **3.41** | 2.31 / **3.38** | 2.30 / **3.36** |
| 13 | 4.67 / **9.07** | 3.80 / **6.70** | 3.41 / **5.74** | 3.18 / **5.20** | 3.02 / **4.86** | 2.92 / **4.62** | 2.84 / **4.44** | 2.77 / **4.30** | 2.72 / **4.19** | 2.67 / **4.10** | 2.63 / **4.02** | 2.60 / **3.96** | 2.55 / **3.85** | 2.51 / **3.78** | 2.46 / **3.67** | 2.42 / **3.59** | 2.38 / **3.51** | 2.34 / **3.42** | 2.32 / **3.37** | 2.28 / **3.30** | 2.26 / **3.27** | 2.24 / **3.21** | 2.22 / **3.18** | 2.21 / **3.16** |

Source: Reprinted by permission from *Statistical Methods*, Seventh Edition, by George W. Snedecor and William G. Cochran, copyright © 1980 by The Iowa State University Press, Ames, Iowa 50010.

**TABLE B.7  The Distribution of F—*Continued***

$f_1$, Degrees of Freedom (for greater mean square)

| $f_2$ | 1 | 2 | 3 | 4 | 5 | 6 | 7 | 8 | 9 | 10 | 11 | 12 | 14 | 16 | 20 | 24 | 30 | 40 | 50 | 75 | 100 | 200 | 500 | ∞ |
|---|---|---|---|---|---|---|---|---|---|---|---|---|---|---|---|---|---|---|---|---|---|---|---|---|
| 14 | 4.60 / 8.86 | 3.74 / 6.51 | 3.34 / 5.56 | 3.11 / 5.03 | 2.96 / 4.69 | 2.85 / 4.46 | 2.77 / 4.28 | 2.70 / 4.14 | 2.65 / 4.03 | 2.60 / 3.94 | 2.56 / 3.86 | 2.53 / 3.80 | 2.48 / 3.70 | 2.44 / 3.62 | 2.39 / 3.51 | 2.35 / 3.43 | 2.31 / 3.34 | 2.27 / 3.26 | 2.24 / 3.21 | 2.21 / 3.14 | 2.19 / 3.11 | 2.16 / 3.06 | 2.14 / 3.02 | 2.13 / 3.00 |
| 15 | 4.54 / 8.68 | 3.68 / 6.36 | 3.29 / 5.42 | 3.06 / 4.89 | 2.90 / 4.56 | 2.79 / 4.32 | 2.70 / 4.14 | 2.64 / 4.00 | 2.59 / 3.89 | 2.55 / 3.80 | 2.51 / 3.73 | 2.48 / 3.67 | 2.43 / 3.56 | 2.39 / 3.48 | 2.33 / 3.36 | 2.29 / 3.29 | 2.25 / 3.20 | 2.21 / 3.12 | 2.18 / 3.07 | 2.15 / 3.00 | 2.12 / 2.97 | 2.10 / 2.92 | 2.08 / 2.89 | 2.07 / 2.87 |
| 16 | 4.49 / 8.53 | 3.63 / 6.23 | 3.24 / 5.29 | 3.01 / 4.77 | 2.85 / 4.44 | 2.74 / 4.20 | 2.66 / 4.03 | 2.59 / 3.89 | 2.54 / 3.78 | 2.49 / 3.69 | 2.45 / 3.61 | 2.42 / 3.55 | 2.37 / 3.45 | 2.33 / 3.37 | 2.28 / 3.25 | 2.24 / 3.18 | 2.20 / 3.10 | 2.16 / 3.01 | 2.13 / 2.96 | 2.09 / 2.89 | 2.07 / 2.86 | 2.04 / 2.80 | 2.02 / 2.77 | 2.01 / 2.75 |
| 17 | 4.45 / 8.40 | 3.59 / 6.11 | 3.20 / 5.18 | 2.96 / 4.67 | 2.81 / 4.34 | 2.70 / 4.10 | 2.62 / 3.93 | 2.55 / 3.79 | 2.50 / 3.68 | 2.45 / 3.59 | 2.41 / 3.52 | 2.38 / 3.45 | 2.33 / 3.35 | 2.29 / 3.27 | 2.23 / 3.16 | 2.19 / 3.08 | 2.15 / 3.00 | 2.11 / 2.92 | 2.08 / 2.86 | 2.04 / 2.79 | 2.02 / 2.76 | 1.99 / 2.70 | 1.97 / 2.67 | 1.96 / 2.65 |
| 18 | 4.41 / 8.28 | 3.55 / 6.01 | 3.16 / 5.09 | 2.93 / 4.58 | 2.77 / 4.25 | 2.66 / 4.01 | 2.58 / 3.85 | 2.51 / 3.71 | 2.46 / 3.60 | 2.41 / 3.51 | 2.37 / 3.44 | 2.34 / 3.37 | 2.29 / 3.27 | 2.25 / 3.19 | 2.19 / 3.07 | 2.15 / 3.00 | 2.11 / 2.91 | 2.07 / 2.83 | 2.04 / 2.78 | 2.00 / 2.71 | 1.98 / 2.68 | 1.95 / 2.62 | 1.93 / 2.59 | 1.92 / 2.57 |
| 19 | 4.38 / 8.18 | 3.52 / 5.93 | 3.13 / 5.01 | 2.90 / 4.50 | 2.74 / 4.17 | 2.63 / 3.94 | 2.55 / 3.77 | 2.48 / 3.63 | 2.43 / 3.52 | 2.38 / 3.43 | 2.34 / 3.36 | 2.31 / 3.30 | 2.26 / 3.19 | 2.21 / 3.12 | 2.15 / 3.00 | 2.11 / 2.92 | 2.07 / 2.84 | 2.02 / 2.76 | 2.00 / 2.70 | 1.96 / 2.63 | 1.94 / 2.60 | 1.91 / 2.54 | 1.90 / 2.51 | 1.88 / 2.49 |
| 20 | 4.35 / 8.10 | 3.49 / 5.85 | 3.10 / 4.94 | 2.87 / 4.43 | 2.71 / 4.10 | 2.60 / 3.87 | 2.52 / 3.71 | 2.45 / 3.56 | 2.40 / 3.45 | 2.35 / 3.37 | 2.31 / 3.30 | 2.28 / 3.23 | 2.23 / 3.13 | 2.18 / 3.05 | 2.12 / 2.94 | 2.08 / 2.86 | 2.04 / 2.77 | 1.99 / 2.69 | 1.96 / 2.63 | 1.92 / 2.56 | 1.90 / 2.53 | 1.87 / 2.47 | 1.85 / 2.44 | 1.84 / 2.42 |
| 21 | 4.32 / 8.02 | 3.47 / 5.78 | 3.07 / 4.87 | 2.84 / 4.37 | 2.68 / 4.04 | 2.57 / 3.81 | 2.49 / 3.65 | 2.42 / 3.51 | 2.37 / 3.40 | 2.32 / 3.31 | 2.28 / 3.24 | 2.25 / 3.17 | 2.20 / 3.07 | 2.15 / 2.99 | 2.09 / 2.88 | 2.05 / 2.80 | 2.00 / 2.72 | 1.96 / 2.63 | 1.93 / 2.58 | 1.89 / 2.51 | 1.87 / 2.47 | 1.84 / 2.42 | 1.82 / 2.38 | 1.81 / 2.36 |
| 22 | 4.30 / 7.94 | 3.44 / 5.72 | 3.05 / 4.82 | 2.82 / 4.31 | 2.66 / 3.99 | 2.55 / 3.76 | 2.47 / 3.59 | 2.40 / 3.45 | 2.35 / 3.35 | 2.30 / 3.26 | 2.26 / 3.18 | 2.23 / 3.12 | 2.18 / 3.02 | 2.13 / 2.94 | 2.07 / 2.83 | 2.03 / 2.75 | 1.98 / 2.67 | 1.93 / 2.58 | 1.91 / 2.53 | 1.87 / 2.46 | 1.84 / 2.42 | 1.81 / 2.37 | 1.80 / 2.33 | 1.78 / 2.31 |
| 23 | 4.28 / 7.88 | 3.42 / 5.66 | 3.03 / 4.76 | 2.80 / 4.26 | 2.64 / 3.94 | 2.53 / 3.71 | 2.45 / 3.54 | 2.38 / 3.41 | 2.32 / 3.30 | 2.28 / 3.21 | 2.24 / 3.14 | 2.20 / 3.07 | 2.14 / 2.97 | 2.10 / 2.89 | 2.04 / 2.78 | 2.00 / 2.70 | 1.96 / 2.62 | 1.91 / 2.53 | 1.88 / 2.48 | 1.84 / 2.41 | 1.82 / 2.37 | 1.79 / 2.32 | 1.77 / 2.28 | 1.76 / 2.26 |
| 24 | 4.26 / 7.82 | 3.40 / 5.61 | 3.01 / 4.72 | 2.78 / 4.22 | 2.62 / 3.90 | 2.51 / 3.67 | 2.43 / 3.50 | 2.36 / 3.36 | 2.30 / 3.25 | 2.26 / 3.17 | 2.22 / 3.09 | 2.18 / 3.03 | 2.13 / 2.93 | 2.09 / 2.85 | 2.02 / 2.74 | 1.98 / 2.66 | 1.94 / 2.58 | 1.89 / 2.49 | 1.86 / 2.44 | 1.82 / 2.36 | 1.80 / 2.33 | 1.76 / 2.27 | 1.74 / 2.23 | 1.73 / 2.21 |
| 25 | 4.24 / 7.77 | 3.38 / 5.57 | 2.99 / 4.68 | 2.76 / 4.18 | 2.60 / 3.86 | 2.49 / 3.63 | 2.41 / 3.46 | 2.34 / 3.32 | 2.28 / 3.21 | 2.24 / 3.13 | 2.20 / 3.05 | 2.16 / 2.99 | 2.11 / 2.89 | 2.06 / 2.81 | 2.00 / 2.70 | 1.96 / 2.62 | 1.92 / 2.54 | 1.87 / 2.45 | 1.84 / 2.40 | 1.80 / 2.32 | 1.77 / 2.29 | 1.74 / 2.23 | 1.72 / 2.19 | 1.71 / 2.17 |
| 26 | 4.22 / 7.72 | 3.37 / 5.53 | 2.98 / 4.64 | 2.74 / 4.14 | 2.59 / 3.82 | 2.47 / 3.59 | 2.39 / 3.42 | 2.32 / 3.29 | 2.27 / 3.17 | 2.22 / 3.09 | 2.18 / 3.02 | 2.15 / 2.96 | 2.10 / 2.86 | 2.05 / 2.77 | 1.99 / 2.66 | 1.95 / 2.58 | 1.90 / 2.50 | 1.85 / 2.41 | 1.82 / 2.36 | 1.78 / 2.28 | 1.76 / 2.25 | 1.72 / 2.19 | 1.70 / 2.15 | 1.69 / 2.13 |

*Continued*

**TABLE B.7  The Distribution of F—Continued**

$f_1$ Degrees of Freedom (for greater mean square)

| $f_2$ | 1 | 2 | 3 | 4 | 5 | 6 | 7 | 8 | 9 | 10 | 11 | 12 | 14 | 16 | 20 | 24 | 30 | 40 | 50 | 75 | 100 | 200 | 500 | ∞ |
|---|---|---|---|---|---|---|---|---|---|---|---|---|---|---|---|---|---|---|---|---|---|---|---|---|
| 27 | 4.21/7.68 | 3.35/5.49 | 2.96/4.60 | 2.73/4.11 | 2.57/3.79 | 2.46/3.56 | 2.37/3.39 | 2.30/3.26 | 2.25/3.14 | 2.20/3.06 | 2.16/2.98 | 2.13/2.93 | 2.08/2.83 | 2.03/2.74 | 1.97/2.63 | 1.93/2.55 | 1.88/2.47 | 1.84/2.38 | 1.80/2.33 | 1.76/2.25 | 1.74/2.21 | 1.71/2.16 | 1.68/2.12 | 1.67/2.10 |
| 28 | 4.20/7.64 | 3.34/5.45 | 2.95/4.57 | 2.71/4.07 | 2.56/3.76 | 2.44/3.53 | 2.36/3.36 | 2.29/3.23 | 2.24/3.11 | 2.19/3.03 | 2.15/2.95 | 2.12/2.90 | 2.06/2.80 | 2.02/2.71 | 1.96/2.60 | 1.91/2.52 | 1.87/2.44 | 1.81/2.35 | 1.78/2.30 | 1.75/2.22 | 1.72/2.18 | 1.69/2.13 | 1.67/2.09 | 1.65/2.06 |
| 29 | 4.18/7.60 | 3.33/5.42 | 2.93/4.54 | 2.70/4.04 | 2.54/3.73 | 2.43/3.50 | 2.35/3.33 | 2.28/3.20 | 2.22/3.08 | 2.18/3.00 | 2.14/2.92 | 2.10/2.87 | 2.05/2.77 | 2.00/2.68 | 1.94/2.57 | 1.90/2.49 | 1.85/2.41 | 1.80/2.32 | 1.77/2.27 | 1.73/2.19 | 1.71/2.15 | 1.68/2.10 | 1.65/2.06 | 1.64/2.03 |
| 30 | 4.17/7.56 | 3.32/5.39 | 2.92/4.51 | 2.69/4.02 | 2.53/3.70 | 2.42/3.47 | 2.34/3.30 | 2.27/3.17 | 2.21/3.06 | 2.16/2.98 | 2.12/2.90 | 2.09/2.84 | 2.04/2.74 | 1.99/2.66 | 1.93/2.55 | 1.89/2.47 | 1.84/2.38 | 1.79/2.29 | 1.76/2.24 | 1.72/2.16 | 1.69/2.13 | 1.66/2.07 | 1.64/2.03 | 1.62/2.01 |
| 32 | 4.15/7.50 | 3.30/5.34 | 2.90/4.46 | 2.67/3.97 | 2.51/3.66 | 2.40/3.42 | 2.32/3.25 | 2.25/3.12 | 2.19/3.01 | 2.14/2.94 | 2.10/2.86 | 2.07/2.80 | 2.02/2.70 | 1.97/2.62 | 1.91/2.51 | 1.86/2.42 | 1.82/2.34 | 1.76/2.25 | 1.74/2.20 | 1.69/2.12 | 1.67/2.08 | 1.64/2.02 | 1.61/1.98 | 1.59/1.96 |
| 34 | 4.13/7.44 | 3.28/5.29 | 2.88/4.42 | 2.65/3.93 | 2.49/3.61 | 2.38/3.38 | 2.30/3.21 | 2.23/3.08 | 2.17/2.97 | 2.12/2.89 | 2.08/2.82 | 2.05/2.76 | 2.00/2.66 | 1.95/2.58 | 1.89/2.47 | 1.84/2.38 | 1.80/2.30 | 1.74/2.21 | 1.71/2.15 | 1.67/2.08 | 1.64/2.04 | 1.61/1.98 | 1.59/1.94 | 1.57/1.91 |
| 36 | 4.11/7.39 | 3.26/5.25 | 2.86/4.38 | 2.63/3.89 | 2.48/3.58 | 2.36/3.35 | 2.28/3.18 | 2.21/3.04 | 2.15/2.94 | 2.10/2.86 | 2.06/2.78 | 2.03/2.72 | 1.98/2.62 | 1.93/2.54 | 1.87/2.43 | 1.82/2.35 | 1.78/2.26 | 1.72/2.17 | 1.69/2.12 | 1.65/2.04 | 1.62/2.00 | 1.59/1.94 | 1.56/1.90 | 1.55/1.87 |
| 38 | 4.10/7.35 | 3.25/5.21 | 2.85/4.34 | 2.62/3.86 | 2.46/3.54 | 2.35/3.32 | 2.26/3.15 | 2.19/3.02 | 2.14/2.91 | 2.09/2.82 | 2.05/2.75 | 2.02/2.69 | 1.96/2.59 | 1.92/2.51 | 1.85/2.40 | 1.80/2.32 | 1.76/2.22 | 1.71/2.14 | 1.67/2.08 | 1.63/2.00 | 1.60/1.97 | 1.57/1.90 | 1.54/1.86 | 1.53/1.84 |
| 40 | 4.08/7.31 | 3.23/5.18 | 2.84/4.31 | 2.61/3.83 | 2.45/3.51 | 2.34/3.29 | 2.25/3.12 | 2.18/2.99 | 2.12/2.88 | 2.07/2.80 | 2.04/2.73 | 2.00/2.66 | 1.95/2.56 | 1.90/2.49 | 1.84/2.37 | 1.79/2.29 | 1.74/2.20 | 1.69/2.11 | 1.66/2.05 | 1.61/1.97 | 1.59/1.94 | 1.55/1.88 | 1.53/1.84 | 1.51/1.81 |
| 42 | 4.07/7.27 | 3.22/5.15 | 2.83/4.29 | 2.59/3.80 | 2.44/3.49 | 2.32/3.26 | 2.24/3.10 | 2.17/2.96 | 2.11/2.86 | 2.06/2.77 | 2.02/2.70 | 1.99/2.64 | 1.94/2.54 | 1.89/2.46 | 1.82/2.35 | 1.78/2.26 | 1.73/2.17 | 1.68/2.08 | 1.64/2.02 | 1.60/1.94 | 1.57/1.91 | 1.54/1.85 | 1.51/1.80 | 1.49/1.78 |
| 44 | 4.06/7.24 | 3.21/5.12 | 2.82/4.26 | 2.58/3.78 | 2.43/3.46 | 2.31/3.24 | 2.23/3.07 | 2.16/2.94 | 2.10/2.84 | 2.05/2.75 | 2.01/2.68 | 1.98/2.62 | 1.92/2.52 | 1.88/2.44 | 1.81/2.32 | 1.76/2.24 | 1.72/2.15 | 1.66/2.06 | 1.63/2.00 | 1.58/1.92 | 1.56/1.88 | 1.52/1.82 | 1.50/1.78 | 1.48/1.75 |
| 46 | 4.05/7.21 | 3.20/5.10 | 2.81/4.24 | 2.57/3.76 | 2.42/3.44 | 2.30/3.22 | 2.22/3.05 | 2.14/2.92 | 2.09/2.82 | 2.04/2.73 | 2.00/2.66 | 1.97/2.60 | 1.91/2.50 | 1.87/2.42 | 1.80/2.30 | 1.75/2.22 | 1.71/2.13 | 1.65/2.04 | 1.62/1.98 | 1.57/1.90 | 1.54/1.86 | 1.51/1.80 | 1.48/1.76 | 1.46/1.72 |
| 48 | 4.04/7.19 | 3.19/5.08 | 2.80/4.22 | 2.56/3.74 | 2.41/3.42 | 2.30/3.20 | 2.21/3.04 | 2.14/2.90 | 2.08/2.80 | 2.03/2.71 | 1.99/2.64 | 1.96/2.58 | 1.90/2.48 | 1.86/2.40 | 1.79/2.28 | 1.74/2.20 | 1.70/2.11 | 1.64/2.02 | 1.61/1.96 | 1.56/1.88 | 1.53/1.84 | 1.50/1.78 | 1.47/1.73 | 1.45/1.70 |

**TABLE B.7    The Distribution of F—*Continued***

$f_1$ Degrees of Freedom (for greater mean square)

| $f_2$ | 1 | 2 | 3 | 4 | 5 | 6 | 7 | 8 | 9 | 10 | 11 | 12 | 14 | 16 | 20 | 24 | 30 | 40 | 50 | 75 | 100 | 200 | 500 | ∞ | $f_2$ |
|---|---|---|---|---|---|---|---|---|---|---|---|---|---|---|---|---|---|---|---|---|---|---|---|---|---|
| 50 | 4.03/7.17 | 3.18/5.06 | 2.79/4.20 | 2.56/3.72 | 2.40/3.41 | 2.29/3.18 | 2.20/3.02 | 2.13/2.88 | 2.07/2.78 | 2.02/2.70 | 1.98/2.62 | 1.95/2.56 | 1.90/2.46 | 1.85/2.39 | 1.78/2.26 | 1.74/2.18 | 1.69/2.10 | 1.63/2.00 | 1.60/1.94 | 1.55/1.86 | 1.52/1.82 | 1.48/1.76 | 1.46/1.71 | 1.44/1.68 | 50 |
| 55 | 4.02/7.12 | 3.17/5.01 | 2.78/4.16 | 2.54/3.68 | 2.38/3.37 | 2.27/3.15 | 2.18/2.98 | 2.11/2.85 | 2.05/2.75 | 2.00/2.66 | 1.97/2.59 | 1.93/2.53 | 1.88/2.43 | 1.83/2.35 | 1.76/2.23 | 1.72/2.15 | 1.67/2.06 | 1.61/1.96 | 1.58/1.90 | 1.52/1.82 | 1.50/1.78 | 1.46/1.71 | 1.43/1.66 | 1.41/1.64 | 55 |
| 60 | 4.00/7.08 | 3.15/4.98 | 2.76/4.13 | 2.52/3.65 | 2.37/3.34 | 2.25/3.12 | 2.17/2.95 | 2.10/2.82 | 2.04/2.72 | 1.99/2.63 | 1.95/2.56 | 1.92/2.50 | 1.86/2.40 | 1.81/2.32 | 1.75/2.20 | 1.70/2.12 | 1.65/2.03 | 1.59/1.93 | 1.56/1.87 | 1.50/1.79 | 1.48/1.74 | 1.44/1.68 | 1.41/1.63 | 1.39/1.60 | 60 |
| 65 | 3.99/7.04 | 3.14/4.95 | 2.75/4.10 | 2.51/3.62 | 2.36/3.31 | 2.24/3.09 | 2.15/2.93 | 2.08/2.79 | 2.02/2.70 | 1.98/2.61 | 1.94/2.54 | 1.90/2.47 | 1.85/2.37 | 1.80/2.30 | 1.73/2.18 | 1.68/2.09 | 1.63/2.00 | 1.57/1.90 | 1.54/1.84 | 1.49/1.76 | 1.46/1.71 | 1.42/1.64 | 1.39/1.60 | 1.37/1.56 | 65 |
| 70 | 3.98/7.01 | 3.13/4.92 | 2.74/4.08 | 2.50/3.60 | 2.35/3.29 | 2.23/3.07 | 2.14/2.91 | 2.07/2.77 | 2.01/2.67 | 1.97/2.59 | 1.93/2.51 | 1.89/2.45 | 1.84/2.35 | 1.79/2.28 | 1.72/2.15 | 1.67/2.07 | 1.62/1.98 | 1.56/1.88 | 1.53/1.82 | 1.47/1.74 | 1.45/1.69 | 1.40/1.62 | 1.37/1.56 | 1.35/1.53 | 70 |
| 80 | 3.96/6.96 | 3.11/4.88 | 2.72/4.04 | 2.48/3.56 | 2.33/3.25 | 2.21/3.04 | 2.12/2.87 | 2.05/2.74 | 1.99/2.64 | 1.95/2.55 | 1.91/2.48 | 1.88/2.41 | 1.82/2.32 | 1.77/2.24 | 1.70/2.11 | 1.65/2.03 | 1.60/1.94 | 1.54/1.84 | 1.51/1.78 | 1.45/1.70 | 1.42/1.65 | 1.38/1.57 | 1.35/1.52 | 1.32/1.49 | 80 |
| 100 | 3.94/6.90 | 3.09/4.82 | 2.70/3.98 | 2.46/3.51 | 2.30/3.20 | 2.19/2.99 | 2.10/2.82 | 2.03/2.69 | 1.97/2.59 | 1.92/2.51 | 1.88/2.43 | 1.85/2.36 | 1.79/2.26 | 1.75/2.19 | 1.68/2.06 | 1.63/1.98 | 1.57/1.89 | 1.51/1.79 | 1.48/1.73 | 1.42/1.64 | 1.39/1.59 | 1.34/1.51 | 1.30/1.46 | 1.28/1.43 | 100 |
| 125 | 3.92/6.84 | 3.07/4.78 | 2.68/3.94 | 2.44/3.47 | 2.29/3.17 | 2.17/2.95 | 2.08/2.79 | 2.01/2.65 | 1.95/2.56 | 1.90/2.47 | 1.86/2.40 | 1.83/2.33 | 1.77/2.23 | 1.72/2.15 | 1.65/2.03 | 1.60/1.94 | 1.55/1.85 | 1.49/1.75 | 1.45/1.68 | 1.39/1.59 | 1.36/1.54 | 1.31/1.46 | 1.27/1.40 | 1.25/1.37 | 125 |
| 150 | 3.91/6.81 | 3.06/4.75 | 2.67/3.91 | 2.43/3.44 | 2.27/3.14 | 2.16/2.92 | 2.07/2.76 | 2.00/2.62 | 1.94/2.53 | 1.89/2.44 | 1.85/2.37 | 1.82/2.30 | 1.76/2.20 | 1.71/2.12 | 1.64/2.00 | 1.59/1.91 | 1.54/1.83 | 1.47/1.72 | 1.44/1.66 | 1.37/1.56 | 1.34/1.51 | 1.29/1.43 | 1.25/1.37 | 1.22/1.33 | 150 |
| 200 | 3.89/6.76 | 3.04/4.71 | 2.65/3.88 | 2.41/3.41 | 2.26/3.11 | 2.14/2.90 | 2.05/2.73 | 1.98/2.60 | 1.92/2.50 | 1.87/2.41 | 1.83/2.34 | 1.80/2.28 | 1.74/2.17 | 1.69/2.09 | 1.62/1.97 | 1.57/1.88 | 1.52/1.79 | 1.45/1.69 | 1.42/1.62 | 1.35/1.53 | 1.32/1.48 | 1.26/1.39 | 1.22/1.33 | 1.19/1.28 | 200 |
| 400 | 3.86/6.70 | 3.02/4.66 | 2.62/3.83 | 2.39/3.36 | 2.23/3.06 | 2.12/2.85 | 2.03/2.69 | 1.96/2.55 | 1.90/2.46 | 1.85/2.37 | 1.81/2.29 | 1.78/2.23 | 1.72/2.12 | 1.67/2.04 | 1.60/1.92 | 1.54/1.84 | 1.49/1.74 | 1.42/1.64 | 1.38/1.57 | 1.32/1.47 | 1.28/1.42 | 1.22/1.32 | 1.16/1.24 | 1.13/1.19 | 400 |
| 1000 | 3.85/6.66 | 3.00/4.62 | 2.61/3.80 | 2.38/3.34 | 2.22/3.04 | 2.10/2.82 | 2.02/2.66 | 1.95/2.53 | 1.89/2.43 | 1.84/2.34 | 1.80/2.26 | 1.76/2.20 | 1.70/2.09 | 1.65/2.01 | 1.58/1.89 | 1.53/1.81 | 1.47/1.71 | 1.41/1.61 | 1.36/1.54 | 1.30/1.44 | 1.26/1.38 | 1.19/1.28 | 1.13/1.19 | 1.08/1.11 | 1000 |
| ∞ | 3.84/6.63 | 2.99/4.60 | 2.60/3.78 | 2.37/3.32 | 2.21/3.02 | 2.09/2.80 | 2.01/2.64 | 1.94/2.51 | 1.88/2.41 | 1.83/2.32 | 1.79/2.24 | 1.75/2.18 | 1.69/2.07 | 1.64/1.99 | 1.57/1.87 | 1.52/1.79 | 1.46/1.69 | 1.40/1.59 | 1.35/1.52 | 1.28/1.41 | 1.24/1.36 | 1.17/1.25 | 1.11/1.15 | 1.00/1.00 | ∞ |

## TABLE B.8   Critical Values of Correlation Coefficients (One- and Two-Tailed Levels of Significance)

The procedures for using Table B.8 are discussed in Chapter 11. The decision rule is as follows: If the computed *r* value is equal to or larger than the value at the intersect of df and the level of significance, reject $H_0$ and accept $H_1$.

| | *Level of significance for one-tailed test* | | | |
|---|---|---|---|---|
| | .05 | .025 | .01 | .005 |
| | *Level of significance for two-tailed test* | | | |
| $df = n - 2$ | .10 | .05 | .02 | .01 |
| 1 | .988 | .997 | .9995 | .9999 |
| 2 | .900 | .950 | .980 | .990 |
| 3 | .805 | .878 | .934 | .959 |
| 4 | .729 | .811 | .882 | .917 |
| 5 | .669 | .754 | .833 | .874 |
| 6 | .622 | .707 | .789 | .834 |
| 7 | .582 | .666 | .750 | .798 |
| 8 | .549 | .632 | .716 | .765 |
| 9 | .521 | .602 | .685 | .735 |
| 10 | .497 | .576 | .658 | .708 |
| 11 | .476 | .553 | .634 | .684 |
| 12 | .458 | .532 | .612 | .661 |
| 13 | .441 | .514 | .592 | .641 |
| 14 | .426 | .497 | .574 | .623 |
| 15 | .412 | .482 | .558 | .606 |
| 16 | .400 | .468 | .542 | .590 |
| 17 | .389 | .456 | .528 | .575 |
| 18 | .378 | .444 | .516 | .561 |
| 19 | .369 | .433 | .503 | .549 |
| 20 | .360 | .423 | .492 | .537 |
| 21 | .352 | .413 | .482 | .526 |
| 22 | .344 | .404 | .472 | .515 |
| 23 | .337 | .396 | .462 | .505 |
| 24 | .330 | .388 | .453 | .496 |
| 25 | .323 | .381 | .445 | .487 |
| 26 | .317 | .374 | .437 | .479 |
| 27 | .311 | .367 | .430 | .471 |
| 28 | .306 | .361 | .423 | .463 |
| 29 | .301 | .355 | .416 | .456 |
| 30 | .296 | .349 | .409 | .449 |
| 35 | .275 | .325 | .381 | .418 |
| 40 | .257 | .304 | .358 | .393 |
| 45 | .243 | .288 | .338 | .372 |
| 50 | .231 | .273 | .322 | .354 |
| 60 | .211 | .250 | .295 | .325 |
| 70 | .195 | .232 | .274 | .303 |
| 80 | .183 | .217 | .256 | .283 |
| 90 | .173 | .205 | .242 | .267 |
| 100 | .164 | .195 | .230 | .254 |

Source: From Sir Ronald A. Fisher and Frank Yates, *Statistical Tables for Biological, Agricultural and Medical Research* (London: Longman Group, 1979), table 7, p. 63. Reproduced by permission of Addison Wesley Longman Ltd.

## TABLE B.9   Transformation of r Values to Z

Procedures for using Table B.9 are discussed in Chapter 11. The Z value corresponding to a given r value is at the intersect of the r values in the left-hand column and across the top of the table. An $r = .712$ has a corresponding $Z = .8912$.

| r | .000 | .001 | .002 | .003 | .004 | .005 | .006 | .007 | .008 | .009 |
|---|------|------|------|------|------|------|------|------|------|------|
| .000 | .0000 | .0010 | .0020 | .0030 | .0040 | .0050 | .0060 | .0070 | .0080 | .0090 |
| .010 | .0100 | .0110 | .0120 | .0130 | .0140 | .0150 | .0160 | .0170 | .0180 | .0190 |
| .020 | .0200 | .0210 | .0220 | .0230 | .0240 | .0250 | .0260 | .0270 | .0280 | .0290 |
| .030 | .0300 | .0310 | .0320 | .0330 | .0340 | .0350 | .0360 | .0370 | .0380 | .0390 |
| .040 | .0400 | .0410 | .0420 | .0430 | .0440 | .0450 | .0460 | .0470 | .0480 | .0490 |
| .050 | .0501 | .0511 | .0521 | .0531 | .0541 | .0551 | .0561 | .0571 | .0581 | .0591 |
| .060 | .0601 | .0611 | .0621 | .0631 | .0641 | .0651 | .0661 | .0671 | .0681 | .0691 |
| .070 | .0701 | .0711 | .0721 | .0731 | .0741 | .0751 | .0761 | .0771 | .0782 | .0792 |
| .080 | .0802 | .0812 | .0822 | .0832 | .0842 | .0852 | .0862 | .0872 | .0882 | .0892 |
| .090 | .0902 | .0912 | .0922 | .0933 | .0943 | .0953 | .0963 | .0973 | .0983 | .0993 |
| .100 | .1003 | .1013 | .1024 | .1034 | .1044 | .1054 | .1064 | .1074 | .1084 | .1094 |
| .110 | .1105 | .1115 | .1125 | .1135 | .1145 | .1155 | .1165 | .1175 | .1185 | .1195 |
| .120 | .1206 | .1216 | .1226 | .1236 | .1246 | .1257 | .1267 | .1277 | .1287 | .1297 |
| .130 | .1308 | .1318 | .1328 | .1338 | .1348 | .1358 | .1368 | .1379 | .1389 | .1399 |
| .140 | .1409 | .1419 | .1430 | .1440 | .1450 | .1460 | .1470 | .1481 | .1491 | .1501 |
| .150 | .1511 | .1522 | .1532 | .1542 | .1552 | .1563 | .1573 | .1583 | .1593 | .1604 |
| .160 | .1614 | .1624 | .1634 | .1644 | .1655 | .1665 | .1676 | .1686 | .1696 | .1706 |
| .170 | .1717 | .1727 | .1737 | .1748 | .1758 | .1768 | .1779 | .1789 | .1799 | .1810 |
| .180 | .1820 | .1830 | .1841 | .1851 | .1861 | .1872 | .1882 | .1892 | .1903 | .1913 |
| .190 | .1923 | .1934 | .1944 | .1954 | .1965 | .1975 | .1986 | .1996 | .2007 | .2017 |
| .200 | .2027 | .2038 | .2048 | .2059 | .2069 | .2079 | .2090 | .2100 | .2111 | .2121 |
| .210 | .2132 | .2142 | .2153 | .2163 | .2174 | .2184 | .2194 | .2205 | .2215 | .2226 |
| .220 | .2237 | .2247 | .2258 | .2268 | .2279 | .2289 | .2300 | .2310 | .2321 | .2331 |
| .230 | .2342 | .2353 | .2363 | .2374 | .2384 | .2395 | .2405 | .2416 | .2427 | .2437 |
| .240 | .2448 | .2458 | .2469 | .2480 | .2490 | .2501 | .2511 | .2522 | .2533 | .2543 |
| .250 | .2554 | .2565 | .2575 | .2586 | .2597 | .2608 | .2618 | .2629 | .2640 | .2650 |
| .260 | .2661 | .2672 | .2682 | .2693 | .2704 | .2715 | .2726 | .2736 | .2747 | .2758 |
| .270 | .2769 | .2779 | .2790 | .2801 | .2812 | .2823 | .2833 | .2844 | .2855 | .2866 |
| .280 | .2877 | .2888 | .2898 | .2909 | .2920 | .2931 | .2942 | .2953 | .2964 | .2975 |
| .290 | .2986 | .2997 | .3008 | .3019 | .3029 | .3040 | .3051 | .3062 | .3073 | .3084 |
| .300 | .3095 | .3106 | .3117 | .3128 | .3139 | .3150 | .3161 | .3172 | .3183 | .3195 |
| .310 | .3206 | .3217 | .3228 | .3239 | .3250 | .3261 | .3272 | .3283 | .3294 | .3305 |
| .320 | .3317 | .3328 | .3339 | .3350 | .3361 | .3372 | .3384 | .3395 | .3406 | .3417 |
| .330 | .3428 | .3439 | .3451 | .3462 | .3473 | .3484 | .3496 | .3507 | .3518 | .3530 |
| .340 | .3541 | .3552 | .3564 | .3575 | .3586 | .3597 | .3609 | .3620 | .3632 | .3643 |
| .350 | .3654 | .3666 | .3677 | .3689 | .3700 | .3712 | .3723 | .3734 | .3746 | .3757 |
| .360 | .3769 | .3780 | .3792 | .3803 | .3815 | .3826 | .3838 | .3850 | .3861 | .3873 |
| .370 | .3884 | .3896 | .3907 | .3919 | .3931 | .3942 | .3954 | .3966 | .3977 | .3989 |
| .380 | .4001 | .4012 | .4024 | .4036 | .4047 | .4059 | .4071 | .4083 | .4094 | .4106 |
| .390 | .4118 | .4130 | .4142 | .4153 | .4165 | .4177 | .4189 | .4201 | .4213 | .4225 |
| .400 | .4236 | .4248 | .4260 | .4272 | .4284 | .4296 | 4308 | .4320 | .4332 | .4344 |
| .410 | .4356 | .4368 | .4380 | .4392 | .4404 | .4416 | .4429 | .4441 | .4453 | .4465 |
| .420 | .4477 | .4489 | .4501 | .4513 | .4526 | .4538 | .4550 | .4562 | .4574 | .4587 |
| .430 | .4599 | .4611 | .4623 | .4636 | .4648 | .4660 | .4673 | .4685 | .4697 | .4710 |
| .440 | .4722 | .4735 | .4747 | .4760 | .4772 | .4784 | .4797 | .4809 | .4822 | .4835 |
| .450 | .4847 | .4860 | .4872 | .4885 | .4897 | .4910 | .4923 | .4935 | .4948 | .4961 |
| .460 | .4973 | .4986 | .4999 | .5011 | .5024 | .5037 | .5049 | .5062 | .5075 | .5088 |
| .470 | .5101 | .5114 | .5126 | .5139 | .5152 | .5165 | .5178 | .5191 | .5204 | .5217 |
| .480 | .5230 | .5243 | .5256 | .5279 | .5282 | .5295 | .5308 | .5321 | .5334 | .5347 |
| .490 | .5361 | .5374 | .5387 | .5400 | .5413 | .5427 | .5440 | .5453 | .5466 | .5480 |

Source: From Albert E. Waugh, *Statistical Tables and Problems* (New York: McGraw-Hill, 1952), pp. 40–41, as adapted in Hurbert M. Blalock, Jr., *Social Statistics* (New York: McGraw-Hill, 1979).

*Continued*

## TABLE B.9  Transformation of *r* Values to Z—*Continued*

| r | .000 | .001 | .002 | .003 | .004 | .005 | .006 | .007 | .008 | .009 |
|---|------|------|------|------|------|------|------|------|------|------|
| .500 | .5493 | .5506 | .5520 | .5533 | .5547 | .5560 | .5573 | .5587 | .5600 | .5614 |
| .510 | .5627 | .5641 | .5654 | .5668 | .5681 | .5695 | .5709 | .5722 | .5736 | .5750 |
| .520 | .5763 | .5777 | .5791 | .5805 | .5818 | .5832 | .5846 | .5860 | .5874 | .5888 |
| .530 | .5901 | .5915 | .5929 | .5943 | .5957 | .5971 | .5985 | .5999 | .6013 | .6027 |
| .540 | .6042 | .6056 | .6070 | .6084 | .6098 | .6112 | .6127 | .6141 | .6155 | .6170 |
| .550 | .6184 | .6198 | .6213 | .6227 | .6241 | .6256 | .6270 | .6285 | .6299 | .6314 |
| .560 | .6328 | .6343 | .6358 | .6372 | .6387 | .6401 | .6416 | .6431 | .6446 | .6460 |
| .570 | .6475 | .6490 | .6505 | .6520 | .6535 | .6550 | .6565 | .6579 | .6594 | .6610 |
| .580 | .6625 | .6640 | .6655 | .6670 | .6685 | .6700 | .6715 | .6731 | .6746 | .6761 |
| .590 | .6777 | .6792 | .6807 | .6823 | .6838 | .6854 | .6869 | .6885 | .6900 | .6916 |
| .600 | .6931 | .6947 | .6963 | .6978 | .6994 | .7010 | .7026 | .7042 | .7057 | .7073 |
| .610 | .7089 | .7105 | .7121 | .7137 | .7153 | .7169 | .7185 | .7201 | .7218 | .7234 |
| .620 | .7250 | .7266 | .7283 | .7299 | .7315 | .7332 | .7348 | .7364 | .7381 | .7398 |
| .630 | .7414 | .7431 | .7447 | .7464 | .7481 | .7497 | .7514 | .7531 | .7548 | .7565 |
| .640 | .7582 | .7599 | .7616 | .7633 | .7650 | .7667 | .7684 | .7701 | .7718 | .7736 |
| .650 | .7753 | .7770 | .7788 | .7805 | .7823 | .7840 | .7858 | .7875 | .7893 | .7910 |
| .660 | .7928 | .7946 | .7964 | .7981 | .7999 | .8017 | .8035 | .8053 | .8071 | .8089 |
| .670 | .8107 | .8126 | .8144 | .8162 | .8180 | .8199 | .8217 | .8236 | .8254 | .8273 |
| .680 | .8291 | .8310 | .8328 | .8347 | .8366 | .8385 | .8404 | .8423 | .8442 | .8461 |
| .690 | .8480 | .8499 | .8518 | .8537 | .8556 | .8576 | .8595 | .8614 | .8634 | .8653 |
| .700 | .8673 | .8693 | .8712 | .8732 | .8752 | .8772 | .8792 | .8812 | .8832 | .8852 |
| .710 | .8872 | .8892 | .8912 | .8933 | .8953 | .8973 | .8994 | .9014 | .9035 | .9056 |
| .720 | .9076 | .9097 | .9118 | .9139 | .9160 | .9181 | .9202 | .9223 | .9245 | .9266 |
| .730 | .9287 | .9309 | .9330 | .9352 | .9373 | .9395 | .9417 | .9439 | .9461 | .9483 |
| .740 | .9505 | .9527 | .9549 | .9571 | .9594 | .9616 | .9639 | .9661 | .9684 | .9707 |
| .750 | .9730 | .9752 | .9775 | .9799 | .9822 | .9845 | .9868 | .9892 | .9915 | .9939 |
| .760 | .9962 | .9986 | 1.0010 | 1.0034 | 1.0058 | 1.0082 | 1.0106 | 1.0130 | 1.0154 | 1.0179 |
| .770 | 1.0203 | 1.0228 | 1.0253 | 1.0277 | 1.0302 | 1.0327 | 1.0352 | 1.0378 | 1.0403 | 1.0428 |
| .780 | 1.0454 | 1.0479 | 1.0505 | 1.0531 | 1.0557 | 1.0583 | 1.0609 | 1.0635 | 1.0661 | 1.0688 |
| .790 | 1.0714 | 1.0741 | 1.0768 | 1.0795 | 1.0822 | 1.0849 | 1.0876 | 1.0903 | 1.0931 | 1.0958 |
| .800 | 1.0986 | 1.1014 | 1.1041 | 1.1070 | 1.1098 | 1.1127 | 1.1155 | 1.1184 | 1.1212 | 1.1241 |
| .810 | 1.1270 | 1.1299 | 1.1329 | 1.1358 | 1.1388 | 1.1417 | 1.1447 | 1.1477 | 1.1507 | 1.1538 |
| .820 | 1.1568 | 1.1599 | 1.1630 | 1.1660 | 1.1692 | 1.1723 | 1.1754 | 1.1786 | 1.1817 | 1.1849 |
| .830 | 1.1870 | 1.1913 | 1.1946 | 1.1979 | 1.2011 | 1.2044 | 1.2077 | 1.2111 | 1.2144 | 1.2178 |
| .840 | 1.2212 | 1.2246 | 1.2280 | 1.2315 | 1.2349 | 1.2384 | 1.2419 | 1.2454 | 1.2490 | 1.2526 |
| .850 | 1.2561 | 1.2598 | 1.2634 | 1.2670 | 1.2708 | 1.2744 | 1.2782 | 1.2819 | 1.2857 | 1.2895 |
| .860 | 1.2934 | 1.2972 | 1.3011 | 1.3050 | 1.3089 | 1.3129 | 1.3168 | 1.3209 | 1.3249 | 1.3290 |
| .870 | 1.3331 | 1.3372 | 1.3414 | 1.3456 | 1.3498 | 1.3540 | 1.3583 | 1.3626 | 1.3670 | 1.3714 |
| .880 | 1.3758 | 1.3802 | 1.3847 | 1.3892 | 1.3938 | 1.3984 | 1.4030 | 1.4077 | 1.4124 | 1.4171 |
| .890 | 1.4219 | 1.4268 | 1.4316 | 1.4366 | 1.4415 | 1.4465 | 1.4516 | 1.4566 | 1.4618 | 1.4670 |
| .900 | 1.4722 | 1.4775 | 1.4828 | 1.4883 | 1.4937 | 1.4992 | 1.5047 | 1.5103 | 1.5160 | 1.5217 |
| .910 | 1.5275 | 1.5334 | 1.5393 | 1.5453 | 1.5513 | 1.5574 | 1.5636 | 1.5698 | 1.5762 | 1.5825 |
| .920 | 1.5890 | 1.5956 | 1.6022 | 1.6089 | 1.6157 | 1.6226 | 1.6296 | 1.6366 | 1.6438 | 1.6510 |
| .930 | 1.6584 | 1.6659 | 1.6734 | 1.6811 | 1.6888 | 1.6967 | 1.7047 | 1.7129 | 1.7211 | 1.7295 |
| .940 | 1.7380 | 1.7467 | 1.7555 | 1.7645 | 1.7736 | 1.7828 | 1.7923 | 1.8019 | 1.8117 | 1.8216 |
| .950 | 1.8318 | 1.8421 | 1.8527 | 1.8635 | 1.8745 | 1.8857 | 1.8972 | 1.9090 | 1.9210 | 1.9333 |
| .960 | 1.9459 | 1.9588 | 1.9721 | 1.9857 | 1.9996 | 2.0140 | 2.0287 | 2.0439 | 2.0595 | 2.0756 |
| .970 | 2.0923 | 2.1095 | 2.1273 | 2.1457 | 2.1649 | 2.1847 | 2.2054 | 2.2269 | 2.2494 | 2.2729 |
| .980 | 2.2976 | 2.3223 | 2.3507 | 2.3796 | 2.4101 | 2.4426 | 2.4774 | 2.5147 | 2.5550 | 2.5988 |
| .990 | 2.6467 | 2.6996 | 2.7587 | 2.8257 | 2.9031 | 2.9945 | 3.1063 | 3.2504 | 3.4534 | 3.8002 |

| r | z |
|---|---|
| .9999 | 4.95172 |
| .99999 | 6.10303 |

## TABLE B.10    Random Numbers

The procedures for using Table B.10 are discussed in Chapter 6.

| | | | | |
|---|---|---|---|---|
| 10 09 73 25 33 | 76 52 01 35 86 | 34 67 35 48 76 | 80 95 90 91 17 | 39 29 27 49 45 |
| 37 54 20 48 05 | 64 89 47 42 96 | 24 80 52 40 37 | 20 63 61 04 02 | 00 82 29 16 65 |
| 08 42 26 89 53 | 19 64 50 93 03 | 23 20 90 25 60 | 15 95 33 47 64 | 35 08 03 36 06 |
| 99 01 90 25 29 | 09 37 67 07 15 | 38 31 13 11 65 | 88 67 67 43 97 | 04 43 62 76 59 |
| 12 80 79 99 70 | 80 15 73 61 47 | 64 03 23 66 53 | 98 95 11 68 77 | 12 17 17 68 33 |
| | | | | |
| 66 06 57 47 17 | 34 07 27 68 50 | 36 69 73 61 70 | 65 81 33 98 85 | 11 19 92 91 70 |
| 31 06 01 08 05 | 45 57 18 24 06 | 35 30 34 26 14 | 86 79 90 74 39 | 23 40 30 97 32 |
| 85 26 97 76 02 | 02 05 16 56 92 | 68 66 57 48 18 | 73 05 38 52 47 | 18 62 38 85 79 |
| 63 57 33 21 35 | 05 32 54 70 48 | 90 55 35 75 48 | 28 46 82 87 09 | 83 49 12 56 24 |
| 73 79 64 57 53 | 03 52 96 47 78 | 35 80 83 42 82 | 60 93 52 03 44 | 35 27 38 84 35 |
| | | | | |
| 98 52 01 77 67 | 14 90 56 86 07 | 22 10 94 05 58 | 60 97 09 34 33 | 50 50 07 39 98 |
| 11 80 50 54 31 | 39 80 82 77 32 | 50 72 56 82 48 | 29 40 52 42 01 | 52 77 56 78 51 |
| 83 45 29 96 34 | 06 28 89 80 83 | 13 74 67 00 78 | 18 47 54 06 10 | 68 71 17 78 17 |
| 88 68 54 02 00 | 86 50 75 84 01 | 36 76 66 79 51 | 90 36 47 64 93 | 29 60 91 10 62 |
| 99 59 46 73 48 | 87 51 76 49 69 | 91 82 60 89 28 | 93 78 56 13 68 | 23 47 83 41 13 |
| | | | | |
| 65 48 11 76 74 | 17 46 85 09 50 | 58 04 77 69 74 | 73 03 95 71 86 | 40 21 81 65 44 |
| 80 12 43 56 35 | 17 72 70 80 15 | 45 31 82 23 74 | 21 11 57 82 53 | 14 38 55 37 63 |
| 74 35 09 98 17 | 77 40 27 72 14 | 43 23 60 02 10 | 45 52 16 42 37 | 96 28 60 26 55 |
| 69 91 62 68 03 | 66 25 22 91 48 | 36 93 68 72 03 | 76 62 11 39 90 | 94 40 05 64 18 |
| 09 89 32 05 05 | 14 22 56 85 14 | 46 42 75 67 88 | 96 29 77 88 22 | 54 38 21 45 98 |
| | | | | |
| 91 49 91 45 23 | 68 47 92 76 86 | 46 16 28 35 54 | 94 75 08 99 23 | 37 08 92 00 48 |
| 80 33 69 45 98 | 26 94 03 68 58 | 70 29 73 41 35 | 53 14 03 33 40 | 42 05 08 23 41 |
| 44 10 48 19 49 | 85 15 74 79 54 | 32 97 92 65 75 | 57 60 04 08 81 | 22 22 20 64 13 |
| 12 55 07 37 42 | 11 10 00 20 40 | 12 86 07 46 97 | 96 64 48 94 39 | 28 70 72 58 15 |
| 63 60 64 93 29 | 16 50 53 44 84 | 40 21 95 25 63 | 43 65 17 70 82 | 07 20 73 17 90 |
| | | | | |
| 61 19 69 04 46 | 26 45 74 77 74 | 51 92 43 37 29 | 65 39 45 95 93 | 42 58 26 05 27 |
| 15 47 44 52 66 | 95 27 07 99 53 | 59 36 78 38 48 | 82 39 61 01 18 | 33 21 15 94 66 |
| 94 55 72 85 73 | 67 89 75 43 87 | 54 62 24 44 31 | 91 19 04 25 92 | 92 92 74 59 73 |
| 42 48 11 62 13 | 97 34 40 87 21 | 16 86 84 87 67 | 03 07 11 20 59 | 25 70 14 66 70 |
| 23 52 37 83 17 | 73 20 88 98 37 | 68 93 59 14 16 | 26 25 22 96 63 | 05 52 28 25 62 |
| | | | | |
| 04 49 35 24 94 | 75 24 63 38 24 | 45 86 25 10 25 | 61 96 27 93 35 | 65 33 71 24 72 |
| 00 54 99 76 54 | 64 05 18 81 59 | 96 11 96 38 96 | 54 69 28 23 91 | 23 28 72 95 29 |
| 35 96 31 53 07 | 26 89 80 93 54 | 33 35 13 54 62 | 77 97 45 00 24 | 90 10 33 93 33 |
| 59 80 80 83 91 | 45 42 72 68 42 | 83 60 94 97 00 | 13 02 12 48 92 | 78 56 52 01 06 |
| 46 05 88 52 36 | 01 39 09 22 86 | 77 28 14 40 77 | 93 91 08 36 47 | 70 61 74 29 41 |
| | | | | |
| 32 17 90 05 97 | 87 37 92 52 41 | 05 56 70 70 07 | 86 74 31 71 57 | 85 39 41 18 38 |
| 69 23 46 14 06 | 20 11 74 52 04 | 15 95 66 00 00 | 18 74 39 24 23 | 97 11 89 63 38 |
| 19 56 54 14 30 | 01 75 87 53 79 | 40 41 92 15 85 | 66 67 43 68 06 | 84 96 28 52 07 |
| 45 15 51 49 38 | 19 47 60 72 46 | 43 66 79 45 43 | 59 04 79 00 33 | 20 82 66 95 41 |
| 94 86 43 19 94 | 36 16 81 08 51 | 34 88 88 15 53 | 01 54 03 54 56 | 05 01 45 11 76 |

*Continued*

Source: Reprinted from the Rand Corporation, *A Million Random Digits with 100,000 Normal Deviates* (New York: The Free Press, 1955), pp. 1–3. Copyright 1955 by the Rand Corporation. Used by permission.

**TABLE B.10    Random Numbers—*Continued***

| | | | | |
|---|---|---|---|---|
| 98 08 62 48 26 | 45 24 02 84 04 | 44 99 90 88 96 | 39 09 47 34 07 | 35 44 13 18 80 |
| 33 18 51 62 32 | 41 94 15 09 49 | 89 43 54 85 81 | 88 69 54 19 94 | 37 54 87 30 43 |
| 80 95 10 04 06 | 96 38 27 07 74 | 20 15 12 33 87 | 25 01 62 52 98 | 94 62 46 11 71 |
| 79 75 24 91 40 | 71 96 12 82 96 | 69 86 10 25 91 | 74 85 22 05 39 | 00 38 75 95 79 |
| 18 63 33 25 37 | 98 14 50 65 71 | 31 01 02 46 74 | 05 45 56 14 27 | 77 93 89 19 36 |
| | | | | |
| 74 02 94 39 02 | 77 55 73 22 70 | 97 79 01 71 19 | 52 52 75 80 21 | 80 81 45 17 48 |
| 54 17 84 56 11 | 80 99 33 71 43 | 05 33 51 29 69 | 56 12 71 92 55 | 36 04 09 03 24 |
| 11 66 44 98 83 | 52 07 98 48 27 | 59 38 17 15 39 | 09 97 33 34 40 | 88 46 12 33 56 |
| 48 32 47 79 28 | 31 24 96 47 10 | 02 29 53 68 70 | 32 30 75 75 46 | 15 02 00 99 94 |
| 69 07 49 41 38 | 87 63 79 19 76 | 35 58 40 44 01 | 10 51 82 16 15 | 01 84 87 69 38 |
| | | | | |
| 09 18 82 00 97 | 32 82 53 95 27 | 04 22 08 63 04 | 83 38 98 73 74 | 64 27 85 80 44 |
| 90 04 58 54 97 | 51 98 15 06 54 | 94 93 88 19 97 | 91 87 07 61 50 | 68 47 66 46 59 |
| 73 18 95 02 07 | 47 67 72 52 69 | 62 29 06 44 64 | 27 12 46 70 18 | 41 36 18 27 60 |
| 75 76 87 64 90 | 20 97 18 17 49 | 90 42 91 22 72 | 95 37 50 58 71 | 93 82 34 31 78 |
| 54 01 64 40 56 | 66 28 13 10 03 | 00 68 22 73 98 | 20 71 45 32 95 | 07 70 61 78 13 |
| | | | | |
| 08 35 86 99 10 | 78 54 24 27 85 | 13 66 15 88 73 | 04 61 89 75 53 | 31 22 30 84 20 |
| 28 30 60 32 64 | 81 33 31 05 91 | 40 51 00 78 93 | 32 60 46 04 75 | 94 11 90 18 40 |
| 53 84 08 62 33 | 81 59 41 36 28 | 51 21 59 02 90 | 28 46 66 87 95 | 77 76 22 07 91 |
| 91 75 75 37 41 | 61 61 36 22 69 | 50 26 39 02 12 | 55 78 17 65 14 | 83 48 34 70 55 |
| 89 41 59 26 94 | 00 39 75 83 91 | 12 60 71 76 46 | 48 94 97 23 06 | 94 54 13 74 08 |
| | | | | |
| 77 51 30 38 20 | 86 83 42 99 01 | 68 41 48 27 74 | 51 90 81 39 80 | 72 89 35 55 07 |
| 19 50 23 71 74 | 69 97 92 02 88 | 55 21 02 97 73 | 74 28 77 52 51 | 65 34 46 74 15 |
| 21 81 85 93 13 | 93 27 88 17 57 | 05 68 67 31 56 | 07 08 28 50 46 | 31 85 33 84 52 |
| 51 47 46 64 99 | 68 10 72 36 21 | 94 04 99 13 45 | 42 83 60 91 91 | 08 00 74 54 49 |
| 99 55 96 83 31 | 62 53 52 41 70 | 69 77 71 28 30 | 74 81 97 81 42 | 43 86 07 28 34 |
| | | | | |
| 33 71 34 80 07 | 93 58 47 28 69 | 51 92 66 47 21 | 58 30 32 98 22 | 93 17 49 39 72 |
| 85 27 48 68 93 | 11 30 32 92 70 | 28 83 43 41 37 | 73 51 59 04 00 | 71 14 84 36 43 |
| 84 13 38 96 40 | 44 03 55 21 66 | 73 85 27 00 91 | 61 22 26 05 61 | 62 32 71 84 23 |
| 56 73 21 62 34 | 17 39 59 61 31 | 10 12 39 16 22 | 85 49 65 75 60 | 81 60 41 88 80 |
| 65 13 85 68 06 | 87 64 88 52 61 | 34 31 36 58 61 | 45 87 52 10 69 | 85 64 44 72 77 |
| | | | | |
| 38 00 10 21 76 | 81 71 91 17 11 | 71 60 29 29 37 | 74 21 96 40 49 | 65 58 44 96 98 |
| 37 40 29 63 97 | 01 30 47 75 86 | 56 27 11 00 86 | 47 32 46 26 05 | 40 03 03 74 38 |
| 97 12 54 03 48 | 87 08 33 14 17 | 21 81 53 92 50 | 75 23 76 20 47 | 15 50 12 95 78 |
| 21 82 64 11 34 | 47 14 33 40 72 | 64 63 88 59 02 | 49 13 90 64 41 | 03 85 65 45 52 |
| 73 13 54 27 42 | 95 71 90 90 35 | 85 79 47 42 96 | 08 78 98 81 56 | 64 69 11 92 02 |
| | | | | |
| 07 63 87 79 29 | 03 06 11 80 72 | 96 20 74 41 56 | 23 82 19 95 38 | 04 71 36 69 94 |
| 60 52 88 34 41 | 07 95 41 98 14 | 59 17 52 06 95 | 05 53 35 21 39 | 61 21 20 64 55 |
| 83 59 63 56 55 | 06 95 89 29 83 | 05 12 80 97 19 | 77 43 35 37 83 | 92 30 15 04 98 |
| 10 85 06 27 46 | 99 59 91 05 07 | 13 49 90 63 19 | 53 07 57 18 39 | 06 41 01 93 62 |
| 39 82 09 89 52 | 43 62 26 31 47 | 64 42 18 08 14 | 43 80 00 93 51 | 31 02 47 31 67 |

**TABLE B.10    Random Numbers—*Continued***

| | | | | |
|---|---|---|---|---|
| 59 58 00 64 78 | 75 56 97 88 00 | 88 83 55 44 86 | 23 76 80 61 56 | 04 11 10 84 08 |
| 38 50 80 73 41 | 23 79 34 87 63 | 90 82 29 70 22 | 17 71 90 42 07 | 95 95 44 99 53 |
| 30 69 27 06 68 | 94 68 81 61 27 | 56 19 68 00 91 | 82 06 76 34 00 | 05 46 26 92 00 |
| 65 44 39 56 59 | 18 28 82 74 37 | 49 63 22 40 41 | 08 33 76 56 76 | 96 29 99 08 36 |
| 27 26 75 02 64 | 13 19 27 22 94 | 07 47 74 46 06 | 17 98 54 89 11 | 97 34 13 03 58 |
| | | | | |
| 91 30 70 69 91 | 19 07 22 42 10 | 36 69 95 37 28 | 28 82 53 57 93 | 28 97 66 62 52 |
| 68 43 49 46 88 | 84 47 31 36 22 | 62 12 69 84 08 | 12 84 38 25 90 | 09 81 59 31 46 |
| 48 90 81 58 77 | 54 74 52 45 91 | 35 70 00 47 54 | 83 82 45 26 92 | 54 13 05 51 60 |
| 06 91 34 51 97 | 42 67 27 86 01 | 11 88 30 95 28 | 63 01 19 89 01 | 14 97 44 03 44 |
| 10 45 51 60 19 | 14 21 03 37 12 | 91 34 23 78 21 | 88 32 58 08 51 | 43 66 77 08 83 |
| | | | | |
| 12 88 39 73 43 | 65 02 76 11 84 | 04 28 50 13 92 | 17 97 41 50 77 | 90 71 22 67 69 |
| 21 77 83 09 76 | 38 80 73 69 61 | 31 64 94 20 96 | 63 28 10 20 23 | 08 81 64 74 49 |
| 19 52 35 95 15 | 65 12 25 96 59 | 86 28 36 82 58 | 69 57 21 37 98 | 16 43 59 15 29 |
| 67 24 55 26 70 | 35 58 31 65 63 | 79 24 68 66 86 | 76 46 33 42 22 | 26 65 59 08 02 |
| 60 58 44 73 77 | 07 50 03 79 92 | 45 13 42 65 29 | 26 76 08 36 37 | 41 32 64 43 44 |
| | | | | |
| 53 85 34 13 77 | 36 06 69 48 50 | 58 83 87 38 59 | 49 36 47 33 31 | 96 24 04 36 42 |
| 24 63 73 87 36 | 74 38 48 93 42 | 52 62 30 79 92 | 12 36 91 86 01 | 03 74 28 38 73 |
| 83 08 01 24 51 | 38 99 22 28 15 | 07 75 95 17 77 | 97 37 72 75 85 | 51 97 23 78 67 |
| 16 44 42 43 34 | 36 15 19 90 73 | 27 49 37 09 39 | 85 13 03 25 52 | 54 84 65 47 59 |
| 60 79 01 81 57 | 57 17 86 57 62 | 11 16 17 85 76 | 45 81 95 29 79 | 65 13 00 48 60 |
| | | | | |
| 03 99 11 04 61 | 93 71 61 68 94 | 66 08 32 46 53 | 84 60 95 82 32 | 88 61 81 91 61 |
| 38 55 59 55 54 | 32 88 65 97 80 | 08 35 56 08 60 | 29 73 54 77 62 | 71 29 92 38 53 |
| 17 54 67 37 04 | 92 05 24 62 15 | 55 12 12 92 81 | 59 07 60 79 36 | 27 95 45 89 09 |
| 32 64 35 28 61 | 95 81 90 68 31 | 00 91 19 89 36 | 76 35 59 37 79 | 80 86 30 05 14 |
| 69 57 26 87 77 | 39 51 03 59 05 | 14 06 04 06 19 | 29 54 96 96 16 | 33 56 46 07 80 |
| | | | | |
| 24 12 26 65 91 | 27 69 90 64 94 | 14 84 54 66 72 | 61 95 87 71 00 | 90 89 97 57 54 |
| 61 19 63 02 31 | 92 96 26 17 73 | 41 83 95 53 82 | 17 26 77 09 43 | 78 03 87 02 67 |
| 30 53 22 17 04 | 10 27 41 22 02 | 39 68 52 33 09 | 10 06 16 88 29 | 55 98 66 64 85 |
| 03 78 89 75 99 | 75 86 72 07 17 | 74 41 65 31 66 | 35 20 83 33 74 | 87 53 90 88 23 |
| 48 22 86 33 79 | 85 78 34 76 19 | 53 15 26 74 33 | 35 66 35 29 72 | 16 81 86 03 11 |
| | | | | |
| 60 36 59 46 53 | 35 07 53 39 49 | 42 61 42 92 97 | 01 91 82 83 16 | 98 95 37 32 31 |
| 83 79 94 24 02 | 56 62 33 44 42 | 34 99 44 13 74 | 70 07 11 47 36 | 09 95 81 80 65 |
| 32 96 00 74 05 | 36 40 98 32 32 | 99 38 54 16 00 | 11 13 30 75 86 | 15 91 70 62 53 |
| 19 32 25 38 45 | 57 62 05 26 06 | 66 49 76 86 46 | 78 13 86 65 59 | 19 64 09 94 13 |
| 11 22 09 47 47 | 07 39 93 74 08 | 48 50 92 39 29 | 27 48 24 54 76 | 85 24 43 51 59 |
| | | | | |
| 31 75 15 72 60 | 68 98 00 53 39 | 15 47 04 83 55 | 88 65 12 25 96 | 03 15 21 92 21 |
| 88 49 29 93 82 | 14 45 40 45 04 | 20 09 49 89 77 | 74 84 39 34 13 | 22 10 97 85 08 |
| 30 93 44 77 44 | 07 48 18 38 28 | 73 78 80 65 33 | 28 59 72 04 05 | 94 20 52 03 80 |
| 22 88 84 88 93 | 27 49 99 87 48 | 60 53 04 51 28 | 74 02 28 46 17 | 82 03 71 02 68 |
| 78 21 21 69 93 | 35 90 29 13 86 | 44 37 21 54 86 | 65 74 11 40 14 | 87 48 13 72 20 |

*Continued*

**TABLE B.10    Random Numbers—*Continued***

| | | | | |
|---|---|---|---|---|
| 41 84 98 45 47 | 46 85 05 23 26 | 34 67 75 83 00 | 74 91 06 43 45 | 19 32 58 15 49 |
| 46 35 23 30 49 | 69 24 89 34 60 | 45 30 50 75 21 | 61 31 83 18 55 | 14 41 37 09 51 |
| 11 08 79 62 94 | 14 01 33 17 92 | 59 74 76 72 77 | 76 50 33 45 13 | 39 66 37 75 44 |
| 52 70 10 83 37 | 56 30 38 73 15 | 16 52 06 96 76 | 11 65 49 98 93 | 02 18 16 81 61 |
| 57 27 53 68 98 | 81 30 44 85 85 | 68 65 22 73 76 | 92 85 25 58 66 | 88 44 80 35 84 |
| | | | | |
| 20 85 77 31 56 | 70 28 42 43 26 | 79 37 59 52 20 | 01 15 96 32 67 | 10 62 24 83 91 |
| 15 63 38 49 24 | 90 41 59 36 14 | 33 52 12 66 65 | 55 82 34 76 41 | 86 22 53 17 04 |
| 92 69 44 82 97 | 39 90 40 21 15 | 59 58 94 90 67 | 66 82 14 15 75 | 49 76 70 40 37 |
| 77 61 31 90 19 | 88 15 20 00 80 | 20 55 49 14 09 | 96 27 74 82 57 | 50 81 69 76 16 |
| 38 68 83 24 86 | 45 13 46 35 45 | 59 40 47 20 59 | 43 94 75 16 80 | 43 85 25 96 93 |
| | | | | |
| 25 16 30 18 89 | 70 01 41 50 21 | 41 29 06 73 12 | 71 85 71 59 57 | 68 97 11 14 03 |
| 65 25 10 76 29 | 37 23 93 32 95 | 05 87 00 11 19 | 92 78 42 63 40 | 18 47 76 56 22 |
| 36 81 54 36 25 | 18 63 73 75 09 | 82 44 49 90 05 | 04 92 17 37 01 | 14 70 79 39 97 |
| 64 39 71 16 92 | 05 32 78 21 62 | 20 24 78 17 59 | 45 19 72 53 32 | 83 74 52 25 67 |
| 04 51 52 56 24 | 95 09 66 79 46 | 48 46 08 55 58 | 15 19 11 87 82 | 16 93 03 33 61 |
| | | | | |
| 83 76 16 08 73 | 43 25 38 41 45 | 60 83 32 59 83 | 01 29 14 13 49 | 20 36 80 71 26 |
| 14 38 70 63 45 | 80 85 40 92 79 | 43 52 90 63 18 | 38 38 47 47 61 | 41 19 63 74 80 |
| 51 32 19 22 46 | 80 08 87 70 74 | 88 72 25 67 36 | 66 16 44 94 31 | 66 91 93 16 78 |
| 72 47 20 00 08 | 80 89 01 80 02 | 94 81 33 19 00 | 54 15 58 34 36 | 35 35 25 41 31 |
| 05 46 65 53 06 | 93 12 81 84 64 | 74 45 79 05 61 | 72 84 81 18 34 | 79 98 26 84 16 |
| | | | | |
| 39 52 87 24 84 | 82 47 42 55 93 | 48 54 53 52 47 | 18 61 91 36 74 | 18 61 11 92 41 |
| 81 61 61 87 11 | 53 34 24 42 76 | 75 12 21 17 24 | 74 62 77 37 07 | 58 31 91 59 97 |
| 07 58 61 61 20 | 82 64 12 28 20 | 92 90 41 31 41 | 32 39 21 97 63 | 61 19 96 79 40 |
| 90 76 70 42 35 | 13 57 41 72 00 | 69 90 26 37 42 | 78 46 42 25 01 | 18 62 79 08 72 |
| 40 18 82 81 93 | 29 59 38 86 27 | 94 97 21 15 98 | 62 09 53 67 87 | 00 44 15 89 97 |
| | | | | |
| 34 41 48 21 57 | 86 88 75 50 87 | 19 15 20 00 23 | 12 30 28 07 83 | 32 62 46 86 91 |
| 63 43 97 53 63 | 44 98 91 68 22 | 36 02 40 09 67 | 76 37 84 16 05 | 65 96 17 34 88 |
| 67 04 90 90 70 | 93 39 94 55 47 | 94 45 87 42 84 | 05 04 14 98 07 | 20 28 83 40 60 |
| 79 49 50 41 46 | 52 16 29 02 86 | 54 15 83 42 43 | 46 97 83 54 82 | 59 36 29 59 38 |
| 91 70 43 05 52 | 04 73 72 10 31 | 75 05 19 30 29 | 47 66 56 43 82 | 99 78 29 34 78 |

# SELECTED ANSWERS
# TO EXERCISES

## Chapter 1

**2.** Interval, dichotomous, nominal, nominal, nominal, interval, nominal, interval, interval, ordinal, nominal

## Chapter 2

**2.** .216   **3.** .235   **4.** .367   **5.** .767   **6.** .311   **7.** 1.11%   **8.** 37.8%   **11.** .156   **12.** .867   **13.** 36.7%
**14.** 93.3%   **16.** 49.5–59.5   **17.** 64.5   **18.** 6.5–13.5   **19.** 10.0

## Chapter 3

**1.** 74, 78, 80.2   **2.** 90, 86, 77   **3.** mean, mode   **4.** mode, mean   **5.** 81.7, 86.7   **6.** (a) 90, 83   (b) 88,
78   (c) 87.0, 78.7   (d) 25, 31   (e) 12, 12   (f) 53.14, 7.29   (g) 83.21, 9.12   (j) 7.29, 14.58, 21.87 and
9.12, 18.24, 27.36   **7.** (a) 54.5   (b) 52.57   (c) 51.15   (d) 100   (e) 545.81, 23.36   **8.** (a) 88.5%
(b) 99.59%   (c) club 2   **9.** 111.88

## Chapter 4

**7.** (a) 164.80, 12.04   **8.** Jennifer   **9.** .025   **10.** .025   **11.** .05   **12.** .005   **13.** .995   **14.** .995
**15.** .005   **16.** .01   **17.** .99   **18.** 2.05   **19.** 2.32   **20.** 2.43   **21.** .67   **22.** (a) 53.35   (b) 21.29
(e) .068   (f) .218   (g) .071   (h) 79   **23.** (a) 32.11   (b) 25.50   **24.** (a) 49.10   (b) 28.94

## Chapter 5

**3.** $p^{10} + 10p^9q + 45p^8q^2 + 120p^7q^3 + 210p^6q^4 + 252p^5q^5 + 210p^4q^6 + 120p^3q^7 + 45p^2q^8 + 10pq^9 + q^{10}$
**4.** .1172   **5.** .0100   **6.** .2150   **7.** .0106   **8.** .0735   **9.** .3602   **10.** .0193   **11.** .006   **12.** .061   **13.** .023
**14.** .164   **15.** (a) 15   (b) 2.7386   (c) 1.28 to 1.64   (d) .1003 to .0505   (e) 2.01 to 2.37   (f) .0222 to
.0089   **16.** (a) 42   (b) 3.5496   (c) –3.24 to –3.52   (d) .0006 to .0002   (e) –.4226 to –.7043   (f) .3372
to .2420

## Chapter 6

**2.** .0833   **8.** .8006   **9.** .50   **10.** (a) 85, 85   (b) 2.280, 9.522   (c) .5887, 2.459   (d) 83.8461 to 86.1539
and 80.1811 to 89.8189   (e) 83.4812 to 86.5188 and 78.6568 to 91.3432   **11.** (a) .0787   (b) .2958 to
.6042   (c) .2470 to .6530

## Chapter 7

**5.** 0174   **6.** .0087   **7.** .0536   **8.** .0069   **9.** .0427   **10.** (a) standard-error-of-the-mean test   (b) $\mu = 122$
(c) $\mu < 122$   (d) –1.15   (e) accept   (f) reject   (h) no risk   **11.** (a) standard-error-of-the-mean
test   (b) $\mu = 122$   (c) $\mu < 122$   (d) –2.309   (e) reject $H_0$, accept $H_1$   **12.** (a) Student's $t$
(b) $\mu = 29,126$   (c) $\mu < 29,126$   (d) –1.67   (e) accept $H_0$   (f) reject $H_1$   (h) none   **13.** (a) 2.38   (b) no
**15.** (a) standard error of proportions   (b) $P = .40$   (c) $P < .40$   (d) –2.14   (e) reject $H_0$   (f) accept
$H_1$   **16.** (a) chi-square   (c) not appropriate   (d) 11.20   (e) 3   (f) .02   (g) not appropriate

## Chapter 8

**1.** (a) Student's $t$   (b) $\mu_1 = \mu_2$   (c) $\mu_1 < \mu_2$   (d) –2.069   (e) 122   (f) yes   (g) .025   **2.** (a) Student's $t$
(b) $\mu_1 = \mu_2$   (c) $\mu_1 < \mu_2$   (d) .809   (e) 17   (f) no   (g) no   **3.** (a) 2.0476   (b) yes   (c) Student's $t$,
unequal variances   (d) $\mu_1 = \mu_2$   (e) $\mu_1 > \mu_2$   (f) 2.533   (g) 52   (h) yes   (i) yes   **4.** (a) Student's $t$
(b) $\mu_1 = \mu_2$   (c) $\mu_1 < \mu_2$   (d) –2.096   (e) yes   (f) yes   **5.** (a) .1825   (b) 5.3923 to 6.1077
(c) .1919   (d) 5.9239 to 6.6761   (e) sample 1   **6.** (a) standard error of proportions   (b) $P_1 = P_2$
(c) $P_1 < P_2$   (d) 1.89   (e) accept   (f) .0294   **7.** (a) Student's $t$ for matched pairs   (b) $\delta = 0$
(c) $\delta > 0$   (d) 2.375   (e) 17   (f) yes   (g) Type I   (h) .025   (i) Type I

## Chapter 9

**1.** (a) Mann-Whitney U   (b) sophomores = juniors   (c) sophomores < juniors   (d) 40.5   (e) yes
(f) yes   **2.** (a) Mann-Whitney U   (b) group 1 = group 2   (c) group 1 < group 2   (d) –3.18
(e) yes   (f) yes   **3.** (a) Wilcoxon   (b) pre = post   (c) pre < post   (d) T = 3   (e) yes   (f) yes
**4.** (a) Wilcoxon   (b) pre = post   (c) pre < post   (d) –2.851   (e) yes   (f) yes   **5.** (a) chi-square
(c) inappropriate   (d) 3.60   (e) no   **6.** (a) chi-square   (c) inappropriate   (d) 6.087   (e) .02
(f) inappropriate   (g) sample size   (h) Type I   **7.** (a) chi-square   (c) inappropriate   (d) 7.29
(e) no   (f) inappropriate   **8.** (a) McNemar's   (b) change to positive   (c) inappropriate   (d) 4.27
(e) yes   (f) inappropriate

## Chapter 10

**1.** (a) $\mu_1 = \mu_2 = \mu_3$   (b) 312, 465, 555   (c) 12,390   (d) 9,874.5   (e) 2,515.5   (f) 33   (g) 2
(h) 299.227   (i) 1,257.75   (j) 4.203   (k) reject $H_0$   **2.** (a) $\mu_{\mu_1} = \mu_{\mu_2} = \mu_{\mu_3}$, $\mu_{T_1} = \mu_{T_2} = \mu_{T_3}$, no
interaction   (b) 312, 465, 555   (c) 670, 440, 222   (d) 12,390   (e) 1,313   (f) 11,077
(g) 2515.50   (h) 8364.67   (i) 196.83   (j) 48.63   (k) 49.21   (l) 1,257.75   (m) 4,182.33
(n) 1.01   (o) no   (p) 25.86   (q) yes   (r) 86.00   (s) yes   **3.** (a) Kruskal-Wallis   (c) 3.0146
(d) 4   (e) chi-square   (f) accept $H_0$

## Chapter 11

**1.** (a) no association   (b) happiness, health   (d) .4776   (e) 2.355   (f) 2.355, 2.833, 3.310, 7.131
(h) 1.2924   (i) 2.341 to 8.100   (j) .409   (k) 4.3100 to 6.1312   (l) 2.6912   (m) 1.0164   (n) 1.6718
**2.** (a) $\rho = 0$   (b) .614   (d) positive   (e) .05   (f) .377   (g) .333   (h) .1000   (i) .062 to .878
(j) .477 to .721

## Chapter 12

**1.** (a) Spearman's rho   (b) no association   (c) positive association   (d) .8071   (e) yes   (f) yes
**2.** (a) gamma   (b) no association   (c) negative association   (d) .5152   (e) no   **3.** (a) gamma
(b) no association   (c) positive association   (d) .5158   (e) yes   (f) yes   **4.** (a) lambda   (b) .424
(d) $\lambda_r$   (e) .509   (f) $\lambda_c$   (g) .357   **5.** (a) $\phi$   (b) .4573   (d) no   (e) 20.91%   **6.** (a) Cramer's V
(b) .2474   (c) moderate   (d) yes

## Appendix A

**1.** (a) 20   (b) –13   (c) –9   (d) –150   **2.** (a) 15   (b) 9   (c) 3   (d) –16   (e) –6   (f) –27   (g) –1
(h) 3   **3.** (a) 8   (b) –54   (c) –42   (d) –14   (e) 18   (f) –24   (g) –24   (h) 108   (i) –24   (j) –30
(k) 12   (l) –168   (m) 480   **4.** (a) 3   (b) –2   (c) –4   (d) 2   (e) .5   (f) –.32   (g) –2.12   **5.** (a) 16
(b) 243   (c) 512   (d) 81   (e) 2,401   (f) 1,024   (g) 1,728   (h) 50,625   (i) 2,187   **6.** (a) 2   (b) 120
(c) 720   (d) 40,320   (e) 39,916,800   **7.** (a) 1.4142   (b) 2.6458   (c) 14.6629   (d) 5.5678
(e) 8.6023   (f) 9.5394   (g) 17.6918   (h) 1   **8.** (a) 25.15   (b) 6.09   (c) 795.84   (d) 2   (e) 8.65
**9.** (a) 9.748   (b) 784.711   (c) 2.491   (d) 32.956   (e) 10   **10.** (a) 3.5198   (b) 26.3780   (c) 13.8230
(d) 10.6006   (e) 8.14

# REFERENCES

Berenson, Mark L., and David M. Levine. *Basic Business Statistics: Concepts and Applications.* Englewood Cliffs, N.J.: Prentice-Hall, 1992.

Blalock, Hubert M., Jr. *Social Statistics.* New York: McGraw-Hill, 1979.

Capon, Anthony. *Elementary Statistics for the Social Sciences.* Belmont, Calif.: Wadsworth, 1988.

Cohen, Jacob. *Statistical Power Analysis for the Behavioral Sciences.* Hillsdale, N.J.: Lawrence Erlbaum Associates, 1988.

Edwards, Allen L. *Statistical Methods.* New York: Holt, Rinehart and Winston, 1967.

Fisher, Sir Ronald A., and Frank Yates. *Statistical Tables for Biological, Agricultural, and Medical Research.* London: Longman Group, 1979.

Freund, John E., and Richard Manning Smith. *Statistics: A First Course,* 4th ed. Englewood Cliffs, N.J.: Prentice-Hall, 1986.

Galton, Francis. "Regression towards Mediocrity in Hereditary Status." *Journal of the Anthropological Institute,* 1885.

Legendre, Adrian L. *Nouvelles methodes pour lat determination des cometes.* Paris, 1806.

McNemar, Quinn. *Psychological Statistics.* New York: John Wiley & Sons, 1969.

Mueller, John H., Karl F. Schuessler, and Herbert L. Costner. *Statistical Reasoning in Sociology.* Boston: Houghton Mifflin, 1970.

Norusis, Marija J. *SPSS 7.5 Guide to Data Analysis.* Englewood Cliffs, N.J.: Prentice-Hall, 1997.

Parsons, Robert. *Statistical Analysis: A Decision-Making Approach.* New York: Harper and Row, 1974.

Popper, Karl R. *The Logic of Discovery.* New York: Harper Torch Books, 1968.

Runyon, Richard P., and Audrey Haber. *Fundamentals of Behavioral Statistics.* New York: McGraw-Hill, 1991.

Runyon, Richard P., Audrey Haber, David J. Pittenger, and Kay A. Coleman. *Fundamentals of Behavioral Statistics.* New York: McGraw-Hill, 1996.

Siegel, Sidney. *Nonparametric Statistics for the Behavioral Sciences.* New York: McGraw-Hill, 1956.

Sigelman, Lee, Timothy Bledsoe, Susan Welch, and Michael W. Combs. "Making Contact? Black-White Social Interaction in an Urban Setting." *American Journal of Sociology* 101 (1996):1306–32.

Snedecor, George, and William G. Cochran. *Statistical Methods,* 7th ed. Ames: Iowa State University Press, 1974.

Stevens, S. Smith. "Measurement." In *Scaling: A Sourcebook for Behavioral Scientists,* edited by Garry M. Maranell. Chicago: Aldine Publishing, 1974.

Substance Abuse and Mental Health Administration. *National Household Survey on Drug Abuse.* Washington, D.C., July 1997.

The Rand Corporation. *A Million Random Digits with 100,000 Normal Deviates.* New York: The Free Press, 1955.

U.S. Bureau of the Census. *Statistical Abstract of the United States, 1978,* 116th ed., Washington, D.C., 1996.

U.S. Bureau of the Census. *1990 Census of Population and Housing.* In U.S. Bureau of the Census, *Statistical Abstract of the United States, 1978,* 116th ed., Washington, D.C., 1996.

U.S. Department of Commerce. Bureau of the Census. *Statistical Abstract of the United States, 1996,* 116th ed., Washington, D.C.

U.S. Department of Commerce. Economics and Statistics Administration. Bureau of the Census. *Current Population Reports, Population Characteristics, The Black Population in the United States,* March 1992 (by Claudette Bennett).

U.S. Department of Education. National Center for Education Statistics. Integrated Postsecondary Data System (IPEDS). *Finance, FY91 Survey.* Washington, D.C.

U.S. Department of Health and Human Services, *Preliminary Results from the 1996 National Household Survey on Drug Abuse:* Substance Abuse and Mental Health Administration, Washington, D.C., July 1997, p. 57.

Waugh, Albert E. *Statistical Tables and Problems.* New York: McGraw-Hill, 1952.

Wilcoxon, F. *Some Rapid Approximate Statistical Procedures.* New York: American Cyanamid Company, 1964.

# INDEX